# Non-Policy Politics

*Richer Voters, Poorer Voters, and the Diversification of Electoral Strategies*

**ERNESTO CALVO**
*University of Maryland*

**MARIA VICTORIA MURILLO**
*Columbia University*

CAMBRIDGE
UNIVERSITY PRESS

# CAMBRIDGE
## UNIVERSITY PRESS

University Printing House, Cambridge CB2 8BS, United Kingdom

One Liberty Plaza, 20th Floor, New York, NY 10006, USA

477 Williamstown Road, Port Melbourne, VIC 3207, Australia

314–321, 3rd Floor, Plot 3, Splendor Forum, Jasola District Centre, New Delhi – 110025, India

79 Anson Road, #06-04/06, Singapore 079906

Cambridge University Press is part of the University of Cambridge.

It furthers the University's mission by disseminating knowledge in the pursuit of education, learning, and research at the highest international levels of excellence.

www.cambridge.org
Information on this title: www.cambridge.org/9781108497008
DOI: 10.1017/9781108683708

© Maria Victoria Murillo and Ernesto Calvo 2019

This publication is in copyright. Subject to statutory exception and to the provisions of relevant collective licensing agreements, no reproduction of any part may take place without the written permission of Cambridge University Press.

First published 2019

Printed and bound in Great Britain by Clays Ltd, Elcograf S.p.A.

*A catalogue record for this publication is available from the British Library.*

Library of Congress Cataloging-in-Publication Data
NAMES: Murillo, Maria Victoria, 1967- author. | Calvo, Ernesto, author.
TITLE: Non-policy politics : richer voters, poorer voters, and the diversification of electoral strategies / Maria Victoria Murillo, Ernesto Calvo.
DESCRIPTION: Cambridge, United Kingdom ; New York, NY : Cambridge University Press, 2019. | Includes bibliographical references.
IDENTIFIERS: LCCN 2018034111 | ISBN 9781108497008 (hardback) | ISBN 9781108739405 (paperback)
SUBJECTS: LCSH: Party affiliation–Chile. | Political parties–Chile. | Political participation–Chile. | Party affiliation–Argentina. | Political parties–Argentina. | Political participation–Argentina.
CLASSIFICATION: LCC JL2698.A1 M87 2019 | DDC 324.282–dc23
LC record available at https://lccn.loc.gov/2018034111

ISBN 978-1-108-49700-8 Hardback

Cambridge University Press has no responsibility for the persistence or accuracy of URLs for external or third-party internet websites referred to in this publication and does not guarantee that any content on such websites is, or will remain, accurate or appropriate.

# Non-Policy Politics

Calvo and Murillo consider the non-policy benefits that voters consider when deciding their vote. While parties advertise policies, they also deliver non-policy benefits in the form of competent economic management, constituency service, and patronage jobs. Different from much of the existing research, which focuses on the implementation of policy or on the delivery of clientelistic benefits, this book provides a unified view of how politicians deliver broad portfolios of policy and non-policy benefits to their constituency. The authors' theory shows how these non-policy resources also shape parties' ideological positions and which type of electoral offers they target to poorer or richer voters. With exhaustive empirical work, both qualitative and quantitative, the research documents how linkages between parties and voters shape the delivery of non-policy benefits in Argentina and Chile.

ERNESTO CALVO is Professor and Associate Chair of the Department of Government and Politics of University of Maryland-College Park. He is the author of *Legislator Success in Fragmented Congresses in Argentina* (Cambridge, 2014), *Anatomía Política de Twitter en Argentina*, and *La Nueva Política de Partidos En La Argentina* (2005). His research has been recognized with the Lawrence Longley Award and the Leubbert Best Article Award from the Representation and the Comparative Politics sections of the American Political Science Association.

MARIA VICTORIA MURILLO is Professor of Political Science and International Affairs at Columbia University, New York. She is the author of *Labor Unions, Partisan Coalitions, and Market Reforms in Latin America* (Cambridge, 2001) and *Political Competition, Partisanship, and Policy Making in Latin American Public Utilities* (Cambridge, 2009). Her research has been supported by the National Science Foundation, Russell Sage Foundation, the Fulbright Foundation, and the Harvard Academy for Area Studies.

*For Anahi Camila Cabrera-Murillo, Emiliano Calvo-Alcañiz,
Lauren Perry, and Camilo Calvo-Alcañiz*

# Contents

| | | |
|---|---|---|
| *Figures* | | *page* ix |
| *Tables* | | xii |
| | Prologue | 1 |
| 1 | Non-Policy Politics | 6 |
| 2 | A Demand-Side Model of Non-Policy Politics | 35 |
| 3 | Tracing Political Preferences and Party Organization in Argentina and Chile | 48 |
| 4 | Mapping Voter Preferences in Argentina and Chile | 64 |
| 5 | Party Organization: How Activists Reach Voters | 82 |
| 6 | Voters' Preferences and Parties' Electoral Offers | 107 |
| 7 | Party Activists and Their Conditional Effect on the Vote | 131 |
| 8 | Targeting Patronage in Argentina and Chile | 160 |
| 9 | Back to Policy Offers | 180 |
| 10 | Non-Policy Politics and Electoral Responsiveness | 214 |
| *Appendices* | | 229 |
| | Appendix to Chapter 2 | 229 |
| | Appendix to Chapter 4 | 235 |
| | Appendix to Chapter 5 | 239 |
| | Appendix to Chapter 6 | 243 |
| | Appendix to Chapter 7 | 257 |

| | |
|---|---:|
| *Appendix to Chapter 8* | 265 |
| *Appendix to Chapter 9* | 271 |
| *Appendix with List of Cited Politicians* | 275 |
| *References* | 277 |
| *Index* | 297 |

# Figures

2.1 Optimal policy offer $L$ with a mixture model where richer and poorer voters give equal weight to policy $[\alpha_P = \alpha_R = -0.2]$    *page* 40
2.2 Optimal policy offer $L$ with a mixture model where richer voters give double the weight to policy than poor voters $[\alpha_P = -0.1, \alpha_R = -0.2]$    41
4.1 Self-reported placement of voters and reported location of parties in Argentina and Chile, 2007    67
4.2 Voters' ideological preferences by socioeconomic status, Argentina and Chile, 2007    70
4.3 Evaluations of economic competence and ideological self-placement, Argentina    72
4.4 Evaluations of economic competence and ideological self-placement, Chile    73
4.5 Distributive expectations and self-reported ideology in Argentina, 2007    78
4.6 Distributive expectations and self-reported ideology in Chile, 2007    79
5.1 Ideological self-placement and number of activists (count) known by voters (2007)    94
6.1 Vote, ideology, and economic competence in Chile    116
6.2 Vote, ideology, and economic competence in Argentina    117
6.3 Linear effect by socioeconomic income, Chile 2007    122
6.4 Linear effect by socioeconomic income, Argentina 2007    124
6.5 Maximum linear effect by socioeconomic income, Chile 2007    125

| | | |
|---|---|---|
| 6.6 | Maximum linear effect by socioeconomic income, Argentina 2007 | 126 |
| 6.7 | Optimal policy offer as a weighted function of the importance that socioeconomic groups attach to policy preferences, $[\alpha_s, \bar{x}_{is}]$ | 129 |
| 7.1 | The effect of targeted distribution on vote choice, conditional on network proximity $(1-\theta_i)$ | 147 |
| 7.2 | The effect of targeted distribution on vote choice conditional on network proximity for voters of lower socioeconomic status (D voters) | 150 |
| 7.3 | The effect of targeted distribution on vote choice conditional on network proximity for voters of higher socioeconomic status (C voters) | 151 |
| 7.4 | The effect of ideological distance on vote choice conditional on network proximity in Argentina and Chile | 155 |
| 8.1 | Private- and public-sector wages in Argentina, 2003–2011 | 166 |
| 8.2 | Private- and public-sector wages in Chile, 1996 through 2009 | 167 |
| 8.3 | Public-sector wage premium by socioeconomic level, Argentina, 2009 | 169 |
| 8.4 | Public-sector wage premium by socioeconomic level, Chile, 2009 | 170 |
| 8.5 | Wage distribution and marginal effect of public-sector employment and education on wages in Argentina, quantile regression estimates for Argentina (EPH, 2009) and Chile (CASEN, 2009) | 173 |
| 8.6 | Effect of education, age, and gender on public-sector wages, Argentina (EPH, 2009) and Chile (Casen, 2009) | 175 |
| 9.1 | Equilibrium location of parties and model parameters | 188 |
| 9.2 | Equilibrium location of parties in Argentina and Chile, 2007 | 194 |
| 9.3 | Changes in party equilibrium in Chile with high alpha | 197 |
| 9.4 | Changes in party equilibrium in Chile as a function of model parameters (all voters) | 201 |
| 9.5 | Elite and voter locations of political parties in Chile | 204 |
| 9.6 | Elite and voter locations of political parties in Argentina | 204 |
| 2.A.1 | Bivariate normal distributions of policy preference $x_i$ and non-policy endowment $T_i$ in the vertical axis, two examples. | 231 |

| | | |
|---|---|---|
| 2.A.2 | Bivariate normal distributions of policy preference $x_i$ and non-policy endowment $T_i$ in the vertical axis, two examples. | 232 |
| 4.A.1 | Competence in dealing with poverty and ideological self-placement in Argentina | 236 |
| 4.A.2 | Competence in dealing with poverty and ideological self-placement in Chile | 236 |
| 4.A.3 | Competence in dealing with crime and ideological self-placement in Argentina | 237 |
| 4.A.4 | Competence in dealing with crime and ideological self-placement in Chile | 237 |
| 8.A.1 | Association between distributive expectations and SES, Chile | 269 |
| 8.A.2 | Association between distributive expectations and SES, Argentina | 269 |

# Tables

| | | |
|---|---|---|
| 1.1 | Non-policy endowments: resources and benefits | page 9 |
| 2.1 | Description of the terms in Equation (2.1) | 37 |
| 3.1A | Effective number of parties and margin of victory in Chile (1891–1925) | 50 |
| 3.1B | Effective number of parties and margin of victory in Argentina (1912–1930) | 51 |
| 5.1 | Activists' networks in Argentina and Chile | 88 |
| 5.2 | Networks of handout recipients, Argentina and Chile (2007) | 102 |
| 9.1 | Parameters and variables in the synthetic dataset | 187 |
| 9.2 | Multinomial estimates of key model parameters, $-\alpha, \beta_1, \beta_2, \beta_{3,1}, \beta_{3,2}, \beta_{3,3}$, from Chapter 6 | 193 |
| 4.A.1 | Ideological self-placement and non-responses in Argentina and Chile | 235 |
| 5.A.1 | Networks of activists compared with volunteers | 239 |
| 6.A.1 | Determinants of the vote in Argentina, conditional (multinomial) choice model | 244 |
| 6.A.2 | Determinants of the vote in Chile, conditional (multinomial) choice model | 248 |
| 6.A.3 | Argentina vote choice model by socioeconomic class, multinomial model (WinBUGS), handouts | 251 |
| 6.A.4 | Argentina vote choice model by socioeconomic class, multinomial model (WinBUGS), patronage | 252 |
| 6.A.5 | Argentina vote choice model by socioeconomic class, multinomial model (WinBUGS), pork | 253 |

| | | |
|---|---|---|
| 6.A.6 | Chile vote choice model by socioeconomic class, multinomial model (WinBUGS), handouts | 254 |
| 6.A.7 | Chile vote choice model by socioeconomic class, multinomial model (WinBUGS), patronage | 255 |
| 6.A.8 | Chile vote choice model by socioeconomic class, multinomial model (WinBUGS), pork | 256 |
| 7.A.1 | The conditional effect of partisan networks on targeted distribution, ideological distance, and competence | 258 |
| 7.A.2 | Effect of networks on distribution and ideological distance by SES in Chile | 260 |
| 7.A.3 | Effect of networks on distribution and ideological distance by SES in Argentina | 262 |
| 8.A.1 | Quantile regression of public employment and education on employee wages (LN) in Argentina, INDEC (2009) | 266 |
| 8.A.2 | Quantile regression of public employment and education on employee wages (LN) in Chile, CASEN (2009) | 267 |
| 8.A.3 | Mean wages by socioeconomic class in the private and public sector | 268 |
| 9.A.1 | Optimal ideological location of parties and expected vote in Chile, 2007 | 272 |
| 9.A.2 | Optimal ideological location of parties and expected vote in Argentina, 2007 | 273 |
| 9.A.3 | Ideological location of parties in Argentina and Chile as reported by legislators, 2006–2010 | 274 |

# Prologue

The paradox of modern democracies is that they level the playing field so that profoundly unequal parties may compete against each other. Political parties in democracies seem to enjoy unfettered freedom to select and advertise the policies of their choosing. However, they have different reputations for competence and honesty, unequal capacity to recruit and mobilize activists, as well as different access to public office and money. While competition for policy may be the paramount goal of democratic representation, most of parties' time and energy is devoted to managing non-policy endowments. There are good reasons for this. Any party can offer policy, but only a handful of them can deliver.

We began this project over a decade ago to explore a simple intuition: not all political parties are created equal. Peronists and Radicals in Argentina have wildly different reputations for managerial competence and honesty as well as different-sized networks of activists, brokers, and clients. In hindsight, Peronists and Radicals differ in non-policy endowments to a larger extent than they do in all policy-related matters. Differences in non-policy endowments also complement ideological distinctions in party competition among Socialists, Christian Democrats, UDI, and RN in Chile. Just as in Argentina, parties differ in style and substance, publicizing what makes them valuable, useful, and an asset to voters. As noted by one of Bachelet's presidential advisors in 2009, "There are more people that think that Bachelet is honest than people thinking their own grandmother is honest. And that is a great political asset to have." Yet, changing public views of her competence and character were crucial in explaining the defeat of her coalition in the 2018 presidential election.

The general theoretical framework we present in this book understands non-policy endowments as an asset to parties and as a boon to voters. On the supply side, parties differ in non-policy endowments, from a good reputation for managerial competence to armies of activists and donors to the advantages holding office provides. On the demand side, voters reveal differences in their taste for non-policy benefits. Some voters care deeply about competence while others value honesty, handouts, and/or public-sector jobs. Differences in party endowments, voter preferences, and party-voter linkages constrain the ability of candidates to deliver benefits. As different groups of voters weigh some of the non-policy endowments in parties' portfolio more heavily, parties disproportionally target benefits to some voters at the expense of others. Who these voters are is a crucial question to understand patterns of electoral responsiveness.

In this book, we focus our attention on the effects of non-policy endowments on electoral politics. We consider three types of non-policy endowments that are of the utmost importance and have already garnered considerable attention among scholars: managerial competence, activists' networks, and patronage resources. We describe these non-policy endowments as a resource to parties as well as a benefit to voters. We develop a general theory of how non-policy endowments interact with each other, constrain policy offers, and provide evidence of large and measurable effects on party vote in Argentina and Chile.

As we develop our theory, we demonstrate that parties with larger non-policy endowments could have lower costs to switch policy offers. Our study of non-policy politics provides answers to important puzzles that characterize elections in Argentina, Chile, and the Americas as a whole. Why are policy switches frequent in Argentina but not in Chile? Why do Peronists have such a stable constituency if policy switches are frequent in Argentina? Why do parties on the left and right of the political spectrum dominate Chilean politics when most voters are centrists? As we analyze asymmetries in non-policy endowments and uncover their effect on policy offers, this book also provides an answer to questions about policy volatility in Argentina and to policy stability in Chile.

As the project evolved, we published some results in specialized journals and developed collaborative efforts to explore new lines of research. The initial impulse for this project was published in the *American Journal of Political Science*, which led to an NSF proposal that financed the surveys in Argentina and Chile. Results on partisan networks, which inform Chapters 5 and 7, were then published in *Comparative Political Studies* under the title "When Parties Meet Voters." The effect of non-policy politics on policy positions also informed collaborative research by Ernesto Calvo with Tim Hellwig and Kiyoung Chang, published in the *American Journal of Political Science* (2011) and in *Electoral Studies* (2015 and 2017). While some of the results in this book have been discussed with colleagues on three continents, most are presented in their current form and published for the first time. As such, they are more the continuation of a long-term research agenda rather than its conclusion.

Because this book was long in the making, in the process, we acquired numerous intellectual and institutional debts, which we would like to acknowledge. We first want to thank the National Science Foundation (#0617659) for financing our surveys in Argentina and Chile. Vicky Murillo would also like to thank Columbia University for institutional support and a friendly intellectual community, as well as the Russell Sage Foundation for an interdisciplinary forum, which was crucial for thinking of the ideas expressed in this book. The Institute of Latin American Studies and the Institute for Social and Economic Research and Policy also provided generous support for her. Ernesto Calvo would like to thank the University of Houston and the University of Maryland for providing research support and two wonderful communities of colleagues that greatly contributed to the completion of this book.

During this long journey, we benefited from the comments of two anonymous reviewers as well as participants in a book conference, generously organized by Erik Wibbels at Duke University. At the conference, excellent comments where provided by our discussants Anna Grzymala-Busse, Pablo Beramendi (who had also been our discussant at Lundt), Herbert Kitschelt, Guadalupe Tuñon (who had also been our discussant at Yale), and Erik Wibbels (who also suggested the title of our book), as well as other participants. We also presented parts of the manuscript at George Washington University, the University of Lundt, Stanford University, the University of Sao Paulo, the University of Tel Aviv, Hebrew University of Jerusalem, Washington University, University of North Carolina, University of Miami, Princeton University, Yale University, Caltech, Columbia University, University of Houston, University of Maryland, Rochester University, University of Chicago, Harvard University, New York University, University of Minnesota, University of Virginia, University of Texas-Austin, Universidad Torcuato Di Tella, Universidad de General San Martin, Universidad de Buenos Aires, Universidad de San Andres, Universidad Catolica de Chile, Universidad Diego Portales, Instituto Tecnologico Autonomo de Mexico, Centro de Investigacion y Docencia Economica, the Inter-American Development

Bank, the World Bank, the 2008 American Political Science Association Annual Meeting, and the Russell Sage Foundation.

We are indebted to many colleagues who provided feedback on the manuscript. Alisha Holland read the whole book and her comments and suggestions were invaluable. We also benefited from feedback from Isabella Alcañiz, Virginia Oliveros, Stephen Kaplan, Karen Remmer, Cecilia Martinez-Gallardo, Jonathan Rodden, Beatriz Magaloni, Alberto Diaz Cayeros, Fernando Limongi, Lorena Barbería, Andrés Malamud, Fernando Guarnieri, Yael Shomer, Orit Kedar, Pazit Ben-Nun Bloom, Guillermo Rosas, Brian Crisp, Norman Schofield, Jonathan Hartlyn, Evelyn Huber, Graeme Robertson, Agustina Giraudy, Santiago Olivella, Merike Blofield, Bill Smith, Jim Adams, Bernie Grofman, Sam Merrill, Andy Gelman, Cristopher McCarty, Noah Kaplan, Gary Cox, Sebastian Saiegh, Peter Smith, Carles Boix, Alicia Adsera, Deborah Yashar, Noam Lupu, Susan Stokes, Statis Kalyvas, Thad Dunning, Steven Wilkinson, Mike Alvarez, Cary Smulovitz, Juan Carlos Torre, Alejandro Bonvecchi, Sebastian Etchemendy, Carlos Gervasoni, German Lodola, Marcelo Cavarozzi, Marcelo Escolar, Ricardo Gutierrez, David Altman, Juan Pablo Luna, Rossana Castiglione, Eric Magar, Juan Pablo Micozzi, Joy Langston, Gabriel Negretto, Mariano Tomassi, Lorena Moscovich, Marcelo Leiras, Carlos Scartascini, Ernesto Stein, Joel Helmman, Greg Wehier, Eduardo Aleman, Andy Baker, Tim Hellwig, Ray Duch, Gergely Ujhelyi, Bin Powell, Gretchen Helmke, David Karol, Hanna Birnir, Mark Lichbach, John McCauley, Kanisha Bond, Antoine Banks, Joel Simmons, John Huber, Isabela Mares, Kimuli Kasara, Kate Baldwin, Mariela Szwarcberg, Rebecca Weitz-Shapiro, Ana de la O, Tulia Falleti, Matt Singer, Maria Escobar-Lemmon, Misha Taylor-Robinson, Gerardo Adrogue, Julia Pomares, Mario Pecheny, Peter Siavelis, Sara Niedzwiecki, Javier Auyero, Terri Caraway, Daniel Gingerich, Robert Kaufman, Mathew McCubbins, Charles Munnel, Patricio Navia, David Samuels, Simeon Nichter, Horacio Larreguy, Steven Levitsky, Amaney Jamal, Daniela Campello, Tariq Tachil, Libby Wood, Thomas Brambor, Rodrigo Zarazaga, Viridiana Rios, Nahomi Ichino, Lisa Wedeen, Phil Keefer, Ken Roberts, Marty Gilens, Andrew Schrank, and the students in Vicky's class on Democratic Responsiveness at Columbia University. We are also thankful to comments and suggestions given to our presentation, whose names we have forgotten. Finally, we benefited from the terrific research assistance of Giancarlo Visconti, Mariana Gutierrez, Iñaki Sagarzazu, Jorge Mangonnet, Pilar Giannini, Alex Micic, Zachary Scott, as well as by the support staff at the Russell Sage Foundation.

## Prologue

We wrote our first joint paper in college at the Universidad de Buenos Aires and since then have discussed politics and political science while sharing a long-term friendship that exceeds scholarly pursuits. We both left Argentina to pursue careers in the United States; we both got married and had families. We benefited from the friendship of each other's partners in the process, and we saw our kids grow up. The support of our partners and friends Isabella Alcañiz and Ernesto Cabrera has kept us going through all these years across both hemispheres and in the process of writing this book. Isabella and Ernesto's intellectual support, feedback, and – more importantly – their love, affection, and senses of humor were crucial in keeping our focus on what is important while working on this book. Our children were dispensed from reading its pages, but they gave us both a sense of how time passed while we were working on this project and how their lives are what matters the most for both of us. For this reason, we dedicate this book to them.

# 1

# Non-Policy Politics

Parties do not focus narrowly on advertising policy proposals. Instead, they use all the resources they have at their disposal to win elections. Parties advertise policies, such as lower taxes and improved access to health services, while also offering non-policy benefits in the form of competent economic management, constituency service, and patronage jobs. Voters value policy and non-policy benefits, and consider all that parties have to offer when deciding their vote. The non-policy benefits, which voters demand and parties supply, are the object of this book.

Non-policy benefits are important for winning elections. Supporters and detractors of New York's Tammany Hall, the political machine that delivered public jobs to allies and services to city residents for over a century, understood this well (Golway, 2014). Non-policy politics also fueled efforts by early reformers that fought Tammany Hall, who trusted that clean politics and competent management would deliver electoral victories (Morris, 2010). Indeed, competing non-policy endowments empowered machine politics in New York as much as they facilitated its demise.

Non-policy politics also shapes the policies parties offer to voters.[1] Consider a contest between two candidates that know the exact tax policy that different groups of voters want, with leftist voters preferring a higher tax rate than conservative voters, $r_L > r_M > r_C$, and a median voter $r_M$ being decisive to the outcome of the election. Consider then that these two

---

[1] See Adams et al. (2005), Londregan and Rommer (1993), Groseclose (2001), Ansolabehere and Snyder (2000), and Schofield (2003) for a literature that describes the effect of valence on policy offers.

candidates advertise the exact same policy, $r_M$, but one of them is perceived by all voters as a more competent candidate (e.g. a better administrator, a more experienced politician, or any other similar trait that denotes competence).[2] If two candidates offer the exact same policy but one of them has a non-policy advantage, shouldn't voters opt for the more competent one on Election Day? More important, if the more competent candidate takes on the median voter's preferred policy, which policy should the disadvantaged candidate offer? As we will argue, non-policy politics is crucial to winning elections not only because it delivers votes, but also because it changes the policy based calculus of candidates with different endowments of non-policy resources.

Once we acknowledge that parties maximize votes by delivering policy and non-policy benefits, a number of interesting questions arise. Which types of non-policy benefits matter most to voters? What happens if voters have heterogeneous assessments of the non-policy benefits provided by different parties? How do parties administer different non-policy endowments, such as a good reputation for managerial competence, the delivery of public-sector jobs, or the energy and time invested by activists during campaigns? How do candidates signal non-policy reputations, such as managerial competence, and how do they administer scarce resources, such as patronage jobs? Finally, what are the electoral consequences of a party holding a non-policy advantage over its competitors, and how does such an advantage shape the policies offered to voters? In short, which combinations of non-policy benefits and policy offers do voters expect to receive and candidates hope to deliver?

## 1.1 NON-POLICY ENDOWMENTS AND RESPONSIVENESS

We conceptualize non-policy endowments as a resource at the disposal of elites, as well as a benefit to voters. There are differences in the type and quantity of endowments held by parties, as well as in the benefits sought by voters. Differences in the parties' endowments result from their capacity to recruit well-trained bureaucrats, control public offices, access financial resources, and attract, energize, and deploy networks of activists. Voters, in turn, recognize the positive value of non-policy benefits but differ on the weight they assign to different endowments in deciding their

---

[2] See Groseclose (2001) and Ansolabehere and Snyder (2000) for a formal treatment of this assumption in two party settings. See Schofield and Sened (2006) and Calvo and Hellwig (2011) for similar findings in multiparty settings.

vote choice. Voters also differ in their ability to observe and benefit from non-policy endowments. Just as partisans (of any ideological position) and independents may give different values to the policies offered by candidates, perceptions of non-policy endowments may also differ across groups.

Some parties, for example, build dense and energetic networks of activists while others parties fail to do so. Some parties have proven records of managerial competence, while others lack the experience, skills, and personnel required to fill public offices and implement even the most basic policies. We argue that while candidates may advertise policy offers without cost, not all parties are equally capable of accessing and delivering non-policy benefits. More important for our research, differences arise on the demand side as well, as voters have different perceptions of parties' non-policy endowments and expect to derive varying benefits from them. Some voters may be close to the parties' networks and value the benefits they deliver, while others may not know a single activist. Voters may vary on their perceptions about the managerial competence of competing parties and care to different extents about its importance.

Similar to factor endowments in economic production, we consider that different non-policy endowments may be pooled together, create synergies, and/or substitute each other. A reputation for managerial competence, for example, serves as a recruiting tool that expands the pool of potential activists. Dense and energized networks of activists may facilitate the delivery of targeted benefits and propagate messages that enhance the reputation of a party candidate. The delivery of patronage jobs may provide activists with financial independence to engage voters. In all, we consider non-policy endowments as a resource to party elites and as a benefit to voters, as illustrated in Table 1.1.

While we acknowledge that both policy offers and non-policy benefits matter, we direct most of our research efforts toward explaining the latter. In particular, we focus on the effect of asymmetries in the perceived supply of non-policy endowments as well as in the voters' heterogeneous demand for non-policy benefits. When deciding their vote, high-income voters may care deeply about managerial competence, unemployed voters may be enticed by public-sector jobs, while voters in slums may value the ability of party brokers to reduce crime in their communities or to deliver clean water and food. Differences on perceived party endowments and on voters' preferences, we posit, are crucial for understanding party competition and electoral performance in democracies around the world.

TABLE 1.1. *Non-policy endowments: resources and benefits*

| Non-policy endowment | As a resource to politicians | As perceived by voters |
|---|---|---|
| Valence | More competent bureaucrats, more personable politicians, less corrupt politicians | "They get things done," "they communicate better," "they are trustworthy" |
| Targeted benefits | Access to office for the delivery of goods, public-sector jobs, and contracts | "They took care of my electric bill," "they got me this job," "they got the money to repair our school" |
| Party organization | Networks of activists | "They answer my questions," "they are always doing things for the community," "they understand my needs" |

Consequently, how parties with different non-policy endowments respond to voters with heterogeneous demands is a critical question.

Non-policy politics is crucial for explaining party and voter behavior in modern electoral democracies where voters weigh all that parties have to offer and candidates struggle to mix and match complex portfolios of benefits to secure the support of voters. Candidates could always do better if they had unlimited resources to tailor policy offers and non-policy benefits to the particular needs of each voter. If one group is likely to change their vote upon observing a particular tax policy offer while another group cares deeply for the delivery of public-sector jobs, parties would gain more votes by tilting tax policy in the direction of the former and delivering more jobs to the latter. How do parties respond to such heterogeneous combinations of voters' demands, given their resource constraints?

Policy offers and non-policy endowments, we argue, should be biased toward the preferences of voters that care more intensely about them: i.e. voters that display larger changes in the probability of voting for a party in response to particular combinations of policy offers and non-policy benefits. Whether such differences are the result of preferences, asymmetries in information, or strategic behavior on the part of voters is an empirical question to be carefully tested. Irrespective of its origin, we expect politicians to bias policy and non-policy offers toward voters who feel more intensely about each of them. Consequently, parties should develop strategies to identify both the content as well as the intensity of the voter's policy and non-policy preferences.

Parties may target distinct policy offers and non-policy benefits toward different groups of voters[3] or focus their efforts on a particularly intense subgroup. We assess such differences empirically and place them in historical context, an important step considering they result from particular distributions of voter preferences and party endowments. Our theory of non-policy politics explains the general mechanisms underlying such differences, as well as their overall effect on electoral strategies.

In the chapters that follow, we provide evidence of asymmetries in the parties' non-policy endowments, of heterogeneity in voters' preferences, and of unequal allocation of non-policy benefits to preferred groups of voters. We discuss the institutional, behavioral, informational, socioeconomic, and identity related factors that explain these differences. In doing so, we follow a significant literature that acknowledges the tailoring of electoral strategies to diverse demographic constituencies, although our work focuses on socioeconomic status as the category of interest.[4] To advance our research goals, we draw from existing scholarship that analyzes the effect of valence issues, targeted distribution, and party organization on the policies offered by parties.[5] At the intersection of these distinct literatures, we build our argument on the determinants and the consequences of non-policy politics.

### a) Non-Policy Endowments and Electoral Responsiveness

Non-policy endowments are key to campaigns and a defining component of voters' electoral behavior. Politicians promise non-policy benefits as often as they promise policy ones, advertising competent management, constituency service, and patronage jobs among a long list of valence-related offers where execution is what matters most to voters. Donald Stokes forcefully argued this point in his classic "Spatial models of party competition," where he criticized Downs's (1957) ideological

---

[3] What Luna (2014) describes as "segmented representation."
[4] Other demographic categories, such ethnic or religious divisions, have also been used for explaining electoral behavior (Baldwin, 2016; Chandra, 2004; Corstange, 2016; Gryzmala-Busse, 2015; Kasara, 2017; Posner, 2005; Thachil, 2014; Wilkinson, 2006).
[5] See Stokes (1963), Cox and McCubbins (1986), Dixit and Londregan (1996, 1998), Ansolabehere and Snyder (2000), and Adams, Merrill, and Grofman (2005), among others.

reductionism by convincingly stating that voters care about many issues that all parties are expected to deliver in "greater quantities" – such as greater managerial competence or lower government corruption – but that some parties deliver *better* than others (Stokes, 1963: 369). It would make little sense for voters to hope for the delivery of lower corruption on the left, rather than lower corruption on the right. Instead, voters hope for as little corruption as possible. Nor is it true that voters are blind to corruption when deciding their vote and focus solely on policy, even if voters sometimes face significant trade-offs between the social goods and social "ills" delivered by parties. On corruption, as in other valence-related issues where voters expect *larger quantities* rather than competing offers, parties are responsive to voters when they deliver more non-policy benefits than their competitors. Voters, consequently, hold parties accountable for the failure to deliver non-policy benefits just as they do for unsuccessfully implementing the voters' preferred policies.

From an information standpoint, however, it is often easier for voters to hold politicians accountable for failures to deliver non-policy benefits than for their policy offers. Significant scholarly works show that voters face difficulties interpreting the consequences of public policies and discerning whether to punish or reward incumbents for complex policy outcomes.[6] In contrast, voters have an easier time observing who distributes handouts, who delivers public- sector jobs, or who executes public works that their communities require. Voters have an easier time connecting heuristics of managerial competence to macroeconomic stability than tracing the complex consequences of monetary and fiscal policy, an area where policy experts and economists have equally profound disagreements. Indeed, most research on economic voting, from Alesina and Rosenthal (1995) to Duch and Stevenson(2008), theorizes that good and bad economic performance by incumbents is interpreted as a signal of managerial competence, rather than as a signal of superior policy choices. A good economy highlights the incumbent's good management qualities, while a poor economy does the opposite. Hence, voters hold incumbents accountable based on competence rather than policy choice.

Trusting competent politicians to deliver whatever policy they deem necessary is generally easier than connecting the dots between policies and

---

[6] Hellwig and Samuels (2008) discuss institutions shaping voters' capacity for attributing responsibility in general whereas Alcañiz and Hellwig (2011) do so for Latin America. A less sanguine view of voters' capacity to assign responsibility for outcomes it taken by Achen and Bartells (2016) for the US and Campello and Zucco (2016) for Latin America.

outcomes. Hence, although non-policy preferences may differ across voters depending on time horizons, life experience, or tolerance for risk, politicians are more likely to be held accountable for their perceived non-policy failures than for their lofty policy goals. Therefore, extending the broad literature on policy responsiveness, we favor a demand-side view of party politics that hinges on non-policy endowments such as managerial competence, constituency service, and the delivery of targeted distribution, although other non-policy benefits, such as partisan identification, could be more relevant in other polities.[7]

Responsiveness in the context of non-policy party asymmetries and voter heterogeneity, however, introduces some interesting theoretical problems. While parties may offer policies on a leveled field, they are not equally capable of delivering non-policy benefits. Competent parties with larger partisan networks and access to office have significant non-policy advantages that are difficult to match by newcomers. When considering non-policy endowments, the electoral field is inclined rather than leveled, much to the delight of candidates with a non-policy advantage and the dismay of those who are disadvantaged. Consequentially, parties cannot be equally responsive to voters even if they are held equally accountable for their successes and failures while in office. Because not all parties are equally capable of delivering non-policy benefits, even if they are equally capable of promising policy, democratic competition may be biased in favor of advantaged candidates and their privileged constituencies.

---

[7] There is a widespread literature on the influence on party identification in shaping electoral decisions in the US. Partisanship as a non-policy resource distinct from policy offers has long been recognized as crucial in American electoral behavior and its influence on vote choice varies across individual voters. The US literature on partisanship is divided among those who consider it a social identity shaping political behavior (Bartels, 2002; Campbell et al., 1964; Green et al., 2004; Greene, 2004; Miller, 1996) and those that view it as running tally (Achen, 1992; Fiorina, 1981). In all cases, it is distinguished from the policy offers of political parties and it is assigned a positive effect on the vote. In the European literature, there is more skepticism on the distinction between partisan identity and vote intention (Bartle and Bellucci, 2009). We do not analyze partisanship because there is evidence that the other non-policy resources we investigate also modify party identification in Latin America. Lupu (2016) shows how party identification is shaped by both policy and economic competence perceptions, Shaffer and Baker (2015) demonstrate how it can be shaped by targeted distribution, while Baker, Ames, and Renno (2006) show how it can be defined by partisan networks. On the evolution of party identity in Argentina, see Lupu (2011, 2013) and, in Chile, see Morales and Navia (2010), Osorio and Navia (2015), and Luna and Altman (2011). For a review of the constituency service literature see Crisp and Simoneau (2018).

Our theory explains how politicians with different non-policy endowments respond to voters' heterogeneous preferences to maximize electoral returns. Based on this theory, we explain biases that result from parties allocating disproportionate non-policy resources to voters who attach more weight to particular types of benefits, while shifting their positions toward the preferences of voters who care more about policy. We propose that parties pay attention to both the content and intensity of voters' preferences, with responsive parties translating voter heterogeneity into biased policy offers and non-policy benefits. Hence, our theory explains policy biases that result from the combination of non-policy endowments and the heterogeneity of voters' preferences.

### b) Parties' Non-Policy Resources

In our analysis, we consider three families of non-policy endowments widely recognized by the literature on Latin American electoral behavior as influential: reputation (*valence*), organization (*activists*), and material inducements (*targeted distribution*). Each of these types of endowments impose different constraints on the agency of parties and their candidates. Different types of party activities are also required to build and sustain the value of these different resources.

Political parties differ in their capacity to deliver non-policy benefits to voters. This is true when we consider valence endowments, organizational capacity, and material inducements. Political parties are constrained by reputational differences on managerial competence (Duch and Stevenson, 2008), with some parties having more credibility regarding their ability for quality governance, while others are perceived as inept and/or untrustworthy. Parties are constrained by differences in organizational endowments as not all parties are equally likely to recruit activists, embed them in competitive communities, or energize them as the election approaches (Grossman and Helpman, 2002; Schofield and Sened, 2006). Parties are also constrained by their institutional access to fiscal resources, as well as in their capacity to use public office for electoral gain (Calvo and Murillo, 2004). Indeed, while advertising policy offers a choice, non-policy politics is an endowments' game.

The distribution of voter preferences and the extent to which policy offers and non-policy benefits vary across subgroups of voters further limit politicians' agency. Parties with privileged access to particular constituencies, through network linkages or control of office, may have better information about their preferences and, consequently, overperform when catering to them (Cox and McCubbins, 1986; Dixit and Londregan, 1998). Hence, parties' electoral offers are not only influenced by voters' desires, but also by politicians' knowledge about these preferences.

As we will discuss in detail later in this chapter, we assume that in the short run all non-policy resources are given – vis-à-vis the next election – while politicians may freely propose or rescind policy offers to voters. While we recognize that voter experiences and party choices alter non-policy endowments over time, endowments change slowly over periods of time. A party cannot change a reputation for poor managerial competence just by promising to be better. Similarly, it cannot update its activist networks or deliver public-sector jobs just by promising to do so when voters demand it. By contrast, we consider that policy offers are instantaneous and credible, with politicians adjusting these offers when external shocks demand. Therefore, we assume that, in the short-term, non-policy endowments are sticky and exogenous, whereas politicians may readily propose or rescind policy offers.

In our view, voters' expectations of a party's managerial capacity are informed by prior experiences as assumed by the literature on retrospective voting since Fiorina (1981). Nevertheless, facing the next election, parties have few resources to alter their reputations for managerial performance. A good reputation is an asset, while a bad reputation is a burden. Reputations are not derivative of ideology and thus a party does not acquire a good managerial reputation by offering the policies that voters want. Some parties have, deservingly or not, a better reputation on valence-related issues, which allows them to claim ownership of particular issue areas even when their policies change (Karol, 2009; Petrocik, 1996).

Similarly, access to private and/or public funds may grant some parties a superior capacity to deliver selective incentives such as handouts, patronage jobs, or public works. Because asymmetries in non-policy endowments provide parties with electoral benefits, they also create incentives for non-policy specialization. Candidates and parties, consequently, advertise non-policy endowments when they have a comparative advantage and target voters who care deeply about those resources. Just as candidates are expected to emphasize policy issues in which they have a comparative advantage – thereby talking about their strengths or "past each other" rather than dialoguing "with each other" on a given issue (Bélanger and Meguid, 2008) – parties should invest in non-policy resources that provide them electoral advantages.[8] That is, parties should more heavily invest and advertise non-policy endowments where they enjoy a comparative advantage.

In sum, the point of departure of this book is that parties make policy offers and deliver non-policy benefits to voters. In turn, voters weigh all policy offers and non-policy endowments in the party's portfolio to decide their vote.[9] Although we acknowledge that endowments change over time, we consider that they do so slowly and, for all practical purposes, non-policy endowments are fixed for politicians facing the next election. By the time the campaign starts, we argue, parties have a good or bad reputation for managerial competence, a record of accomplishments for delivering handouts, public jobs, and public works; and a network of activists with a size and structure that is difficult to alter. Consequently, we consider non-policy endowments as exogenous and relatively fixed for parties facing an electoral campaign, to the benefit of those enjoying abundant resources and the despair of those facing scarcity.

### c) Exogenous Non-Policy Endowments and Endogenous Policy Offers

Whereas we assume that non-policy endowments are sticky, policy offers are not. Politicians face few constraints to shift their policy stances. Such changes may carry a hefty electoral price tag or they may be costless, but they do not require building party capacity, nor do they necessitate greater resources or skills. Policy offers, defined as a promise for future implementation, are effective the moment a party or a candidate makes the announcement to the public. Voters may question the credibility of these policy offers or consider them at face value. In so doing, voters may weigh whether these policy offers deviate from past party behavior or

---

[8] Issue-ownership models (Petrocik, 1996) argue that parties should publicize issues on which they have an advantage among voters (issues on which they are perceived as more capable) but should not raise the salience of issues on which they do not have an advantage. Therefore, candidates should talk about different things ("past each other") rather than engaging in dialogue ("to each other"). Bélanger and Meguid (2008), extending the model implications, show that parties should talk "past each other" on issues that either of them owns but they should engage in dialogue in regards to issues that are less salient or unknown to voters. As in our model, voters have preferences about issues but, as important, weight some of those issues more heavily than others.

[9] We borrow the concept of portfolio diversification from Diaz-Cayeros et al. (2016) but while they apply it to targeted distribution, we expand its use to refer to both policy and non-policy offers. Moreover, whereas they distinguish voters according to past electoral behavior, we focus on demographic categories.

affirm the party's previous stances. Politicians, however, have the ability to make policy offers on the spot, irrespective of whether they follow through with them or not. The cost of defaulting on policy promises comes into play in the future, be it in the form of less trust in the party and candidate or lower marks for managerial competence. However, as Stokes (2001) showed in her study of policy switches, parties often change policy playbooks without having to previously build institutional capacity and voters sometimes learn to love the policies they thought they hated. Therefore, we assume that non-policy endowments are exogenous from policy considerations, while policy offers are endogenous and need to take into account the non-policy endowments available to parties.[10]

In considering non-policy endowments as relatively fixed and exogenous, even for targeted distribution, we distance ourselves from much of the vote-buying literature, where politicians promise future emoluments in exchange for voting for the party today (Brusco, Nazareno, and Stokes, 2004; Gonzalez-Ocantos et al., 2010; Nichter, 2008; Schaffer, 2007). Instead, we see the delivery of goods as a road to building capacity and voter support, in line with Finan and Schechter (2012: 1), who note, "most standard models of elections would suggest that vote-buying should not exist. With secret balloting, votes are unobservable, while a politician's promises are unenforceable. With this double commitment problem, there is no formal way to contract for votes in an election." Like Finan and Schechter, we assume that parties may deliver handouts *ex-ante* but have little capacity to monitor or enforce vote agreements. They may also promise to pay *ex-post*, which would be equally unenforceable and, at that time, woefully unnecessary. Instead, we consider electoral benefits such as handouts, jobs, and public works as faits accomplis, with parties being held accountable for past actions and expected to deliver in the future only insofar as it reflects their record of current accomplishments.[11] Therefore, in our view, voters' expectation

---

[10] While it may be true that prior policies already in place may affect current endowments, we posit that current policy offers have no effect on existing party endowments. The fact that a candidate promises higher or lower taxes, we posit, has no effect on whether voters perceive that that candidate as a good manager. The fact that voters may perceive her as a good public manager, by contrast, affects the electoral calculus of offering higher or lower taxes.

[11] While we acknowledge that brokers often police voters in elections, and that voters often believe that brokers may sanction them for defecting, the costs of disloyalty is banishment from future delivery networks rather than repayment or litigation.

about targeted distribution should be based on parties' prior accomplishments and capacity to deliver.[12]

Methodologically, our decision to consider non-policy endowments as exogenous is also based on evidence that voters perceive parties as having distinct non-policy endowments. While we acknowledge that non-policy endowments could be modeled as endogenous, both affecting and being affected by the policy choices of parties, we take the explicit methodological decision of simplifying our assumptions, hopefully gaining clarity without sacrificing much in the way of substance.

### d) Voter Heterogeneity: Connections between Non-Policy Resources and Policy Offers

Although separate dimensions, the policy offers and the non-policy endowments of parties may be orthogonal to each other or intertwined in the mind of voters. Voters that perceive particular party candidates as more capable, for example, may also embrace their policy choices as if they were their own.[13] This is the logic underlying *follow-the-leader* theories of policy attitudes, which see voters' policy preferences as shaped from above by both party insiders and by policy motivated activists. Leaders, some argue, frame issues for public consumption and marshal evidence in support of their arguments.[14] Policy attitudes, consequently, may develop from cues rooted in constitutive traits such as party identification, ethnic membership, or religious beliefs.[15] In these cases, non-policy endowments may permeate to policy assessments, reducing dimensionality in the minds of voters as well as in the data of researchers.

---

[12] Our view is supported by our own field research where we find evidence that politicians deliver selective incentives to grow communities of voters rather than to buy votes, in line with other scholars conducting ethnographies of clientelistic politics (Auyero, 2001; Szwarcberg, 2012, 2015; Zarazaga, 2015).

[13] Notice that in this description we are still assuming that non-policy endowments affect policy choices by parties and policy perceptions by voters. That is, we are still assuming that non-policy endowments are exogenous while policy choices are not. The question of whether a party that advertises a policy position is perceived as more capable, reversing the causation arrow, is not addressed by our own research and cannot be answered by our research design.

[14] See Iyengar (1994, 2010), Karol, (2009), Bawn et al. (2012), and Rahn (1993).

[15] See Bartels (2002), Wattenberg (2009), Eifert et al. (2010), and Campbell (1964).

Similarly, preference for a particular set of policies adopted by parties in the past may inform voters' assessments of managerial competence.[16] We cannot emphasize enough that, by assumption, we do not expect that current policy offers will inform managerial competence even if past policy implementations may do so. We still hold non-policy endowments, such as managerial competence, to be exogenous to policy offers. However, prior policies implemented by incumbents could inform on a party's perceived competence, thereby reducing dimensionality in the data. Therefore, although policy and non-policy dimensions of the vote are theoretically separate and empirically distinct, they may correlate with each other.

In other cases, however, voters perceive policy offers and non-policy endowments as distinct and unrelated (orthogonal) to each other. As we will show, whether voters perceive policy and non-policy dimensions as closely related or not is an important empirical question. The fact that the policy and non-policy dimensions may be dependent or independent from each other has important consequences, which are described in detail in Chapters 2 and 9 of this book. Our theory shows that when the policy and non-policy dimensions of the vote are not strictly independent from each other, parties have incentives to keep stable policy offers across elections. By contrast, when the policy and non-policy dimensions of the vote are independent from each other, parties will be able to switch their policy offers in response to exogenous shocks and changes in the preferences of the median voter. Our theory of non-policy politics, therefore, is able to explain the stable and informative character of party labels in Chile, as well as the ability of some Argentine parties to switch policies.

## 1.2 NON-POLICY ENDOWMENTS: COMPETENCE, PARTISAN NETWORKS, AND TARGETED DISTRIBUTION

As noted earlier, we consider three families of non-policy endowments based on reputation, party organization, and access to resources. Our framework begins with the testable assumption that voters consider both the policy offers and non-policy endowments of parties and candidates when deciding their vote. Both vary across and within political systems. In

---

[16] We still consider current policy choices as endogenous and current non-policy choices as exogenous. Prior policies are in this case observed by their outcome as in most of the economic voting literature.

each polity, different parties have distinct non-policy advantages and policy positions, with voters of different socioeconomic backgrounds (or other demographic categories) displaying heterogeneous preferences regarding each component of parties' electoral portfolio.

For any given country, we may consider a plethora of potential non-policy endowments, including a long list of reputation targets (honesty, transparency, managerial competence), organization endowments (activists, candidate networks, corporate linkages), and resources (money, food, jobs, contracts). We consider three different families of non-policy endowment, which are rather general and apply across different cases. They also feature prominently in the current comparative scholarship on political behavior and its applications to Latin America. For each of the three types of endowments, we consider the most salient and studied examples in the literature on political behavior. Hence, in our analyses of reputation endowments, we consider *managerial competence*, broadly understood as the perceived capacity to manage the economy, deal with unemployment, and reduce crime. When considering organizational endowments, we focus on the perceived linkages between the voters and the party – *partisan networks* – which candidates and voters use to collect and deliver information and goods through direct and personal contacts. Finally, when analyzing the access and delivery of resources, we consider expectations on *targeted distribution*, related to the parties' ability to deliver handouts, public-sector jobs, and pork to voters. We proceed to describe each of them in detail.

### a) Managerial Competence

For many years, the political science literature has recognized managerial competence as the ability to solve commonly agreed problems as a critical determinant of vote choice (Clarke et al., 2011; Duch and Stevenson, 2008). Inter-party differences in competence result from bureaucratic recruitment and experience (Alcañiz, 2016), choice of policy instruments, institutional trajectories, prior policy implementation experiences, and even serendipity, as is the case when a particular party holds the presidency at the time of unanticipated and exogenous shock (Achen and Bartels, 2004, 2016; Campello and Zucco, 2016). These differences have resulted in increasing interest on valence politics in comparative research (Adams, 2012; Clark, 2009; Clarke et al., 1992), which in most countries tend to be a better predictor of vote choices than ideological proximity due to is lower informational demands (Clark, 2009).[17]

As previously noted, we see voters as capable of distinguishing information that reveals ideological preferences from clues capturing the relative competence of parties, although we assume the latter to be easier.[18] Voters use this information to select parties, taking into consideration issue positions expressed in the candidates' policy offers as well as perceived managerial competence.

In this book, we consider *perceptions* of competence rather than actual measures of competence. The literature suggests that voters can associate parties with expertise in particular issue areas, which influences their perceptions of parties' competence. Voters in the United States, for example, perceive Democrats as having an advantage in ensuring economic growth, due to a partisan message that has long described how spending and progressive taxation results in superior economic performance. By contrast, an extensive literature on issue ownership has shown that Republicans have an advantage when advancing tough security policies (Kaplan, Park, and Ridout, 2006; Petrocik, 1996). As a result, if both parties propose similar hawkish policies in security matters, voters are likely to give lower implementation marks to Democrats, whereas if both parties propose growth-promoting policies, voters are likely to grant Democrats better grades.[19] Given that reputations for competence in issue areas evolve slowly over time, parties trespassing on issues owned by other parties may fail to recruit the voters they seek (Vavreck, 2009), making issue trespassing and issue realignment infrequent (Karol, 2009: 1630). As a result, the distribution of parties' competence assessments may be uneven across issue areas. Moreover, the slow evolution of issue

---

[17] Even in African countries, where the literature has traditionally emphasized ethnic identities and networks as the crucial non-programmatic dimension providing information for electoral choices (Habyarimana et al., 2009; Posner, 2005), valence issues have been shown to have a crucial effect on the vote, certainly stronger than positional issues (Bleck and Van de Walle, 2013).

[18] Indeed, in coining the "issue-valence" concept, Stokes (1992) argues that information to assess managerial competence should be easier to acquire than when assessing issue positions. In later chapters, we confirm this assumption empirically, with respondents reporting fewer non-responses on competence and network questions than when reporting the ideological location of parties in Chapter 4.

[19] From the recognition that parties differ in perceived competence to carry out mandates, a broad literature sprung analyzing information effects (Blais, Martin, and Nadeau, 1998; Granberg and Brent, 1980; Zaller and Feldman, 1992) and issue dominance across parties in the US (Petrocik, 1996; Vavreck, 2009).

ownership makes it harder for political parties to change their reputations; for this reason, parties seek to make salient issues on which they enjoy better competence perceptions.

In assessing the managerial competence of political parties, we consider three distinct issue areas: (i) the economy, (ii) poverty, and (iii) crime.[20] In both countries, the ability to manage the economy had the strongest effect on voting, and therefore we use it as our default measure when referring to political parties' competence in our empirical analyses. The salience of economic competence we find in our cases resonates with an extensive literature on economic voting, which has identified retrospective economic performance assessments as one of the most important determinants of vote choice in Latin America. A positive reputation for dealing with the economy is an asset, whereas a negative reputation is a liability (Alcañiz and Hellwig, 2011; Alesina and Rosenthal, 1995; Duch and Stevenson, 2008; Hellwig and Samuels, 2008).

The literature on economic voting assumes that voters can draw competence signals from economic outcomes by distinguishing the expected distributive consequences of policies from the relative competence of politicians in economic outcomes. Alesina and Rosenthal (1995) model how voters distinguish ideological content and competence signals from objective economic data to process economic shocks. Duch and Stephenson (2008) provide a general framework that shows cross-national differences in competence signals when evaluating incumbents based on conditions that shape their agency regarding economic performance. Hellwig and Samuels (2008) focus on how different institutions filter signals explaining the attribution of economic responsibility. A more recent literature questions voters' ability to distinguish outcomes directly attributable to the actions of incumbents from those resulting from exogenous conditions (Achen and Bartels, 2016; Campello and Zucco, 2016). Regardless of voters' capacity to adequately evaluate economic competence, their perceptions of politicians' ability to manage the economy remain a crucial component of electoral behavior when measured using individual attitudes. Voters prefer parties with greater economic competence. We therefore measure parties' competence using voters'

---

[20] The Latin American literature has shown the impact of economic performance on voting behavior (Campello, 2013; Kaplan, 2016; Lewis-Beck and Ratto, 2013; Murillo, Oliveros, and Vaishnav, 2010; Murillo and Visconti, 2017; Remmer, 2012). There is also an emerging literature on the impact of crime on electoral behavior in Latin America (Bateson, 2012; Holland, 2013; Perez, 2015; Visconti, 2017).

attitudes, which allows us to both sidestep the debate on their capacity to elaborate on those views and distinguishes between assessments of incumbent and opposition parties.[21]

While ideology and competence are distinct dimensions, political parties often package them as part of a single message, advertising policy goals not by their distributive consequences but as improvements for voters as a whole. That is, parties routinely present policies that separate voters into winners and losers as superior in general. For instance, a right-wing party, as a way to boost employment that will benefit the poor, offers a reduction on taxes that benefits the wealthy. A left-wing party describes an expansion of unemployment benefits as a strategy for economic growth, which also benefits businesses. Ideology and policy competence, consequently, could become intertwined in the communication strategies of parties and subsequently entangled in the minds of voters. We remain agnostic about whether the policy preferences and the competence assessments by voters are intertwined or not, which we consider an empirical question to be tested across political environments. Similarly, we have no expectation regarding the distribution of competence assessment by socioeconomic status, although we do expect most voters would provide such evaluations given the relatively low information requirements.

### b) Targeted Distribution

Following a burgeoning literature on electoral behavior in young democracies, we analyze the impact of targeted distribution as a crucial non-policy resource.[22] We view targeted distribution as a stream of resources that voters receive or expect to receive in-between elections. We do not believe that parties buy elections by delivering a payoff sum before or after the fact to a restricted menu of voters. Instead, we contend that parties offer a schedule of payments that is contingent on controlling office. Different parties offer different transfer schedules to voters, who

---

[21] To assess voters' perception of political parties' competence of both incumbents and challengers, we follow Sanders et al. (2011) who propose using measures of voters' perception instead of relying on prior performance. This strategy allows measures of competence for both incumbents and challengers.

[22] The large literature on electoral behavior and targeted distribution is summarized by Stokes et al. (2013: table 1.1) who discuss more than forty recent pieces, covering studies of the US, Europe, Asia, Latin America, and Africa and building on Stokes's (2007) earlier review of this scholarship.

consider both the value of the offer and the probability, $\pi$, that parties will win and make good on their payment schedule.[23] That is, for any given individual, a schedule for the allocation of targeted goods by party $k$ raises the utility of voting for that party, conditional on their sensitivity to receiving such benefit. Furthermore, different distributive expectations about targeted goods yield different returns, contingent on the weight that voters attach to each benefit in the portfolio of politicians.[24]

Attention to voters' expectations about targeted distribution and their influence in shaping their electoral calculus has a long tradition departing from the seminal contributions of Cox and McCubbins (1986) and Dixit and Londregan (1996). Formal models focus on the ideal distributive strategy conditional on voters' ideological preferences or the core-swing dilemma: whether to focus targeted distribution on loyal or swing voters. Building on their insights, the literature on new democracies proposed new explanations for the apparent contradiction between parties targeting core voters and formal models suggesting the advantages of focusing on swing voters (Diaz-Cayeros et al., 2016; Stokes et al., 2013). For the most part, this literature expects organizational specialization on targeted distribution contrasting clientelistic and programmatic parties.[25] In consonance with those expectations, this view assumes a weak association between expectations about targeted distribution and voters' policy preferences. Instead, because we see all parties as combining policy and non-policy benefits in their electoral portfolios, we suggest that such correlation needs to be empirically tested.

We expect voter heterogeneity to be more extensive for targeted distribution than for perceived economic competence, given that only a subset of voters will expect benefits from targeted distribution. Empirical results demonstrate that a large share of voters do not anticipate receiving private goods, such as handouts or public-sector jobs, thus rendering a

---

[23] Notice that, after the election, parties can always stop payment to voters and forfeit on the expected delivery of targeted goods. Such a decision would lower the value of targeted returns in the next election, as voters would update and reduce the probability, $\pi$, of future allocations of benefits. In our model, without winning office there are no payments and without payments the utility of targeted distribution in future elections declines.

[24] Some scholars have argued that the delivery of targeted benefits to a sub-group of voters may drive away those voters that feel excluded from that party (Weitz-Shapiro, 2012). Our model accommodates such "disincentives," which will behave much in the same way that positive incentives do, and we control for attitudes about distribution in our empirical analyses.

[25] See Kitschelt (2000), Kitschelt and Wilkinson (2007), Shefter (1994), Keefer and Vlaicu (2008), Chandra (2004).

value of zero to expectations about targeted distribution. While a larger share of voters expects to benefit from public works, this is still a subset of all voters. We also expect greater variation regarding the weight voters attach to distributive expectations based on their labor market constraints and opportunities. Vote-seeking politicians, consequently, will be better off if they select clients that are more sensitive to targeted distribution; i.e. voters that provide the most bang for their buck.

### c) Partisan Networks

Partisan networks signal a party's capacity to mobilize for electoral campaigns, disseminate party messages, deliver targeted benefits, and reach voters to collect and communicate information. Activists allow voters to attach familiar faces to candidates, forge descriptive ties, interpret party messages, relay preferences, and access benefits. Voters recognize differences among partisan networks due to their personal contact with party activists who are mobilizing, campaigning, sharing policy messages, asking voters about their wants and needs, or delivering resources to them. Therefore, a large and dense network of activists is an asset that increases the party's vote. By contrast, a small and sparse network of activists threatens a party's electoral viability.

The literature on political parties has long recognized the electoral value of activists emphasizing their ability to get out the vote, communicate party positions to voters, and deliver targeted goods. These different tasks are often associated with distinct type of activists in the literature. Kitschelt (1994) argues that activists can be policy-oriented, office-oriented, or pragmatic according to their incentives to join party ranks. Schofield and Sened's (2006) model features activists providing electorally valuable labor and being paid through policies, in line with Kitschelt's policy-oriented category.[26] Shifting the focus to the supply side, Shefter (1994) distinguishes parties with access to patronage jobs – which should attract "office-oriented" activists – from policy-oriented parties lacking these resources because they originated in the opposition, or after the

---

[26] In analyzing why European left-wing parties remained anchored to their policy positions rather than chasing the median voter in the 1990s, Kitschelt (1994) focuses on the ideological intransigence of policy-oriented activists, whereas Tsebelis (1990) argues that activists were playing a second, or *nested*, game to discipline the party today to ensure their preferred policies tomorrow.

establishment of civil service. The Latin American literature focuses on the territorial reach of activists networks, which seek to mobilize voters and deliver targeted distribution, rather than investigating activists' policy preferences (Auyero, 2001; Diaz-Cayeros et al., 2016; Levitsky, 2003; Szwarcberg, 2015).

In our own investigation of activists' contribution to parties' electoral efforts, we build on the existing literature and focus on two distinct types, which we associate with different network structure, recruitment patterns, information mechanisms, and connection to voters. We call those "ideological" and "territorial" and assume that their electoral activities are similar and that a portion of activists in each category seeks to gain access to elected office or the public sector.[27] The former type of activist requires skills for policy persuasion and thereby recruitment is likely to rely on ideological connections to professional or educational organizations. The latter type is dedicated to serving the needs and wants of voters in their own neighborhoods and should be more likely to attract local community leaders and activists embedded in their localities. We expect these different types of activists' networks to be distinguished in their structure and connections to voters.

To measure the importance of activist networks, as well as the opportunities and constraints they provide to parties, we propose a novel methodology using a survey-based measure of linkages between voters and party activists. Our empirical measure allows us to model the size and structure of activists' networks, measure inter-party asymmetries in their activist endowments, and assess their effect on vote choice. A closer connection between voters and activists, we will show, increases the electoral returns of targeted distribution, while simultaneously constraining parties' ability to deviate from their prior distributive strategies and policy offers. However, such a connection need not be defined in ideological terms, therefore our analysis of network structure will show whether or not activists are more likely to know voters who share their policy views. We expect ideological activists' networks to have stronger connections to voters who share their policy views, thereby making voters vary on their proximity to activists depending on their ideological self-placement and thus intertwining both dimensions. By contrast, we do not have such expectations about territorial networks, which should be more embedded in activists' communities.

---

[27] What Kitschelt labels "office-oriented."

This book provides a unique methodology for measuring activists-type by focusing on network structure while assessing their expected effect on voting behavior, by analyzing how activists can influence voters' perception of parties' policy offers and non-policy endowments. In doing so, we point to how activists provide new opportunities and constraints to politicians seeking to gain office. The empirical analysis of these effects, we argue, is a crucial contribution to scholarly debates about policy adaptation, as well as to current debates on the allocation of distributive benefits to core or swing voters as described in Chapter 7.

## 1.3 VOTER PREFERENCES AND PORTFOLIO DIVERSIFICATION STRATEGIES

Our research begins with the assumption that the policy and non-policy preferences of voters explain their electoral choices. Voters weigh the policies and non-policy benefits offered by candidates, inducing parties to tailor different packages to distinct groups of constituencies. Heterogeneity in voters' preferences provides vote-seeking candidates with opportunities to mix and match electoral offers to voters who are more sensitive to particular policy offers and non-policy benefits. Asymmetries in non-policy endowments, therefore, create opportunities and constraints for different parties which may provide systematic advantages over their rivals.

### a) Asymmetries on Non-Policy Endowments

Asymmetries in non-policy endowment could benefit different parties across constituencies, such as when left-wing voters perceive progressive parties as more competent, or when right-wing voters identify conservative parties as more capable. This is a common finding in US surveys, where conservative voters consider Republicans as more capable of managing the economy, whereas progressive voters give better marks to the Democrats on that dimension. Similarly, Chilean voters on the left and right of the political spectrum perceive parties that are ideologically more proximate as having non-policy advantages in managing the economy, poverty, and crime than other, more ideologically distant, parties. A majority of voters, however, could also perceive a party as being more competent, more attuned to the needs of voters, or better at providing services and benefits. A majority of survey respondents in Argentina, for example, have consistently ranked Peronists as more competent administrators than their rivals.

Whether groups of voters perceive different parties as having a non-policy advantage – as in Chile – or perceive that one party is simply better, has important implications for our theory. If parties make the same policy offer, but voters perceive one of them as "better" in some non-policy dimension, voters should opt for the party with a non-policy advantage on Election Day. In such a case, if all parties advertise the same policy to voters, the advantaged party should perform better, as it can take on the position of the median voter (Groseclose, 2001).

If a party has a non-policy advantage and seeks to maximize voters, it should constantly change its policy offers to match the preferences of the median voter. If a majority of voters swing to the left, the party should follow them toward the position of the median voter. If a majority move rightward, the party should shift its ideological positioning in that direction. Indeed, if there are no costs associated with policy switches, something that we will discuss shortly, a non-policy advantage should always result in the advantaged party chasing the median voter. Wherever the median voter goes, the advantaged party should follow.

The disadvantaged party, however, faces a dilemma: if it offers the policy preferred by the median voter, signaling the same ideology as that of the advantaged party, all voters would be better off selecting the "better" party. This is the case for voters on the left or the right who would be equally distant from both parties but perceived one of them as "better" in some non-policy dimension. As a result, the disadvantaged party should move away from the median voter to a location where its ideological proximity to at least a subgroup of voters offsets the aggregate non-policy disadvantage. While the disadvantaged party will not win the election, it will at least collect the largest possible minority of the vote, rather than losing all votes.[28]

The theoretical implications of the proposed model are that a party with a non-policy advantage has fewer constraints to taking on the position of the median voter, rapidly adapting to external shocks or changes in voter preference. As a result, the disadvantaged parties should

---

[28] For this result to hold, the policy and non-policy dimensions of the votes should not be strictly independent from each other, which would result in all parties collapsing to the location of the median voter and no policy equilibria. Heterogeneity in non-policy assessments will also be necessary to prevent the advantaged party from mimicking the policy offer of the disadvantaged party. See Adams, Merrill, and Grofman (2005) and the appendix to Chapter 4.

be crowded out of the median voter location, pushed centrifugally to the left or right of the median voter depending on the distribution of voter preferences and the location of rival parties.

### b) Non-Policy Asymmetries and Electoral Strategies

A key insight of our research is that parties with a non-policy advantage among a subgroup of voters (voter heterogeneity) will benefit from delivering policy offers that disproportionally benefit that same group (biased responsiveness). As a result, when the non-policy and policy dimensions of the vote correlate with each other, policy will become sticky and parties will develop stable and informative party labels. By contrast, when the non-policy and policy dimensions of the vote are orthogonal to each other, the advantaged party will face weaker constraints to changing its policy offers in response to changes in the preferences of the median voter.

Heterogeneity with regards to voters' ideological positions in the distribution of non-policy resources across groups of voters matters because when policy preferences and non-policy endowments correlate with each other, the returns of policy offers are conditional on non-policy endowments. More generally, the correlation between policy and non-policy resources constrains parties from modifying their policy offers. To illustrate this mechanism, consider a progressive party with ideological activists who have more linkages to leftist voters with whom they share greater affinity. That is, consider a polity where left-wing voters have more linkages to the activists of leftist parties, so that the non-policy endowments (activists) correlate with policy preferences. If the party moderates its policy offers toward the median voter, these ideological activists will be less efficient at gathering information and delivering benefits to moderate voters, both because of cognitive dissonance as well as because they have fewer connections to moderate voters. Because these activists are more connected to ideologically akin voters than to moderate ones, moderate voters will not be informed of changes in the party's policy offers as rapidly as those who favored leftist policies. As a result, vote losses incurred among progressive voters will grow faster than gains among moderate ones. The result is a non-policy advantage among leftist voters that makes changing policy offers costly, as it reduces the overall vote by losing old voters at a faster rate than new ones are acquired. In the long run, if non-policy endowments grow to connect with moderate voters, the party may recover. In the short run, however, moving away from past policy offers is costly and detrimental to the party's electoral performance.

Our argument is similar to those of Cox and McCubbins (1986) and Dixit and Londregan (1996), who note that more linkages to core voters, whom the party knows better and to whom it can deliver benefits more efficiently, should make activists more responsive to their preferences and increase the electoral benefits of allocating disproportionate amounts of benefits to them. Hence, non-policy endowments that disproportionally benefit a subgroup of voters constrain parties from modifying the offers given to those voters.

This type of connection emerged empirically in our data. For example, our survey results show a close connection between ideological preferences and perceptions of economic competence among Chilean voters, with leftist voters giving higher economic competence marks to progressive parties, whereas conservative voters grant higher competence marks to right-wing parties. In Argentina, by contrast, voters across the ideological spectrum perceived the Peronists as a more competent party at managing the economy, above and beyond its rivals, thereby showing that reported ideological self-placement does not inform voters on managerial skill but is a separate dimension altogether. We also observe internal country differences, as Argentine voters on the right of the political spectrum give higher competence marks to the center-right PRO (Republican Proposal) than voters on the left. Therefore, inter-voter asymmetries on perceptions of parties' economic competence are not associated with voters' policy preferences for the Peronist's voters, but they are associated for voters of the PRO.[29] We therefore expect competence assessment to anchor Chilean political parties ideologically, but to grant further opportunities for shifting policy offers to the Argentine Peronist than to their PRO rivals.

## 1.4 TESTING THE ARGUMENT: CASE SELECTION AND RESEARCH STRATEGY

To develop our non-policy politics framework, we consider the cases of Argentina and Chile because the literature suggested that political parties had different policy and non-policy endowments. These are two middle-

---

[29] The data on our 2007 survey shows that the correlation between ideological distance and evaluations of economic competence was 0.40 for the Chilean Socialist Party, 0.09 for the Argentine Peronists, and 0.16 for the conservative PRO.

income democracies with well-established multiparty systems and free and fair elections, a scope condition of our argument. Moreover, large socioeconomic differences among voters in each country allow us to explore how parties deliver distinct types of policy and non-policy offers across voters with distinct policy and non-policy expectations. In so doing, we take advantage of two large national surveys of our own design (including an innovative measure to assess the impact of partisan networks), supplemented by semi-structured interviews with politicians and publicly available statistics. Using these tools, we measure voters' preferences and their impact on the opportunities and constraints of parties. In particular, we assess which voters are most sensitive to diverse policy and non-policy offers in the portfolio of political parties. We complement our analysis of voters' preferences with politicians' own framing of their electoral strategies as well as measures of the behavior of public officials (derived from publicly available data) and elite attitudes (relying on the Political Elites of Latin America surveys).

Argentina and Chile are both located in Latin America, the developing region with the broadest democratic experience since the Third Wave. In both countries, free and fair elections generate incentives for politicians to respond to voters' preferences. Indeed, compulsory voting in both countries may have broadened such responsiveness. Two middle-income countries with relatively high levels of socioeconomic inequality provide the conditions that make them comparable to both more advanced and emerging democracies, while allowing the identification of a crucial category in terms of electoral behavior: socioeconomic status. The established literature on Latin American political parties, moreover, suggests significant variation in parties' policy and non-policy offers – especially with regards to targeted distribution and the value of ideological shortcuts for voters in these countries – which leads us to investigate variation in the crucial independent variable of our argument: voters' policy and non-policy preferences.[30] Finally, common historical legacies of Spanish colonization, early democratization, the experience of brutal military dictatorships in the 1970s, and similar demographics are useful to control for other factors that could shape electoral competition in both countries.

---

[30] See, for instance, Alcantara and Freidenberg (2001), Torcal and Mainwaring (2003), Roberts (2013), Levitsky (2003), Luna (2014), Kitschelt et al., (2010); Mainwaring and Scully (1995).

## a) Argentine and Chilean Voters

In both countries, policy differences regarding the role of the state are crucial ideological dimensions separating voters, whereas socioeconomic inequality produced crucial political cleavages.[31] As a result of residential segregation, socioeconomic status is a crucial category used to organize political preferences and electoral strategies.[32] The scholarship on both countries documents how parties' electoral strategies for the poor and the middle classes diverge.[33] We investigate this source of voter heterogeneity in this book, uncovering patterns that do not always coincide with the conventional wisdom. For instance, we find that although policy preferences for richer and poorer voters differ in both countries, the pattern of variation is not identical. Richer voters are more conservative than poorer voters in Chile, while the opposite is true in Argentina.

In defining non-policy dimensions, we relied on an extensive literature highlighting the influence of targeted distribution, economic competence, and partisan networks on the vote in both countries.[34] Our survey includes empirical indicators based on questions about parties' competence in managing the economy, crime, and poverty, as well as about distributive expectations regarding handouts (clientelism), public jobs (patronage), and public works (pork). We measure both the number of activists and their connections to voters using questions about the different number of activists from each party known personally by respondents, with the assumption that if they know more activists, they are more connected to the party organization and therefore have an advantage in

---

[31] See Levitsky and Roberts (2011), Flores-Macias (2012), Kitchelt et al. (2010), Mainwaring and Scully (1995), Zeichmester and Corral (2013).

[32] There is a vast literature that analyzes the effect of federal institutions and residential sorting on the allocation of public resources. For readers interested on this line of reasoning, see Beramendi and Rueda (2014), Chen and Rodden (2013), Rodden (2002, 2006), Wibbels (2000).

[33] For Chile, see Luna (2014) and Barozet (2004, 2006). For Argentina, see Weitz-Shapiro (2014) and Brusco et al. (2004). For Perú, see Muñoz (2018).

[34] On targeted distribution see Stokes et al. (2013), Weitz-Shapiro (2014), Luna (2014), Auyero (2001), Levitsky and Roberts (2013), Kitchelt et al. (2010), and Calvo and Murillo (2004). On party activists see Calvo and Murillo (2013), Levitsky (2003), Stokes et al. (2013), Szwarcberg (2015), Luna, Rosenblatt, and Toro (2011); Luna (2014); and Espinoza and Madrid (2010). The effect of competence has not been studied directly, but see Ratto (2011, 2013), Alcántara and Tagina (2013), Lewis-Beck and Ratto (2013), and Murillo and Viscontti (2017) on the impact of economic performance on incumbent support.

exchanging information with activists regarding targeted distribution or policy positions. Our surveys are further discussed in Chapters 4 and 5.[35]

To summarize, we selected Argentina and Chile seeking variation on parties' policy and non-policy benefits as well as voters' preferences on those dimensions, while keeping other variables theorized to affect electoral competition relatively constant. Additionally, our choice of the three non-policy resources was supported by the literature on electoral behavior in both countries. Finally, in both countries, socioeconomic status was a crucial electoral category, allowing us to assess biases derived from electoral responsiveness to poorer and richer voters.

## b) Scope Conditions

We assume that politicians have electoral incentives to be responsive to voters' preferences, and thereby our framework is restricted to democracies with free and fair elections. It also requires fluid flows of information between voters and parties. Information is crucial for voters to recognize party offers and for parties to react to voters' preferences. Additionally, parties should survive between elections and therefore allow voters to establish expectations about their behavior. These are standard scope conditions of the demand-side literature on electoral behavior.[36] In our view, the limits to apply our argument to some new democracies are not derived from the lack of policy offers (which may weigh zero in the decision of some voters, according to our framework), but from the lack of adequate information flows and relatively stable parties.

A stronger critique to our argument comes from supply-side theories of voting behavior derived from the American context, where responsiveness to public opinion is limited.[37] Building on Converse's (1962a, 1962b) distrust of the American electorate, this literature suggests that politicians shape voters' preferences rather than respond to them.[38] According to

---

[35] See also Calvo and Murillo (2013).
[36] The demand-side literature on electoral behavior assumes responsiveness of parties seeking to maximize the vote (e.g. Adams, Merrill, and Grofman, 2005; Schofield and Sened, 2006) even when adjudicating different degree of strategic behavior to voters conditional on political institutions (e.g. Ames, 1987; Calvo and Hellwig, 2011; Cox, 1999; Kedar, 2005.)
[37] Analyzing policy responsiveness, Gilens (2012: 71) shows that issues require more than two-thirds of public opinion support to produce policy change by US legislators.
[38] According to Converse, US voters "simply do not have meaningful beliefs, even on issues that have formed the basis for intense political controversy among elites"(1964: 245).

Zaller (1992), voter preferences – although stable once measurement error is considered – are molded by elites conditional on political awareness and education.[39] Other scholars suggest that politicians are reactive only to core voters' views and seek to shape median voters' preferences by relying on ambiguity or "pandering" to them to mask their behavior.[40] More recently, Achen and Bartels (2016) question the ability of voters to even discern politicians' responsibility over outcomes – despite the lower information demands of competence – and submit that their social identities, namely partisanship in the American context, shape their policy preferences.

Partisanship, as explained before, could be considered a non-policy resource, and its correlation with policy preferences is consistent with our framework as parties with larger endowments would be less constrained to move in the policy space. Remember that we take non-policy resources as given (at least in the short-term) whereas policy switching is endogenous to non-policy advantages that are not correlated with voters' ideological preferences. Moreover, we are agnostic about the origin of voters' preferences – even when we hypothesize about possible historical origins in Chapter 3 – and could incorporate political identities as a source for their origin. As a result, our main difference with this literature refers to our expectations on parties' attention to the opportunities and constraints generated by diverse distribution of voters' preferences. Politicians, in our interviews, recognized the importance of voters' policy and non-policy preferences in defining their short-term strategies. Indeed, the fixed timing of elections and expansion of information has made politicians increasingly aware of voters' preferences and made them rely on different sources to gauge them. However, in the US context, other institutional mechanisms may be at play in reducing responsiveness, as already discussed by the American literature on electoral behavior.[41] In the non-US context,

---

[39] Zaller (1992) argues that there is a non-monotonic relationship between political awareness and sensitivity to political messages with increasing sensitivity at intermediate levels of political attention because voters pay attention to messages, but do not have strong enough predispositions to make them resistance to new information.

[40] Tomz and Van Howelling (2009) show to that "ambiguity" is more effective when voters already have partisan identities, which shape their interpretation of unclear policy positions or when they have weaker policy priors. Lax and Phillips (2009) find support for legislators' responsiveness to core, rather than median, voters using state-level data, whereas Jacob and Shapiro (2000) argue that American politicians are more responsive to core voters and donors than to the median voter, but "pander" to the latter through their messages.

[41] See Bartels (2008), Baumgartner and Jones (1993), Brooks and Manza (2006), Gilens (2012), Carnes and Lupu (2015), and Schlozman, Verba and Brady (2012).

electoral responsiveness tends to be higher and the challenges for our theory are derived from the weakness of political parties and the difficulties such weakness may generate for voters to form preferences over their policy and non-policy offers (Brader, Tucker, and Duell, 2013; Roberts, 2013).

### c) Roadmap

Chapter 2 expands on our explanatory framework and develops its operationalization by introducing the statistical model used to measure the influence of each dimension on voters' electoral decisions. We provide a brief history of Argentine and Chilean political parties and trace possible sources of voters' preferences in Chapter 3. In Chapters 4 and 5, we present the distribution of voters' policy and non-policy preferences in both countries. We investigate the extent to which policy and non-policy offers weigh on voters' electoral choices, identifying distinct socioeconomic patterns in Chapter 6. We expect variation on the weight attached by voters to diverse preferences to create opportunities for political parties to target distinct groups with the type of benefit to which they are most electorally sensitive. In Chapter 7, we focus on the operation of partisan networks in relation to such heterogeneity and the distinct types of activists we identify, whereas Chapter 8 analyzes the disbursement of public-sector employment expenditures to favor particular groups of voters who were identified as most sensitive to these non-policy benefits in Chapter 6. Chapter 9 focuses on the discussion of parties' policy responsiveness to diverse groups of voters and the potential bias it generates on policymaking as well as its implications for understanding the evolution of party systems in the two studied countries. Chapter 10 concludes with a discussion of our contributions to the literature, as well as the normative implications derived from our broader conceptualization of electoral responsiveness.

# 2

# A Demand-Side Model of Non-Policy Politics

This chapter presents our explanatory framework and introduces a statistical model of vote choice, with individual-level variation on policy offers and non-policy endowments. In our framework, voters assess the non-policy endowments of parties and their policy offers. As described in Chapter 1, heterogeneity in the weight that voters attach to benefits results in some groups of voters providing larger electoral returns to parties. Therefore, responsiveness should be biased toward those voters that feel more intensely about distinct policy and non-policy benefits in the portfolio of parties.

A formal presentation of the model[1] will further show that parties with a comparative non-policy advantage will benefit from taking policy positions that are more central, closer to the median voter. Meanwhile, parties with a comparative non-policy disadvantage advertise more extreme policy offers. As parties are constrained by their different non-policy endowments, they will deliver different combinations of benefits to distinct groups of voters. Therefore, differences in non-policy endowments and in the weights that voters attach to benefits will bias electoral competition, to the benefit of more intense voters and that of better-endowed parties.

---

[1] In this chapter, we provide a Stackelberg model that describes political parties' behavior predicted by our model, thus anticipating results in Chapter 9. Critical to our results is that the policy preferences of voters and the non-policy endowments of parties are not strictly orthogonal to each other. We discuss extensively this assumption and introduce measures of empirical association in later chapters. Additionally, the models described in this chapter identify both the opportunities and constraints that shape the policy and non-policy strategies of political parties and their expected effect on voters.

## 2.1 VOTING WITH POLICY AND NON-POLICY OFFERS

We model voters' electoral behavior using a utility function with policy and non-policy preferences. The utility function of voters considers policy offers in the left–right scale as well as non-policy endowments, such as a party's managerial competence or its capacity to deploy activists. The electoral importance or weight that voters associate with policy offers and non-policy endowments affects the probability that they will vote for a party on Election Day.

Taking a page from the notebook of Bayesian statistics (Gelman and Hill, 2007), we consider policy offers and non-policy endowments as observable variables, while weights are unobservable variables with proper distributions and substantive interpretations. The observed variables describe assessments of ideological proximity and non-policy endowments. The unobserved variables describe how much each voter cares about policy proximity and the non-policy benefits provided by parties.

Consider the frequently used specification of the voters' utility function with proximity and valence terms:[2]

$$U(V_{ik}) = -\alpha_i(x_i - L_k)^2 + \beta_i T_{ik} + \gamma_{ik} \qquad \text{(Eq. 2.1)}$$

In Equation (2.1), $x_i$ is the self-reported policy preference of voter $i$ on the left–right scale; $L_k$ is the policy proposal $L$ of party $k$; $(x_i - L_k)^2$ describes the quadratic distance between voter $i$'s preferred policy and the party proposal; the parameter $\alpha_i$ describes a voter-specific disutility for a policy that is further removed from their ideal policy preference $x_i$; $\beta_i T_{ik}$ describes a voter-specific weight $\beta_i$ for the non-policy trait $T_{ik}$; and $\gamma_{ik}$ describes a random utility term that is both voter and party specific. (See Table 2.1.)

Existing models generally consider the disutility $\alpha$ as fixed and identical for all voters. That is, when party $k$ offers a policy that is further removed from the preference of any voter $i$, the utility of voting for that party declines at the same fixed rate, $\alpha$, for each and every voter. We relax this assumption, acknowledging that there is heterogeneity in how much

---

[2] Since Alesina and Rosenthal (1995), a number of authors have used variations of this equation, including Dixit and Londregan (1996, 1998), Ansolabehere and Snyder (2000), Adams, Merrill, and Grofman (2005); Schofield and Sened (2006); and Calvo and Hellwig (2011).

TABLE 2.1. *Description of the terms in Equation (2.1)*

| Term | Description |
|---|---|
| $x_i$ | Ideological location of voter $i$ on a left–right dimension (taxes, health benefits, social rights, etc.) |
| $L_k$ | Policy offer by party $k$ on a left–right dimension (taxes, health benefits, social rights, etc.) |
| $(x_i-L_k)^2$ | Distance from the voter's preferred location to the policy offer made by party $k$ |
| $-\alpha_i$ | Importance or weight that voter $i$ attaches to policy proximity. We index the disutility $\alpha_i$ by voter $i$, allowing heterogeneity among voters |
| $\beta_i$ | Importance or weight that voter $i$ attaches to the non-policy benefit $T$ provided by party $k$, $T_{ik}$. We index the disutility $\beta_i$ by voter $i$, allowing heterogeneity among voters |
| $T_{ik}$ | Non-policy endowment $T$ of party $k$ as assessed by voter $i$ (managerial competence, access to party networks, selective benefits, etc.) |
| $\gamma_{ik}$ | Voter- and party-specific random utility term, drawn from a type I extreme value distribution (multinomial logit) |

different voters care for the policy and non-policy benefits delivered by parties.

We may index $\alpha_i$ by the socioeconomic status, ethnicity, or religious affiliation of a group of voters. In its more general form, however, our notation makes explicit that individuals attach different weights to policy and non-policy benefits. Further, individuals can be grouped in a number of different categories. Accordingly, Equation (2.1) allows ideological distance weights to vary, with the disutility term $\alpha_i$ being indexed by voter $i \in I$.

Our theory also models heterogeneity in the weight $\beta_i$ that each voter attaches to non-policy endowments. A wealthy voter, for instance, may care a great deal more than a poor voter about ideological distance, $\alpha_R > \alpha_P$, whereas a poorer voter may care a great deal about party networks, $\beta_R < \beta_P$.[3] Such heterogeneity is crucial to our argument, as it enters into the calculus of politicians and drives the parties' incentives to

---

[3] The fact that voters care to a different degree about ideological proximity and non-spatial determinants of the vote such as targeted distribution or competence also explains that parties gain benefits from allocating different types of targeted goods among distinct groups of voters (Cox and McCubbins, 1986; Dixit and Londregan, 1996; Gans-Morse, Mazzuca, and Nichter, 2014; Stokes, 2005).

tailor their policy and non-policy portfolio to distinct groups of voters. Finally, $T_{ik}$ describes the perceived non-policy endowments of parties, which in the cases we study are managerial competence, network capacity, and targeted distribution.

Political parties differ in their capacity to acquire and deliver non-policy benefits such as managerial competence or selective incentives. For example, parties may have more or less latitude to allocate patronage jobs while in office. Parties may also differ in their capacity to identify voters with intense preferences for those jobs. Some endowments may be easier to allocate to new constituencies, such as public-sector jobs, while others may be more difficult to change, such as a reputation for managerial competence. In the short run, however, we consider that endowments are relatively fixed and difficult to acquire.

Our model considers the utility of voting for a party as resulting from the combination of policy and non-policy benefits expected by voters, as well as the weight they attach to each of those benefits. Given that candidates are more likely to infer inter-group differences rather than individual differences in the weight that voters attach to benefits, we may model aggregated, rather than individual, heterogeneity.[4] Still, at a conceptual level, we can think of heterogeneity as an individual trait and the decision to target groups of voters as a best possible approximation to the preferences of individuals when such information is not available.

## 2.2 POLICY AND NON-POLICY BIASES: RESPONSIVENESS TO INTENSE VOTERS

Our theory assumes that the heterogeneity in the weight that voters attach to policy and non-policy benefits will bias parties' responsiveness to them. That is, voters who are more sensitive to a particular policy or non-policy offer (and change their vote accordingly) are likely to be more influential in parties' decisions on the allocation of those benefits. In this section, we provide a simple formalization of this intuition, describing the expected biases in benefits provided by parties.

Consider two equally sized groups, one composed of poorer voters and another one of richer voters, with a different disutility for policy offers

---

[4] We assume that parties can tailor distinct policy and non-policy offers to diverse groups of voters but do not assume that parties need to segment their offers in a particular way, as argued by Luna (2014) and Thachil (2014).

## A Demand-Side Model of Non-Policy Politics

(different $-\alpha$ in Equation (2.1)).[5] As we show, optimal policy offers should deviate from the policy preferences of the median voter to the benefit of voters with more intense policy preferences. Optimal policy moves toward the preference of the *median-weighted voter*, with weights provided by the relative importance that voters attach to policy and non-policy benefits. Our results also provide a simple formula to compute the expected biases, which we report to readers using survey data in Chapter 6.

Let us begin with two equally sized groups of voters, a group of poorer voters and a group of richer voters, with normally distributed and symmetric preferences lined up on a single policy dimension. The median poorer voter is located to the left of the overall median voter, whereas the median richer voter is situated to the right of the median voter:

$$x_{Pi} \sim N(\mu_{Pi}, \sigma_P^2),$$

$$x_{Ri} \sim N(\mu_{Ri}, \sigma_R^2)$$

$$\bar{x}_{Pi} < \bar{x}_{Mi} < \bar{x}_{Ri}$$

For simplicity, we exemplify policy biases and hold non-policy weights at zero. Therefore, we assume that voters perceive no benefits from the non-policy weight parameter $\beta_i = 0$ for all $\in I$, and consider a plain, vanilla policy model, $U(V_{ik}) = -\alpha_i(x_i - L_k)^2$. An identical model with non-policy terms yields similar results. In the previous section, we defined the parameter $-\alpha_i$ as the disutility experienced by voter $i$ when party $k$ makes a policy offer that is different from its preferred policy. Consider, for example, that the preferred policy of the median poorer voter is $\bar{x}_P = 3$ and the preferred policy of the median richer voter is $\bar{x}_P = 7$.

If party $k$ makes a policy offer $L_k = 4$, with the disutility parameter arbitrarily set to $-\alpha_i = 0.2$ for each voter, then the proposed party offer would yield a disutility for the median poorer voter equal to $U_{\bar{x}_P} = -0.2*(3-4)^2 = -0.2$. Meanwhile, the expected disutility for the median richer voter would be $U_{\bar{x}_R} = -0.2*(7-4)^2 = -1.8$. That is, a leftist policy would yield a larger disutility to the richer median voter than to the poorer one. Let us now consider a candidate that wants to maximize the aggregate policy benefits of all voters (minimize the overall disutility) and

---

[5] We may accommodate groups with different sizes with a second set of weights. For simplicity, we assume that both groups are of equal size, which is not very different from our empirical measures in the studied countries, where half of the respondents to our survey were middle income and half were lower-income voters.

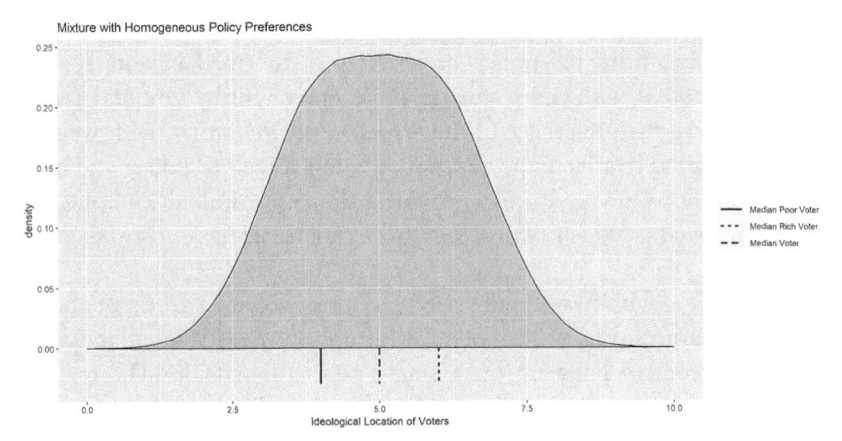

FIGURE 2.1. Optimal policy offer $L$ with a mixture model where richer and poorer voters give equal weight to policy $[\alpha_P = \alpha_R = -0.2]$

make an optimal offer that makes voters, on average, better off. We would then differentiate the following equation:[6]

$$\frac{d}{dx} f(L_k) = -\alpha_P(\bar{x}_P - L_k)^2 - \alpha_R(\bar{x}_R - L_k)^2 \quad \text{(Eq. 2.2)}$$

$$0 = 2\alpha_P(\bar{x}_P - L_k) + 2\alpha_R(\bar{x}_R - L_k) \quad \text{(Eq. 2.3)}$$

and solve for $L_k$

$$L_k = \frac{\alpha_P \bar{x}_P + \alpha_P \bar{x}_R}{\alpha_P + \alpha_P} \quad \text{(Eq. 2.4)}$$

Readers can verify that the optimal offer in Equation (2.4) is a weighted function of the mean preference of each group $[\bar{x}_P, \bar{x}_R]$, with weights given by the importance that voters attach to policy, $[-\alpha_P, -\alpha_R]$.

If the disutility that each group attaches to policy is identical, $-\alpha_P, -\alpha_R$, then all voters are valued equally by parties when making an offer. Figure 2.1 shows the combined density of poorer and richer voters, with a mixture of normal distributions that yields an optimal and unbiased policy offer located on the position of the median voter, $L_K = \frac{-0.2*3 - 0.2*7}{-0.2 - 0.2} = 5$. That is, a policy that is not given more weight to the preferences of some voters. However, if richer voters care for policy $L_K$ more intensely that poorer voters, $[\alpha_P = -0.1, \alpha_R = -0.2]$, then the

---

[6] The relative size of each group is the same so that we may disregard population weights.

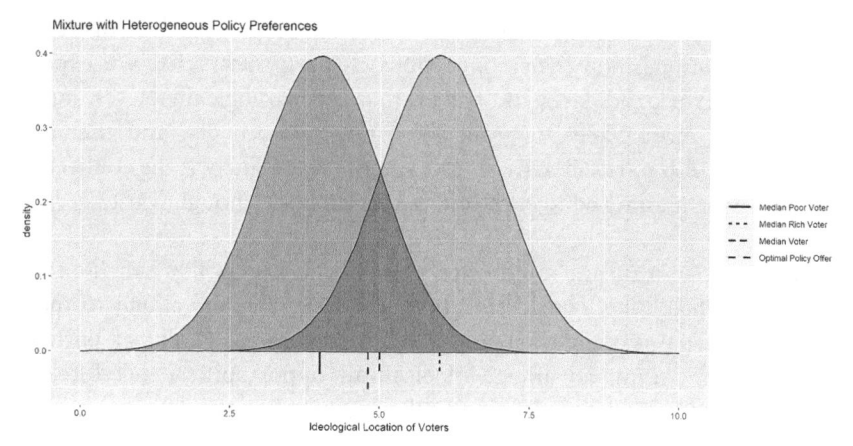

FIGURE 2.2. Optimal policy offer $L$ with a mixture model where richer voters give double the weight to policy than poor voters $[\alpha_P = -0.1, \alpha_R = -0.2]$

optimal policy offer will shift to the right of the median voter preference, to $L_K = \dfrac{-0.1^*3 - 0.2^*7}{-0.1 - 0.2} = 5.66$, as it is shown in Figure 2.2.

Our theory indicates that parties that maximize vote shares should not give equal voice to voters that care about policy with different intensity. Indeed, if an electorally minded politician offers an optimal policy that minimizes the distance to all voters, differences in the weights that voters attach to policy should bias policy offers in the direction of the most intense group. In Chapter 6, we provide statistical estimates of $[-\alpha_P, -\alpha_R]$ for voters from different socioeconomic groups, showing variation on the incentives of politicians seeking to define their optimal policy and non-policy offers in both countries. In the appendix to this chapter, we provide a two-party Stackelberg model that describes the effect that non-policy endowments have in the optimal policy offers made by parties. We now turn our attention to describing differences in the type of non-policy endowments provided by parties.

## 2.3 VOTERS' PREFERENCES, PARTY ENDOWMENTS, AND POLITICIANS' ELECTORAL PORTFOLIOS

Given our framework, we expect inter-party asymmetries in non-policy endowments to generate opportunities and constraints for parties regarding their policy offers. In calculating these incentives, we consider the policy preferences of voters, parties' policy offers, and their non-policy endowments. In the two cases we study, these non-policy resources were defined by voters' evaluations of managerial competence, their distributive expectations, and their connections to party networks. We expect voters to favor candidates and parties that are ideologically closer, more competent, more likely to grant them targeted benefits, and that are associated with partisan activists the voter is more likely to be connected to. The weight attached to each of these dimensions, though, varies across voters.

Politicians, in turn, should offer policies and non-policy benefits that maximize their vote, considering both the weight voters attach to their offers, as well as their own non-policy endowments. Political parties' capacity for taking advantage of electoral opportunities, therefore, is constrained by the type of benefits at their disposal and by the distribution of non-policy benefits expected by voters. In what follows, we identify how heterogeneity in preferences and asymmetries in endowments shape the electoral calculus of parties.

### a) Political Agency and the Distribution of Non-Policy Resources

Asymmetries in the endowment of non-policy resources are not only crucial to defining the ability of politicians to win elections, but also the policy offers they should make to maximize their vote. Such asymmetries imply that advantaged parties have, on average, more non-policy resources than disadvantaged parties. Further, asymmetries in non-policy endowments can either be perceived by most voters, or vary across sub-groups, with some voters perceiving different parties as better in some non-policy dimensions than others. This distinction has important consequences for both voter and party behavior. Such differences in the distributions of non-policy resources constrain the agency of politicians in terms of their ability to deliver non-policy resources and, consequentially, their opportunities for modifying their policy offers.

Vote-seeking politicians, faced with exogenous shocks such as changing population demographics or economic crises, seek to change their policy offers to cater to the evolving needs of the electorate. External shocks provide incentives to change policy offers and, if parties have the freedom to do so, may induce significant policy switches and even new party branding (Lupu, 2016; Stokes, 2001). Policy shocks may also provide new incentives to allocate non-policy resources, as when rises in unemployment make it more attractive to create new public-sector jobs or deliver handouts (Robinson and Verdier, 2002). Asymmetries in non-policy resources, however, shape parties' ability to both change policy and to respond to shocks by delivering non-policy benefits.

The distribution of preferences among voters generates unequal opportunities for political parties to tailor their portfolio of electoral offers. When the distribution is uneven, voters may perceive some political parties as better than their competitors. Voters who perceive parties as better on some non-policy dimension may also relate advantages on other preference dimensions, either policy or non-policy. Hence, modifying the allocation of one type of benefit may shape the returns of the associated one as well.

Empirically, as we show in Chapters 4 and 5, there are groups of voters that perceive some non-policy and policy dimensions of the vote as closely related. To illustrate the opportunities generated by different distributions of voters' preferences, we start here with an example derived from our vote equation and the incentives created by the association between a voter's policy positions and their connection to activists from a particular party. In Equation (2.1), voters have ideological preferences $x_i$ and know $T_{ik}$ activists of party $k$. There are historical, institutional, and socioeconomic reasons why voters with close ideological affinity to each other may also be more likely to know activists from particular political parties, as described in Chapter 1, for ideological networks of activists. First, parties often recruit activists from among their voters and, consequently, we should expect them to share common traits such as social, economic, and district-level origins. Second, voters may want to avoid cognitive dissonance by being more receptive to messages from activists that share similar ideological beliefs. Consequently, voters may be more likely to welcome and interact with activists that share similar political beliefs. Third, party activities used for recruitment and persuasion, such as rallies, festivals, and fundraising will benefit from economies of scale. Therefore, increasing the number of contacts among individuals embedded in dense networks facilitates the reduction of cognitive consonance among participants.

Different reasons drive parties to search and connect with ideologically distant voters. First, party growth often depends on incorporating new members and getting the party message out to uncommitted voters. Outreach efforts to connect with out-members are not very different from allocating selective incentives to ideologically uncommitted (swing) voters rather than to core constituencies (Lindbeck and Weibull, 1987; Stokes, 2005). Second, partisan networks may develop along non-ideological traits in group membership, such as the territorial networks we described in Chapter 1, which are deeply embedded in the local communities.[7] When activists' networks are unrelated to left–right policy positions, parties can effectively connect voters who do not share policy positions.

The opportunity faced by political parties varies in either case. First, we expect political parties with activists who are connected to voters located in particular ideological positions to derive lower electoral returns from updating policy offers. For instance, if Socialist activists are more connected to left-wing voters, a moderation of the party policy position will be relayed more efficiently to leftist voters than to moderate and conservative voters. Whereas left-wing voters are more likely to perceive the increasing policy distance to the party, given the personal connection to activists, moderate voters will not perceive a higher proximity at similar rates. Differences in the connections to party activists thus reduces the electoral returns from policy updating among leftist voters, without offsetting them with new moderate ones. The net effect of moderation to approach the median voter may be negative as a result. Hence, such a distribution of voters' preferences constrains the agency of political parties in terms of modifying their policy offers.

Second, asymmetries in voters' perceptions of party non-policy endowments, even if not associated with other preferences, can constrain the party's capacity to tailor their electoral portfolio. For instance, an uneven distribution of competence evaluation, which cannot be modified in the short-term, should result in politicians relying on other non-policy or policy offers to compensate for their weakness in this area. By contrast, those with a non-policy advantage have an opportunity to tailor their electoral portfolio, taking advance of their larger share of resources for targeting voters who are sensitive to them. Thus, vote-maximizing strategies that involve the updating of electoral offers can be constrained by asymmetries in the distribution of non-policy resources perceived by voters.

### b) Electoral Responsiveness: Parameter and Compositional Effects

We argue that voters' sensitivity to and the composition of their policy and non-policy preferences shape political parties' opportunities for

---

[7] Other dimensions that are not ideological and which the literature has analyzed in terms of their influence in building activists' networks are ethnicity and religion. As in the other two cases, patterns of recruitment and the organization of electoral activities are crucial in defining network dimensions.

tailoring particular resources to high-yield voters. On the one hand, sensitivity is crucial to define the returns to either policy or non-policy returns in electoral terms (the *parameter* effect). For instance, if poorer voters weigh expectations to receive a public job more than richer voters in their electoral calculus, politicians should target patronage distribution to those voters while delivering other resources to richer voters to maximize their returns to invested resources. Composition, on the other hand, defines the content of preferences. Regardless of the salience attached to policy proposals, for instance, richer and poorer voters may prefer lower or higher tax rates, more or less state intervention. For instance, richer voters are more conservative than poorer voters in Chile, but their counterparts are more progressive than poorer voters in Argentina (*composition effect*). Yet, richer Chilean voters are more *sensitive* to policy offers (*parameter effect*), thereby, generating incentives for all political parties to shift policies in a conservative direction, as we show in Chapter 9. In short, the compositional preferences of the most sensitive voters are more likely to be influential on parties' electoral portfolios.

Our general framework is in line with an existing literature, which recognizes that some voters are more likely to change their vote in response to policy offers, whereas others are more sensitive to non-policy offers. Part of this literature also relies on socioeconomic distinctions in sensitivity to diverse electoral offers including variation in the value assigned by higher- and lower-income voters to economic competence (Duch and Stevenson, 2008), targeted distribution (Weitz-Shapiro, 2012), ideology (Luna, 2014), or partisan networks (Calvo and Murillo, 2013). These arguments could be modeled as special cases of our general framework, explaining parties' decisions to allocate electoral resources based on variation on voters' preferences.

Finally, in addition to the *compositional* and *parameter* effects, parties' strategies are also shaped by the asymmetries in the distribution of voters' preferences described in the prior section. Asymmetries in parties' non-policy endowments can generate advantaged players with more capacity to tailor those extra resources to specific categories of voters who are the most sensitive to them. As these asymmetries are based on the composition of preferences, the effects they generate are heightened by parameter effects.

For instance, if a party has higher competence marks associated only with ideologically proximate voters, modifying its policy offer may result in a decline in its high managerial assessments among those voters. In this case, sensitivity to competence assessments should heighten the effect of ideological salience on the vote, thus giving more sway to the compositional preferences of these voters and further reducing politicians' incentives for updating policy offers. If those sensitive voters also share a common socioeconomic status, the influence of their compositional preferences would bias electoral responsiveness as described in Chapter 4.

The proposed empirical framework, therefore, allows us to estimate the opportunities and constraints generated by the different weights voters grant to policy and non-policy offers, as well as variation in the preferences of diverse groups of voters, which we operationalize in Equation (2.1). The individual voter in Equation (2.1) can be aggregated to the group level into any type of category. We choose to use socioeconomic categories, which are the most relevant in the countries we study. Additionally, Equation (2.1) allows for variation in voters' views of parties' non-policy endowments and in their association between those endowments and other terms in the equation, creating further opportunities and constraints for parties' electoral strategies.

## 2.4 EMPIRICAL IMPLICATIONS OF OUR ARGUMENT

Our explanatory framework assumes variation in voter preferences and sensitivity regarding policy and non-policy offers, as well as asymmetries in parties' non-policy endowments. This variation generates opportunities and constraints for politicians seeking to maximize electoral support. We presented Equation (2.1) in this chapter, which we use to calculate the different dimensions in the voter utility function and the incentives these dimensions should generate in competing political parties, given the distribution of voter preferences. In this concluding section, we state our expectations regarding policy and non-policy offers – to be tested in later chapters – and point to some potential trade-offs generated by this broader conceptualization of electoral responsiveness.

We do not have expectations about the distribution of the three main components of our analysis: the content of voters' preferences, their salience, and their distribution across voters of different socioeconomic status. Instead, we investigate them empirically in Chapters 4 and 5. In Chapter 6, we use Equation (2.1) to establish the components of voting decisions in both countries, which we disaggregate by socioeconomic status. Following the existing literature, we expect ideological distance to have a higher salience in Chile than in Argentina, although we do not anticipate particular patterns of variation across social class. Similarly, we anticipate distributive expectations to be more influential in Argentina, with handouts having a higher marginal value for poorer voters. Unexpectedly, we find that sensitivity to public jobs is higher among Chilean middle-income voters and poorer Argentine voters. These differences in electoral sensitivity leads us to expect policymakers to target public-sector employment toward these groups of voters in either country, an expectation that we test in Chapter 8 by investigating public-sector wage differentials with administrative data from both countries.

Our investigation of partisan networks in Chapter 5, moreover, provides a crucial contribution to this book as we analyze both network size and structure, a vital element in identifying the type of activists that predominate in each country. Chilean ideological activists are more connected to voters with similar policy preferences but are less embedded into their local communities than Argentine territorial activists. Both types of activists provide different information to politicians, which affect the electoral returns derived from targeted distribution in each country. The positive effect of territorial activists in this task should be particularly strong for voters deriving larger marginal returns from targeted distribution and for goods that can be more excludable at the individual level. By contrast, ideological activists should provide better information for policy persuasion (see Chapter 7).

Finally, we expect variation on the salience assigned to policy preferences and its association to non-policy endowments in the minds of voters to shape parties' incentives to adopt diverse ideological offers. Chapter 9 investigates these incentives and how they operate in cases in which voters' policy views are connected or unconnected with their non-policy preferences, using a combination of synthetic data and data derived from our surveys. The expectations derived from the analysis are then used to assess the policy positions adopted by politicians of diverse parties in both countries, relying on the surveys from the Political Elites of Latin America project.

In sum, the policy influence granted to more sensitive voters and, in particular, when influential non-policy resources are associated to their own ideological views, may bias political parties' policy responsiveness. There are many biases in terms of policy responsiveness associated with the financing of politics, differences in turnout and other forms of participation, as well as the influence of interest groups. Here, we point to another possible source of bias, stemming from voters' own preference distribution and the electoral incentives of politicians to seek their electoral support. In a sense, it is electoral responsiveness that biases policy toward the preferences of particular voters. In the conclusion, we discuss more extensively the normative implications of this broader conception of electoral responsiveness.

# 3

# Tracing Political Preferences and Party Organization in Argentina and Chile

This chapter traces the origin of party organizations and voters' political preferences in Argentina and Chile. It adds background information that is critical to properly placing our empirical cases in their historical context and facilitates the analyses in later chapters. As noted in Chapter 1, we consider, in the short-term, the preferences of voters and the endowments of parties are fixed. In the long run, however, preferences and endowments change. What the short-term calculus of parties takes as given in a given election is also the result of larger political trends that need to be properly described.

In what follows, we discuss how the long-term historical evolution of electoral competition shapes the parties' non-policy endowments and their linkages to voters. We focus most of our attention on the period after re-democratization which, since the 1980s, has shaped the evolution of voters' preferences in Argentina and Chile.

## 3.1 LONG-TERM LEGACIES OF ELECTORAL COMPETITION

Argentina and Chile were early democratizers. Both countries enacted constitutions and electoral rules of democratic competition in the nineteenth century, based on plurality block lists for the election of Congress members, as well as Electoral Colleges for the selection of presidents. Both countries also shared a history of fraudulent elections at the hand of party bosses.

Argentina and Chile's early democratic periods, however, differed in important ways. While Chile imposed stringent suffrage property requirements, replaced in later years by literacy restrictions, Argentina enfranchised most adult males from the onset, as reflected in its 1853 constitution.[1] Different patterns of electoral competition in each country explain their distinct reliance on ideology as a crucial resource for party differentiation. Whereas multiparty and nationalized competition characterized the early regime in Chile, a predominant party system of provincial alliances emerged in Argentina. Such country differences generated diverse incentives for policy differentiation that carried on well into the new democratic period, as most of the post-authoritarian parties could trace their roots to the earlier period of electoral competition.

In Chile, Conservatives and Liberals competed until 1857 when a conflict between the State and the Church led to the creation of the National or Montt-Varista and Radical Parties (Scully, 1992:56). In 1874, to rein in the electoral advantage of Liberals, the opposition parties pushed for the adoption of a cumulative voting formula for Congress, along with minority representation in municipal assemblies, while granting control of voter rolls to the richest voters in each municipality (Scully, 1992:56; Valenzuela, 1985, 1997: 219).[2] Successive institutional reforms further reinforced multiparty competition. An 1891 reform empowered Congress and local party leaders. A 1925 reform introduced D'Hont proportional representation and abolished the Electoral College (Valenzuela, 1977:10, 1998; Valenzuela, 1985, 1999: 198; Gamboa and Morales, 2015).

As a federal country, Argentina delegated electoral responsibility to the provinces, allowing provincial elites to coalesce into a loose confederation, which under the name of National Autonomist Party (PAN) won all presidential elections from 1862 to 1912 (Alonso, 2010; Botana, 1984; Castro, 2008; Sabato, 2001). Facing their inability to compete electorally, excluded politicians established the Radical Civic Union (UCR) in 1891, with the goal of ending electoral fraud and opening competition. To achieve electoral reform, Radical politicians supported a military rebellion in 1905. In response, PAN elites adopted electoral reform, which imposed secret ballots and obligatory universal male suffrage, with automatic registration using the draft rolls of military service in 1912 (Alonso, 2010; Botana, 1984; De Privitellio, 2011; Rock, 1975). The reform also

---

[1] The most populated province, Buenos Aires, established universal male suffrage in its 1821 constitution and that precedent was influential (Sabato, 2001; Sabato and Ternavasio, 2015).

[2] In the 1864–1873 period, the Liberals had between 44–58 percent of seats in the lower chamber. By contrast, the Conservatives had between 16–32 percent, the Mont-Varistas between 4–25 percent, and the Radicals between 6–19 percent (Scully, 1992: 58).

TABLE 3.1A. *Effective number of parties and margin of victory in Chile (1891–1925)*

Table 3.1a
Chile's lower chamber: ENP (votes) & margin of victory

| Year | ENP | Margin (%) | Winner | Runner-up |
|---|---|---|---|---|
| 1891 | 3.37 | 0 | Liberals | Conservatives |
| 1894 | 4.09 | 2 | Conservatives | Liberals |
| 1897 | 4.42 | 8 | Liberals | Liberal Democrats |
| 1900 | 5.05 | 1 | Liberal Democrats | Conservatives |
| 1903 | 5.50 | 6 | Liberal Democrats | Conservatives |
| 1906 | 5.69 | 7 | Conservatives | Liberal Democrats |
| 1909 | 5.62 | 4 | Conservatives | Nationals (Montt-Varistas) |
| 1912 | 5.96 | 2 | Liberal Democrats | Conservatives |
| 1915 | 6.11 | 0 | Conservatives | Radicals |
| 1918 | 5.81 | 5 | Radicals | Liberals |
| 1921 | 5.61 | 11 | Radicals | Conservatives |
| 1925 | 4.13 | 1 | Democrats | Radicals |

*Source:* Nohlen (2005), Valenzuela (1992).

introduced minority representation with an incomplete list system, where parties left a third of the positions without candidates to be occupied by the runner-up in each electoral district. Although PAN politicians were attempting to include the UCR as a minority partner with this reform, the Radicals won all elections between 1916 and 1930, when a military coup resulted in the end of fair and competitive elections. The UCR won using a catch-all electoral strategy that crowded out the smaller Conservative and Democratic Progressive Parties (heirs of the PAN) to its right and the Socialist Party to its left. Therefore, Argentina shifted from one predominant party to another.

Tables 3.1a and 3.1b illustrate these historical patterns for the 1891–1925 period in Chile and the 1914–1930 in Argentina (to keep electoral systems constant in each case). The effective number of parties in the Chilean lower chamber (measured on legislative votes) was around five, whereas in Argentina it was lower than two. Margins of victory were also significantly different as many parties took the lead in Chile, while the Radicals won repeatedly in Argentina. The different patterns of electoral competition in both countries engendered distinct incentives for parties. Ideological shortcuts became more useful for party differentiation in Chile, whereas catch-all strategies helped successive parties to keep their electoral predominance in Argentina.

TABLE 3.1B. *Effective number of parties and margin of victory in Argentina (1912–1930)*

Table 3.1b
Argentina's lower chamber:
Effective number of parties & margin of victory (1912–1930)

| Year | ENP (provincial average) | Margin (%) | Winner | Runner-up |
| --- | --- | --- | --- | --- |
| 1912 | 3.73 | 0.05 | Conservatives | UCR |
| 1914 | 1.90 | 21.9 | UCR | Conservatives |
| 1916 | 1.95 | 25.18 | UCR | Conservatives |
| 1918 | 1.91 | 30.11 | UCR | Conservatives |
| 1920 | 2.09 | 24.11 | UCR | Conservatives |
| 1922 | 1.91 | 33.22 | UCR | Conservatives |
| 1926 | 1.93 | 27.15 | UCR (Av de Mayo) | Conservatives |
| 1928 | 2.13 | 35.96 | UCR | UCR (antipersonalista) |
| 1930 | 2.09 | 22.7 | UCR | UCR (antipersonalista) |

*Note*: the ENP in Argentina is an average of the provincial ENP, given that provincial conservative parties will coordinate both for presidential elections and in legislative caucus.
*Source*: Nohlen (2005), Interior, M. d. (2008); Tow (2016).

### a) The Legacies of Multiparty Competition in Chile

In the post-1925 period, multiparty competition relied on ideological cues at the national level and clientelism at the local level. As the number of parties increased, so did electoral volatility, prompting the adoption of another electoral reform. The 1958 reform introduced the single ballot (rather than party-made ballots) to make the vote effectively secret. It also banned local-level electoral coalitions differing from those established at the national level, thereby ending opportunistic municipal alliances between parties lacking ideological affinity (Gamboa, 2011: 173; Valenzuela, 1977). The immediate consequence was a reduction in the number of parties and the organization of electoral competition around three ideological blocks on the right, center, and left (Gamboa, 2011: 167).[3] Although increasingly relying on ideological shortcuts for electoral competition, Chilean parties continued using targeted distribution, delivered

---

[3] The effective number of parties declined from 11.9 in 1953 to four in 1965, and electoral volatility came down from 51 percent between the elections of 1953 and 1957 to 21 percent between the elections of 1961 and 1965 (Gamboa, 2011: 167).

through territorial and functional networks across the territory in this period (Borzutzky, 2002; Valenzuela, 1977).

Ideological shortcuts organized electoral competition with the Communist (PC) and Socialist (PS) Parties on the left, the Christian Democratic (DC) Party on the center, and National Party (PN) on the right. The PS, founded in 1933, was a center-left party not aligned with the Socialist International, which developed an extensive organization, reaching 5,000 party branches and 3,500 chapters of the Socialist Youth Federation by 1937 (Drake, 1978: 106–107; Roberts, 1998: 87). In the elections of 1938 and 1942, the Socialists joined a coalition with the Communists, the Democrats, and the Radicals to support two Radical candidates, who each became president (Drake, 1978: 160). In 1956, the PS joined the Communists and other left-wing groups in an electoral coalition, which would bring the Socialist Salvador Allende to the presidency, after literacy requirements were abolished in 1970 (Roberts, 1998; Valenzuela, 1978).

In 1957, a splinter of the Conservative Party founded the Christian Democratic (DC) party, seeking to occupy the ideological center to compete with the Socialists and Communists on the left and the Conservatives, Liberals and Nationals on the right (Scully, 1992: 151–160). Based on religious connections, it built strong territorial and functional networks, whereas the weakening of clientelism produced by the 1958 electoral reform enhanced its reach among the peasants who had previously been a crucial Conservative constituency (Scully, 1992: 146). Fearful of an Allende victory, the right-wing parties supported DC presidential candidate Eduardo Frei in 1964, who ultimately received 55 percent of the vote. Frei's social policies and agrarian reform facilitated the expansion of DC's organization among workers and peasants but alienated the right. In response, the Conservative, Liberal and National Parties merged into the National Party (PN) in 1966 and presented their own candidate in the 1970 presidential election, dividing the vote in thirds and allowing the victory of Allende with 36 percent of the vote. In a context of heightened ideological polarization, the PN led the opposition to Allende through legislative gridlock, street protests, and calls for a military coup after losing the 1973 midterm elections (Valenzuela, 1978).

The Allende presidency was characterized by deep ideological polarization framed in a Cold War context. Right-wing legislative obstruction encountered left-wing social mobilization, including peasants taking over estates and workers occupying factories (Bascuñán, 1990: 67–71; Gamboa and Salcedo, 2009: 675; Valenzuela, 1978, 1999). In 1973, General Augusto Pinochet led a military coup, which was supported by DC and the PN. The military killed Allende, banned all political parties, and brutally repressed left-wing politicians and activists. In response to the left-wing policies of Allende, Pinochet led a process of dramatic economic transformation including adjustment policies, trade liberalization, school choice, privatization of state-owned enterprises, public utilities, and pensions while reforming labor regulation to prevent unionization.

There was no electoral competition during military rule. Yet, the two right-wing parties we study can trace their origin to this period. The Independent Democratic Union (UDI) was established in 1983 and the National Renovation (RN) followed not long after in 1987. Whereas RN was a successor to the traditional right-wing parties, the UDI's original cadre was formed by government personnel and young professionals, who had met in the *gremialist* student movement at the Catholic University following the call of Jaime Guzmán, the charismatic intellectual behind Pinochet's 1980 constitution (Huneeus, 2000: 334; Loxton, 2016).[4] Taking advantage of their connections with the government and local majors, UDI activists disseminated information about eligibility for social assistance, while providing professional services and performing charity activities in shantytowns. Their call was ideological as they sought to build networks reaching to poorer voters to replace their left-wing loyalties (Morales and Bugueño, 2001; Pinto, 2006: 164, 169; Pollack, 1999; Soto, 2001).

Pinochet's 1980 constitution established a plebiscite on democratic transition for 1988. Confident that sustained economic growth of almost 7 percent between 1984 and 1988 (World Bank, 2015) in contrast to a regional recession would give him a victory, Pinochet called a transition plebiscite in 1988. The left-wing Socialists came together with the Christian Democrats, the Radical Democrats, and other smaller groups in the Coalition of Parties for Democracy or *Concertacion*, which campaigned for transition to democracy: the "no" vote. Yet as the Socialists were banned, they established the Party for Democracy (PPD) as a front for the PS. The right-wing politicians in RN and UDI supported the "yes" vote. After the transition, which was triggered by the victory of the "no" vote, these two coalitions continued defining electoral competition until the time of our study, partially helped by a counter majoritarian electoral

---

[4] Its original group occupied positions in the General Secretary of Government (especially the National Youth Secretariat), the National Development Planning Office (ODEPLAN), as majors in city governments, and in the Commission that created the 1980 Constitution (Huneeus, 2000: chapter 7; Morales and Burgeño 2001; Pinto, 2006: 48; Soto, 2001).

system with two-member electoral districts, where the first seat went to the plurality winner and the second seat to the runner-up, unless the former doubled the votes of the latter (Carey and Siavelis, 2006; Navia and Rojas, 2005).[5]

In sum, multiparty competition facilitated the use of ideological differentiation among parties during the twentieth century. In the 1970s, ideological polarization heightened so much that it ended party competition when both the center and right-wing parties supported a military coup. The transition to democracy reactivated these cleavages as the right-wing parties sought to run on the successful economic legacy of a brutal dictatorship they perceived as having saved the country from communism. After the transition to democracy, however, the Christian Democrats joined a coalition with the left-wing parties, serving as a moderating force. Even as polarization declined, the relative ideological positioning of political parties remained, facilitating their identification by voters after democratization.

### b) The Legacies of Electoral Predominance in Argentina

The UCR won all presidential elections from 1916 until the 1930 military coup. After a period of conservative restoration sustained by electoral fraud, the Peronist or Justicialista Party (PJ) became the dominant national party when free elections were allowed. Both parties had built their success on dense organizational networks and access to fiscal resources rather than ideological differentiation, as both shared a preference for import-substitution industrialization policies in the postwar era.

The UCR built its electoral success in the most affluent, urbanized, and educated electoral districts in the early twentieth century (Alonso, 2000: 11; Rock, 1975). Its pyramidal organization was based on committees established at the provincial, city, and neighborhood level, where ward bosses delivered patronage and favors while providing local safety nets in return for electoral support (Rock, 1975: 56–57, 252). The intense activity of its political networks and party bosses became salient at the time of

---

[5] This electoral system overrepresents the losing coalition at the district level unless there is a landslide in favor of the winner, thus generating incentives to sustain the two electoral coalitions because each could secure a seat given that under open-list rules, the most voted candidate of each coalition will be selected. It was supposed to favor the representation of the minority, in this case right-wing parties (Magar, Rosemblum, and Samuels, 1998; Navia, 2004; Scully and Valenzuela, 1993; Torcal and Mainwaring, 2003).

primaries, characterized by high turnout (Horowitz, 2010; Rock, 1972: 246–247). The non-ideological nature of their work is illustrated in the following quote from a Radical newspaper:

The speaker mentioned that in the 7th ward alone ... there had been sold at reduced prices and on a daily average 855 kilos of bread, 298 liters of milk and 3200 kilos of meat, which represents a daily economy of 900,400 pesos. This figure multiplied by the number of wards in the municipality yields an average daily saving of 18,000 pesos or 6,588,000 annually, equivalent over 15 years to 98,820,000 pesos. Over the same period, the Socialists, making the same rigorous calculation, would have gushed out 117,992,000 words from which the working classes would have obtained not the least benefit. (*El Radical*, August 30, 1915, cited by Rock, 1972: 252)

Radicals took advantage of their access to an expanding public sector to deliver patronage, while relying on federal interventions to broaden their geographic reach by attracting conservative groups in the provinces and shifting the vote of their poorer constituencies toward the UCR (Lupu and Stokes, 2009; Persello, 2005: 32). The Radical electoral dominance (see Table 3.1b) ended in 1930 with a military coup. The Conservatives returned to power by resorting to electoral fraud while banning the UCR from electoral competition (Cantú and Saiegh, 2011).

In 1943, another coup ended this conservative restoration and established a military government. The Secretary of Labor of that administration was Colonel Juan Perón, who issued regulations that favored collective bargaining, restricted work hours, established welfare benefits, and expanded labor rights. Fearful of Perón's increasing popularity with workers, his colleagues sent him to prison. A massive worker mobilization brought about Perón's release and a transition to democracy (Luna, 1972; Portantiero and Murmis, 1971; Torre, 2006). In 1946, Perón won the presidential election running as the candidate of a Laborist party, created by labor unions, in a coalition with some Conservative factions and splinters from the UCR (MacKinnon, 2002; Mora y Araujo and Llorente, 1980). He defeated the Radical candidate by a 10-point margin, starting a period of Peronist electoral dominance which lasted until 1983 (Cavarozzi, 1984).

Perón used fiscal resources and his personal charisma (as well as that of his wife, Eva) to build a catch-all party with a vague ideology, even though his policies represented a dramatic break with the past. He promoted import-substitution industrialization, delivered on labor rights and social welfare, nationalized public utilities, and fostered state intervention in the economy (Mackinnon, 2002; Murmis and Portantiero,

1974; Torre, 1974). These policies benefitted the working class and the poor, who developed a strong allegiance to Peronism (McGuire, 1997; Torre, 1974).

As in the case of the UCR, the Peronist or Justicialist party (PJ) was anchored in the work of political networks organized in local "base units," which used public resources to serve as hubs for the distribution of private goods as well as forums for political and social interaction (Bianchi and Sanchís, 1988; Ciria, 1983: 151; Levitsky, 2003: 39–40; Tcach, 1991: 161). These networks reached into both the rich and industrialized provinces, as well as into the less urbanized and poorer hinterland, more dependent on patronage (Mora y Araujo and Llorente, 1980). After reforming the constitution to allow immediate re-election in 1949, Perón won the 1951 presidential election while obtaining absolute control of Congress, thanks to gerrymandering and the imposition of single-member electoral districts (Abal Medina and Suarez Cao, ND: tables 3 and 4). His electoral predominance contributed to the alienation of the opposition. In 1955, a military coup ousted Perón and sent him into exile. Until 1973, he was not allowed to return to Argentina and his party was banned from electoral competition.

Between 1955 and 1973, underground political networks sustained Peronist partisan loyalties and allowed Perón to influence elections, leading to weak civilian presidencies, which ended with military coups (Cavarozzi, 1984; McGuire, 1997; Pirro, 2009; Rouquié and Zadunaisky, 1984). In 1973, the military allowed the PJ to compete while instituting a run-off election for the presidency and D'Hont proportional representation for the lower chamber in an effort to reduce Peronist electoral dominance (Abal Medina, Suárez Cao, and Cavarozzi, 2002). Nonetheless, Perón was elected president with a substantial margin of victory and his party controlled a majority of seats in the lower house as well as two-thirds of the Senate (Abal Medina, Suarez-Cao, and Cavarozzi 2002: tables 5 and 6). Perón died in 1974, while the country was experiencing economic distress and political violence. Amidst heightening political polarization, the rule of his third wife and vice-president was cut short by a military coup in 1976. The subsequent military dictatorship was modelled after Pinochet's in terms of political repression and economic policies. The Argentine military, however, could not match the Chilean economic success. In response to negative growth of more than 5 percent in 1981 and 1982 (World Bank, 2015), the Argentine military invaded the Malvinas/Falkland Islands, which had been in dispute with Britain, seeking a rally-around-the-flag effect. Their defeat triggered democratization. In the 1983 presidential election, the two main contenders were the PJ and the UCR.

In short, Argentina's two main parties, the PJ and the UCR, were born as catch-all parties. They both acquired predominant electoral status and used its access to state resources to build political networks that expanded their reach from the richer and urbanized areas into the poorer hinterland. These political networks combined the provisions of goods and services with social and political activities anchored in their local and functional communities that would re-emerge after democratization.

## 3.2 ELECTORAL COMPETITION SINCE DEMOCRATIZATION IN CHILE AND ARGENTINA

After democratization, while both countries experienced competitive elections, ideological shortcuts had a stronger force on party differentiation in Chile than in Argentina. We associate this pattern to the historical legacies described above, along with the impact of economic shocks on parties' incentives for policy switching. In Chile, the economy continued growing after the center-left *Concertación* gained power, thereby providing evidence of economic competence across the ideological spectrum, which facilitates the association of policy preferences with competence assessments described in Chapter 4. Ideological differentiation was aided by networks of activists who specialized in political persuasion. Finally, in line with the expectations derived from Grzymala-Busse (2007), the even legislative balance of power between the center-left *Concertación* and the electoral alliance of the right-wing parties along with the bureaucratic legacies of the military dictatorship (Luna and Mardones, 2017) reduced the politicization of the public sector as well as governmental ability to abuse public resources, which could generate asymmetric distributive expectations.

By contrast, economic volatility prompted the two Argentine catch-all parties to switch their policy offers, thereby weakening the value of ideological shortcuts (Lupu, 2016). The policy switching did not erode their political networks because these were developed around territorial connections associated with incumbency and the need to provide safety nets for poorer voters facing the consequences of economic volatility. Finally, the coincidence of two deep economic crises with Radical administrations had a dramatic effect on evaluations of economic competence for this party, whereas the Peronists benefitted from having been in power during times of economic recovery.

In Chile, the "*Concertación*" won all presidential elections until the time of our survey, but the Alliance (of UDI and RN) controlled a significant proportion of municipalities and legislators. The first two *Concertación* presidents were Christian Democrats Patricio Alwyn (1990–1994) and Eduardo Frei (1994–2000), both of whom won with electoral majorities. They were followed by two Socialist presidents – Ricardo Lagos (2000–2006) and Michelle Bachelet (2006–2010) – who faced tougher electoral competition and won in runoff elections.[6] Both were highly popular at the end of their mandates but could not run for immediate re-election due to a constitutional ban.

The long stretch of incumbency over four administrations helped the *Concertación* rebuild and sustain political networks, which were mostly based on professional connections and privileged ideological proximity, as described in Chapter 5. During this period, the *Concertación* expanded pension and health coverage, while increasing the education expenditures and the regulatory power of the state. Meanwhile, it kept prudent macroeconomic policies, which were accompanied by continued economic growth (Dávila, 2010; Garretón, 2012; Kaufman, 2011; Murillo, 2009; Pribble and Huber, 2011; Weyland, 1997).[7] While its reforms were moderated – either due to the legislative power of right-wing parties or to its own coalitional dynamics (Fuentes, 1999; Gamboa, Lopez, and Baeza, 2013; Garreton, 2012; Luna, 2008; Siavelis 2000), Chilean voters did not experience the economic volatility that characterized most of the rest of the region. Instead, Chile maintained its strong economic performance both under a right-wing military dictatorship and under its center-left successors. Without incentives to switch policy offers, political parties kept their relative ideological positions, facilitating voters' use of ideological shortcuts. That is, even though the Socialist Party (PS) moderated after a process of ideological revision in exile (Gamboa and Salcedo, 2009: 671, 674–675; Hite 2000,), which may have reduced the distance between parties in comparison to the 1970s, their relative positions remained unchanged.

The PS was to the left of the DC, which claimed its centrist position in the coalition, and the PPD, which had become a party of its own when it ended double membership with the PS in 1992 and moved to occupy the

---

[6] A constitutional amendment reduced the duration of presidential mandates to four years in 2005.
[7] Between 1990 and 1998, GDP growth averaged 7.2 percent per year, and despite a mild recession in 1999 when the economy declined by less than 1 percent, between 2000 and 2008, yearly growth averaged 8.8 percent (World Bank, 2015).

center-left space between the other two parties in the coalition. Due to its youth, the PPD had smaller networks, thereby emphasizing its message of post-material policy offers, whereas its candidates relied more on the media and personal distribution (Luna, 2014; Plumb, 1998: 99–101). Based on their ideological affinity and a common history, the PPD and the PS formed a sub-pact within the *Concertación*, avoiding competition in the same electoral districts and collaborating in electoral campaigns.

The two right-wing parties have keep their ideological location even though RN is more liberal on social issues and less associated with Pinochet than the UDI (Pollack, 1999: 136–137). Their access to municipal governments and private donors was crucial in sustaining their partisan networks, whereas limits to discretionary public spending allowed them to keep an even playing field with the *Concertación* on distributive expectations (Luna, 2014; Luna and Mardones, 2017). The UDI activists were united by a coherent ideology built by Jaime Guzmán and expanded the political networks, originally established when Pinochet was in power, by relying on rich donors to finance distribution to poorer voters (Barozet, 2004; Luna, 2014; Pollack, 1999: 128–132). The success of this strategy allowed its disciplined legislative delegation to overtake that of RN by 2010. By contrast, RN had a less hierarchical and smaller organization with weak legislative discipline (Barozet and Aubry, 2005: 5, 17; Luna, 2014; Visconti, ND) even when its presidential candidate, Sebastián Piñeira, was the first to defeat the *Concertación* in 2010.

In Argentina, democratization opened with the presidential election of 1983, when the Radical candidate, Raúl Alfonsín, defeated the PJ for the first time in competitive elections. During the campaign both catch-all parties crowded the political center, bringing smaller parties to compete on their left (Intransigent Party or PI) and right (Union for a Democratic Center or UCEDE). The UCR and PJ sustained class-based electoral loyalties, with poorer voters being more attached to the Peronists and middle-class voters to the Radicals. Moreover, Peronist electoral support in less populated provinces allowed it to control the Senate, even when the Radicals won both the presidency and the lower chamber (Calvo and Murillo, 2005).

The Alfonsín administration (1983–1989) started during an economic crisis and ended in another one after experimenting with heterodox policies, before moving toward macroeconomic adjustment (and even failed attempts at privatization).[8] The 1989 presidential election took

---

[8] The Argentine GDP fell by more than 7 percentage points in both 1984 and 1989 (World Bank, 2015).

place amidst hyperinflation and food riots, which prompted the early inauguration of Peronist president Carlos Menem. Menem had initially campaigned as a populist, but pursued policies of economic adjustment – trade liberalization, privatization of state-owned enterprises, and market deregulation – which represented a turnaround from the traditional Peronist support for state-led growth (Stokes, 2001). According to Lupu (2016), the mild policy shift of Alfonsín and the more dramatic one of Menem weakened voters' capacity to use ideological shortcuts for party differentiation. Menem was able to keep poorer voters loyal to the PJ by relying on territorial activists' networks, which provided access to dwindling social services and delivered publicly financed targeted distribution (Auyero, 2001; Giraudy, 2007; Levitsky, 2003). Additionally, by achieving macroeconomic stability, he generated positive income effects for all voters, heightening their views of Peronist capacity for macroeconomic management, and thereby increasing his popularity (Gerchunoff and Torre, 1992; Smith, Acuña, and Gamarra, 1994). To achieve re-election, Menem made a pact with Alfonsín to reform the constitution. The reform allowed immediate re-election, abolished the Electoral College, and shortened the presidential period to four years (Acuña, 1995).

In 1999, Menem was unable to run for re-election and the economy was contracting in response to international shocks. Radical candidate Fernando de la Rúa (UCR), in an alliance with a new center-left party called FREPASO (Front for a Country in Solidarity), defeated Peronist Eduardo Duhalde. Under De La Rúa's watch, economic deterioration turned into a full-blown crisis, which evaporated electoral support for the incumbent coalition in the 2001 midterm elections, producing a run on the currency, massive protests, and looting.[9] Amidst a major economic recession, President De la Rúa resigned on December 20, 2001, two years into his four-year term, becoming the second Radical president who could not finish his full mandate. Congress appointed Peronist Eduardo Duhalde as his successor because his vice-president had already resigned. As economic decline accelerated, public perceptions of Radical macroeconomic competence collapsed.[10]

In 2003, the UCR collapsed and the PJ fragmented, running three presidential candidates. Peronist Carlos Menem received 25 percent of the vote. The runner-up was Peronist Governor Néstor Kirchner, who

---

[9] For analyses of protest events in Latin America see Moseley (2018), Machado, Scartascini, Tommasi (2011), and Calvo and Moscovich (2017).

[10] The GDP contracted by 4.4 percent in 2001 and 11 percent in 2002 (World Bank, 2015).

obtained 22 percent. In response to survey predictions of a Kirchner victory in a runoff, Menem conceded. The electoral collapse of the Radicals prompted the emergence of new political parties seeking to attract their former voters (Torre, 2003). We study two of these parties in our 2007 survey: the ARI or *Alternativa por una República de Iguales* (Alternative for a Republic of Equals) on the center-left and PRO or *Propuesta Republicana* (Republican Proposal) on the center-right.[11] PRO candidate Mauricio Macri won the government of the City of Buenos Aires in 2007 and he was re-elected as mayor in 2011. In 2015, allied with the UCR and Civic Coalition (successor to ARI), he won the presidential election in a run-off.

Peronist Néstor Kirchner (2003–2007) returned to his party's traditional policies of state intervention, protectionism, and increasing public spending while denouncing Menem's neoliberal reforms of the 1990s (Malamud and De Luca, 2015). His policy switching coincided with the commodities boom and the turn to the left across the region (Murillo et al., 2011). After the 2002 devaluation of the currency, the price of agricultural exports rapidly hiked starting in 2003, thereby benefiting his administration with strong economic growth.[12] The economic recovery heightened perceptions of Peronist capacity for macroeconomic management found in our survey. Based on this economic performance, his wife Cristina Fernandez de Kirchner (2007–2015) was elected president in 2007 and re-elected in 2011 riding a wave of sympathy, which followed the death of Néstor Kirchner.

The 2000s bonanza also filled the fiscal coffers, enhancing asymmetric expectations of targeted distribution in favor of the Peronists. At the time of our study, the PJ and UCR had sustained a long period of activists' network development, whereas the youth of ARI and PRO put them in a disadvantageous situation. Electorally, these two parties were still heavily concentrated in the City of Buenos Aires and lacked access to fiscal resources because they did not have any incumbency experience, making them more dependent on policy offerings, which can be delivered on shorter notice. Only after the PRO won the government of the City of

---

[11] The ARI founder was former Radical Elisa Carrió whereas the PRO originated in 2005 from the confluence of two other new right wing political parties established in 2003: *Commitment to Change* founded by Mauricio Macri and *Recreate for Growth* created by former Radical Ricardo Lopez Murphy.

[12] Between 2003 and 2007, yearly growth averaged 8.7 percent (World Bank, 2015).

Buenos Aires in 2007 could it take advantage of its incumbency to expand its political networks (Vommaro, Morresi, and Bellotti, 2015).[13]

## 3.3 SUMMARY

This chapter traces the historical conditions behind the distribution of voter preferences analyzed in Chapters 4 and 5. Different historical trajectories were crucial in defining distinct patterns of electoral competition reinforced over time. In Chile, we hypothesize, a larger number of competing parties generated incentives for ideological differentiation, which was heightened by subsequent electoral reforms until peaking in the 1970s before the military dictatorship. After democratization, the cleavages generated by democratic transition and the binomial electoral system contributed to sustaining the relative ideological positions of political parties, while furthering the value of ideological shortcuts and its connection to both party organization and competence evaluations in the minds of voters. Good economic performance before and after the transition did not hurt either coalition with negative evaluations of macroeconomic competence. Finally, limits to discretionary spending contributed to maintaining an even field across parties in terms of distributive expectations.

In Argentina historical catch-all parties, which embarked on policy switching in response to economic volatility after democratization, weakened the informational value of ideological shortcuts. Because the two major economic crises happened under Radical incumbents and subsequent recoveries under Peronist presidents, perceptions of economic competence were biased in favor of the PJ.[14] Discretionary targeted distribution, which had emerged in the 1990s to compensate for economic adjustment policies (Giraudy, 2007; Levitsky, 2003; Lodola, 2005), continued in the 2000s, alongside generalized social policies

---

[13] Vommaro et al. (2015: chapter 3) describes the expansion of PRO networks – originally developed by NGOs and right-wing parties – by building on PJ and UCR pre-existing networks in the City of Buenos Aires after winning the government of this district.

[14] Campello and Zucco (2015) emphasize the impact of external factors, such as US interest rates and commodities prices, on the growth of South American economies. They suggest that economic ups and downs are more related to "luck" than government competence. However, as voters do not have other sources of information, they still rely on prior economic performance as their main indicator in judging the party of the president. We infer that evaluations of competence, thereby, are based on the experience in office of different political organizations in both countries.

targeted to individuals such as cash transfers for parents and non-contributory pensions for the elderly (Etchemendy and Garay, 2010; Garay, 2007).[15] As a result, the PJ's ample access to subnational executive offices facilitated the discretionary use of public funds, thus fostering expectations about its distributive capacity and the expansion of partisan networks (Calvo and Murillo, 2013). Finally, the two new political parties, which emerged from the 2001 crisis and had no incumbency experience at the time of our survey, were endowed with smaller political networks and lower distributive expectations, inducing them to rely on policy offers to attract voters.

In short, voters' preferences in 2007 reflect prior patterns of electoral competition in both countries. Economic volatility, which created distinct incentives for policy switching, along with historical legacies associated with the origin of political parties were crucial in defining the weight of ideological shortcuts in each country described in Chapter 4. Moreover, the stability of ideological shortcuts not only sustained party brands, but also facilitated the connection between policy preferences and competence evaluations, as shown in the following chapter. These different electoral trajectories were also associated with the investment in ideological networks of activists in Chile and territorial ones in Argentina – as described in Chapter 5.

---

[15] For a general discussion on the politics of cash transfer programs see De La O (2013), Zucco (2013), and Diaz-Cayeros et al. (2016).

# 4

# Mapping Voter Preferences in Argentina and Chile

This chapter describes the political attitudes of Argentine and Chilean voters based on the data collected in our original surveys. We provide evidence here of socioeconomic heterogeneity in voters' policy views and perceptions of parties' ideological positions, managerial competence, and capacity to generate expectations of targeted distribution in each country. This heterogeneity is crucial to defining diverse constraints and opportunities for parties seeking to advance their electoral goals. Voters' assessments of parties' policy and non-policy resources as well as the connections they establish between both types of endowments, we argue, created distinct incentives for parties to choose particular electoral strategies when seeking to maximize the vote.

Our survey results provide evidence of large asymmetries in the perceived non-policy endowments of Argentine parties. Argentine voters perceive the Peronists as having significant non-policy advantages in terms of macroeconomic competence and capacity to deliver selective incentives, which provides the party with opportunities that are not available to its rivals. More importantly, these non-policy endowments are perceived in a similar fashion irrespective of voters' ideological position.

By contrast, our descriptive data shows that Chilean voters perceived the policy location and non-policy endowments of parties as intertwined, with voters on the left and right of the political spectrum perceiving parties that are ideologically closer as more competent managers of the economy. This close association between the policy and non-policy perceptions of voters, we argue, constrains political parties from departing from their previous policy offers. The influence of ideological shortcuts is further reinforced by political activists who, as described in Chapter 5, are more connected to voters' who share their policy views.

## 4.1 THE SURVEYS

This section presents the surveys, which provide the data presented in Chapters 4 and 5 and are used to test our argument in subsequent chapters. Between March and May of 2007, we conducted two very large national surveys in Argentina and Chile.[1] Each survey included 2,800 respondents for a combined 5,600 units. Survey samples were drawn from cities with populations larger than 10,000 in Argentina and 40,000 in Chile (see the appendix to this chapter for sampling details). The survey included three modules measuring (i) the preferences and political behavior of voters, (ii) the size and structure of partisan networks, and (iii) other sociodemographic controls.[2]

Behavioral questions included the respondent's vote choice in the prior election, as well as the likely vote for the president and Congress "if the election were to take place next week."[3] It also included assessments of parties' competence to manage the economy, deal with crime, poverty, and unemployment; feeling thermometer questions on each of the main five parties in each country; expectations of receiving handouts, a public-sector job, or public works from each political party; and other behavioral controls. We also measured the size and structure of partisan networks using a novel design, which requires each respondent to count party members they personally know (McCarty et al., 2000; McCarty, Killworth, and Rennell, 2007), as described in the Chapter 5.

The following sections present descriptive measures for each of the components of our theoretical framework, as well as grouped categories based on socioeconomic status. We start with voters' views of political parties' ideological offers and continue by focusing on competence assessments and expectations about targeted distribution. We complete the analysis of the crucial elements on the voters' utility function by focusing on partisan networks in the Chapter 5. We show variation both across and within countries, which include asymmetries in voter policy and non-policy

---

[1] Surveys where generously financed by a grant from the NSF, NSF 0617659.
[2] The survey was carried out by KNAK S. A. in both Argentina and Chile under the supervision of Gerardo Adrogue. All survey data, codebook, and survey materials are available at www.gvpt.umd.edu/calvo/.
[3] Surveys took place six months prior to the general elections in Argentina and eighteen months prior to the election in Chile.

preferences, as well as different attitudes across poorer and richer voters in each country. These preference distributions, we claim, generate diverse incentives for parties when targeting policy and non-policy benefits to distinct groups of voters.

In distinguishing voters by socioeconomic status, we rely on marketing measures which include income, educational attainment, possession of certain goods (as a proxy for wealth), and employment situation. The socioeconomic scale used for these indicators utilizes the survey industry standard ABCD socioeconomic categories and is comparable across countries. As expected, there are few wealthy respondents from the AB categories, given their low numbers in each country and even lower response rates to face-to-face surveys. Consequently, all responses from ABC1 are folded into the same C1 category.

Our socioeconomic groups in Chile are: upper-middle-income (C1), middle-income (C2), lower-middle-income (C3), and lower-income (D) respondents. In Argentina, we use the same three upper categories for middle-income respondents but are able to further disaggregate the lower-income (D) respondents between those who are upper-lower-income (D1) and lower-income (D2) respondents, as well as the very small category of indigents, who fall below the poverty line (E). In each country, the middle-income (in all C categories) and the lower-income (in all D categories) respondents represent around half of the sample. We present our measures of voters' preferences, distinguishing poorer or lower-income voters (D) from middle-class or richer voters (C), terms that we use interchangeably in the rest of the book.

## 4.2 POLICY PREFERENCES: THE IDEOLOGICAL LOCATION OF PARTIES AND VOTERS

The comparative literature suggests that Chilean voters are more likely to define themselves in ideological terms and can more easily identify the ideology of political parties and candidates than Argentine voters (Kitschelt et al., 2010) – for historical reasons explored in Chapter 3 – and our survey results conform to this conventional wisdom. Although the levels of self-reported ideological identification are relatively high in both countries, non-responses reach 33.2 percent of the sample in Argentina, compared to 22.3 percent in Chile. Logistic analyses of non-responses show that female, less-educated, and poorer voters are considerably less likely to identify themselves in ideological terms, although the effect of education is stronger in Chile, while socioeconomic

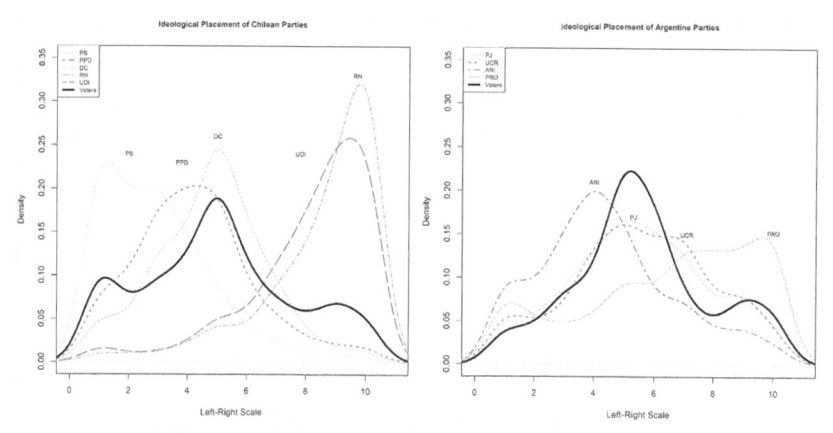

FIGURE 4.1. Self-reported placement of voters and reported location of parties in Argentina and Chile, 2007

status has a larger magnitude in Argentina. Parties' electoral portfolios are shaped by socioeconomic distinctions in a way that likely makes them more attentive to the policy views of richer voters.

Our survey includes questions about the five main Chilean political parties described in Chapter 3. We include the three main parties of the *Concertación* (Coalition of Parties for Democracy) – the Socialist Party (PS), the Party for Democracy (PPD), and the Christian Democratic Party (DC) – as well as the two right-wing parties in the Alianza por Chile (Alliance for Chile): National Renovation (RN) and the Independent Democratic Union (UDI). As shown in Figure 4.1, Chilean voters are able to recognize the ideological location of all five parties. A majority identifies the PS on the left of the political spectrum, with 70 percent of respondents placing the party as outright left (40.3 percent) or center-left (30 percent). Seventy-six percent of respondents identify the DC in the center and locate the PPD as center-left, between the PS and the DC. Respondents also clearly identify the RN and UDI as right-wing parties in their ideological placement. By contrast, voters place themselves mostly in the center, as shown by the dark line distribution in Figure 4.1, although two small peaks emerge in the left and right.

The political parties in the Argentine survey are the Radical Civic Union (UCR) and the Partido Justicialista (PJ), as well as the newer ARI (Alliance for a Republic of Equality) and PRO (Republican Proposal). Given policy switching since democratization, Argentine respondents have difficulties placing the two catch-all parties, the UCR and the PJ, on the ideological spectrum. Non-responses rates are higher than in Chile and there is high variability in the placement of parties, as shown in Figure 4.1. The ideological mode of the PJ, located in a centrist position, only includes 21 percent of respondents; this increases to 47 percent if we combine the categories of center, center-left, and center-right. Similarly, the UCR mode includes only 18.4 percent of respondents, increasing to 45 percent if we include the categories of center, center-left, and center-right. Additionally, there were 36 percent of non-responses for the PJ and 40 percent for the UCR, further confirming that respondents had difficulty in describing the ideological locations of these parties. By contrast, both the ARI and the PRO display better defined ideological profiles, catering to voters on the center-left and center-right, respectively, as shown in Figure 4.1. Finally, Argentine voters, like their Chilean counterparts, tend to place themselves in the center of the ideological spectrum as shown by the solid darker lines in Figure 4.1.

### a) Socioeconomic Status and Ideology: Self-Reported Ideology and Non-Reponses

Our framework assumes a voter utility function, where voters want to minimize their ideological distance from parties when they go to the ballot box $(x_i-L_k)^2$ but where the intensity of preferences varies across individuals ($\alpha$ is indexed by voter $i$). To calculate that distance, we therefore measure voters' assessments of party locations in the ideological spectrum and their own self-placement. To measure the intensity of their policy preferences, we assess the impact of this ideological distance on their vote choice. Using those individual measures, we are able to cluster voters by socioeconomic status to calculate the average preferences of middle- and lower-income voters in each country, as well as the average intensity of such preferences on their electoral choices.

In setting up our analyses, it is important to consider the impact of socioeconomic status on the frequency of non-responses to the self-placement question as mentioned above (and shown in Table 4.A.1 in the appendix to this chapter). In Argentina, 33 percent of respondents failed to report an ideological position in contrast to 22 percent in Chile. These patterns of non-response were shaped by socioeconomic status to a much larger extent than in Chile. Only 11.8 percent of Argentine voters in the upper-middle-income (C1) category failed to report an ideological preference, compared to 36–47 percent for voters in the low-income categories (D1 through E). Indeed, the rate of non-response for upper-middle-income voters (C1) was lower in Argentina (12 percent) than in

Chile (23 percent), whereas for lower-income voters (D), it ranges from 36–40 percent in Argentina in contrast to 23 percent in Chile. More remarkably, in Chile there are no large socioeconomic differences in the non-response rate (see Table 4.A.1 in the appendix to this chapter).[4]

In analyzing the ideological preferences of poorer and middle-class voters, we find different patterns in each country. These empirical results are not in line with a literature that has long assumed that socioeconomic status shapes policy preferences in a homogenous way across countries, based on economic models of redistribution. Since the Meltzer-Richard (1981) model (Meltzer and Richard, 1981), it is often assumed that voters from distinct socioeconomic groups vary systematically on their preferred level of taxation (Acemoglu and Robinson, 2005; Boix, 2003; Steinmo, 1993). High-income voters may be interested in preserving their income and support lower taxation, whereas low-income voters may be interested in higher levels of taxation. Thus, if a composite index of policy preferences shapes their ideological location, we should expect diversity in the average location of voters based on socioeconomic status. Additionally, as socioeconomic status is associated with education, it may influence the ability of respondents to use ideological cues to define parties' policy positions, thus shaping the salience of this term in the voter utility function for different categories of voters, as discussed in Chapter 6.[5]

What is remarkable in our results is that we find cross-national variation in socioeconomic patterns. Our surveys show systematic differences in the self-reported ideological preferences of voters by socioeconomic income in both Chile and Argentina, but the differences in ideological placement by socioeconomic status run in opposite directions in either country. Middle-class voters are more conservative than poorer voters in Chile, but they are more progressive in Argentina. Figure 4.2 uses the responses separated by socioeconomic status (Table 4. A.1 in the appendix to this chapter) to disaggregate the dark lines in Figure 4.1 and present two plots of middle- and lower-income voters' ideological self-placement in either country.

Figure 4.2 illustrates the contrasting patterns just described. In Argentina, upper-income voters place themselves toward the center-left of the ideological scale, whereas lower-income voters place themselves closer to the middle of the scale. Richer voters locate themselves around five, on

---

[4] Socioeconomic differences in non-responses do not affect results in later chapters.
[5] Bishop (1976) and Jacoby (1991) show the effect of education on ideological consistency or identification in the US.

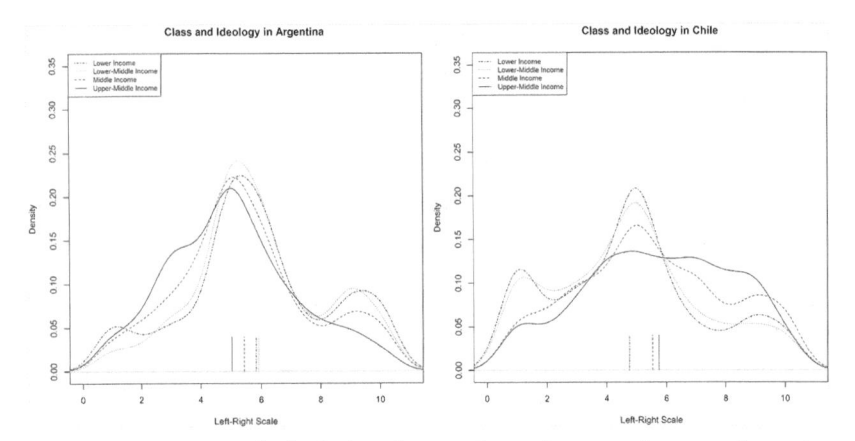

FIGURE 4.2. Voters' ideological preferences by socioeconomic status, Argentina and Chile, 2007
*Note*: Low-income voters = D; low-middle-income voters = C3; middle-income voters = C2; upper-middle-income voters = C1.

average, whereas the mean of poorer voters' self-placement is around six. The distribution of each group of voters is spread in opposite directions. By contrast, in Chile conservatism increases with income; fewer upper-middle income voters place themselves on the left of the political spectrum, whereas lower-income voters are more likely to define themselves as centrist or to the left on the political spectrum. The average position for higher-income voters in Chile is almost six, whereas for lower-income voters it is below five, with distributions tilted in opposite directions for each group of voters in Figure 4.2.[6]

In short, Argentine and Chilean voters display different capacities to locate the main political parties in the ideological space in line with the conventional wisdom. Additionally, in both Argentina and Chile, the policy preferences of middle-class and poorer voters differ significantly. More surprisingly, the association between socioeconomic status and ideological preferences differed between the two countries. In addition, socioeconomic differences had a stronger effect in explaining non-responses in Argentina than in Chile.

---

[6] Our results show similar trends to those described by Luna (2014: 128–129), although he analyzes the impact of education on the self-location of voters by party. He shows that more educated voters of the same party placed themselves more to the right and less educated voters more to the left, in line with the general distribution by socioeconomic status that we find in Chile.

## 4.3 VOTERS' NON-POLICY PREFERENCES

Parties' non-policy resources are crucial to defining electoral behavior in our framework. We focus here on competence assessments and expectations about targeted distribution, whereas Chapter 5 is dedicated to partisan networks. Both non-policy resources exhibit similar patterns across countries. In Argentina, we found inter-party asymmetries that favored the Peronists in terms of evaluations of macroeconomic competence and expectations about targeted distribution. We associate this unevenness with the timing of economic cycles and the impact of incumbency, combined with discretionary use of public resources respectively. In Chile, by contrast, there are no significant inter-party differences in the endowments of these non-policy resources. However, whereas competence assessments are associated with voters' ideological self-placement in Chile, they are unrelated in Argentina. For distributive expectations, we find no association with voters' policy preferences in either country.

### a) Competence: Voters' Perceptions in Argentina and Chile

Competence is a crucial non-policy dimension to the vote. It is a valence issue because all voters prefer more (rather than less) competent politicians. As discussed in Chapter 1, the literature on retrospective voting is based on voters' assessments of prior incumbent performance, which are especially influential with regards to economic outcomes in Latin America (Campello and Zucco, 2015). Our results in Chapter 6 confirm that competence on macroeconomic management is the single most important determinant of the vote in both countries. However, we also show here that perceptions of macroeconomic competence vary within and across countries. Although our survey inquired about competence in three areas which have been shown to be relevant for the vote – the economy, crime and security, and poverty – this book focuses on macroeconomic competence, due to its electoral impact in the two countries we study.[7] In all cases, we gauged these attitudes by asking respondents: "In your opinion, how capable are the politicians of Party X to manage [the economy/crime and security/poverty]." Responses to this ordered categorical variable ranged in a four-value scale including "very," "somewhat," "little," and

---

[7] We report results for the other two indicators in the appendix to this chapter.

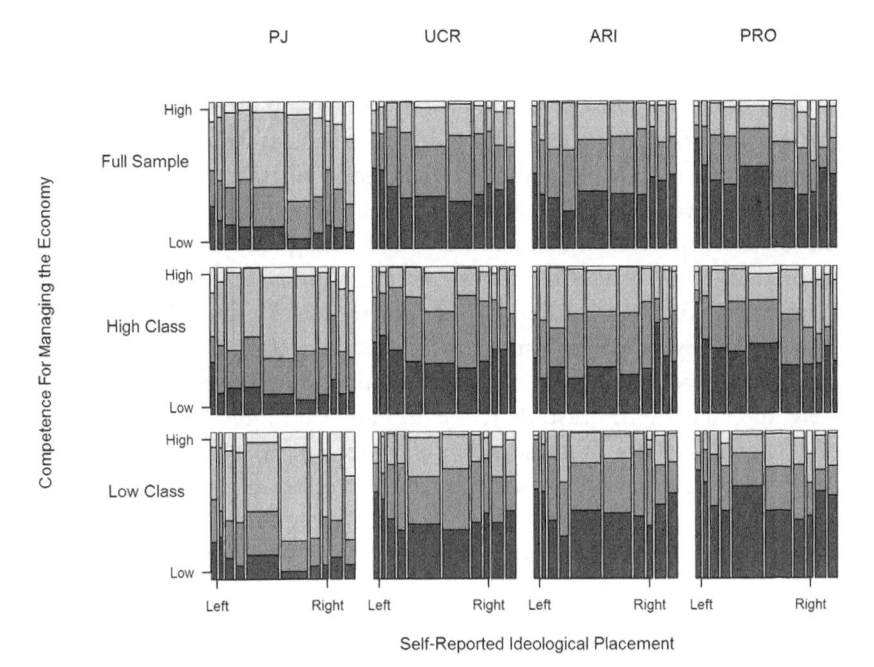

FIGURE 4.3. Evaluations of economic competence and ideological self-placement, Argentina
*Note*: Mosaic plot with self-reported ideological location in the horizontal axis and perceptions of economic competence by class.

"not at all" capable. We asked the exact same question for each of the top five parties in each country. Non-response rates were low, ranging between 5–15 percent, thereby showing that valence questions are easier to answer than self-ideological placement questions and provide voters with a more effective information shortcut in both countries.

In presenting voters' competence perceptions about economic management, we analyze the distribution across three categories: by political party, by socioeconomic status, and by the degree to which they overlap with voters' ideological positions. Asymmetries in the distribution along these dimensions, we argue, generate opportunities and constraints for political parties. Figures 4.3 (Argentina) and 4.4 (Chile) summarize this information. First, to show whether perceptions of economic competence vary across political parties within each country, there are four columns in each figure corresponding to the largest party in each country.[8] Second,

---

[8] We exclude the PPD in Chile and the provincial parties in Argentina for simplification.

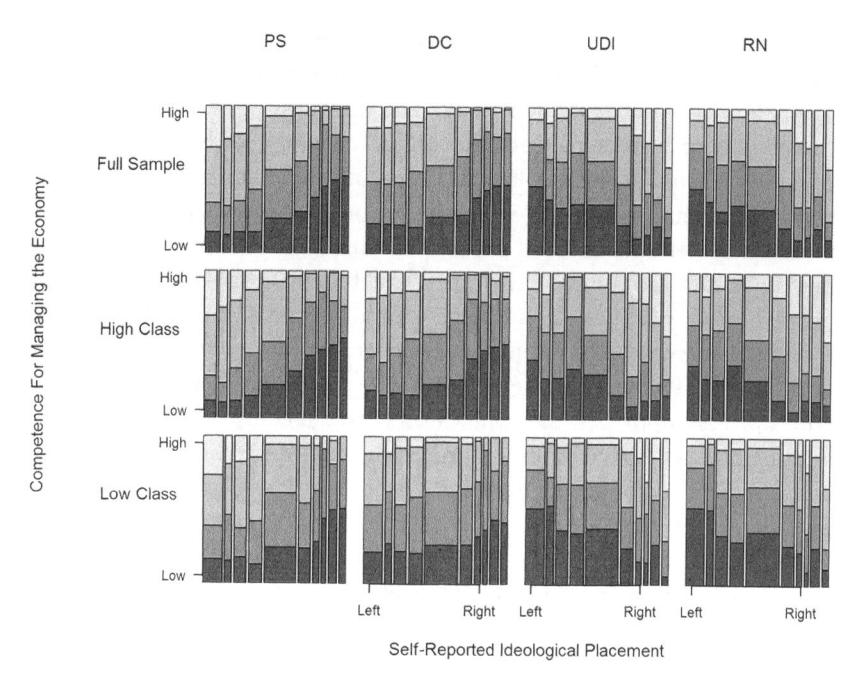

*Mapping Voter Preferences in Argentina and Chile*

FIGURE 4.4. Evaluations of economic competence and ideological self-placement, Chile
*Note*: Mosaic plot with self-reported ideological location in the horizontal axis and perceptions of economic competence by class.

to assess the degree to which these preferences vary by socioeconomic status, we divide each country-sample in two approximate halves with middle-income voters (the C categories) in one and low-income voters (the D categories) in the other. We then present three rows of information, with the top row including all voters, the middle row representing the middle-income voters, and the bottom row representing the poorer voters. Third, to show the extent to which these competence evaluations are associated with voters' self-ideological location, the x-axis locates all voters in the left–right ideological spectrum with the y-axis establishing a four-point scale of perceived macroeconomic competence.

Let us describe the three rows in Figure 4.3. Each shows the correlation between voters' self-ideological placement on the horizontal axis and the four-point scale of perceived macroeconomic competence for each party on the vertical axis. The top row presents this information for all voters, whereas the middle row is restricted to middle-income voters and the bottom row to poorer voters. Because we eliminated non-responses, the four reported categories add up to 100 percent. Each of the shades corresponds to one of the four ordinal categories described above. The lighter is the color, the higher the macro-economic competence assessments among voters for each party. The thickness of each bar describes the share of individuals in each ideological category, with larger numbers of voters located at the ideological center in both countries.

In Argentina, Figure 4.3 shows that voters perceive the Peronists as more competent than other parties. Peronists receive higher marks for managing the economy, with more than half of respondents reporting positive or very positive assessments of the Peronists managerial competence. This asymmetry diminishes when regarding competence dealing with crime, as shown in the appendix to this chapter, which is in line with our assumption of the connection between competence assessments and the economic recoveries under Peronist administrations in the 1990s and 2000s. The contrast with the UCR is remarkable as very few voters give this party high marks on macroeconomic competence and almost half of voters consider Radicals as "not competent at all" in this area. As a result, the column with plots for this party is darker. Again, this finding aligns with our expectations derived from the coincidence between Radical administrations and the two deep economic crises. The two smaller parties with no incumbency experience, ARI and PRO, fall right in the middle of the larger parties, with slightly over half the voters holding negative assessments of their competence to manage the economy. The Peronists, therefore, hold an advantage in macroeconomic competence perceptions.

More importantly, these plots suggest that macroeconomic competence assessments are not associated with voters' ideological self-positioning in Argentina, in line with our expectations about the weakness of ideological shortcuts as a result of policy switching. This is the case not only for the larger Peronists and Radicals, but also for the smaller and more ideological ARI and PRO. Indeed, although voters tend to place the ARI at the center-left of the political spectrum and the PRO at the center-right, there is little spillover from ideological considerations to competence considerations. Only in the case of the right-wing PRO do we observe lower marks among left-wing voters.

Finally, the plots that separate richer and poorer voters do not show significant differences on macroeconomic competence assessments. The advantage of Peronists in this dimension is roughly the same across middle-income voters in the middle row and low-income voters in the bottom row; it is also not associated with voter self-defined ideology for either group. For example, almost 50 percent of upper-middle-class voters

(C1) and 46 percent of lower-income voters (D2) consider the Peronists are "very" or "somewhat" competent at managing the economy. By contrast, the percentage that chooses those answers for the Radicals is 26 and 27 percent, respectively. Overall, the most significant difference is that competence assessments are almost twice as large for the PJ than for the UCR. This asymmetry is only slightly more pronounced among the high-middle-income voters (C1), but not the rest of the middle-income voters. Neither do we observe different patterns of association between perceptions of competence and ideological self-placement for either middle- or lower-income Argentine voters.

Figure 4.4 presents the distribution of macroeconomic competence evaluations among Chilean voters. In contrast to Argentina, we do not observe large asymmetries in perceptions of economic competence across the four main political parties, as there is not much difference in the predominance of lighter colors across columns. However, these perceptions are clearly associated with the ideological location of voters. Consider, for example, perceptions of economic competence for the Socialist Party (PS) in the plots on the left of the figure. A majority of left-wing and center-left voters provide mostly positive or very positive assessments of Socialist competence to manage the economy (top row). By contrast, approximately 80 percent of voters on the right of the political spectrum provide negative or very negative assessments of the Socialist capacity for macroeconomic management. More conservative voters, in contrast, give higher marks to the UDI and RN in the right columns of Figure 4.4. Although we do not show these results here, the correlation between ideology and assessments of crime and poverty issues are significant as well (see Figures 4.A.1, 4.A.2, 4.A.3 and 4.A.4 in the appendix to this chapter).

Ideology informs views on parties' competence for middle- and lower-income voters, as shown by the middle and bottom rows respectively. However, we do observe asymmetries on the evaluation of parties' competence across social class. Whereas poorer voters give higher marks to the PS and the DC on macroeconomic competence (predominance of lighter colors in the bottom row), middle-income voters more positively evaluate the two right-wing parties (as shown by lighter colors in the medium row). For example, 40 percent of lower-income voters (D) consider the PS as "very" or "somewhat" capable of managing the economy, compared to 36 percent among the upper-middle-class voters (C1). We observe the opposite effect among conservatives, with almost 33 percent of poorer voters (D) considering the UDI "very" or "somewhat" capable of managing the economy, compared to 40 percent among the upper-middle-income voters (C1). Hence, competence assessments are associated with ideological self-placement for all Chilean voters, although results are larger for relatively better-off Chilean voters – a fact that shapes their policy influence as discussed in Chapter 9. Among the richer half of voters, a comfortable majority in the left have positive competence assessments of the PS, while a large majority of voters on the right have negative assessments of the PS. Interestingly, the effect of ideology on competence assessments for the conservative UDI and RN are slightly less pronounced.

### b) Targeted Distribution: Voters' Expectations in Argentina and Chile

In analyzing the impact of targeted distribution on voting behavior, we focus on voters' expectations of receiving handouts, public-sector jobs, and/or public works. We show here that, in contrast to competence assessments, these expectations do not correlate with the respondents' ideology in either country, although we observe larger inter-party asymmetries in Argentina.

To measure distributive expectations, we use a battery of questions on the respondents' perceived likelihood of receiving handouts, public-sector jobs, and/or the public works that the community demands if each of the main competing parties were to win the election. The questions are prospective and do not involve an explicit "quid pro quo" even if respondents internalize that their electoral support may increase the odds of electoral victory and grant the mentioned party access to resources for targeted distribution. Respondents answered on a ten-point scale, from "not at all likely" to "extremely likely" that each party would deliver each type of good ("clothes, food, or money;" "a public-sector job;" or "public works needed by the community"). We do not include instruments to deal with sensitive questions (Corstange, 2009; Gingerich, 2010), leading to results that should be conservative. The response rate was above 90 percent for all parties in both countries, with close to a third of respondents indicating some degree of probability that they would receive handouts, or a public-sector job and significantly higher likelihood for public works.

The data we gathered on distributive expectations provides a different picture than the one depicted by conventional wisdom. First, in contrast with the conventional wisdom, our data shows few differences in terms of distributive expectations between Argentina and Chile. In fact, expectations of receiving handouts in Chile are higher than in Argentina, expectations of a public-sector job are roughly similar, and Argentine respondents were marginally more likely to expect parties to deliver local public works.[9] These descriptive results are in line with earlier findings (Barozet, 2004, 2006; Luna, 2010; Luna and Mardones 2017) about targeted distribution in Chile. A starker contrast between both countries can be found in the polarized reactions that are generated by expectations for targeted distribution. A higher proportion of Chilean respondents dislike targeted distribution than their Argentine counterparts, thus suggesting a different stigma associated with targeted distribution in each country.[10]

We start by describing voter expectations of receiving handouts, which has been the focus of most of the literature on clientelism. Indeed, based on these measures, clientelism is presented as an alternative to policy (Kitschelt, 2000; Kitschelt and Wilkinson, 2007; Luna 2014; Stokes et al., 2013). Handout expectations are described in the top rows of Figures 4.5 (Argentina) and 4.6 (Chile). The middle rows correspond to distributive expectations about public jobs, which are essential to the literature on patronage, whereas the bottom rows refer to hopes regarding the distribution of public works, the main indicator of pork. As before, Figures 4.5 (Argentina) and 4.6 (Chile) present four columns to assess inter-party asymmetries on distributive expectations, while placing respondents according to their ideological self-placement in the horizontal axis. Lighter colors refer to higher expectations and darker colors to lower expectations based on our ten-point scale in each of the plots.

Figure 4.5 shows no correlation between ideological self-placement and distributive expectations for any of the three types of goods in

---

[9] In later chapters we will show that, although the expectation of receiving selective incentives is similar across countries, the effect of targeted benefits on the vote varies across countries and across groups of voters, not just based on socioeconomic status, but also on connections to partisan networks.

[10] We measure the positive or negative perception of parties' redistributive intent and found considerable variation in this variable with more negative views in Chile, especially regarding public works. For instance, 43 percent of Chileans considered it totally inappropriate or not very appropriate that political parties provide public works, whereas only 18.5 percent of Argentines hold that view. These differences are more pronounced than the socioeconomic differences within each country. For instance, Weitz-Shapiro (2014: 128) predicts positive views of distribution using our measure as a dependent variable and controlling for age, gender, general views of redistribution, and government role in Argentina. She finds that 47 percent of upper-middle-income voters (C1) had positive views of targeted distribution in contrast to 66 percent of lower-income voters (D2). See also Mares and Young (2016).

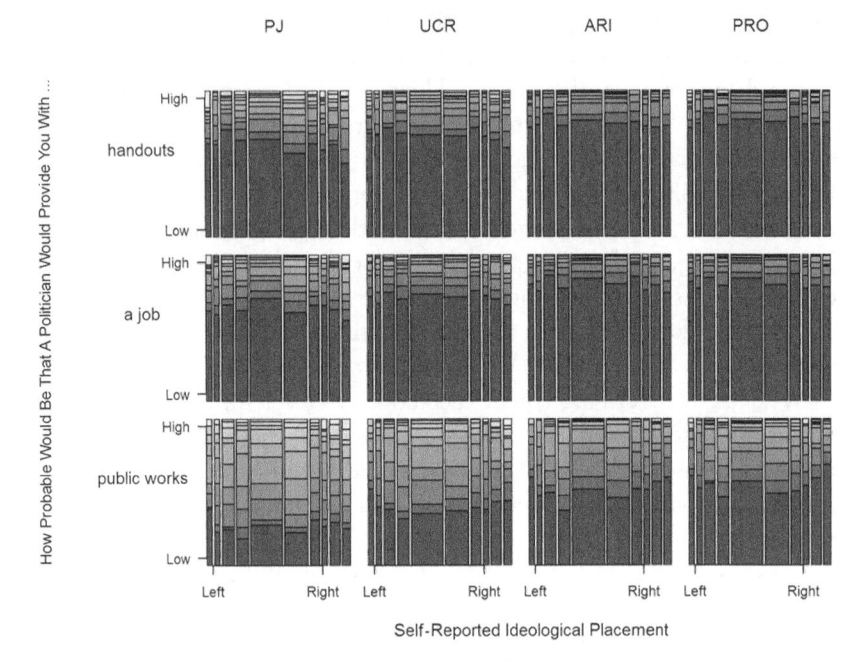

FIGURE 4.5. Distributive expectations and self-reported ideology in Argentina, 2007

*Note*: Mosaic plots of selective incentives and ideology. Darker colors represent lower likelihood of receiving the benefit from zero (not likely) to ten (extremely likely). Thickness of the bar describes the share of voters in each of the ideological categories, from left (one) to right (ten).

Argentina – i.e. there is no correlation in either row – across any of the political parties. However, respondents considered the PJ as more likely to deliver handouts, public-sector jobs, and public works than any of the other parties. Hence, as shown by the lighter colors in the PJ column across all rows, and especially in the bottom one, this party has a non-policy advantage regarding targeted distribution. Indeed, we show in Chapter 5 that the number of handout recipients by different parties follows a similar distribution. Distributive expectations are higher for the UCR than for the smaller ARI and PRO. At the time, both the PJ and the UCR had more governorships and mayoralties, and thereby access to discretionary fiscal resources for targeted distribution. Indeed, while the ARI and PRO – with no incumbency experience – received considerably higher marks in economic competence than the UCR, the Radicals have an advantage over them in terms of distributive expectations.

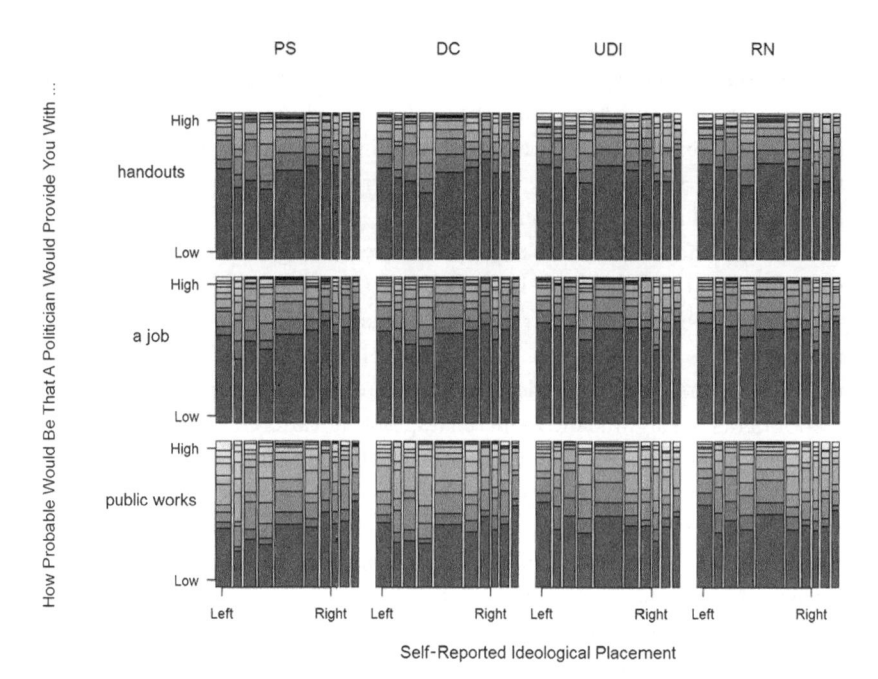

Mapping Voter Preferences in Argentina and Chile 79

FIGURE 4.6. Distributive expectations and self-reported ideology in Chile, 2007
Note: Mosaic plots of selective incentives by ideology. Darker colors represent lower likelihood of receiving the benefit from zero (not likely) to ten (extremely likely). Thickness of the bar describes the share of voters in each of the ideological categories, from left (one) to right (ten).

Figure 4.6 shows a lack of association between voter ideology and distributive expectations in Chile, which contrasts with the patterns described above for competence evaluations. Indeed, it is noteworthy that, similar to Argentina, there is little association between handout distributive expectations and ideological positions in Chile for any political party. Another interesting descriptive result is that voters on the extreme right tend to have lower distributive expectations. Only in the case of the PS does there seem to be a slight association between ideological self-placement and public-work distributive expectations. Hence, we find considerable similarity on the lack of association between distributive expectations and voters' ideological self-placement across both countries.

The literature suggests that voters of different incomes have diverse distributive expectations associated with the marginal return they perceive of receiving the good. Whereas we find moderate and oftentimes statistically insignificant differences in the distributive expectations of poorer and richer voters in either country, we observe more socioeconomic variation in Argentina than in Chile. Inter-class differences in distributive expectations are larger among Argentine voters than for Chilean voters. Inter-class differences are also more noticeable for handouts and negligible when considering pork.

In Argentina, distributive expectations regarding handouts and public-sector jobs are higher for lower-income (D) than middle-income (C) voters, but more meaningful for the former. While 57 percent of lower-income voters considered it highly unlikely that Peronists would offer them handouts, the proportion goes up to 69 percent for middle-income respondents – a significant 12-percentage-point difference. This difference remains, albeit smaller, when considering the odds of receiving handouts from the Radicals. Among lower-income respondents, 66 percent consider it highly unlikely that the UCR would deliver handouts to them, compared to 73 percent among middle-income voters. We detect no statistically significant effect among other parties. By contrast, among Chilean respondents, differences in the expectation of receiving handouts between lower-income and higher-income voters was a much smaller 0.3 percentage points for the PS – with 62.2 percent of lower-income respondents reporting that it was highly unlikely that Socialists would offer them a handout, compared to 62.5 percent for middle-income voters. This difference was also small and statistically insignificant for all other major Chilean parties.

Inter-class differences in the expectation of receiving a public-sector job were also small in Argentina. A mere 5-percentage-point difference was reported when considering jobs delivered by Peronists, while the difference declined to just 2 points when considering jobs delivered by the UCR. Inter-class differences in expected jobs delivered by Chilean parties were below 2 percentage points and statistically insignificant. Remember, we are describing here the content of voters' preferences, whereas Chapter 6 presents the sensitivity of diverse groups of voters to targeted distribution, which varies more across socioeconomic categories, driving the partisan responses we identify in Chapter 8 for public-sector jobs.

Finally, inter-class differences among Argentine voters all but vanished when considering public works, representing less than 1 percent for the Peronists and less than 3 percent for the Radicals. Differences were statistically insignificant and small for all parties in Argentina. Inter-class differences in distributive expectations were also small and statistically insignificant in the case of public works in Chile, showing less than a

3-percentage-point difference between lower- and middle-income voters across all Chilean parties.

In short, in line with the conventional wisdom, we find that distributive expectations do not correlate with ideology in either country. However, two results are worthy of notice. First, distributive expectations by respondents are similar across parties in Chile, but larger for the PJ and, to a lesser degree, the UCR in Argentina. Second, expectations of receiving handouts and public-sector jobs – but not public works – are reported as higher for poorer voters in Argentina, but not in Chile.

## 4.4 SUMMARY

This chapter describes survey evidence on the distribution of policy and non-policy preferences among Argentine and Chilean voters. We present here the content of those preferences, whereas our measurements of sensitivity are introduced in Chapter 6. Here we describe significant within- and across-country variation in voters' policy positions, as well as in their non-policy assessments of economic competence and distributive expectations. Descriptive evidence provides a wealth of information that is consistent with larger asymmetries in the competence assessments of parties in Argentina and a closer correlation between voters' self-reported ideology and their non-policy assessments of parties in Chile. However, for distributive expectations, voters' self-reported ideological positions provide little information in either country. Additionally, we show variation in heterogeneity across richer and poorer voters in terms of ideological preferences, competence assessments, and distributive expectations. We turn to analyzing party networks in Chapter 5.

# 5

## Party Organization

### How Activists Reach Voters

Partisan networks are a crucial non-policy resource granting political parties the capacity to connect with voters. Party activists serve a variety of important party functions. They persuade undecided voters, deliver handouts, gather information about voters' preference to be shared with the party, mobilize voters on Election Day, and provide a personal face to parties. That is, party activists provide a mechanism for reaching voters and implementing the electoral strategies defined by politicians. Given the array of incentives that can make activists join a political party, the literature distinguishes whether they are motivated by policy preferences, by their ambition to hold public office, or by a pragmatic desire to access resources. Kitschelt (1994) classifies activists based on those incentives as policy-oriented, office-oriented, or pragmatic. In Chapter 1, we provide our own classification of activists. We distinguish two types of activists' networks: those specialized in ideological persuasion and those dedicated to serving the wants and needs of voters in their own communities. We label the former as *ideological* and the later as *territorial*. Ideological networks are more likely to attract policy-oriented activists and to rely on ideological connections for recruitment, often in schools and professional associations. Territorial networks, by contrast, are more likely to be based on the co-optation of local community leaders when seeking to expand their party organization. Among both groups of activists, a portion is oriented toward electoral office-seeking and the other aspires to join the public sector, adding political loyalty to the skills they bring to the job.

Shefter (1994) investigates the impact of history on partisan networks, associating ideological activists to opposition parties and those established after civil service curtailed patronage. Instead, we focus on historical legacies of electoral competition along with the distribution of public resources in the post-democratization period, as described in Chapter 3. For instance, we hypothesize that in Chile, multi-party competition facilitated the use of ideological shortcuts for party differentiation, whereas the reliance of political parties on fiscal discretion for local-level clientelism – which had characterized the pre-1973 period – was severely curtailed in the new democratic period by the administrative legacies of the military dictatorship and the strength of the right-wing opposition (Garay, 2016; Luna and Mardones, 2017; Luna and Rosenblatt, 2017). Given these conditions, activists' networks were more likely to be ideological.

In this chapter, we rely both on our surveys and on in-depth interviews with politicians and local campaign managers to describe the size, structure, and type of activist networks in each country, emphasizing variation across and within countries. We present our behavioral measurement strategy first and then describe the size, structure, and type of political networks in each country, paying special attention to inter-party differences. We illustrate our survey findings with excerpts from our interviews.

## 5.1 WHEN PARTIES MEET VOTERS

Activists establish crucial personal connections between political parties and voters. In assessing the connections between activists and voters, we develop a strategy to measure both network size and the proximity of individual voters to activists of different parties. This latter measure allows us to assess whether voters of distinct policy preferences or socioeconomic categories are more or less connected to activists of different parties in each country. Hence, we rely on *behavioral* measures to assess the impact of this crucial non-policy resource, whereas we used attitudes for competence evaluation, ideological position, and distributive expectations in Chapter 4. Thanks to this strategy, we are able to assess both the direct impact of partisan networks on the vote in Chapter 6 and their conditional effect on other policy and non-policy resources as they provide parties' with personal connections in Chapter 7.

Our survey relies on a battery of instruments, based on reported counts of activists by voters to reconstruct the size and structure of party networks. We investigate asymmetries in the size and structure of partisan networks in each country. We evaluate whether activists are better connected to voters of particular ideological leanings, as well as possible heterogeneity distinguishing middle- and lower-income voters. These differences can generate opportunities and constraints for parties seeking to respond to the preferences of distinct groups of voters through the work of activists.

### a) Measuring Activists' Networks

Our survey design considers every respondent as an observer who discloses information about the number of ties with various party member categories. The questions are worded as, "how many X do you know?" with respondents providing counts of groups whose frequencies in the population are known (i.e. "How many individuals do you know whose name is Silvia?") and counts of groups whose frequencies in the population we seek to estimate ("How many activists from the Socialist Party do you know?"). We instructed respondents to interpret knowing someone as indicating that "you know them, they know you, you may contact them by phone, letter, or in person and you have had some contact during the last two years." A connection between the voter and a member of the target group, consequently, implies that there is an acquaintance relationship and that some type of interaction has occurred within the last two years.

We used information about the frequencies of known groups in the populations as offsets to rescale the parameters that measure the size of the respondents' personal networks. For example, if a respondent knows two Silvias, given that the relative prevalence of the name Silvia in the population in Argentina is 0.86 percent, a naïve estimate of the respondent's personal yearly network would be approximately ≈232 individuals, $\left(N_p = \frac{2}{0.0086}\right)$. Using a battery of questions about populations whose frequencies we know and a slightly more sophisticated statistical model, we estimate the size of each respondent's personal network.[1]

---

[1] For this research, we selected names as reference categories that display minimum variance across electoral districts. This ensures that estimated territorial differences in the prevalence of different political categories are not a function of the distribution of names in the population. To select the names used as reference categories, we used the complete list of registered voters in both countries (approximately 18 million registered voters in Argentina and approximately 8 million voters in Chile). By knowing the distribution of the reference categories in the population, we can ensure that estimated differences in the prevalence rates of partisans are properly measured.

Once we estimate the size of the respondents' personal networks, a different set of questions asks about populations whose frequencies we are interested in retrieving, such as the number of activists or candidates from each relevant political party. We use this information both to estimate the prevalence of each group in the population and to estimate how closely connected voters are to each group. For example, if the same respondent who knows two Silvias also knows one UCR activist, we could measure the relative prevalence of UCR activists as a fraction of the respondent's personal network, $(Activist_{UCR} = \frac{1}{PersonalNetwork})$. Given that we previously estimated the respondent's personal network to be ≈232, we could then estimate the number of UCR activists to be ≈0.43 percent of the Argentine population, $\left(Activist_{UCR} = \frac{1}{232}\right)$: approximately 166,000 activists. The primary advantage of the proposed survey strategy is that we may retrieve valid estimates with regards to populations whose prevalence does not allow for direct measurement.

It is important to note that we expect the reference categories (i.e. "Silvia") will not correlate with the substantive group categories we are retrieving. By knowing the frequency distribution of "name" categories across different localities and populations, we may draw proper estimates of personal network size. By contrast, we do not expect the frequencies of partisan activists to be the same across electoral districts and socioeconomic categories. Proper estimates of the personal network, consequently, allow us to explore such substantive variation in the size, structure, and territorial distribution of the substantive network categories.

### b) The Statistical Strategy: An Overdispersed Poisson Model

Once we collect reported data on the raw counts of each subgroup for each respondent, we need a statistical model that will estimate all the parameters of interest. Zheng, Salganik, and Gelman (2006) propose an overdispersed Poisson model that estimates both the size of the personal network and also allows the exploration of the social structure in the data. The model estimates three sets of parameters: the relative size of each respondent's personal network, the relative prevalence of each group in the population, and a parameter that explores individual-level deviations from the personal network and group prevalence. The overdispersed Poisson model uses the count of individuals known to each respondent as the dependent variable and estimates three sets of latent parameters:

$$y_{ik} \sim Poisson\left(e^{\alpha_i + \beta_k + \delta_{ik}}\right) \quad \text{(Eq. 5.1)}$$

where $\alpha_i$ describes the size of the personal network of respondent $i$, $\beta_k$ describes the expected prevalence of group $k$ in the population, and the overdispersion parameter $\delta_{ik}$ estimates a multiplicative factor with individual- and group-level deviations from the personal network $\alpha_i$ and group prevalence $\beta_k$ (Gelman and Hill, 2007). The vector of overdispersed parameters, $\delta_{1k}, \ldots, \delta_{nk}$, provides critical information about individual-level deviations from the overall group prevalence, allowing us to study the social structure of networks – how different political categories relate to each other – by comparing the overdispersion parameters of individuals for different groups. That is, we can assess whether respondents with more ties to a party network, conditional on the size of their personal network, are also associated with other political attitudes that we want to explore (e.g. their ideological distance from a political party).[2]

A battery of questions asked respondents about populations with known frequencies (i.e. names, professions, life events) and that satisfied three criteria: respondents easily and unambiguously identified them, category frequencies were roughly similar across electoral districts, and the category had prevalence ranges between 0.1–2 percent in the overall population (ideally around 0.5 percent) to minimize recall distortions. We chose these rates because respondents tend to under-recall categories that are very common in the population and over-recall group categories that are very uncommon (Gelman and Hill, 2007; McCarty et al., 2000). Based on those criteria, we used approximately fifteen questions referring to categories for which we knew the prevalence rate.[3]

---

[2] It is important to note that model estimates that use the normalized proximity produced substantively similar estimates than those obtained using the raw data. In fact, the normalized results are conservative when compared to those using the raw counts of party members. Still, estimates using the raw counts carry information about differences in network size and should be expected to be biased. Consequently, we consider that the correct estimates need to be normalized, as proposed by Gelman and Hill (2007).

[3] The reference categories are not the same in both countries in order to minimize socioeconomic and regional biases and to adjust for differences in prevalence rates. In Argentina, the names used were Silvia, Patricia, Antonio, Francisco, and Angel. Other categories included the number of individuals the respondent knows who work for the police, as a teacher, or as a medical doctor; who receive work programs; had a son within the last year; married within the last year; or have a physical disability. In Chile, the names were Gladys,

We then asked respondents to report counts of the populations whose frequencies we were interested in retrieving, such as the number of political activists from the most important parties and the number of individuals receiving handouts from each party. The following two modules center on political attitudes, including ideological self-placement and ideological placement of the main political parties, whereas the last module includes questions about sociodemographic characteristics that should affect distributive preferences. The survey, thus, allowed us to retrieve the main variables of interest to measure the impact of ideological distance, partisan networks, distributive expectations, competence evaluations, and socioeconomic status of voters in Chile and Argentina.

## 5.2. THE CONTOURS OF PARTY ORGANIZATIONS: SIZE, STRUCTURE, AND TYPE

In measuring partisan networks in both countries, we found inter-party asymmetries in Argentina which furthered the non-policy advantages of the PJ. In Chile inter-party differences were minor, but we found stronger connections between activists and ideologically akin voters than in Argentina. These findings sustained the distinction between ideological and territorial networks that we presented earlier, which we associated with different strategies for gathering electoral information and delivering targeted distribution.

### a) Counting Activists in Argentina and Chile

Although the estimates from our model led to a similar number of political activists across both countries, there are important inter-party and cross-national distinctions. The total number of activists is roughly 1.4 percent of the population in Argentina and 1.2 percent in Chile (Table 5.1). Our measure is conservative in comparison with studies, which used direct questions, and does not include those defined by respondents as volunteers, who participated in electoral activities but with a lower level of involvement. Those were approximately 0.73 percent of

Veronica, Marta, Sergio, Jaime, Ricardo, Eduardo, and we asked the respondent for the number of individuals they know who work as a professor, in the military, as a medical doctor, or as a maid; receive Chile Solidario; had a son within the last year; died within the last year; married within the last year; or took their college entrance examination. The names were taken from electoral rolls in each country, while other prevalence rates were obtained from census data.

TABLE 5.1. *Activists' networks in Argentina and Chile*

| Total number of members || Percent of Population ||
| CHILE | | ARGENTINA | | CHILE | | ARGENTINA | |
|---|---|---|---|---|---|---|---|
| Activist PS | 53,880 | Activist PJ | 290,930 | Activist PS | 0.356 | Activist PJ | 0.766 |
| Activist DC | 45,221 | Activist UCR | 159,684 | Activist DC | 0.299 | Activist UCR | 0.420 |
| Activist PPD | 30,257 | Activist ARI | 21,463 | Activist PPD | 0.200 | Activist ARI | 0.056 |
| Activist UDI | 30,031 | Activist PRO | 10,853 | Activist UDI | 0.199 | Activist PRO | 0.029 |
| Activist RN | 22,283 | Activist PPP | 41,079 | Activist RN | 0.147 | Activist PPP | 0.108 |

*Note:* Estimates from the network model in (Eq. 5.1).

the population in Chile and 1.28 percent in Argentina (Table 5.A.1, in the appendix to this chapter).[4]

Table 5.1 presents the distribution of activists across parties, showing that it is roughly even in Chile but asymmetric in Argentina. All five Chilean political parties have similar contingents of activists – although those are slightly larger for the older PS and DC – whereas the Peronists, and to a lesser extent the Radicals, hold organizational advantages in Argentina. In Chile, although the Socialist Party has the largest network with approximately 45,000 activists (0.36 percent of the Chilean population), it is not much larger than other parties given the size of activists' networks for the Christian Democrats (0.30 percent), the PPD (0.20 percent), the UDI (0.20 percent), and the RN (0.15 percent). By contrast, the PJ has around 291,000 activists (0.77 percent of the population), which is twice as many as the number of UCR activists ($\approx$160,000, or 0.42 percent of the population). Furthermore, both the PJ and the UCR are several times larger than the PRO and ARI.[5] The inter-party differences in both countries were very similar when considering volunteers rather than activists (see Table 5.A.1 in the appendix to this chapter). In sum, our survey suggests that, in 2007, although parties in both countries had political organizations that they could deploy for connecting voters, the asymmetries we found in Argentina gave the Peronist an organizational advantage in reaching constituencies.

The differences in size of political networks that we gauged with our survey reflect both the longevity of political party organizations, as well as

---

[4] Evidence from a large household survey of social indicators (SIEMPRO) conducted by the Argentine statistical agency (INDEC) in 1997 provides evidence that conforms well to our results. The survey of 24,160 respondents includes the question: "Do you participate in a political party?" and allows respondents to answer "1-Yes, and I am a leader," "2-Yes, but I am not a party leader," "3-Ocasionally," "4-Never," and "5-In the past, but not now." In the survey, 1.36 percent of the unweighted sample self-reported as an activist in a political party (category 2) compared to 1.40 percent in our survey. Similarly, 0.60 percent of INDEC respondents indicated that they were party leaders (category 1) compared to 0.57 percent in our survey. Overall, estimates of the size of partisan networks conform to those found in the INDEC-Siempro Survey (www.siempro-isfam.gov.ar/archivos/evaluaciones_realizadas_1996_2007.pdf). In the 2008 LAPOP surveys, 10 percent of respondents in Argentina and 3 percent in Chile claimed to have work in the last electoral campaign – presidential elections were in 2007 in Argentina and 2005 in Chile – a figure that is higher than the combination of activists and volunteers in our measurements for both countries. There may be bias in the direct answer and our measurement strategy is better at capturing their effective connection with voters.
[5] For Argentina, all references to PPP in tables and figures correspond to the main provincial party in the province of the respondent. However, as we group all these parties together despite wide differences among them, we do not draw inferences from these findings.

the resources derived from incumbency; the former results from the slow-moving process of building political networks, whereas the latter incentivizes the participation efforts of office-seeking activists. Both features were more unevenly distributed across Argentine than Chilean political parties.

In Argentina, both the PJ and the UCR inherited political networks from the pre-authoritarian period. Indeed, during the 1983 electoral campaign, the Peronist claimed 3 million party members while the Radicals claimed 2.5 million (Escudero, 2001: 58; Levitsky, 2003: 49). Their political networks were rejuvenated by the incentives provided by public employment for incumbent parties during alternation in the executive, along with control of provincial and municipal governments (Gibson and Calvo, 2001; Grindle, 2012; O'Donnell, 2005; Oliveros, 2013; Pedrosa, 2005; Torre, 2003). Governments had a preference for partisan public workers who aligned their preferences with incumbents because turnover may affect their work conditions and job continuity, especially when holding temporary contracts (Oliveros, 2013; Bambaci, Spiller, and Tommasi, 2007: 174). Finally, public-sector jobs not only provide salaries for activists, but also granted them access to public resources and information they could deploy in connecting to voters.

Our interviewees in both parties recognized the value of incumbency in building partisan networks (bold added by us for emphasis). We were told by a Radical provincial legislator that "... we, in the municipality, for instance, there was a time when among the 10,000 employees, there were 2,700 affiliated to the Radical Civic Union. **We had been in the city government for 16 years...**" (Argentina 01. August 5, 2009). Similarly, a Radical national representative told us that with the 2001 crisis, "The party weakened nationally and there was a stage of municipalization or regionalization of the party. In the process, obviously **where the party was the incumbent, the networks were more extensive...**" (Argentina 02. July 7, 2009).

The Peronists similarly emphasized the importance of incumbency. As described by a Peronist National Representative,

> ... **usually the minister or public official of high rank who lives in the area is in charge**, is the one organizing the activity... In the City of [name], we have 22 circuits and each has at least between two and five basic units. And each of them has an executive committee... with at least ten people... Additionally, we have the labor unions, the NGOs, the party bureaucracy... because we are the incumbents, **public employees have a commitment as activists. Many public employees originally come from the party**, from the political training courses, is a system of recruitment, to reach the youth ...
> 
> (Argentina 03. July 14, 2009).

Another Peronist National Representative also explained to us:

... where the party is the incumbent, the structure of the state is usually at the service of incumbent candidates ... where the mayor was Peronist [in the province of Buenos Aires] there was a strong mobilization of what is called the 'municipal machine'... and where the PJ was not in the government, there were activists.

(Argentina 04. July 15, 2009)

The impact of incumbency is crucial for understanding asymmetries of partisan network size that favored the PJ – and to a lesser degree the UCR – at the expenses of the ARI and the PRO, which lacked such experience before 2007, although the PRO will expand these networks from incumbent positions subsequently (Vommaro et al., 2015). Their smaller networks could not provide the same type of information flows, thereby making these political parties more dependent on the media and professional services during electoral campaigns. As described by a National Representative of Coalicion Civica/ARI, "... **electoral campaigns are professionalized, the campaigns are focused on the TV proposal, the radio proposal, the internet proposal, the use of the media and the activists are only to put tables on the street** ..." (Argentina 07. July 26, 2009). As the ARI changed its name in 2009 to Coalicion Civica and entered a coalition with the UCR in some electoral districts, a Radical National Representative elected as part of the alliance made the following comparison between the strategies of both parties to reach voters:

... Civic Coalition/ARI likes to organize activities in coffee stores **calling the media to present their proposals, for instance of environmental policies** ... Yet, they dislike public meetings...Another example, they distribute the ballots by mail ... [whereas] we [the UCR] deliver the ballots by hand in some neighborhoods, especially in poor neighborhoods where we have a strong activist organization.

(Argentina 08. July 29, 2009)

Indeed, the impact of incumbency was felt by the PRO when it achieved control of the fourth electoral district in the country and its major city. A PRO politician and campaign manager, relayed to us that,

**In the first mayoral election, it was free. Now some of them are working in the city government.** We make it clear that both things are not related. Some of those working in the city government feel a moral obligation to do it. We clarify 200 times that they are not required to do it ...but there is an incentive because we are in the government....

(Argentine 06. July15, 2009)

In Chile, access to the public sector also favored the development of activists' networks, especially at the local level. However, this access was more evenly distributed than in Argentina and public employment was not as extensive or as imbricated in society, as described in Chapter 8. Indeed, our survey measured the number of public employee relatives and found those to be 50 percent larger in Argentina than in Chile. As a result, Chilean political networks were more symmetrical than the Argentine ones we have just described. The three *Concertación* parties that headed the national executive until 2007 had slightly larger networks favored by incumbency both in the national and regional administrations, to be expected as Chile is a unitary country. Whereas opposition parties were limited to municipal incumbency, these units had more hiring discretion in terms of resorting to temporary employment (Luna and Rosenblatt, 2017).

Our interviews also highlighted how incumbency mattered in Chile for partisan network building. A PS city councilor explained that "... **in the municipalities there is a strong party base for employment because there is no High Management System**. Instead, they have a fiction about competition of the employees that are already there but in general **many local [political] operators have taken refuge in the municipality**." (Chile 07. April 13, 2009). The importance of public employees in political networks is further confirmed by a PPD local campaign manager/activist, who told us that "... **of those going door to door about a 10, 20 percent are public employees who occupy their free time to support the candidate...the rest are activists**." (Chile 04. July 17, 2009). A RN mayor confirmed the political character of municipal public employment when he explained to us,

I have not retired from [current municipality of which he is mayor] because this is a very large municipality... There is a very **large team of people working with me here, they depend directly from me, and therefore I cannot make the decision on my own. If I leave, around 500 people fall [lose their jobs]**....

(Chile 06. July 7, 2009)

In short, we associate the difference we found in size of partisan networks to party age and incumbency experience. We found asymmetries on activists' network size in Argentina, which favored the PJ, and a more even inter-party situation in Chile. We now turn to the structure of party networks and the asymmetries in terms of which voters are more connected to party activists.

### b) Partisan Network Connections

The differences in the size of partisan networks should be analyzed together with their structure to understand the opportunities and constraints they provide to vote-maximizing political parties. To assess the social structure of networks – how different political categories relate to each other – we can take advantage of the matrix of the overdispersion parameters drawn from estimates in Eq. (5.1), $H \equiv \{\delta'_{11}, \ldots, \delta'_{ik}\}$.[6] Each parameter, $\delta'_{ik}$, provides information about the degree to which a respondent knows more individuals from a particular group $k$ than what would be expected given their personal network size and the overall group prevalence in the population. For example, we can compare the deviation in the number of PJ activists known by respondent 1 and respondent 2, e.g. $\delta'_{R1, PJ(activists)}$. Using these parameters, we may also assess whether individuals who know more PJ activists also know, on average, more PJ candidates, i.e. $correlation\left(\delta'_{i, PJ(candidates)}, \delta'_{i, PJ(activists)}\right)$.

In assessing the structure of partisan networks and their relationship with voters' self-reported ideological location, we rely on similar measures as before. Figure 5.1 includes one plot for each country, with the horizontal axis describing the self-reported left–right ideology of voters and the vertical axis describing the mean number of activists from each party known by each voter.[7] The differently dotted lines, meanwhile, plot the differences for each of the main political parties.

There are significant within- and across-country differences in the total number of activists from each party known to voters. As shown in Figure 5.1, Chilean left-wing voters are considerably more likely to know activists from the Socialists, followed by activists from the Christian Democrats. Meanwhile, leftist voters have fewer interactions with activists from the conservative UDI and RN. By contrast, right-wing voters are considerably more likely to know activists from the UDI and RN than from the Socialists and Christian Democrats. Finally, voters are, on average, more likely to know activists from the Socialist Party and the Christian Democrats, indicating that these parties have larger networks of activists than the RN and UDI, as described by Table 5.1.

---

[6] See Zheng et al. (2006: fn. 7). Gelman and Hill (2007: fn. 7) approximate $H \equiv \{\delta'_{11}, \ldots, \delta'_{ik}\}$ by the absolute difference between the predicted and estimated counts in the Poisson model. In our beta binomial specification, we estimate the full set of overdispersion parameters using the model in appendix 3.B. Consequently, we compute the inter-group correlation directly. Both strategies yield substantively similar correlation matrices, which can be provided upon request.

[7] Figure 5.1 presents mean predicted lines of a quadratic Poisson specification estimating the mean number of party activists by the ideological location of voters.

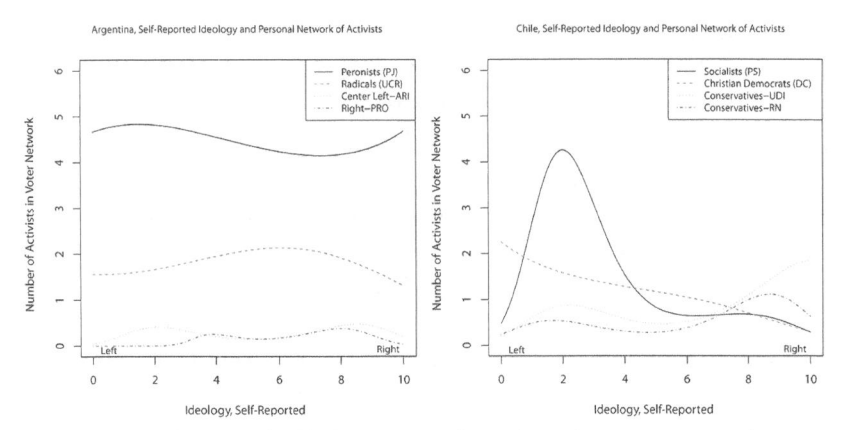

FIGURE 5.1. Ideological self-placement and number of activists (count) known by voters (2007)
*Note*: Generalized Linear Models with splines (k = 4), Poisson distribution. Lines describe the total number of activists that each respondent knows, conditional on self-reported ideological location.

In contrast with their Chilean counterparts, Argentine voters' ideological preferences were not associated with their connection to Peronist or Radical activists, even when all respondents were more likely to know Peronist activists than those of any other political party. Regardless of their ideology, voters were likely to know between five and six Peronist activists and more likely to know a Peronist than an activist of another party. We found a small association between conservatism and the number of PRO activists known by voters. However, the most noticeable characteristic of the Argentine party system was the previously described asymmetry in the size of partisan networks. In short, whereas there is significant variation in the number of party activists known by voters across the ideological spectrum in Chile, in Argentina voters' ideological self-placement is not associated with their proximity to party activists.

Socioeconomic heterogeneity emerged when we divide the sample between middle- and lower-income voters as before. Different patterns also appeared in each country with regards to the number of activists known to voters from different socioeconomic groups. In Chile, richer voters knew more activists than poorer voters. Within each group, voters on the left were considerably more likely to be acquainted with activists from the Socialists and Christian Democrats, just as voters on the right were with UDI and RN activists. Poorer left-wing voters knew, on average, around four Socialist activists, whereas progressive middle-income voters knew around five activists. The contrast is starker for the UDI. Whereas poorer right-wing voters knew less than one activist on average, richer voters were likely to be acquainted with approximately three. Socioeconomic status, thus, proved to be a strong determinant of political connections for Chilean voters across the ideological spectrum. By contrast, in Argentina, all voters are likely to know more Peronist activists than those of other parties. However, among low-income voters, those on the left were more likely to know Peronist activists than those on the right, whereas among middle-income voters, conservatives knew considerably more Peronist activists than progressives.[8]

The different effect of ideological self-placement on connections to party activists across both countries lies within the expectations derived from the historical legacies described in Chapter 3. Multi-party competition in the pre-authoritarian period, reinforced by the binominal electoral system since the transition to democracy, maps the value of ideological shortcuts in Chile. This is confirmed by the connection between ideological self-placement and competence assessments described in Chapter 4, as well as the influence of policy preferences on connections with activists of different parties presented here. By contrast, in Argentina, the catch-all nature of the PJ and the UCR, along with the impact of policy switching in the new democratic period, weakened the informative value of ideological shortcuts, explaining its weak association not only to competence assessments, but also to connections to party activists.

Chilean activists, who were more connected to ideologically akin voters and to richer voters, are recruited among educated voters, with universities playing a crucial role in the process, given the weakness of civil society organizations during this period (De la Maza, 2010; Espinoza and Madrid, 2010; Rhodes, 2005). Chilean ideological networks followed partisan electoral strategies, but were organized around candidates, who acquired more independence when they were incumbents (Luna, 2017; Luna and Rosenblatt, 2017). Because young activists recruited at universities are educated and have skills, they offered in-kind services during electoral campaigns (Espinoza and Madrid, 2010). Taking advantage of its network of young students and professionals, as well as its access to private donors, the UDI developed the model of

---

[8] This was an unexpected finding, which led us to conduct a significant number of robustness tests to make sure that the results were not driven by outliers in the data. Sensitivity analyses censuring outliers above 10, 20, 30, 40, and 50 activists show that the relationship is extremely robust. Data and code are available from the authors.

using high-skilled activists to provide services and resources in poorer neighborhoods during electoral campaigns, and other parties imitated it (Luna, 2014; Pinto, 2006). The in-kind offers to voters delivered by networks operating during the electoral campaign included legal, medical, veterinary, and dental services and even hair-cuts. Candidates delivered gifts such as boxes of food, sports clothing for soccer teams, glasses for farsighted senior citizens, and prizes for auctions to raise money for local projects. This targeted distribution strategy was mostly financed with the private funds and in-kind contributions of activists; its goal was to reach voters seeking to persuade them to vote for their candidate.

Ideological activists providing in-kind resources and privately financed targeted distribution restricted their work to electoral campaigns because they were not part of the communities where they campaigned (Espinoza, 2008: 2164; Luna, 2014; Luna and Altman, 2011). The intermittent nature of the relation produced weaker information flows than those resulting from territorial networks, especially as limited discretion on fiscal resource distribution reduced a crucial incentive for voters to strengthen such flows (Aguero et al., 1998; Luna and Mardones, 2017). As a result, as shown by Aguero et al. (1998: 175–176), party activists routinely failed in their get-out-the-vote efforts, did not connect well with low-income voters, and were unsuccessful in contacting two-thirds of voters with clearly reported party identification.

Although some studies emphasize the role of temporary employment programs (Barozet, 2006), our interviews confirmed the influence of privately financed goods and services for electorally motivated distribution and the fact that those exchanges were carried out by activists who were not embedded in the targeted communities. A PPD National Representative told us:

... we provide medical services to people, 'please, come in; let me know where it hurts?', pharmacies distribute medicines that I either buy or receive from friends who are doctors. Veterinarians disinfest pets, lawyers provide legal advice, and teachers play with the kids. They paint the kids' faces while radio personalities or karaoke machines provide entertainment. All of it on Saturday morning in my headquarters.

(Chile 01. April 14, 2009)

Similarly, a DC National Representative said to us:

... only during electoral campaigns, I bring lawyers to voters who cannot afford them, even though some of those lawyers help me all year around. But there are services that are restricted to the electoral period, such as doctors' services in medical campaigns, with midwives, with veterinarians; veterinarians have the highest impact.

(Chile 03. April 13, 2009)

This is also what a right-wing UDI National Representative explained in describing his campaign strategies:

With the young activists we make a lot of actions, but they are very simple. We have psychologists, veterinarians, hairdressers, very simple. Basically, we take advantage of the youth initiative to do social work ... we mostly drive the legal problems to public offices, which can resolve legal issues. If they have health problems, we can advise them or send them to the public agents in charge ... I have also position myself as someone who facilitate sports activities. Thus, I am permanently collaborating with local sports activities. ...

(Chile 02. April 13, 2009)

The more educated activists that form ideological networks in Chile specialized in policy persuasion – who should be effective among ideologically akin voters – especially as coalitional politics makes parties within each coalition compete with each other. Because ideological shortcuts influence vote choice behavior, as will be shown in Chapter 6, activists who can persuade voters are electorally valuable. As a result, it is not surprising that ideology played an important role in the recruitment of activists, as reported by Espinoza and Madrid (2010) and confirmed by our interviews. A RN National Representative discussed the activists who participate in his electoral campaign: "They [the activists] were from the center-right without partisan distinction. In the rural communities, different from the metropolitan area, there is not much distinction between RN and UDI ... most of them were paid, so it was enough that they were from your political sector for them to feel comfortable working with you" (Chile 08. April 13, 2009). We heard a similar description from an UDI City Councilor when he told us that "They [the activists] were proximate to us. People who are jobless for some circumstance, these are our activists, they are our people... I can also recall whom I can call ... In [NAME], the UDI has a list of all its activists. We never lose contact with them" (Chile 05. July 7, 2009).

We received similar testimonies from the center-left parties in the *Concertación*. The Chief of Staff of a PS National Representative who had run his campaign said to us "I have always been on the left, but I wasn't an activist [of the Socialist party] ..." (Chile 10. July 7, 2009) whereas a PPD activists told us "... to persuade someone to change the vote you have to send someone who understands politics." (Chile 04. July 17, 2009). Similarly, a Socialist activist who had been campaign manager explained to us: "It is impossible [that a right-wing person works with them] ... a friend who was in charge of a campaign hired sympathizers in the University, our friends. You can win some money working for the candidate ... there were **several people, all Concertación sympathizers** ... activists also helped her" (Chile 09. July 16, 2009). Finally, a former DC City Councilor confirmed that for the DC, "... volunteers and paid activists are the perfect combination. I had been a candidate in a poor neighborhood ... **I paid DC activists** and youth to walk from door to door; you hire activists" (Chile 11. April 5, 2009).

In Argentina, voters' policy preferences were not associated with their proximity to activists of different parties because political networks are territorial. Territorial activists in Argentina are embedded in their communities. Although, historically, the PJ and the UCR had strong influence in labor unions and student/professional associations, respectively, after democratization parties relied increasingly on territorial networks organized around electoral units. Territorial organization was crucial because parties were in charge of providing, distributing, and keeping the supply of paper ballots as well as monitoring each other on Election Day. Thus, territorial activists were crucial to mobilizing voters and preventing electoral fraud. They distributed party-made ballots, dedicated themselves to door-to-door canvassing, delivered political publicity, and organized meetings to spread the party message. These tasks are described by a Radical National Representative in the following way:

> ... the activist is engaged in all the activities: distribution of material, tables on the street, adds on the walls, canvassing door to door, organizing networks, monitors elections ... the UCR has always had a strength in its own political networks, conformed by activists and the face-to-face contact, more than in taking advantage of the media ....
>
> (Argentina 02. July 20, 2009)

Territorial networks increased their influence during the process of state retrenchment in the 1990s as the Menem administration relied on clientelism to foster its electoral support, prevent social unrest, and maintain electoral allegiances to Peronism despite economic adjustment and market-oriented policies (Auyero 2001; Garay, 2016; Levitsky, 2003). In poor neighborhoods, political parties sought to co-opt local community organizers who were seeking resources to help their neighbors. As a result, activists were embedded in those communities and worked year-round to provide services and access to scarce resources in contrast to the more intermittent relationship between communities and Chilean ideological activists. The literature has recognized the importance of the continuous delivery of publicly financed benefits as well as information in building electorally valuable relations, which provide thick information flows (Auyero, 2001; Garay, 2016; Giraudy, 2007; Szwarcberg, 2015; Stokes et al., 2013; Weitz-Shapiro, 2014; Zarazaga, 2016). Political connections become crucial. Partisan brokers' reputation are built on their capacity to mediate with the party and the state bureaucracy to advance solutions for voters' problems (Auyero, 2001; Zarazaga, 2015).

Territorial networks, embedded in their communities, attract activists who provide a constant stream of information to the party and therefore play a crucial role in targeting the delivery of goods and services, as referred to in our interviews. A former-Peronist mayor in the province of Buenos Aires explained the role of territorial activists as problem solvers at the local level to us by saying:

[the basic unit of the party] **is all the time accompanying the people. If someone has a problem,** if this person needs to go to the hospital or to obtain an identification card or to get a bureaucratic procedure done… **the activists are the ones who help solving the problem.** If someone dies being indigent and the family needs a coffin and burial. **There are so many things and the territorial activists are in charge of these issues.**

(Argentina 08. July 27, 2009)

A Peronist National Representative also emphasized the permanent role of activists when he described that "… **our activists work all year around. We never stop. They are the transmission belts between the people and the party**…the party is a transmission belt, not only of ideas, of recruitment, of human resources, and also of services" (Argentina 04. July 15, 2009). Similarly, a Radical provincial legislator emphasized that, "**The activists transfer information**, seek party members, participate in meetings, try to make the party known, they visit local community centers, they visit schools, they visit sports clubs, they **try to find solutions to their problems** …" (Argentina 01. UCR provincial legislator, August 5, 2009).

It is important to understand that this permanent role is not only the result of discretion in the use of public funds, but also of strategies of cooptation that bring community organizers to the party – as described by Szwarcberg (2015) – and illustrated in the comments of a Peronist broker of the Great Buenos Aires area:

Many people know me, I do social work with children from poor neighborhoods … People who attend the club or live in the area knows me and I also live there during my childhood, I have a lot of connections. I work in a big supermarket in another area where many people live. I am embedded in that community of [NAME]… My role is to receive the problems that the people bring to me, which are many and diverse...I have a group of 250 activists divided by neighborhoods... they work with the people, they get **the requests for help from anyone who has a need** ... including zinc plaques, bricks, sand, cement, milk, bags of food, medicines ....

(Argentina 10. August 10, 2009)

A similar account was given to us by a Radical broker, who had less access to public resources,

... we **help people get their identification cards**...At some point, they needed to go to Buenos Aires. **I borrowed a bus to bring the people to the City of Buenos Aires for the procedure** ... before there was fruit and vegetable market and I had a friend working there and she told me that on Saturdays they threw away the left overs. I took my own truck and carry those **leftovers and bring them to the party office and we distributed them to the people** at the UCR local office.

(Argentina 11. August 5, 2009)

In sum, their continuous presence, local embeddedness, and access to public resources allowed Argentine territorial activists to generate strong information flows, especially with poorer voters for whom they serve as crucial access points to scarce resources. Thanks to this information, activists could identify voters' needs – e.g. avoiding the delivery of glasses to a voter who needs hearing aid devices – as we show in Chapter 7 when testing the conditional effects of partisan networks. Moreover, thanks to incumbency, the PJ and UCR had more extensive and informative networks than those of the PRO and ARI. Additionally, the territorial embeddedness of activists, along with the subsequent policy changes by both the PJ and the UCR since the transition to democracy, weakened the connection between proximity to activists and ideological self-placement. By contrast, Chilean activists' networks are ideological and more likely to be connected to voters sharing their policy preferences. Each of these two types of networks is associated with diverse mechanisms for gathering electoral information and deploying targeted distribution to which we now turn.

### c) Activist Type, Information, and Handout Distribution

Our model allows us to measure the networks of those receiving handouts in both countries, a crucial indicator of efforts associated with clientelism. Although conceptually distinct from the attitudinal measure of distributive expectations regarding handouts, we use the same methodology employed to measure activists' networks to gauge the number of handout recipients connected to each party. Networks of handout recipients are slightly larger in Argentina (0.79 percent of the population) than in Chile (0.58 percent of the population). We distinguish which parties are delivering to these recipients. As before, there are few inter-party differences in Chile. By contrast, the Argentine PJ has a substantial numerical advantage over its rivals associated with the asymmetry on distributive expectations we described in Chapter 4. The number of individuals receiving handouts from the Peronists (0.48 percent of the population) is two-and-a-half times larger than those receiving handouts from the UCR (0.19 percent of the population) and many times larger than those of all other parties. The large number of Radical recipients, unexpectedly large given its electoral support at the national level by 2007, corresponds to its reach at the subnational level and the work of its partisan networks.

Table 5.2 shows that Chilean political parties are relatively even regarding the distribution of handouts, although the UDI has a small advantage in the reported number of handout recipients even with a smaller network of activists than the PS and the DC (Table 5.1). Our findings are in line with Luna's (2014) description of the UDI as the Chilean party that most actively distributes clientelistic goods. However, the UDI network of handout recipients is smaller than those of Peronists and Radicals, even as a share of each country's population.

These differences in terms of the reach of targeted distribution are related to the access to fiscal resources and information about voters' needs. In Argentina, territorial networks embedded in their communities take advantage of discretion over fiscal resources to target core voters, as will be shown in Chapter 7, and in line with the findings of Stokes et al. (2013). Their access to fiscal resources is facilitated by their connections to the public sector, thereby explaining the larger networks of handout recipients of the PJ and, to a lesser extent, the UCR. To the contrary, Chilean political parties' dependence on private resources (financial or in-kind) for targeted distribution and their weaker information flows with respect to the need of communities receiving those goods and services generates the need to rely on alternative technologies for defining how to allocate their electoral efforts.

Politicians used those alternative technologies to gather information for allotting their electoral efforts and allocating targeted distribution, both of which were crucial in their attempt to persuade voters. Hence, politicians sought to identify undecided voters by purchasing electoral rolls, studying prior electoral results, gathering data from surveys of voter attitudes and focus groups, etc. (Luna and Rosenblatt, 2012). Because voter registration was requisite (which made it compulsory to vote),

TABLE 5.2. *Networks of handout recipients, Argentina and Chile (2007)*

| | Total number of members | | | Percent of Population | |
|---|---|---|---|---|---|
| Goods PS | 17,249 | Goods PJ | 185,052 | Goods PS | 0.114 | Goods PJ | 0.487 |
| Goods DC | 19,485 | Goods UCR | 72,472 | Goods DC | 0.129 | Goods UCR | 0.191 |
| Goods PPD | 11,614 | Goods ARI | 10,074 | Goods PPD | 0.077 | Goods ARI | 0.027 |
| Goods UDI | 23,377 | Goods PRO | 6,535 | Goods UDI | 0.155 | Goods PRO | 0.017 |
| Goods RN | 16,479 | Goods PPP | 23,893 | Goods RN | 0.109 | Goods PPP | 0.063 |

*Note*: Estimates from the network model in (Eq. 5.1).

electoral rolls provided politicians with crucial personal information about voters.[9] Moreover, the stability of the vote facilitated the mapping of prior electoral results to voting stations, whereas voter surveys allowed politicians to assess partisan attachments and to seek loyal and undecided voters in particular districts. The literature suggests the value of such efforts. Whereas 80 percent of Chilean voters identify with a party in this period, a third of those voters shifted party identification from the *Concertación* to the Alianza between 2005 and 2008, suggesting a sizeable number of swing voters (Agüero et al., 1998; Luna and Altman, 2011; Navia and Osorio, 2015).

Based on electoral rolls, surveys, and gifts to hook constituents' attention, Chilean politicians deployed ideological activists to search for persuadable undecided voters. Indeed, according to our interviews, the search for these voters even resulted in the duplication of gifts (uniforms for soccer teams, prizes for auctions, etc.) to avoid negative comparisons with rivals. The focus on undecided voters using these technologies is described in our interviews. A RN mayor told us that he "... made a **study of the electoral rolls,** this is a municipality where in many areas nobody votes because these are poor people who have moved but did not change their electoral registry. Therefore, **I concentrate myself on the old part of my municipality where most people vote.**" (Chile 06. July 7, 2009). The importance of electoral rolls is mentioned by an UDI National Representative who told us that he "... used the **electoral roll that was public and where every voter was classified by occupation**" (Chile 02. April 13, 2009) and a National Representative from the same party told us that,

...the **party uses surveys, studies, focus groups.** These are the mechanisms that the electoral council has to make a decision about who will be the candidate...I had no link to my district...We made a study that measure the "UDI label" and how many votes a candidate from the party could get. It was between 15–19 percent...if we pursue certain strategies I was told that I could reach 27–28 percent. I got 27.5 percent.

(Chile 12. April 14, 2009)

The *Concertación* politicians used similar strategies. A Socialist National Representative explained to us that they "... **also look at surveys** in addition to speaking with the people who can provide another look at reality, and keep you grounded" (Chile 13. April 14, 2009).

---

[9] Our survey only included registered voters.

Meanwhile, a DC National Representative pointed to the DC reticence to get on board with what he defined as the predominant way of gathering electoral information when he said that "... the party gave me a minimum of votes, like 15 percent ... Different from other parties, like the PPD and the UDI, which decide everything with surveys, **the DC only exceptionally relies on surveys, it is more the internal machine.**" (Chile 03. April 13, 2009).

The focus on undecided voters was clear. A RN National Representative told us that he "... **started with the people who were ideologically proximate**, our voters, as a strategy when I compete with someone of our coalition. But as soon as I can leave that sector, **I target the more centrist voters, who can be persuaded.**" (Chile 08. April 13, 2009). A campaign manager for a UDI National Representative said to us: "... we know that there is a voter that is ours, who is not going to change his vote for X ... we know we shouldn't concentrate there but **where most voters live, which is where the election will be defined** ..." (Chile 14. July 9, 2009). Similarly, the Chief of Staff of another National Representative from the same party told us: "We always start the campaign in the **weaker sectors of the district, where we know voters are not our sympathizers** ..." (Chile 15. July 6, 2009).

The search for undecided voters was also apparent in an interview with a PPD activist who explained to us that they "... **start with the most difficult to persuade and then move to the easier to persuade.** Where the Concertación always wins you go last" (Chile 04. July 17, 2009). A mayor from the DC similarly described that he,

... went **door to door in all households of my district without discrimination and we used a statistical study based on prior electoral behavior to target** those areas where there had been a vote for [President] Lagos and for [right-wing politician], who was the former major, my rival. That is, I concentrated in areas where there had been split voting in my second wave of door to door, but in the first one I did not discriminate.

(Chile 16. April 15, 2009)

A National Representative from the same party illustrates how searching for undecided voters brought him to deliver targeted distribution in areas where registered voters were more abundant:

... **we went to activities where there were many voters**, the fairs, the public square on Saturdays, the rural fairs... [we provide services to anyone] because there was always a percentage of people who may vote for us, **there were many independents, undecided,** people who perceived the politics as something alien...and they were waiting to receive something.

(Chile 03. DC National Representative, April 13, 2009)

To sum up, because Chilean political networks are not very informative, politicians rely on alternative technologies in seeking to identify undecided voters to be persuaded. They use the door to door campaigning and targeted distribution to attract voters' attention when searching for undecided voters. By contrast, the efforts of Argentine territorial activists are more informed by their embeddedness in the community. Their access to discretionary resources when their party is incumbent is crucial to explain asymmetries on distributive capacity, in line with expectations described in Chapter 4.

## 5.3 SUMMARY AND EXPECTATIONS

In comparing the size of partisan networks in both countries, we noticed symmetry across Chilean party organizations, which contrasted with the predominance of the Peronist partisan network in Argentina. Chilean partisan networks are also more connected with ideologically akin voters than those in Argentina. These conditions match to ideological activists in Chile, who specialize in persuasion and are more connected to voters with similar policy preferences. These are relatively educated activists, who often develop their electoral activities outside their own neighborhood and mostly during electoral campaigns. Indeed, they are more connected to middle-class rather than-lower-income voters, even when targeted distribution is one of their tasks. Having less information about those communities, they rely on technical sources of data and often use targeted distribution as a hook to attract undecided voters they want to persuade. By contrast, territorial networks in Argentina are not associated with ideology but rather with voters in their home community, which provide them with thick flows of information, especially as these are seen as mechanisms to access scarce public resources among the poor. Peronist and Radical networks are thus territorial and more extensive than those of ARI and PRO, which rely to some extent on ideological activists as they had not developed strong territorial connections at the time of our study.

We have finished describing the content of voters' preferences that we use for testing our argument. The following chapters are dedicated to gauging their sensitivity to distinctive parties' offers and to assessing the implications of our argument, starting with electoral behavior then shifting to the supply side. Given the description of policy and non-policy endowments provided in Chapters 4 and 5, we expect ideological distance to have a stronger effect on the vote in Chile than in Argentina and to weight more for middle-income than for lower-income voters in that country. Distributive expectations should, by contrast, weight more in Argentina than in Chile, whereas – following the literature on economic voting – we expect economic competence to matter significantly in both countries. The distinct types of party activists described in this chapter lead us to expect different conditional effects across countries. Partisan networks should heighten the effect of targeted distribution among Argentine lower-income voters, as well as that of ideological persuasion among the same voters in Chile. Chapters 6 and 7 test these expectations regarding voting behavior while assessing differences in voter sensitivity to party offers, before we analyze parties' responsiveness to the incentives created by voters' preferences.

# 6

# Voters' Preferences and Parties' Electoral Offers

Whereas Chapters 4 and 5 described the distribution of voters' preferences in Argentina and Chile, this chapter focuses on the determinants of vote choice, which are crucial to assessing the heterogeneity on voters' sensitivity to parties' policy and non-policy offers. We provide evidence that ideological proximity, competence for managing the economy, distributive expectations, and connections to partisan networks shape electoral behavior in both countries. Subsequently, we introduce a utility function that models the weight that voters attach to the policy and non-policy determinants of their vote choice. We end by describing how the heterogeneity of voters' preferences provides parties with opportunities and constraints to tailor their electoral strategies toward different groups of voters.

In both countries, perceptions of economic competence are the strongest determinant of the vote. Ideological proximity, we show, is also a predictor of vote choice in both countries, although it weighs more heavily in the decision of Chilean voters. Distributive expectations matter in both countries, although pork and patronage display larger effects than handouts. In fact, once we control for all variables, expectations about the distribution of handouts fail to achieve statistical significance, indicating that vote-buying strategies based on small sums of money, food, or clothing have little impact on the vote despite their widespread documentation in the literature.[1] Instead, the vote for a party increases significantly as expectations of receiving public-sector jobs and local investment in

---

[1] While we find no statistically significant relationship between handouts and vote once we control for other factors, our analyses are restricted to party votes in legislative elections. It

public works grow. In both countries, connections to partisan networks are also important determinants of vote choice.

A core intuition of our theory is that voter heterogeneity provides opportunities and constraints to parties seeking to tailor their policy and non-policy offers to voters. After providing evidence that voters care about policy, competence, selective incentives, and network proximity, we present models that estimate separate parameters for voters in each socioeconomic category. We show that not all voters derive the same utility from the policy and non-policy offers of parties and, consequently, that parties should be attuned to those differences in defining their electoral strategies.

Regarding ideological distance, results show that richer voters care more about ideological distance in both countries, although Chilean voters allot more weight to this dimension than their Argentine counterparts. Similarly, we find significant inter-class differences in the importance that different voters attach to economic competence. In Chile, better-off voters value macroeconomic competence more than poorer voters. By contrast, poorer Argentine voters care more about parties' ability to manage the economy than their richer counterparts. Even for distributive expectations, we show different patterns across countries in terms of the weight assigned by poorer and richer voters to public-sector job expectations in their electoral decision. Indeed, these are more salient for poorer Argentine voters and middle-class Chilean voters. This variation generates incentives for politicians to mix and match policy and non-policy offers to different groups of voters.

## 6.1 VOTING FOR POLICY AND NON-POLICY BENEFITS

In this section, we focus on how voters decide for whom to vote. Existing models have considered the effect of policy preferences expressed by voters on a range of issues, as well as the policy offers made by parties. Indeed, the list can be diverse, (see Chapter 2), because voters care – and parties promise to provide – a diverse assortment of policy and non-policy benefits in deciding whom to support on Election Day.

We use the information collected in our Argentine and Chilean mass surveys to measure the preferences, behavior, and social context of voters

---

is likely that the effect of handouts would be larger when considering candidate-centric rules rather than overall party brand.

and the weight they assign to policy and non-policy benefits. In both countries, we requested that respondents answer the following question: "If national legislative elections were to take place next Sunday, what party would you vote for?" Responses were open-ended and non-responses were followed up with a one-time insistence. This provided us with a sample of 1,584 Chilean respondents and 1,696 Argentine respondents that indicated a vote choice for a top five parties in their respective country.[2] We imputed missing values for the independent variables using multivariate imputation by chain equations (MICE)[3] and estimated models with five alternatives in Argentina – PJ,[4] UCR, ARI, PRO, and the main provincial party (PPP)[5] – and five alternatives in Chile: the Socialist Party (PS), the Christian Democrats (DC), the PPD, UDI and the RN.

To predict party vote, we considered four main independent variables that report on the key traits discussed by our model: the *ideological distance* between respondent $i$ and party $j$, the respondent's *perceived party competence* to manage the economy,[6] the number of connections respondents have to the *network of activists of each party*, and the respondents' *distributive expectations* of receiving handouts, a public sector job, or the public works required by their community. These variables augment the standard model of ideological proximity (Downs, 1957) by incorporating valence components (Stokes, 1963), selective

---

[2] We did not provide a closed menu of parties to respondents and non-responses prompted a one-time insistence. Undecided voters represented 27 percent and 20 percent of respondents in Argentina and Chile, respectively. Blank votes represented another 10 percent and 14 percent, respectively. Finally, votes for smaller parties represented 3.3 percent of the vote in Argentina and 11 percent of the vote in Chile.

[3] While we deleted non-responses, blank, and small-party votes in both countries, we also replicated all analyses with a full dataset, drawing votes randomly to replace missing observations with multivariate imputation by chained equation (MICE in R 2.9). Results of alternative models are similar and available upon request.

[4] The survey was structured so that voters could select their preferred Peronist faction. This included the Frente para la Victoria (FPV) of former President Kirchner, allies of Carlos Menem, Rodriguez Saa, and a generic Peronist party. Because the survey question was "undirected," we recoded as Peronists all responses that described any of the party factions.

[5] Due to the importance of provincial parties in Argentina, the fifth party choice varies per province. Seeking to retrieve information on the main provincial party, its partisan network, and its distributive intent, we coded all provincial parties as PPP when conducting our analyses.

[6] Our analyses concentrate on the effect of competence in managing the economy (rather than dealing with poverty or crime) because it yields the largest electoral effects.

incentives (Cox and McCubbins, 1986), and network capacity (Dixit and Londregan, 1996).

We measured ideological distance as the squared distance from the self-reported ideological location of each respondent to the reported location of each party, $(x_i - L_{ki})^2$. Ideological placements were measured on an eleven-point scale, from zero to ten, with low numbers describing locations on the left of the political spectrum and high numbers representing placement on the right. We expect parameter estimates of ideological distance to be negative, with larger ideological distance reducing the probability of voting for a party.

Second, we measure the effect of competence to manage the economy on the vote using a four-point variable that ranged from "not competent at all" to "very competent." As described in Chapter 4, there are significant inter- and intra-country differences in the perceptions of competence in Argentina and Chile. Furthermore, as in the case of ideology, each voter reports distinct competence assessments for each of the parties, giving us a set of five competence responses per country. We expect that higher competence ratings for a party result in a positive probability of support for it electorally.

Third, we measure personal linkages between voters and each party, taking advantage of our measure of *proximity to the network of activists of each party* described in Chapter 5. This distance is calculated using survey questions "how many people do you know, and they know you, who are activists of party x?" Following Gelman and Hill (2007), we estimated individual parameters, reporting distances from respondents to each party network, were estimated using a negative-binomial design with individual- and group-specific overdispersion parameters (Gelman and Hill, 2007; McCarty et al., 2000; McCarty et al., 2007). Those overdispersion parameters report that the respondent knows more/less members of a group than the prevalence rate (in standard deviations), which is our crucial measure of "proximity." As with ideological distance, network proximity is alternative specific for respondent $i$ and party $k$. We expect this variable to have a positive effect on vote choice, where a respondent who knows more activists from a party will be more likely to vote for that party.

A fourth set of independent variables describes the self-reported unconditional expectation of *receiving handouts, a public-sector job, or the public works* from an elected member of party $k$. The questions read: "On a scale from one to ten, where one is very unlikely and ten is very likely, how likely would it be that an elected member of the (*party*) would provide you with (type of good)?" The 1–10 ordinal index was used to measure the expected probability. The question was worded so as to solicit unconditional expectations of receiving goods and did not imply a quid pro quo exchange before, during, or after an election.[7] The respondent was presented with this question prior to questions on vote behavior in a survey module that assesses party performance. Consequently, survey instruments did not prompt respondents to assume that the delivery of goods was conditional on voting for a candidate who, once in office, would deliver the benefits. These questions are also alternative specific, inquiring on the likelihood of receiving different goods from members of each party $k$. We expect higher distributive expectations from a particular party to increase electoral support at the ballot box.

We also include respondent-specific controls measuring the relative size of the respondents' personal network (ln),[8] as well as the gender and economic income of respondents. We also control for the respondent's normative views about targeted distribution and, in the case of Argentina, the size of locality, which has been associated with vote monitoring and distributive strategies.[9]

### a) Model Specification

We use a Conditional (Multinomial) Logit design with alternative- and respondent-specific variables. Alternative-specific variables estimate the effect of variables that vary by choice (each party $k$ in our model). For

---

[7] The survey instrument was also worded to prevent voters from disclosing information under the false assumption that the interviewer could provide any link or connection to a party that was in position to deliver goods. The question was inserted in a module assessing the expected performance of parties in office, together with questions about the parties' capacity to manage the economy, to respond to voter preferences, etc.

[8] The size of the personal network had a mean of 200 and 203 in Argentina and Chile respectively. Estimates of network size are similar to those measured in France and the USA (McCarty et al., 2000, 2007).

[9] To measure support for distribution, the survey inquires: "How adequate is it for political parties to distribute [food, money, clothing, jobs, and public works]." Responses were coded on a ten-point scale, from completely inadequate to completely adequate to control for the potential negative impact of distribution among non-beneficiaries (Weitz-Shapiro, 2012). In Argentina, district size was measured using the natural log of the voting age population in the voters' district, following a large literature on the impact of district size on both the vote and the allocation of targeted transfers in Argentina (Calvo and Escolar, 2005; Calvo and Murillo, 2005; Gibson and Calvo, 2001). In Chile, we did not use a variable measuring district size, given that district sizes for the lower house are roughly equal by design in two-member districts.

example, the ideological distance between a respondent $i$ and the PS enters into the utility function of voting for the Socialists but not in the utility function of voting for other parties such as the UDI or the RN. That is, each voter reports different ideological distances from her or his preferred position $x_i$ to the location of each of the parties, $S_{ki}$. Consequently, the ideological distance variable differs by party and voter, $(x_i-L_{ki})^2$ and the conditional logit model estimates a single parameter to assess the effect of distance on all vote choices.

Respondent-specific variables, on the other hand, take the same value across alternatives. For example, wealthy voters do not change their income category because they decide to vote for a different party. A wealthy voter remains wealthy independently of whether she or he votes for the PS, the DC, or the UDI. However, wealthy voters exhibit a different propensity of voting for the Peronists, the Radicals, the PRO, etc. Consequently, the same wealth score for voter $i$ yields a different expected linear effect – different vote probabilities – of voting for a party. The respondent-specific variable in the multinomial choice model, consequently, estimate separate parameters for $k-1$ parties.

The alternative-specific choice (e.g. ideological distance from a party) is often mentioned in the literature as a conditional logit model, whereas the respondent-specific choice (e.g. wealth of a voter) is often referred to as a multinomial logit model. Our specification includes both alternative-specific variables that vary by choice, such as ideological distance or competence, and respondent-specific variables with traits that remain constant by voter, such as gender or socioeconomic status (SES). To avoid confusion, consequently, we describe the statistical estimate as a multinomial (conditional) logit model:

$$U(V_{ik}) = -\alpha(x_i-L_{ik})^2 + \beta_1 Competence_{ik} + \ldots + \beta_2 SES_i + \gamma_{ik} \quad \text{(Eq. 6.1)}$$

$$\Pr(V_{ik_1}) = \frac{e^{U(V_{ik_1})}}{\sum_{k_j=1}^{J} e^{U(V_{ik_j})}} \forall i,j \quad \text{(Eq. 6.2)}$$

As readers will note, in Equation (6.1) the alternative specific variable "Competence" is indexed by respondent $i$ and alternative $k$, describing respondents that provide separate assessments of competence for each of the parties. Similarly, the ideological distance $(x_i-L_{ik})^2$ also varies by respondent $x_i$ and party position $L_k$. For these two variables, a single parameter $\beta_1$ or $-\alpha$ summarizes the full effect of competence or ideological distance on party choice. By contrast, the variable socioeconomic status is indexed by respondent, $SES_i$, given that income does not vary by choice. Instead, a different parameter, $\beta_{2k}$, is estimated for each choice, $k-1$, with one party as a baseline. In all analyses in this book, we kept the incumbents, PJ or Peronist (Argentina) and the PS or Socialist (Chile) parties, as the baseline categories.

## b) Model Results

We discuss our results here and report all coefficients in the appendix to this chapter in Tables 6.A.1 and 6.A.2. To facilitate the interpretation of these results, we provide a visual presentation of the marginal effects in Figures 6.1 and 6.2, as well as of the coefficient parameters by socioeconomic class in Figures 6.3 and 6.4. Our results conform to the theory that the determinants of the vote are similar in both countries. Results show that ideology matters for both Argentine and Chilean voters, although the linear effect of ideological proximity on vote choice is significantly larger among Chilean voters. Indeed, the linear predictor is twice as large and – as important given that assessments of party positions are much more precisely defined in Chile than in Argentina – confirms that ideological shortcuts are more valuable to Chilean than Argentine voters.

Evaluations of competence to manage the economy have very large and significant effects on party vote in both countries. In Tables 6.A.1 and 6.A.2 in the appendix to this chapter, the linear estimate of competence on the log-odds ratio of party vote is almost identical for both countries (1.002 in Chile compared to 1.009 in Argentina). While the effect of competence seems much larger than that of ideology, the range of ideological distance is [0,100], while competence is [1,4]. Consequently, the maximum effect of ideology and competence on the vote is very similar in Chile. However, the maximum effect of economic competence on the vote is almost twice as large as that of ideology among Argentine voters.

Proximity to the network of activists also has a large and significant effect on party vote in both Argentina and Chile, although the maximum linear effect on voting is 25 percent larger in Argentina. Given that the total number of activists is almost 17 percent larger in Argentina than in Chile (1.4 percent of the voting age population in Argentina compared to 1.2 percent in Chile), our results are in line with a conventional wisdom that emphasizes the importance of party machines in Argentina.

Our results for distributive expectations are important given the literature on clientelism in both countries. Both patronage and pork are important determinants of the vote in Argentina and Chile, although the maximum possible linear effect is almost a third larger in Argentina. However, as noted in the introduction to this chapter, once we control for the delivery of all three types of goods (handouts, patronage, and pork), results fail to produce statistical significance for expectations regarding the delivery of handouts in either Chile or Argentina. Handouts associated to vote buying in the literature do not have a significant effect on the vote in either country, even when distributing them may be a common practice of electoral campaigns.[10]

The effects of the respondent-specific controls are also of interest. It is worth reminding readers that the effects of respondent-specific variables on party vote describe changes in the log-odds ratios of voting for a party vis-à-vis the model baseline – the Peronists in Argentina and the PS in Chile. For example, voters of the ARI and PRO in Argentina are considerably more likely to live in large districts than those of the Peronist PJ. By contrast, voters of the UCR are considerably less likely to live in large districts than those of the Peronist PJ.[11]

Given that the baseline party in Argentina is the Peronist PJ, estimated parameters already provide a glance of the voters' behavior even before we provide readers with model probabilities. For example, we can observe that middle-income voters in the C2 category are not statistically less likely to vote for the ARI or the PRO than for the Peronist PJ, everything else held constant. However, among lower-income voters we see a statistically significant decline in the log-odds of voting for the ARI, and the PRO, when compared to the Peronist baseline. The negative effect of class on the ARI and PRO becomes larger as the respondents' income declines. The negative effect of class on the PRO and ARI vote is statistically significant even after we control for all other components of the vote such as ideology, competence, network capacity, and selective incentives. Indeed, the pro-Peronist vote among the poor extends beyond all other parameters in the model, confirming the continuous association of the Peronist party with low-income voters.

---

[10] The next chapter investigates this finding and shows that there are groups of voters who are electorally sensitive to expectations about handout distribution in Argentina.

[11] Indeed, since the 2001 crisis, the UCR voter has become a party that is more dependent on the vote of the smaller peripheral provinces (Calvo and Escolar, 2005; Leiras, 2007).

By contrast, in Chile the effect of class on the vote is not statistically significant.[12] That is, once we control for differences in ideology, competence, selective incentives, and network proximity there is no direct effect that is measured by the socioeconomic indicators. Indeed, the pro-PS vote among the poor is explained by inter-class differences in behavioral determinants such as ideology or competence and, once we control for those variables, there is little else to be explained by socioeconomic status.

In Argentina, we can see that larger personal networks increase the log-odds of voting for the UCR in all models and for the UCR and the ARI in the full model when compared to the Peronists: i.e. model 4. In Chile, larger personal networks increase the log-odds ratio of voting for the RN, compared to the leftist PS. Although we expect large networks to correlate with socioeconomic status, we do not have any particular theoretical expectation in regards to the effect of personal network size on vote choice. Personal attitudes toward targeted distribution have no significant effect on the vote on either country, except for the ARI in Argentina. Favorable views about targeted distribution for all three types of selective incentive are negatively correlated with the probability of voting for the ARI, a party whose electoral campaign was strongly based on denouncing government officials for corruption. Finally, results show that women are less likely to vote for the ARI and the PRO in Argentina, when compared to the Peronists. In Chile, women are more likely to vote for the conservative UDI.

To clarify the implications of our argument about the impact of voters' preferences on the vote and the electoral influence of non-policy determinants of the vote, Figures 6.1 and 6.2 provide readers with an intuitive description of different scenarios, with probabilities drawn from the conditional logit estimates in model 4 of Tables 6.1 and 6.2. In all plots, the vertical axes describe the probability of voting for each of the parties and the horizontal axes describe the self-reported ideological placement. For example, the plot in the upper-left of Figure 6.1 describes the probability of voting for the PS, DC, PPD, UDI, or RN, with all independent variables set to their means except those of ideology and perceived competence to manage the economy. For all parties, we fixed mean

---

[12] The Chilean literature on electoral behavior finds no evidence of socioeconomic-driven voting despite the tendency of the upper-middle-class and rich voters to vote for the right and of the poorer voters to support the Concertación (Barrueto and Navia, 2015; Luna, 2008). Altman (2004) analyzes the vote by municipalities and finds that both the poor and the rich support the right, but does not distinguish voters within those geographical units. Luna (2014) suggests that the rich are more likely to vote for the right and the middle classes for the Concertación, with poor voters being pivotal.

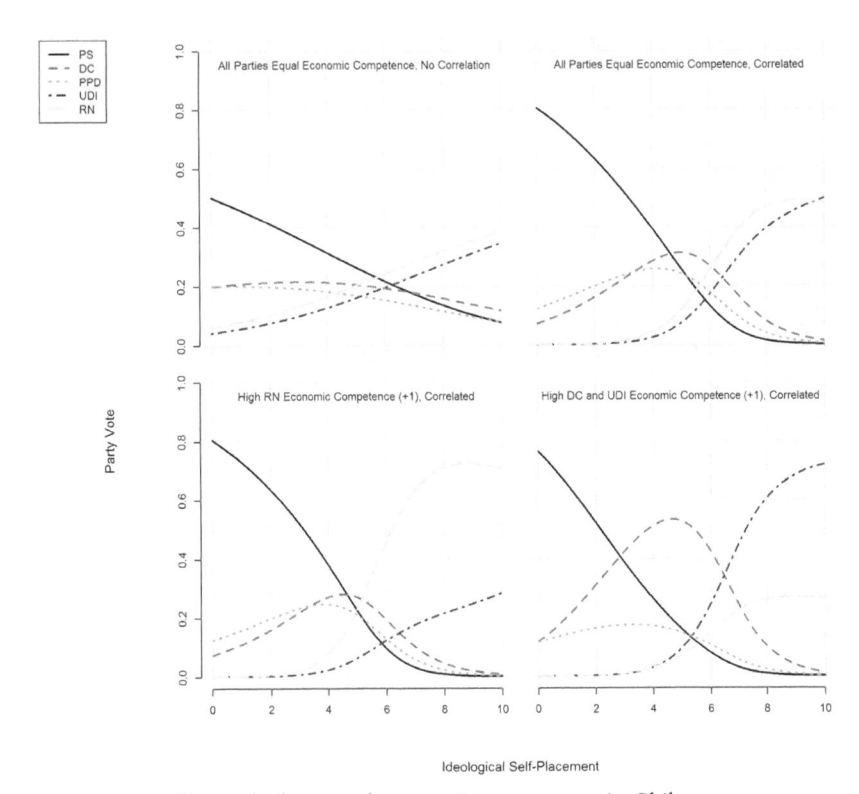

FIGURE 6.1. Vote, ideology, and economic competence in Chile
*Note*: Probability estimates from Table 6.1, model 4, with varying competence scores.

perceived competence equal to five, and estimate the expected probability of voting for a party for voters located in different locations of the policy space using the real distribution of our survey.

In the upper-left plot of Figure 6.1, competence evaluations are uncorrelated with ideological positions; this allows us to isolate the independent effect of each of the benefits offered by parties, assuming equal levels of economic competence. Voters' assessments of competence are set to an average of five for all parties, and therefore voters on the left select the PS, PPD, and DC in larger numbers, while voters on the right are more likely to prefer the UDI and RN. A voter located on the extreme left, a zero in the scale, would display a 51 percent probability of voting for the PS, a 20 percent probability of voting for the DC or for the PPD, and less than 5 percent probability of voting for the conservatives UDI or RN. Similarly, holding mean competence equal to five for all parties, we observe

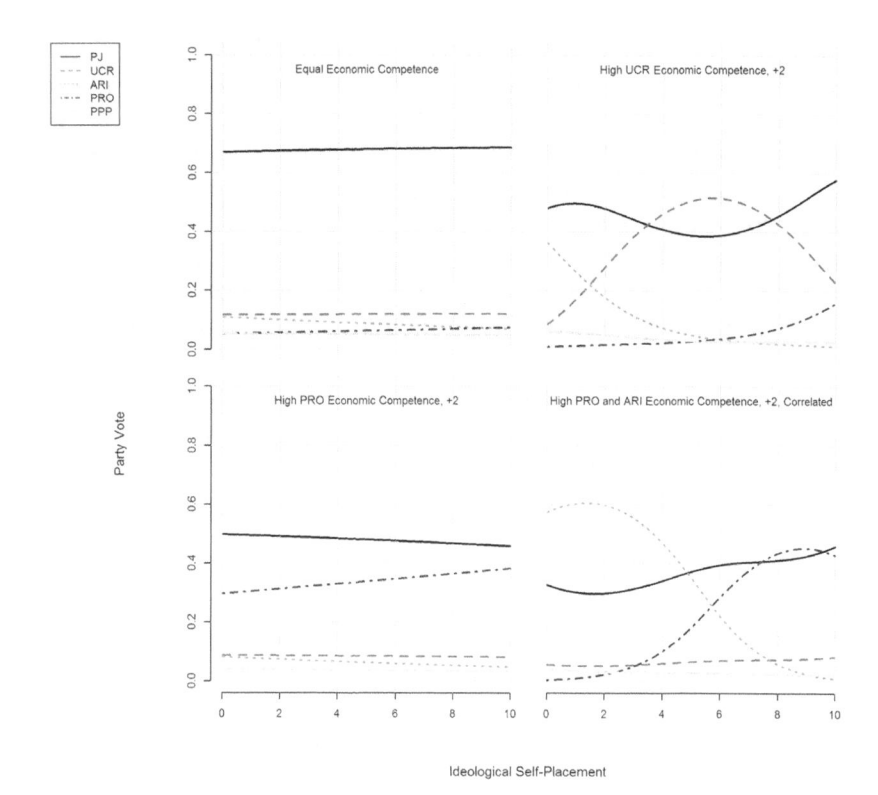

FIGURE 6.2. Vote, ideology, and economic competence in Argentina
*Note*: Probability estimates from Table 6.2, model 4, with varying competence scores. The plot in the lower right has competence assessments correlated with self-reported ideology, as was the case in Chile.

that a voter on the extreme right – a ten on the ideological scale – would display a 37 percent probability of voting for the RN, a slightly lower probability of voting for the UDI (approximately 35 percent), and much lower probabilities of voting for the DC, PPD, and PS.

The upper-right plot of Figure 6.1 considers self-reported ideological placement and evaluations of partisan competence to manage the economy to be highly associated with each other for the Chilean voters in our data. Consequently, the upper-right plot gives, on average, equal competence to all parties, but allows the voters' assessments of competence to be correlated with ideological distances.[13] When assessments of competence

---

[13] Mean correlation was set to the mean values described in Chapter 4.

and ideology are correlated, predicted vote choice shows a more ideological – and polarized – party system, with well-defined parties on the left and right of the political spectrum. Indeed, voters on the extreme left (a zero on the scale) increase their probability of voting for the PS by almost 30 percentage points – from 51 percent to 80 percent – and voters on the right increase their probability of voting for the UDI and RN by almost 12 percentage points each, from around 37 percent to almost 50 percent. Therefore, we show here how the association between ideology and competence assessments by Chilean voters generates incentives for parties to stick to their policy positions because their policy offers also shape how voters perceive a crucial non-policy benefit such as competence. This association thus reduces politicians' incentives to move centripetally in the policy space toward the median voter.

To illustrate the influence of competence on the vote, the lower plots in Figure 6.1 show how small increases in perceived capacity to manage the economy generate dramatic changes in votes. The lower-left plot shows that a mean advantage of one unit (out of ten) in perceived competence ensures that the RN wins even among centrist voters located slightly above five in the ideological space. Furthermore, the advantage of the RN is particularly large among conservative voters. Indeed, differences in perceived competence have a more dramatic effect among parties that are ideologically closer, yielding significant vote losses to the disadvantaged party, which is marked in the electoral decline of the UDI. Similarly, the lower-right plot shows that an increase in competence for the DC and the UDI hurts their closest ideological competitors: the PPD and RN, respectively. In both cases, voters reward higher competence within the boundaries of their proximate ideological space, given the weight of both variables on the electoral decision in Chile. The association between ideological preference and competence evaluations and the weight of policy preferences on Chileans' electoral decisions highlights both the limits it creates for parties' policy shifts and the value of ideological persuasion by activists, to which we return in Chapter 7.

In Figure 6.2, we repeat this exercise for Argentina, where the effect of economic competence on the vote is also very large and significant as shown by Table 6.2 and previously shown by Ratto (2013) and Tagina (2012).[14] In Figure 6.2, the upper-left plot describes our baseline results,

---

[14] Ratto (2013: 371–373) shows the strong impact of perceptions of economic performance among Argentine voters (higher than in Europe or the rest of the region) and associated it to the experience with recurrent economic crises since democratization. Tagina (2012:

with a very large electoral advantage for the Peronist PJ when all values are set at their means and competence fixed to the same score of five for all parties. This is the case because the Peronists benefit from considerable advantages in other non-policy endowments, such as distributive expectations, and a more extensive network of activists.

Results become more interesting once we increase mean competence for the UCR (keeping others constant), allowing the Radicals to overtake the Peronist PJ among moderate voters in the upper right plot. More interesting, we can see that once Peronists no longer enjoy this non-policy advantage, the more ideological traits of the smaller ARI and PRO translate into a party system with better defined policy traits. In the lower-left plot, we keep Peronist competence at five but increase the competence of the PRO, still not allowing ideological correlation. We see the improvement of the PRO in terms of vote share, especially among right-wing voters. This is an electoral result that informs our understanding of the 2015 election when the PRO received a third of the vote in the presidential election, but was able to win the runoff by 2 percentage points in a context of deteriorating evaluations about the Peronist macroeconomic competence, due to high inflation and weak growth. Finally, in the lower-right plot, we increase the relative competence of the ARI and the PRO, while also allowing ideological proximity and competence to correlate with each other, also using the mean values in our data described in Chapter 4 (which mainly affect the ARI and PRO). Predicted probabilities show that positive assessments of competence for the more ideological ARI and PRO alter the ideological space for all voters, with higher Peronist electoral returns on the right of the ideological space, but also higher gains for the PRO in that policy area as its competence increases.

In Argentina, the impact of competence evaluations as a non-policy resource, which are mostly uncorrelated to voters' ideological preference – especially for the PJ and UCR – were crucial to understanding the PJ electoral success and its capacity to attract voters of differing ideological positions and to modify its policy offers. By contrast, in Chile the weight of competence and its association with ideological space anchors parties in their policy positions. That is, if parties modify their electoral offers, they risk affecting voters' perception of their economic capacity – a crucial non-policy determinant of the vote. Hence, the impact of competence on

---

362) finds that the effect of economic performance is even stronger in 2007 than in the prior presidential election when the Peronist had three presidential candidates and responsibility was harder to assign.

the vote is high in both countries, but in the case of Chile, given its correlation with voters' policy preferences, it further restricts politicians' agency to modify their ideological offers.

In all, the empirical results in this chapter show that, in both Chile and Argentina, ideological proximity, competence assessments, network connections, and selective incentives (except for handouts) are predictors of electoral behavior. Second, we find comparable effects across countries for all four types of benefits in the portfolio of politicians, although ideological proximity is a stronger predictor of party vote in Chile than in Argentina. Third, we illustrate how advantages in non-policy endowments result in large vote gains, how disadvantages in non-policy endowments result in steep vote losses, and how these effects operate when policy and non-policy preferences are correlated or uncorrelated. While these patterns generate different expectations for political behavior to be tested in the following chapters, we first analyze variation in voters' electoral behavior by socioeconomic category. Our goal is to uncover variation in preferences over policy and non-policy offers in the electoral portfolio of political parties across poorer and richer voters and to identify the opportunities generated by such diversity in content and sensitivity for parties seeking to mix and match electoral offers.

## 6.2 VOTER HETEROGENEITY AND SOCIOECONOMIC STATUS IN ARGENTINA AND CHILE

In the previous section, we present readers with models of vote choice which estimate changes in the probability of voting for each party, given parties' policy and non-policy offers. These models, however, do not consider whether voters in different socioeconomic groups attach different importance or weight to the policy and non-policy benefits provided by parties. In this section we move one step further, estimating the extent to which different groups of voters develop distinct preferences for different types of benefits in the portfolio of politicians. As in the previous model, we consider alternative-specific and respondent-specific variables, but this time we allow model estimates to vary by socioeconomic status:

$$U(V_{ik}) = -\alpha_{[class]}(x_i - L_k)^2 + \beta_{[class,1]} Competence_{ik} + \ldots + \delta_{[class,k]} Gender_i + \gamma_{ik}$$

(Eq. 6.3)

We compute this model via MCMC Bayesian estimation in WinBUGS 1.4.1 with uninformative priors, as described by the code in Section 6.A in the appendix to this chapter. Tables with model estimates are also given in Section 6.A of the appendix (Tables 6.A.1 through 6.A.8). For presentation purposes, Figure 6.3 and 6.4 present readers with plots of the coefficients for our four key variables of interest, i.e. ideology, competence (to manage the economy), network proximity, and distributive expectations (regarding a public-sector job). Coefficients describe linear changes in the log-odds ratios of voting for a party for each of the income categories, with 90/10 credible confidence intervals.

The interpretation of model results for the alternative-specific parameters is straightforward: the importance or weight that voters within each of the different socioeconomic categories attach to their ideological proximity to parties, their assessments of competence to manage the economy, the size of party networks, and the expectation of receiving a public-sector job. Model results in Argentina distinguish respondents by income categories, from the middle-income respondents (in all three C categories) to lower-income voters (in categories D1 through E). For Chile, results distinguish the middle-income voters (in all three C categories) from the lower-income respondents (in category D). The different classifications respond to how data was collected and do not represent different groupings on our part. In both countries, the cut-off between voters in the C and D categories divides the population approximately in halves.

Consider, for example, Figure 6.3, which describes coefficient estimates for the different socioeconomic categories in Chile. The upper-left plot shows that ideology is an important determinant of vote choice for all four different socioeconomic categories. However, differences are only statistically significant at the 0.1 level when comparing the upper-middle-income (C1) and lower-income (D) voters, with ideological distance leading to a larger decline in the probability of voting for a party among upper-middle-income (C1) voters – an estimate of –0.55 for those voters – compared to –0.33 for lower-income (D) voters, although the statistical difference between the coefficient estimates is barely significant at $p = 0.09$.

The upper-right plot shows larger differences in the weight that voters of different classes attach to managerial competence. Among the upper-middle-income (C1) voters, the linear effect is 1.49 units of change in the log-odds ratio of voting for a party per one-unit increase in perceived competence. By contrast, the effect for the lower-income respondents (D) is only 0.95, with the difference being statistically significant at the 0.01 level.

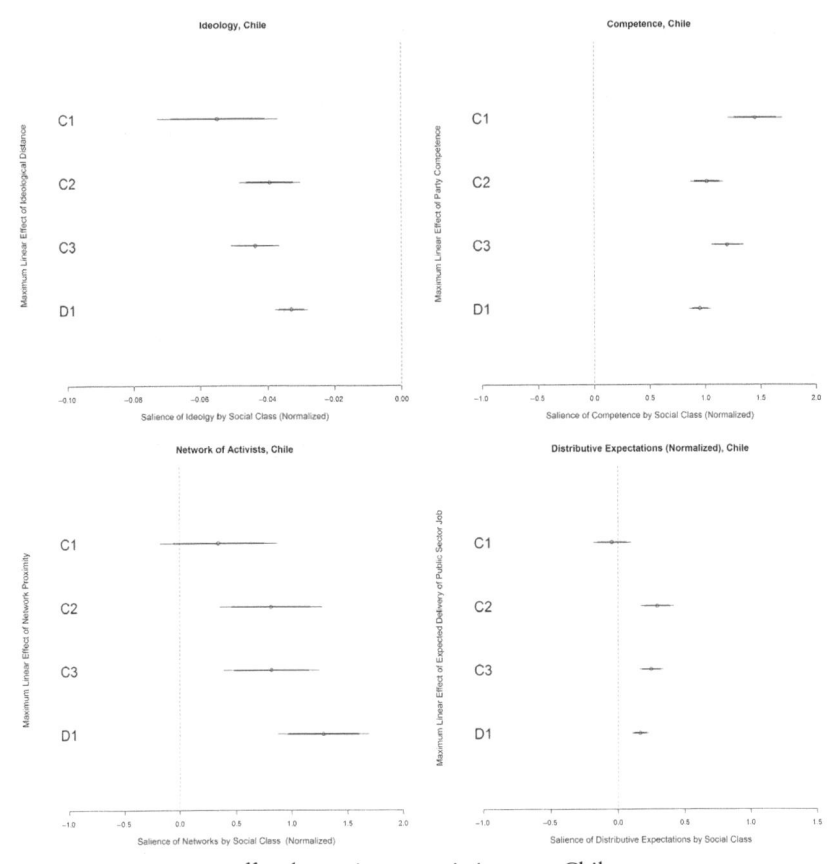

FIGURE 6.3. Linear effect by socioeconomic income, Chile 2007
*Note*: Plots describe the estimated coefficients from Table 6.A.1 in the appendix. Lines describe the [20,80] interval around the estimated coefficients.

The importance voters attach to their relative proximity to party networks and to selective incentives also differs by socioeconomic status, although differences are not particularly dramatic except between upper-middle-income (C1) and lower-income (D) voters. Interestingly, network proximity fails to achieve statistical significance for the former, whereas it matters a great deal for the latter. We analyze this effect more fully in Chapter 7, where we measure the conditional effect of networks connections by socioeconomic status. Results show that personal contacts with party members have a larger impact on poorer voters' decisions in both countries, although through different mechanisms. Finally, distributive expectations for public-sector jobs increase the log-odds of voting for a party among middle-income (C2) through lower-income (D) voters, but have no effect on upper-middle-income (C1) voters. Readers, however, can readily observe that the relatively well-off middle-income (C2) voters are the ones that give the largest weight to public-sector jobs. We will come back to this finding when we analyze public-sector wages in Chile and Argentina in Chapter 8. To conclude, results in Chile show that the better-off upper-middle-income (C1) voters care a great deal about ideology and competence, while they give little weight to party networks and selective incentives. By contrast, lower-income (D) voters are receptive to both the policy and non-policy determinants of the vote.[15]

Within-country variation for Argentina is presented in Figure 6.4, in this case with more discrimination within lower-income voters, which are separated into three categories. Our results show that ideological proximity is a considerably weaker predictor of vote choice in Argentina, resulting in changes in the log-odds vote that are half of those observed in Chile. Moreover, class differences regarding the weight of ideological distance on the vote are smaller than in Chile and estimates are not statistically different for the relatively better-off upper-middle-income (C1) voters and the lower-income voters (from D1 to E).

By contrast, Figure 6.4 shows not only that Argentine voters care a great deal about economic management competence, but also that low-income voters are particularly sensitive to differences in perceived competence – perhaps an effect of the dire consequences they suffered during the two macroeconomic crises experienced since democratization. Indeed, differences in the effect of economic competence on the vote among upper-middle-income (C1) voters and lower-income (D) voters are large and statistically significant. By contrast, there is little socioeconomic difference in the impact of partisan networks on the vote when comparing across all voter categories in Argentina, with estimates only achieving statistical significance for voters in the middle-income (C2) and the lower-income (D2) categories. While network capacity was statistically significant when considering the full sample, the smaller samples by socioeconomic group results in less precise estimates that sometimes fail to achieve statistical significance. However, we explore this effect with more precision in Chapter 7, where the larger impact of networks on lower-income (D2) voters is associated with their capacity to provide information that makes targeted distribution more efficient. Finally, the bottom-right graph shows that distributive expectations about public-

---

[15] We are not considering the electoral impact of their size here, as lower-income (D) voters constitute 45 percent of our sample and upper-middle-income (C1) voters only 9 percent.

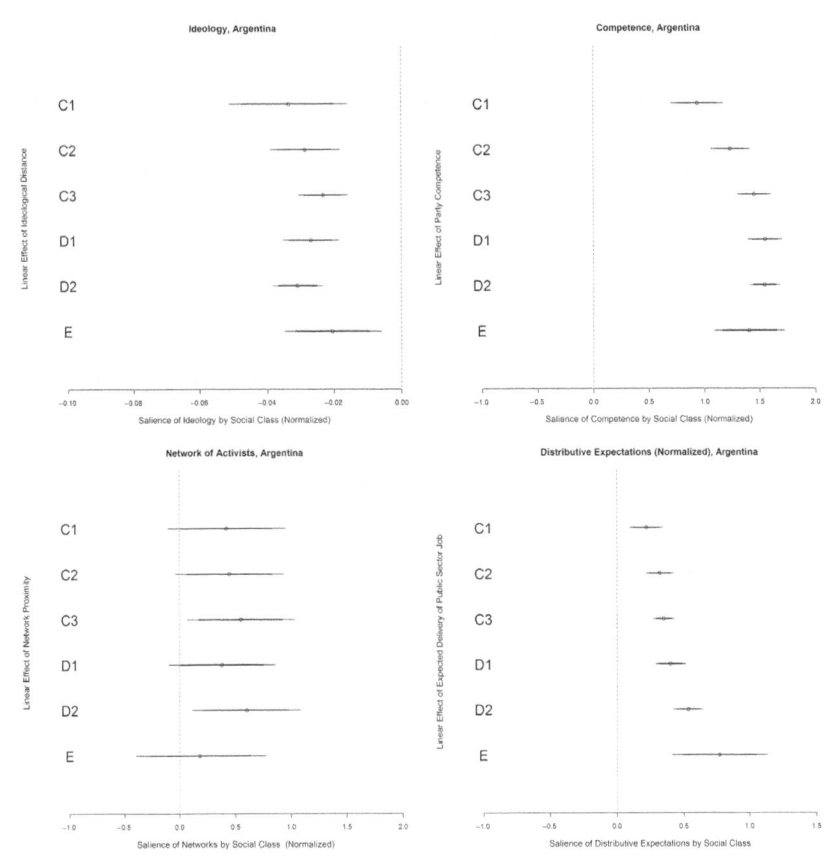

FIGURE 6.4. Linear effect by socioeconomic income, Argentina 2007
*Note*: Plots describe the estimated coefficients from Table 6.A.2 in the appendix. Lines describe the [20,80] interval around the estimated coefficients.

sector jobs significantly affect vote choice and that the effect of allocating public-sector jobs is considerably larger than in Chile for all groups, although more dramatic among poorer voters: an effect that will be further explored in Chapter 8 when we analyze public-sector wages.

To facilitate the comparison among the different types of benefits provided by parties, Figures 6.5 and 6.6 present maximum effects plot, describing the maximum linear change in the log-odds ratio from each type of policy and non-policy benefit. For example, while the decline in vote probability that results from ideological distance seem small, −0.055 among upper-middle-income (C1) voters in Chile, the total range of the squared ideological distances goes from zero through eighty-one. By contrast, while the linear effect of competence to manage the economy seems large, the variable has the much smaller range of one through four. Consequently, comparing the effect of the different policy and non-policy strategies may be difficult. In Figures 6.5 and 6.6 we present the maximum possible linear effect of each benefit by multiplying the estimated

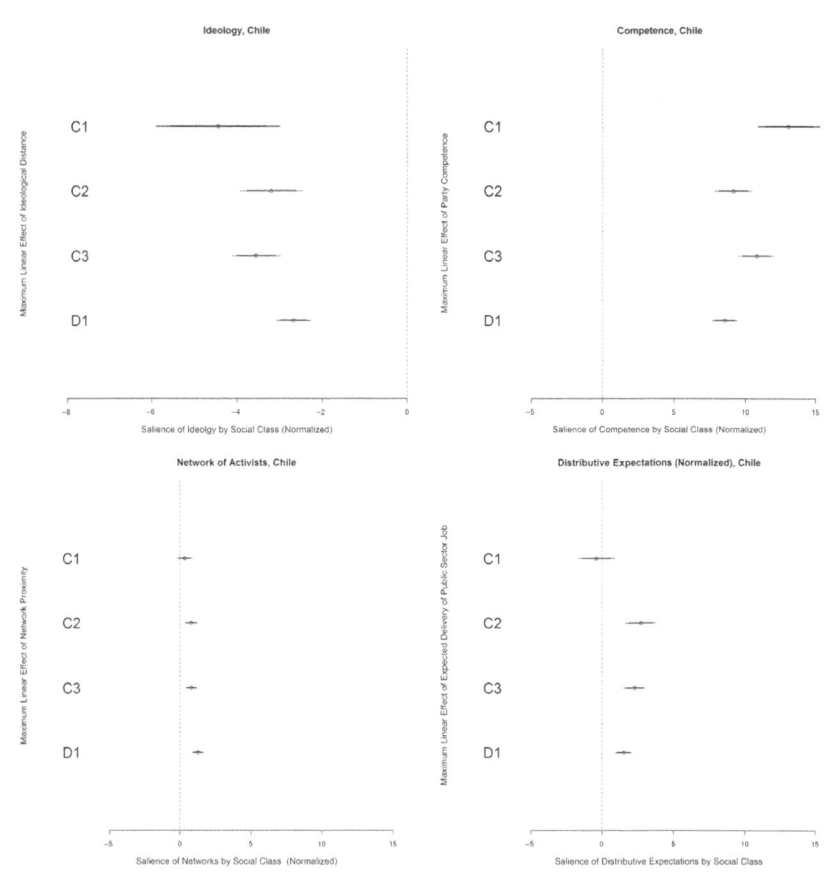

FIGURE 6.5. Maximum linear effect by socioeconomic income, Chile 2007
*Note*: From Table 6.A.2 in the appendix. Maximum effect describes the maximum possible linear effect of the coefficient, multiplying the parameter estimate by the range of the independent variable. For example, the linear effect of one-unit change in ideology for the relatively well-off respondents of C1 is −0.055 and the maximum in-sample range is $9^2 = 81$, resulting in a maximum effect of −4.4. Similarly, the effect of a one-unit increase in perceived PS competence to manage the economy is 1.45 and the maximum range is four, for a maximum effect of 5.81. We can see that in Chile the maximum linear effect of perceived competence is larger than the maximum linear effect of ideological distance among the C1 respondents.

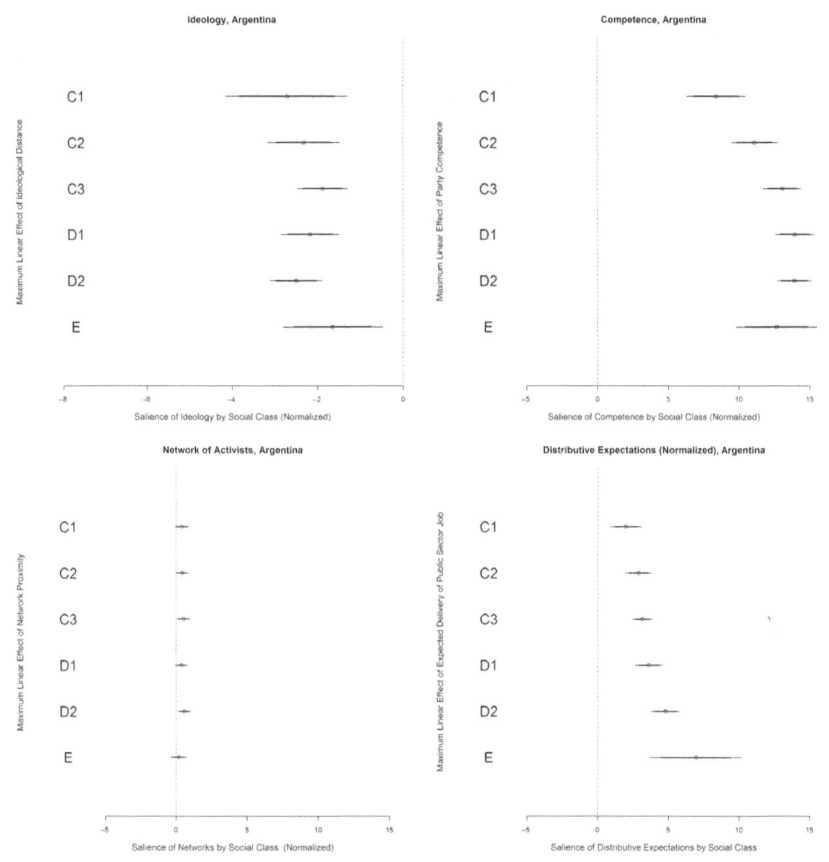

FIGURE 6.6. Maximum linear effect by socioeconomic income, Argentina 2007
*Note*: From Table 6.A.2 in the appendix. Maximum effect describes the maximum possible linear effect of the coefficient, multiplying the parameter estimate by the range of the independent variable. For example, the linear effect of one-unit change in ideology for the relatively well-off respondents of C1 is −0.0335 and the maximum in-sample range is $9^2 = 81$, resulting in a maximum effect of −2.72. Similarly, the effect of a one-unit increase in perceived PS competence to manage the economy is 0.93 and the maximum range is four, for a maximum effect of 3.73. We can see that in Argentina the maximum linear effect of perceived competence is larger than the maximum linear effect of ideological distance among the C1 respondents.

coefficient by its possible range to facilitate the comparison of the impact of policy and non-policy benefit on electoral choice by voters of diverse socioeconomic categories.

In comparing the impact of different benefits in politicians' electoral portfolios, the perceived competence to manage the economy is of the outmost importance among both Chilean and Argentine voters. However, other dimensions do not follow the same pattern. In Chile, economic competence is most important to voters, followed by ideological proximity, distributive expectations for public-sector jobs, and connections to partisan networks (Figure 6.5). By contrast, in Argentina, larger weights are given to competence for managing the economy, followed by public-sector jobs, ideological distance, and partisan networks (Figure 6.6).

These figures show that, in both countries, there are socioeconomic differences in the maximum effect of policy and non-policy benefits on perceptions of macroeconomic competence and distributive expectations. Given the difficulty political parties have in shaping perceptions about competence, this cross-class difference should have implications in terms of public-sector job expectations. Because politicians have more agency over public-sector employment and these expectations are uncorrelated with voters' ideological preferences, we expect politicians to respond with distinct patterns of targeting in terms of public-sector spending toward the most electorally sensitive groups of voters in each country. Chapter 8 investigates these patterns.

Figure 6.5 shows that, for all voters in Chile, competence and ideological distance are more important than distributive expectations, even though competence affects richer voters more than it influences poorer voters and the effects of distributive expectations for public-sector jobs are comparatively larger among middle-class than among poorer voters. The weight of inter-class differences in Chile is more moderate for both ideological distance and the impact of personal connections to activists. In Argentina, ideological distance has a very limited effect on party vote among low-income voters, whereas distributive expectations have a very limited effect among wealthy voters. Competence effects remain the strongest of all and considerably stronger among poorer voters (Figure 6.6). Hence, Argentine politicians should make more use of targeted distribution in terms of their electoral strategies and Chilean politicians should emphasize ideological persuasion.

## 6.3 VOTER SENSITIVITY AND BIASED RESPONSIVENESS

In Chapter 2, we proposed that differences in the weight that voters attach to policy offers should lead to biases in the optimal offer by parties. To gauge the biases generated by these incentives, we measure the median voter preference against the weighted-median voter, using as weights the importance given by respondents from different groups to the different components of their vote. Even if we do not factor in party competition and consider a leader that seeks to minimize overall policy distances to voters, voters with more intense preferences should bias the optimal outcome in their favor.

Equation (2.4) provides a two-groups weighted median, which can be easily generalized to a larger number of socioeconomic categories, $\alpha_s$, with distinct preferred means indexed by voter $i$ and socioeconomic group $s$, as shown below:

$$L_k = \frac{\sum_s \alpha_s \bar{x}_{is}}{\sum_s \alpha_s} \qquad \text{(Eq. 6.4)}$$

Consider, for example, results from the vote choice model in Chile where wealthier voters give more importance to ideological considerations than poorer voters. We also know from the descriptive data in Chapter 4 that the wealthier voters have preferences to the right of the median voter, which is also to the right of the poorer voters. While the overall median voter is located at 4.99 on the left–right scale, wealthier voters give 24 percent more weight to ideological consideration than the average voter while poorer voters give ideological considerations 68 percent less weight than average. As a result, the optimal policy offered to the median weighted voter will be to the right of the ideological scale, shifting policy from 4.99 to 5.25. It is worth noticing that a 0.25-point difference is also the distance between the median poor voter and the overall median voter, a very large substantive drift in policy offers. Further, the weighted optimal offer falls between the preferences of the median middle-income (C2) and the median upper-middle-income (C1) voters, to the right of the overall median of the middle-income (all C) voters. Figure 6.7 provides a visual representation of the results, displaying the density of preferences of the poorer (D) voters in red and the preferences of better-off (C) voters in yellow, with intersecting densities in orange.

Here, we focused on the different weights attached to policy offers by richer and poorer voters. It is important to remember that we argue that those preferences should shape the strategies of electorally minded politicians in a way that biases policy benefits and non-policy resource allocation to more sensitive voters. The potential for policy biases included in our argument is tested in Chapter 9 using data from our survey, as well as legislators' surveys fielded by the Political Elites in Latin America project.

## 6.4 SUMMARY AND EMPIRICAL EXPECTATIONS

This chapter provides evidence that the electoral choices of Argentine and Chilean voters are shaped by a number of policy and non-policy offers in

## Voters' Preferences and Parties' Electoral Offers

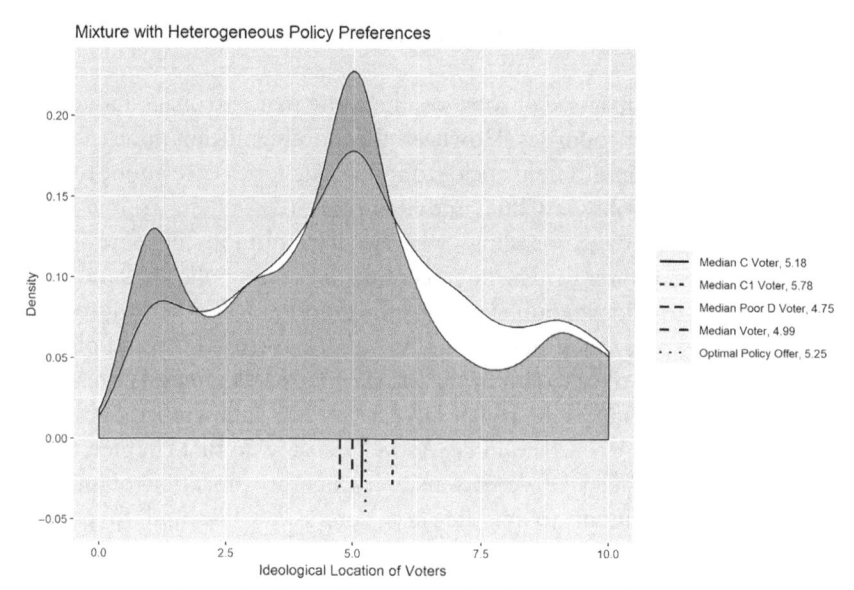

FIGURE 6.7. Optimal policy offer as a weighted function of the importance that socioeconomic groups attach to policy preferences, $[\alpha_s, \bar{x}_{is}]$
*Note*: Optimal policy offer computed from Equation (6.1), with preference density from the Chilean survey and parameter estimates from Table 6.A.4 in the appendix to this chapter.

the portfolio of party candidates, as suggested by our theoretical framework. We provide evidence that ideological proximity, competence for managing the economy, distributive expectations, and connections to partisan network are critical determinants of vote choice in Argentina and in Chile.

We also provide evidence of inter- and intra-country differences in the determinants of the vote. Findings in this chapter show that competence is a critical determinant of vote choice, but it has a greater influence on the electoral decisions of better-off voters in Chile and low-income voters in Argentina. The weak agency of political parties for reshaping competence evaluations, however, suggests that it would be hard for them to react to those inter-class differences.

Our results also show that ideological distance matters in Argentina and Chile, but that Chilean voters care more about ideological proximity when deciding their vote. The larger effect of ideology among Chilean voters adds to the fact that non-policy benefits such as managerial competence correlate with ideology. In this chapter, we illustrate how the effect of competence evaluations on the vote varies depending on whether or not non-policy endowments correlate with ideological preferences.

In allocating public-sector jobs, results show that patronage influences vote choice in both countries. However, there are significant differences in how much voters in different socioeconomic categories care about receiving public-sector jobs. In Chile, middle-income (C2) voters are the most sensitive to patronage spending, whereas its effect on the vote is the largest among poorer voters in Argentina. Because policymakers have more agency to allocate public-sector jobs than in most other non-policy benefits, we expect that differences in how much voters care about public-sector jobs will be reflected in the targeting of those resources. We test this expectation in Chapter 8, using income survey data gathered by the statistical agencies of each country. As we will show in that chapter, there are measurable effects of voter sensitivity on the allocation of public-sector wage premiums to middle-class voters in Chile and to poorer voters in Argentina.

Finally, in our analysis, the effect of connections to activists on the vote is positive but moderate in both Argentina and Chile. However, we find estimates that are more pronounced for low-income voters and among Argentine voters. The next chapter investigates the conditional effect of partisan networks on redistribution, expecting Chilean political networks to be more electorally effective at ideological persuasion while the Argentine ones will specialize at targeted distribution.

# 7

# Party Activists and Their Conditional Effect on the Vote

This chapter and Chapters 8 and 9 test different implications of our theory regarding the allocation of non-policy benefits and policy offers. Chapter 7 measures the influence of activists' networks on parties' electoral strategies. In particular, we measure the conditional effect of network connectivity on targeted distribution and policy persuasion. Chapter 8 assesses whether or not politicians use public-sector employment to target voters who care more intensely about those jobs: poorer voters in Argentina and middle-income voters in Chile, as described in Chapter 6. Finally, Chapter 9 investigates how the association between policy and non-policy preferences constrains policy switches; we test whether non-policy politics enables or constrains the capacity of politicians to modify policy positions.

## 7.1 PARTISAN NETWORKS AND INFORMATION

Partisan activists persuade voters and deliver targeted benefits through a significant number of political activities. Activists interact locally with voters, gather preferences, and deliver information. They deliver goods and services, rally voters, monitor ballots and are a critical safety net in the tally of votes on Election Day. Partisan networks provide parties with crucial resources to target individual voters with distinct policy and non-policy offers. They also possess and produce significant local knowledge that allows the party to distinguish profitable from unprofitable investments of campaign time and money among voters. In this chapter, we focus on the conditional effects of activists' networks on both distributive expectations and ideological persuasion to gauge their direct and indirect influence on electoral behavior in support of their parties.

The deployment of activists, however, is heavily influenced by prior legacies of recruitment and specialization, since party organizations – and social relationships – take time to build and time to change. In Chapter 5, we described party networks as specializing in different types of activists, with different levels of embeddedness in local communities across the Andes. Partisan networks, or at least the larger partisan networks, operate differently in Argentina than in Chile, with the former specializing on territorial activists and the latter on ideological ones. Here we explore the electoral impact of these differences and how they act on richer and poorer voters in each country. In doing so, we focus on the conditional effect of partisan networks on both distributive expectations and ideological preferences and how these effects influence the electoral behavior of poorer and richer voters in the two countries we study. Hence, our analysis focuses on the informational impact of partisan networks and the indirect effects they generate in terms of shaping the electoral efficiency of targeted distribution and ideological persuasion. Extending the models from Chapter 6, we measure the electoral benefits of expectations about targeted distribution and ideological distance conditional on network proximity, distinguishing the effects for poorer and richer voters.

Territorial networks that are embedded in poorer communities and provide access to goods generate incentives for voters to share information, as described in Chapter 5. In turn, these informative partisan networks increase the electoral returns of targeted distribution. This information effect declines when the selective incentives analyzed are public goods, which cannot be discriminated among individual voters. We show here, in line with the description in Chapter 5 that these informational effects are stronger for Argentina where the PJ, but also the smaller UCR networks, are embedded in local communities and work year-round. Inter-voter differences reinforce our findings since poorer Argentine voters, who receive higher marginal returns from distribution and information, are the only ones for whom the effects of handout expectations conditional on connections to partisan networks are significant.

We also explore the conditional effect of partisan networks on ideological distance, which is a stronger determinant of the vote in Chile than in Argentina. In Chapter 5, we described Chilean activists as more educated and ideological than voters. These ideological activists were expected to focus on policy persuasion. Because less-educated voters have weaker priors, making them more malleable to new information and more sensitive to ideological persuasion, the conditional impact of activists should be stronger. In effect, we find that the conditional effect of partisan networks on ideological distance in Chile is mainly driven by the electoral behavior of poorer voters who are more likely to vote for the party that is more ideologically akin to them if they are more connected to party networks. Hence, partisan networks do not necessarily operate in the same way in either country due to the different specialization of activists, even though they provide parties in both countries with a mechanism for targeting individual voters.

While the main goal of this chapter is to assess the impact of party organization on the targeting of electoral offers to distinct groups of voters, our results also contribute to larger debates in the literature on clientelism. We provide an answer to the question of whether parties should target individuals that are close to the party (*core voters*) or individuals that are removed from the party (*non-core voters*).[1] Our answer to this question builds on previous research by Cox and McCubbins (1986) and Dixit and Londregan (1996), who have shown that parties should deliver benefits to core voters when there are informational advantages: when parties can effectively know what core voters want and, consequently, are in position to more efficiently deliver benefits to them. In the absence of privileged information, by contrast, parties will benefit from allocating selective incentives to non-core voters. Party activists can provide that crucial information for targeted distribution.

## 7.2 PARTISAN NETWORKS AND THE TARGETING OF ELECTORALLY SENSITIVE VOTERS

Given that some voters have more intense preferences for distinct benefits, party elites understand that these should not be randomly allocated to voters when seeking to maximize electoral support. However, whereas policy benefits or macroeconomic competence cannot be discriminated as public goods, some non-policy benefits such as targeted distribution can be delivered to subsets of voters. These non-policy benefits lend themselves to allocation to more sensitive voters in order to maximize the

---

[1] There are a large number of definitions for non-core voters, such as swing, uncommitted, semi-loyal, etc. In our analyses we will consider a single, underlying dimension that connects voters to parties, from core voters to non-core voters, based on their personal proximity to activists.

party's vote. One strategy to identify high-yield voters is by distinguishing voters' responses by particular socioeconomic traits, as we did in Chapter 6. Consequently, parties have the opportunity to target distinct offers to voters from the socioeconomic groups that provide the highest return per unit of investment. The fact that parties should invest in voters with the right socioeconomic background, however, does not provide much guidance regarding which individual voters should be targeted.

From the standpoint of the party, the critical issue to be sorted out is which voters are more likely to change their vote if and when targeted with a particular benefit. In the literature on distributive politics, this question is akin to the core-swing voter debate: should parties target *core voters* who are already connected to the party and have a prior relationship with the party members, or should parties allocate resources to voters that are comparatively removed from the party's network and less committed to vote for the party on Election Day? That is, how should parties deploy their organizations and resources in the search for votes? We have argued in this book that parties should deliver benefits to those voters who experience the largest change in their likelihood of voting for the party after receiving a particular electoral promise. The problem is determining who those voters are.

In assessing parties' capacities to identify individual voters who are more sensitive to targeted distribution, we follow the contributions of an extensive literature discussing the "core-swing" dilemma.[2] In developing our statistical model, we take Dixit and Londregan's (1996) influential model, which jointly models the policy and non-policy preferences of voters to explain how two parties simultaneously make policy offers and allocate private goods to voters. While Dixit and Londregan model targeted distribution in a two-party setting, the utility function of voters is a familial relative of the one provided in Chapter 2. A critical contribution of Dixit and Londregan to the literature on targeted distribution is the recognition that the delivery of targeted benefits is not perceived equally by all voters. Heterogeneity in the value that voters attach to targeted delivery, in their case, was modeled as the result of deadweight losses in the allocation of benefits. These deadweight losses described lower returns to targeted distribution that resulted from parties misallocating resources

---

[2] Beginning with Cox and McCubbins' (1986) seminal article "Electoral politics as a distributive game," a number of authors have built models including the policy and non-policy components of the vote (Cox, 2007; Cox and McCubbins, 1986; Dixit and Londregan, 1996, 1998; Lindbeck and Weibull, 1987; Stokes, 2005; Stokes et al., 2013).

to voters. Imagine, for instance, a targeted distribution of glasses to elderly and less well-off voters (as happens in Chile), which does not shape the electoral behavior of a particular voter who, instead, needed a hearing aid. Distinguishing group features is not sufficient for avoiding deadweight losses in the allocation of benefits. We show here that party activists can provide this crucial individualized information that increases the electoral effectiveness of targeted distribution reducing "leakage from the bucket," to use Dixit and Londregan's metaphor.

Dixit and Londregan model electoral competition in an environment with two parties that make policy offers and, simultaneously, distribute targeted benefits to members of two different groups: poor voters and rich voters. Further, they show that the decision to allocate targeted benefits varies as a function of three different and important voter traits: (a) group differences in policy preferences, (b) differences in the marginal value of targeted distribution (non-policy preferences), and (c) deadweight losses in the allocation of private goods to members of the group that are poorly known to politicians. Such deadweight losses in the allocation of benefits – derived from information asymmetries – resulted in some voters perceiving a lower utility for targeted goods ("leaky bucket") and, consequently, providing fewer electoral gains per dollar spent.

The idea that not all voters perceive "in full" the targeted good allocated by parties allowed Dixit and Londregan to solve a riddle in the literature: A model where the utility for non-policy benefits was identical across voters yielded results where parties would benefit from targeting selective incentives to non-core voters who are ideologically indifferent, i.e. *swing voters* (Lindbeck and Weibull, 1987; Stokes, 2005). However, a large literature showed that parties had a distinct preference for allocating selective incentives to party loyalists: *core voters* (Cox and McCubbins, 1986; Magaloni, Diaz-Cayeros, and Estevez, 2007; Stokes et al., 2013)

The model proposed by Dixit and Londregan provided a solution by allowing voters to differ both in the extent to which they benefit from targeted distribution (marginal returns) and the efficiency of such distribution (how much spending reaches individual voters or is lost in a "leaky bucket"). Whereas the marginal impact could be easily calculated relative to income, researchers have not measured the efficiency of distribution in terms of the returns derived from allocating the goods to voters who were the most electorally sensitive to targeted distributions. Hence, Dixit and Londregan's two-party model considers both ideological proximity and the efficiency of distribution and allows inter-group differences in deadweight losses to explain the party's decision to strategically allocate goods to core voters (voters that are "better known" to the party) or swing voters (voters that are "poorly known" to the party).[3] Yet they fall short of describing the mechanisms that account for inter-group differences in efficiency losses during distribution, or how politicians distinguish individual voters within these groups who are more sensitive to distribution. We argue that informed party activists can distinguish individual voters within categories of voters to maximize the electoral returns of targeted distribution. Thus the targeting of particular voters would depend on the information that parties have about groups of voters and about individual voters within these groups. When partisan networks are informative, parties should target "core" or connected voters to minimize the waste in the distribution, and when partisan network are not informative, parties should try to target their distribution to swing voters.

Not all partisan networks are informative, however, and there's specialization as suggested by the Chapter 5 discussion of party organizations, where we distinguish between territorial and ideological activists. What do partisan networks that are not attuned to the immediate wants and needs of voters do? We suggest here that such networks may specialize in different electoral strategies and focus on ideological persuasion. Although policy distribution cannot discriminate across individual voters, there is still considerable ideological persuasion labor performed during electoral campaigns. Voters and political elites may share policy goals, but not necessarily policy instruments. Activists play an important role in explaining the party's policy offers to gain electoral support. In deciding how to target their efforts, activists should seek voters who would be the most sensitive to their persuasion efforts. In a sense, this is the reverse of the core-swing question: who should be reached for persuasion, keeping distributive expectations constant? We investigate this question by assessing the conditional impact of partisan networks on ideological distance in both countries and across different groups of voters. We expect those with weaker priors but more attention to be more malleable to the information; that is, we expect ideological activists to be more effective at persuading voters who are less educated and ideologically closer.

---

[3] "Dixit and Londregan show that, when the parties have no special relationships with any groups [...], the parties' allocations are driven by the density of swing voters in each group – as in the Lindbeck-Weibull model. As larger and larger asymmetries in the parties' abilities to deliver benefits arise, however, the parties' allocations are driven more and more by the core voter logic of promising benefits to those groups to which the party can most effectively deliver benefits" (Cox, 2007: 345).

## 7.3 OPERATIONALIZATION OF TARGETING BY PARTY NETWORKS

The model provided by Dixit and Londregan (1996) is a relative of the one presented in Chapter 2. While it imposes some additional constraints on the choice made by parties, the utility function of voters has a policy and non-policy component that explains the voters' decision. Similar to Dixit and Londregan, we also posit an equation with a policy and non-policy component (Eq. 2.1).

$$U(V_{ik}) = -\alpha_i(x_i-L_k)^2 + \beta_i T_{ik} + \gamma_{ik} \qquad (\text{Eq. 2.1})$$

Furthermore, similar to Dixit and Londregan, we also consider the special case where the utility of the targeted good $T_{ik}$ may be discounted by a deadweight function ($\theta_{ik}$) with a [0,1] range, where only a fraction of the initial benefit reaches voters (Eq. 7.1).

$$U(V_{ik}) = -\alpha_i(x_i-L_k)^2 + \beta_{1i}(\theta_{ik})T_{ik} + \gamma_{ik} \qquad (\text{Eq. 7.1})$$

For example, a corrupt broker may appropriate 20 percent of the money that was marked for a voter, so that only the fraction $0.8T_{ik}$ is effectively delivered. Alternatively, a voter may experience a lower utility for the good $T_{ik}$ if it is delivered by a violent broker (V) rather than a non-violent broker (Szwarcberg, 2014), so that $\beta_{1i}(\theta_{iV})T_{ik} < \beta_{1i}(\theta_{i\ddot{A}V})T_{ik}$. This new source of voter heterogeneity will shift the benefits from targeted distribution toward those voters with lower deadweight loses.

Our conceptualization of partisan networks, as described in Chapter 5, is crucial to understanding Dixit and Londregan's emphasis on deadweight losses among voters ($\theta_{ik}$), which are based on differences in the extent to which parties have information about the needs of voters. Like us, Cox and McCubbins (1986), also highlight the privileged role of networks in relaying information from clients to brokers. Indeed, as the information transmitted by political networks increases, the efficiency of targeted distribution allows strategic politicians to maximize electoral returns by selecting the most sensitive voters. Consequently, the efficiency of targeted distribution depends critically on the availability of party mechanisms to collect and process information for the delivery of private goods. We identify territorial networks as crucially performing that role.

In Chapter 6, we have shown that voters' intensity of preferences for distribution varies by socioeconomic status in each of the two studied countries – and not necessarily as expected given marginal returns. Following Dixit and Londregan's model, we expect the information carried by partisan networks to shape the electoral efficiency of targeted distribution across individual voters within these categories. Parties can supplement or complement activists' personal information with alternative technologies, but we expect these less "informed" activists to be less electorally effective in reaching individual voters with targeted distribution. Moreover, if partisan networks are the crucial conduit of information to reduce "leakage" in the bucket, we expect their value to be higher for private goods that can be discriminated at the individual, rather than district, level; that is to say less valuable in the distribution of local public goods. Hence, our measurement accounts for variation in deadweight losses by considering both (i) the informational efficiency of partisan distribution networks and (ii) and how easy it is to target the type of good being delivered to individual voters.

### a) Hypotheses about Targeted Distribution

According to our argument, electoral returns to targeted distribution are a function of the extent to which voters attach distinct value to targeted benefits and of the capacity of parties to allocate those benefits based on voters' needs and wants. To distinguish among voters, we ask whether or not parties can effectively use networks to collect information and deliver benefits to those voters who are most sensitive to targeted distribution: not all partisan networks are equally informative. This new source of voter heterogeneity indicates that parties should allocate a disproportionate share of targeted benefits to core voters if and when party networks are informative, or alternatively attempt to target swing voters. Hence, we take party networks as the intervening mechanism that explains strategies of targeted distribution.

In this model specification, different groups of voters and activists (nodes) are connected to each other, with networks of different density affecting information flows as well as the access and delivery of resources. Informative networks of party activists should transfer information and benefits between voters and parties and thereby reduce deadweight losses when allocating targeted benefits. By contrast, political parties without networks or whose networks do not provide the relevant information about voters' needs and wants should seek to target among non-core voters those who are ideologically pivotal (swing). The first hypothesis derived from our argument is thus that *voters who are more connected to informative partisan networks should provide larger electoral returns to targeted distribution (hypothesis 1: network information effect)*. Hence, we expect political parties with informative political networks to derive higher electoral returns by selecting core voters for targeted distribution.

However, not all goods can be targeted exclusively to high-yield voters who are well connected to party networks. Indeed, club goods and local public goods, such as roads or parks, can only be allocated to groups or collections of individuals in a locality. In contrast to excludable goods such as cash transfers or public-sector jobs, local public goods cannot be calibrated to the needs of individual voters even in information-rich environments (Diaz-Cayeros et al., 2016). While public-sector jobs or handouts can be allocated to individuals that give maximum electoral returns per unit transferred (high sensitivity and very low deadweight losses, $\theta_{ik}$), local public goods have to be allocated to a collection of individuals, with mean deadweight loss $\bar{\theta} = \frac{1}{n}\sum_{i}^{n} \theta_{ik}$.

Because we expect higher variance in deadweight losses among individuals and lower variance among groups, the conditional effect of networks on distribution should be attenuated for goods that can only be targeted to groups of voters. Hence, we expect that the benefits of targeted distribution, conditional on party networks, will be less significant for local public goods that depend on aggregate-level – rather than individual-level – information. Therefore, the second hypothesis derived from our argument predicts the attenuation of network information effects for local public goods. We expect the *conditional effect of information networks on voters to be larger for goods that can be targeted to individual voters than for goods that are distributed to groups of voters, given that there is at least a subgroup of voters* $i \in I$ *for which* $(\theta_{ik})T_{ik} \geq (\bar{\theta}_{ik})T_{i\in I}$ *(hypothesis 2: attenuation effect)*.

To summarize, we expect that (i) information advantages in the delivery of non-policy goods will result in parties with informative networks targeting (connected) *core voters* to maximize electoral returns. These information advantages should decline (ii) when targeting local public goods, whose benefits cannot be discriminated among individuals. Empirically, it means that our expectations regarding the conditional effect of partisan networks on targeted distribution are different across countries and types of goods.

First, the weaker information capacity of Chilean political networks should make the efficient targeting of core voters less feasible than in Argentina (information effect). We have described in Chapter 5 how territorial activists in Argentina are embedded in their communities, how they work year round, and how their role in providing access to publicly financed goods and services increases voters' incentives to sustain information flows with them. Poorer voters, in particular, rely heavily on the information and access to resources provided by Peronist (and to a lesser extent Radical) activists, thereby generating information-rich networks. By contrast, Chilean ideological activists tend to campaign in communities different from their own and are not embedded in poorer communities, forcing parties to rely more heavily on alternative information technologies to identify undecided voters.

Second, we also expect stronger information effects for handouts and public-sector jobs, which can be discriminated across individual voters using activists' information, than for public work. Public works are local public goods that benefit a particular locality including voters of other parties in that community, thus reducing the value of the information transmitted by partisan networks (attenuation effect). Given our expectation of stronger information effects in Argentina, the attenuation effect should also be stronger in this country than in Chile.

## b) Empirical Analysis of Targeted Distribution

In this section, we estimate a vote model with separate policy and non-policy components. Further, we now interact the measures of network proximity and distributive expectations to assess the effect of handouts, patronage, and pork conditional on network connectivity. We test for the determinants of vote choice using the following linear approximation of our multinomial choice model, described in Chapter 5, with a utility function that is similar to that of Dixit and Londregan[4]:

---

[4] We can show that the model we propose is equivalent to that of Dixit and Londregan (1996). Let us begin with equation (4) in their article:

$$U(V_{iL}) = -\alpha(x_i-L_j)^2 + \frac{k_i(C_{ij})^{1-\epsilon}}{1-\epsilon}$$

Given that epsilon $\epsilon$ may be considered fixed for all voters (Dixit and Londregan, 1996: 1138) we drop this term from the multinomial equation so that $U(V_{iL}) = -\alpha(x_i-L_j)^2 + k_i C_{ij}$. We unpack $C_{ij} = k_i[Y_i + (1-\theta_{ik})T_{iL}]$ and allow separate estimates of $k_i$ for each of the relevant variables. Consequently, we estimate a model with main parameters $U_{ik} = -\alpha (x_i-L_k)^2 + \delta y_i + \beta(1-\theta_{ik})T_{ik}$. We assume that network proximity allows parties to gather information about voters, so that $N_{ik} \equiv 1-\theta_{ik}$. Adding the constituent terms for network, $N_{ik}$, targeted distribution $T_{ik}$, other controls $Z_{ik}$ and assuming a stochastic error we obtain the model in Equation (7.2).

$$U(V_{ik}) = -\alpha_i(x_i-L_k)^2 + \beta_1 T_{ik} + \beta_2 N_{ik} + \beta_3 N_{ik} T_{ik} + \ldots + \gamma_{ik} \quad \text{(Eq. 7.2)}$$

The first term in the right-hand side of the equation describes the effect of ideological proximity, with voters assessing the relative distance from their self-reported placement $x_i$ to the reported location of each party $L_k$. The effect of targeted distribution on vote choice is captured by the parameter $T_{ik}$ while the effect of connectivity to party networks is described by $N_{ik}$. We expect targeted distribution $T_{ik}$ to have a positive effect on party vote, conditional on network proximity. Consequently, together with the base terms, $\beta_3 N_{ik} T_{ik}$ describes the conditional effect of targeted distribution $T_{ik}$ on party $k$ vote, subject to deadweight losses as voters become further removed from party network $N_{ik}$. This "leaky bucket" describes information losses that make distribution less efficient.

Our model also includes variables to assess the conditional effect of networks on ideological distance and on competence evaluations. We omitted the full set of interactions and parameters from Equation (7.2), which are estimated and described in the results of the following section. Model measures of the conditional effect of partisan networks on ideological distance, $-\alpha_i N_{ik}(x_i-L_k)^2$, and the conditional effect of partisan networks on competence, $\beta_3 N_{ik} C_{ik}$, operate as controls in this part of the analysis. The model also includes a variety of individual-level controls as described below.

As in Chapter 6 and in the following section, we use the reported vote if a legislative election "were to take place next week" as our dependent variable. We deleted observations where the dependent variable yielded non-responses, resulting in a sample of 1647 respondents in Argentina and 1497 in Chile.[5] We imputed missing values for the independent variables using *multivariate imputation by chain equations* (MICE)[6] and estimated models with five alternatives in Argentina – PJ,[7] UCR, ARI,

---

[5] We did not provide a closed menu of parties to respondents and non-responses prompted a one-time insistence. Undecided voters represented 27 percent and 20 percent of respondents in Argentina and Chile, respectively. Blank votes represented another 10 percent and 14 percent, respectively. Finally, votes for smaller parties represented 3.3 percent of the vote in Argentina and 11 percent of the vote in Chile.

[6] While we deleted non-responses, blank, and small party votes in both countries, we replicated all analyses with a full dataset, drawing votes randomly to replace missing observations with multivariate imputation by chained equation (*MICE in* R 2.9). Results of alternative models are similar and available upon request.

[7] The survey was structured so that voters could select their preferred Peronist faction. This included the Frente para la Victoria (FPV) of former President Kirchner, allies of Carlos Menem, Rodriguez Saa, and a generic Peronist party. Because the survey question was

PRO, and the main provincial party (PPP)[8] – and five alternatives in Chile – the Socialist Party (PS), the Christian Democrats (DC), the PPD, UDI and the RN.

Like in Chapter 6, our three main independent variables are: (i) the *ideological distance* between each respondent *i* and party *j*; (ii) the proximity of respondent *i* to the *network of activists of party j*; and (iii) the *distributive expectations* that a respondent will receive handouts, a public-sector job, or the public works required by their community. We measure *ideological distance* as the squared distance between the self-reported ideological preference of each respondent and the reported location of each party, $(x_i - L_{ki})^2$. Ideological placements were measured on a ten-point scale, from one to ten, with low numbers describing locations on the left of the political spectrum and high numbers representing placement on the right. The ideological distance variable is alternative specific, assessing the ideological distance between each respondent *i* and each party *k*. We expected a negative effect on vote choice, as further ideological distance reduces the probability of voting for a party.

Second, as in Chapter 6, we measure the connection between voters and parties using the *normalized proximity between respondents and the network of activists of each party*, from the overdispersion parameters described in Chapter 5, which report whether the respondents know more/less members of a group. We rescaled this measure to be bounded between zero and one. We expect this variable to have a positive effect on vote choice, where a respondent who knows more activists from a party will be more likely to vote for that party.

A third set of key independent variables is the self-reported unconditional expectation of *receiving handouts, a public-sector job, or public works* in the community from an elected member of party *k*, as used in Chapter 6. The questions read: "On a scale from one to ten, where one is very unlikely and ten is very likely, how likely would it be that an elected member of the (*party*) would provide you with (*type of good*)?" The 1–10 ordinal index measures the expected probability. The wording of the question solicits the unconditional expectations of receiving goods, as described in Chapter 6. These questions are also alternative specific,

---

"undirected," we recoded as Peronists all responses that described any of the party factions.

[8] Due to the importance of provincial parties in Argentina, the fifth party choice varies per province. Seeking to retrieve information on the main provincial party, its partisan network, and its distributive intent, we coded all provincial parties as PPP when conducting our analyses.

inquiring on the likelihood of perceiving different goods from members of each party $k$. We expect distributive expectations to increase a party's vote.

The most important parameter for testing our hypothesis about whether voters who are more connected to partisan networks provide larger electoral returns (information effect) is measured on the expected party vote *conditional on expectations about the delivery of goods and network proximity*. Consequently, we interact network proximity and distributive expectations to obtain predictions about the marginal change in party vote when goods are targeted to voters that are more closely connected to party networks. We expect the information effect to be stronger in Argentina than in Chile, given differences on partisan network structure and operation, described in Chapter 5. We also expect the positive effect of the interaction to decline for goods that can only be allocated to groups of voters when informative networks are present; that is, to be stronger for handouts and public jobs than public works (attenuation effect). In short, we expect larger electoral gains when targeting goods to voters that are better connected to an informed party's network – i.e. stronger effects in Argentina – and we expect larger core-voter effects when delivering goods that can be targeted to individuals rather than groups – i.e. for handouts and patronage, rather than pork.

As in Chapter 6, we include other controls measuring the relative size of the respondents' personal network (ln), a performance question about parties' capacity, the attitudinal view of respondents on distribution, and gender.[9] The size of the personal network had a mean of 200 and 203 in Argentina and Chile, respectively. To assess the impact of valence on voting decisions, the alternative-specific performance question asks respondents "how capable is [the party] of managing the economy." To control for biases on the self-reported expectation of receiving goods, we ask respondents to indicate, on a scale from one to ten, "how adequate is it that the government provides [type of good]" to citizens. We also include the interaction of partisan networks with ideological distance – which will be analyzed in the next section – and with competence evaluations to assess other ways in which networks can operate on the vote. Table 7.A.1 in the appendix to this chapter presents results with all

---

[9] We also estimated a number of alternative models that included the size of the locality- and regional-specific variables and the results were almost identical. To avoid the proliferation in parameters, our models do not include territorial variables, but data, code, and alternative specifications can be requested from the authors.

controls, which do not change the main results presented here. While these effects have been discussed in Chapter 6, it is important to remember that we are controlling for socioeconomic status, which has no effect on the vote in Chile, but has a negative relationship with voting for the PJ in Argentina (the poorer the voter, the more likely to vote PJ). This control is relevant for the analysis of targeted distribution as it indicates the marginal utility of received benefits for richer or poorer voters. We find the same effects controlling for socioeconomic status as we find in the simpler model we present, as can be seen in Table 7.A.1 in the appendix to this chapter.

### c) Results

As in Chapter 6, we use a Conditional (Multinomial) Logit design with alternative- and respondent-specific variables. Alternative-specific variables vary by voter and respondent-specific variables do not vary by voter but have different effects on each choice. Alternative-specific variables estimate the effect of variables that vary by choice (each party $k$ in our model). Each survey respondent, consequently, reports different ideological distances to each of the parties and the estimated parameter associates distances with vote choice. Respondent-specific variables, such as gender or wealth, take the same value across alternatives, even if voters of different gender or income have a different propensity to vote for different parties.

Here, we describe the results of restricted models in Table 7.A.1 of the appendix that include only the key variables testing our hypotheses: ideological proximity, network proximity, expected delivery of targeted goods, and the interaction of network proximity and distribution, as well as the other interactions with partisan networks. The main results are presented in Table 7.A.1 and the conditional effects of partisan networks on targeted distribution for the three different types of goods we analyze are plotted in Figure 7.1.

Our six restricted models in Table 7.A.1 have the Peronists and the Socialists as the base categories in Argentina and Chile, respectively. Because the alternative-specific parameters (such as ideological distances) describe overall changes in the log-odds ratio of vote choice for any party, readers may interpret the direction and significance of the linear estimates directly, without a baseline parameter or their transformation into probabilities. Individual specific variables such as party membership, on the other hand, need to be interpreted relative to the base categories (PJ in

Argentina and PS in Chile). For instance, voters are, on average, less likely to vote for parties other than the PJ in Argentina or the PS in Chile, as shown by the negative signs for all other parties.

Results in Table 7.A.1 reinforce those described in Chapter 6. Evaluations of economic competence are a crucial determinant of choice and the expected performance of a party vis-à-vis the economy has a very large and positive effect on party vote both in Argentina and Chile, regardless of the type of good included in the model. Both ideological distance and distributive expectations have significant effects on vote intention, although the former has a stronger effect in Chile, while the latter is more impactful in Argentina. Readers should note that because the proximity to networks has been interacted with the other two terms, the baseline coefficients for Chile seem larger than those of Argentina.

Our estimates indicate that further ideological distance decreases the probability of voting for a party in both Argentina and Chile, whatever the type of good (handout, job, public work) included in the model. However, the linear effect of ideological distances remains larger in magnitude in Chile than in Argentina, important to understanding the specialization of Chilean ideological activists analyzed in the next section.[10]

Table 7.A.1 also shows that targeted distribution has a larger effect when respondents have more connections to territorial activists in Argentina (hypothesis 1). *Proximity to the network of activists* is positive and significant in all models, describing the vote gains from a denser network of activists, whether as a result of distribution or through persuasion, although the effect is larger in Argentina than in Chile. Estimates of the *expectation of receiving targeted goods* are significant in all models that include patronage and public works, but not for handouts in either Chile or Argentina, as reported in Chapter 6. Hence, distributive expectations on patronage and pork are more electorally valuable in both countries – although we qualify the analysis of handouts below. The analysis of conditional effects of political networks provides a more nuanced picture, however. Although *interaction terms* are always positive, they are statistically significant for handouts, public jobs, and public work only in Argentina. These results suggest that parties receive larger electoral gains when allocating these goods to respondents who are closer to a party's network in Argentina, but not in Chile.

---

[10] Notice that the log-odds linear predictions do not allow us to compare the substantive impact across models. We provide a more intuitive description in the following figures.

Figure 7.1 facilitates the visualization of our results by providing a more intuitive view of model estimates, plotting the marginal change in the log-odds ratio of voting for a party $k$ conditional on the expectation of targeted distribution and network proximity (Brambor, Clark, and Golder, 2006). The horizontal axis in Figure 7.1 describes network proximity, $N_{ik} = (1-\theta_{ij})$, with a range from −2 – indicating that the respondent is removed from the partisan network – through 2 for respondents that are well connected to the party's network. The vertical axis in Figure 7.1 describes the marginal change in the log-odds ratio of voting for a party $j$ (the linear change or slope that a one-unit change in targeted distribution has on party vote).

The plot in row 1, column 1 in Figure 7.1 describes the marginal change in the log-odds ratio of voting for a party $k$ in Argentina per unit of increase in the expectation of receiving handouts and conditional on network proximity. The positive slope of the marginal effect provides support for the informative effect of networks, with returns from handouts increasing for respondents that are closest to the party network. Meanwhile, effects are not significant for voters removed from the party's network. Consequently, aggregate results in Argentina show that the delivery of handouts significantly increases party vote among *in-network* (core) voters but has no effect on *out-of-network* (non-core) voters. This finding aligns well with the extant literature on clientelism in Argentina: although the mean effect of handouts on votes is not significant, the conditional effect is large and significant. We further explore this effect below in our analysis of poorer and richer voters.

The effect of handouts on Chile's party vote, conditional on proximity to party networks, is in row 1, column 2 of Figure 7.1. Although the results are in the expected positive direction (as shown by the upward slope), they fail to achieve statistical significance, suggesting that political networks do not reduce deadweight losses associated with non-policy distribution. This is in line with our description in Chapter 5 of such networks as not being very informative. This difference confirms our expectation in hypothesis 1 about the information effect of networks and its impact on reducing deadweight losses in distribution.

Figure 7.1 also provides a more intuitive description of the attenuation effect (hypothesis 2) supported by our results. As we move from more excludable goods (handouts and public jobs) to less excludable local public goods (public works), the slope becomes flatter in both countries, but the attenuation effect is stronger in Argentina, where political networks are more informative. That is, while the expectation of receiving

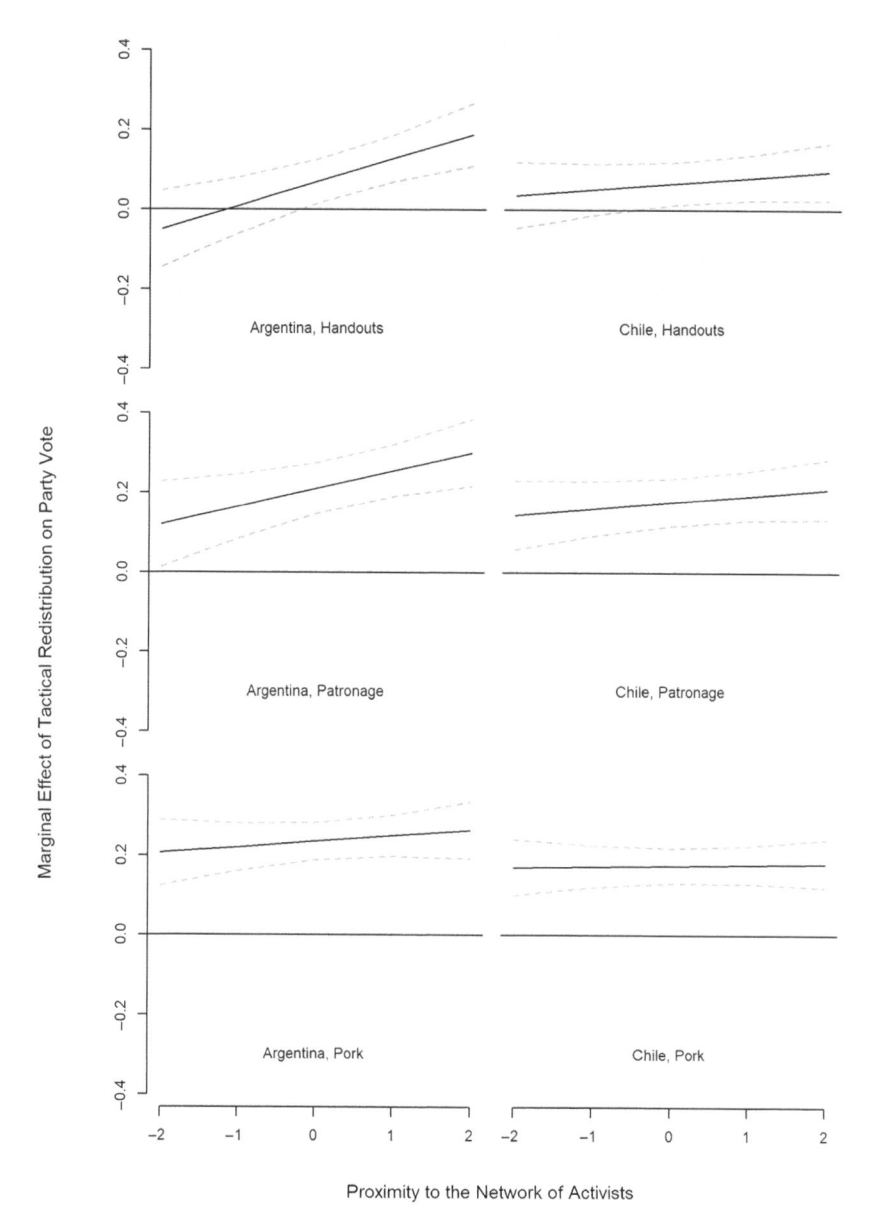

FIGURE 7.1. The effect of targeted distribution on vote choice, conditional on network proximity $(1-\theta_i)$
*Note*: Marginal effects estimated from the Var-Cov Matrices of the models in Table 7.A.1 in the appendix.

public-sector jobs and public works increases party vote, the flatter slope for public works shows that smaller benefits result from targeting *in-network* voters with less excludable goods. Hence, the delivery of pork provides roughly similar electoral benefits when targeting *in-* or *out-of-network* voters, suggesting that the information provided by partisan networks to distinguish core voters is less relevant when delivering local public goods, which are less excludable.

To summarize, whereas Chapter 6 shows that both policy and non-policy offers increase the probability of voting for a party, we focus here on the informational impact of political networks in reducing the deadweight losses of targeted distribution. We show that the effect of distribution conditional on party networks is only significant in Argentina, with electoral returns to non-policy distribution being higher for core, or in-network, voters. This effect is attenuated when access to the delivered goods cannot be discriminated among individual voters, thereby reducing the informative gains that political networks provide in Argentina. Before shifting our analysis to the conditional effect of partisan networks on ideological distance, we turn to differences between richer and poorer voters.

### d) Targeting Distribution to Poorer and Richer Voters

Socioeconomic status is a crucial source of heterogeneity among voters in Argentina and Chile, given patterns of geographic segregation and access to public resources. Additionally, it affects the marginal value of targeted distribution for voters – given labor market differentials (Calvo and Murillo 2004) – and their incentives to provide information to activists given their access to alternative networks, as discussed in Chapter 5. In Chapter 6, we showed how voters of diverse socioeconomic status had distinct sensitivity to the policy and non-policy benefits offered by parties. Given these differences, in this section we estimate the electoral impact of targeted distribution conditional on connections to partisan networks for poorer and richer voters.

Our interviews provide illustrations of the diverse functions developed by partisan networks for voters of diverse socioeconomic status. Richer voters with extensive personal networks are less dependent on political networks to access scarce resources and information, whereas political networks embedded in communities of low-income voters offer valuable avenues for expressing demands and accessing resources. These differences generate incentives, affecting the flow of information between low-income voters and political activists, which is particularly large and significant in Argentina where territorial activists are embedded in their communities. This information, in turn, is crucial to reducing deadweight losses in targeted distribution. Hence, although the marginal value of targeted distribution is higher for poorer voters in both countries, we expect that information effects should be stronger among poorer voters in Argentina. Given the politicization of public resources experienced by Argentine voters, they have stronger incentives for keeping robust information flows with activists that should reduce "leakage" in the distribution (Calvo and Murillo, 2013).

To test this expectation, we run the same models of Table 7.A.1 but separate our sample by socioeconomic status in approximate halves: poorer voters who correspond to respondents in the D categories and middle-income voters who correspond to respondents in the C categories. Our results are graphically represented in Figures 7.2 and 7.3, derived from Tables 7.A.2 and 7.A.3 in the appendix. As in Figure 7.1, each plot describes the linear marginal effect of targeted distribution on vote choice, with the horizontal axis describing ideological distance from the respondent self-reported location to the reported location of each party. In each plot, the horizontal axis ranges from zero (the voter is located in the same ideological position as the party) to a maximum of 100 (the voter is at the other extreme of the ideological scale). The first column describes results for Argentina and the second column does so for Chile, with each row corresponding to a different type of private good.

The contrast between Figures 7.2 and 7.3 is telling, as the information and attenuation effects are much stronger for poorer, rather than richer, voters in Argentina, whereas these differences lose substantive significance in Chile. The upper-left plot in Figure 7.2 shows strong effects for expectations of receiving handouts, gifts, or favors conditional on proximity to partisan networks for poorer voters in Argentina. The effect is significantly negative (at 0.2 decrease) for voters who are not connected to the network and significantly positive (at 0.4 increase) for in-network voters. By contrast, in the second column corresponding to Chile, the effect of expecting the delivery of handouts remains insignificant regardless of proximity to the party network.

Here again, our findings align with the Argentine literature on clientelism, as discussed in Chapter 4, and illuminate the results of Chapter 5, where handout expectations had no aggregate effect on vote intention. The subset of Argentine voters who are likely to change their electoral behavior in response to this strategy are poorer and better

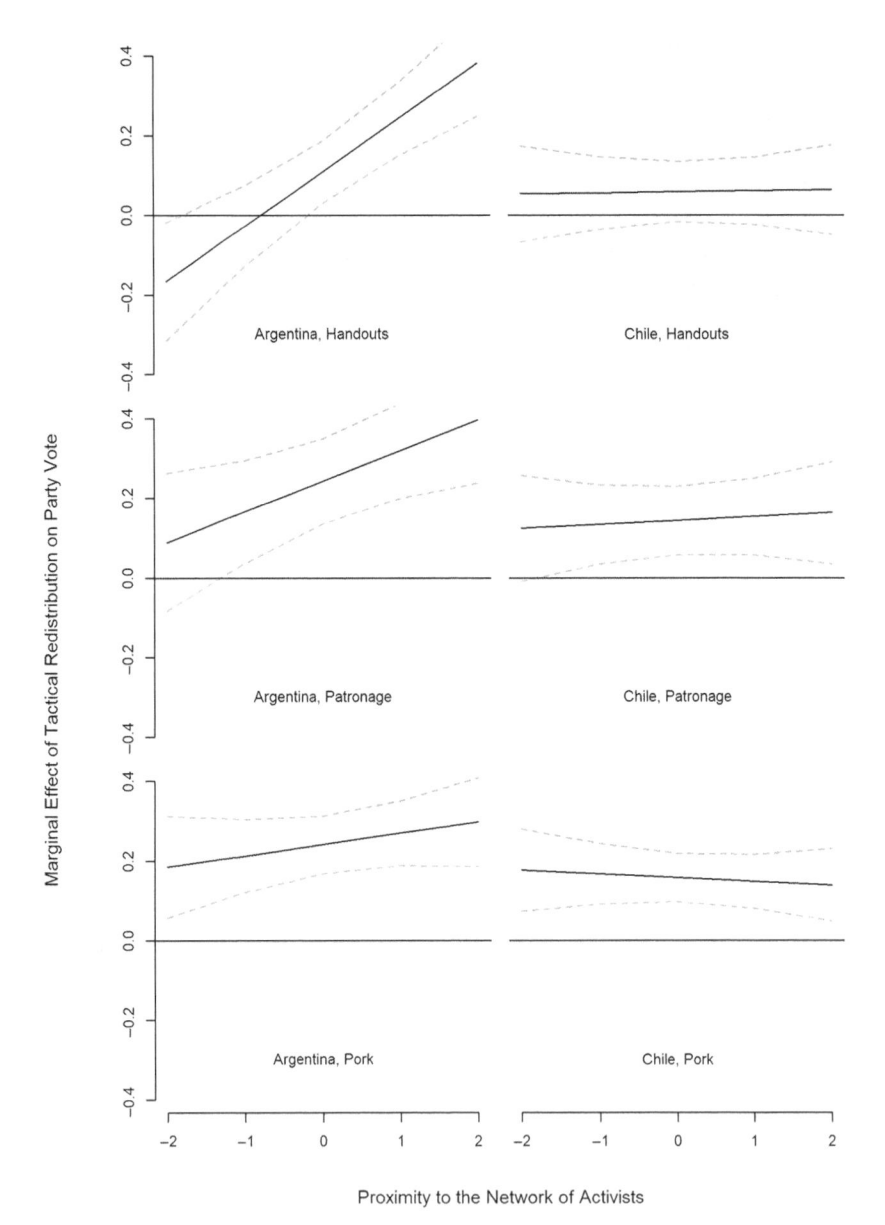

FIGURE 7.2. The effect of targeted distribution on vote choice conditional on network proximity for voters of lower socioeconomic status (D voters)

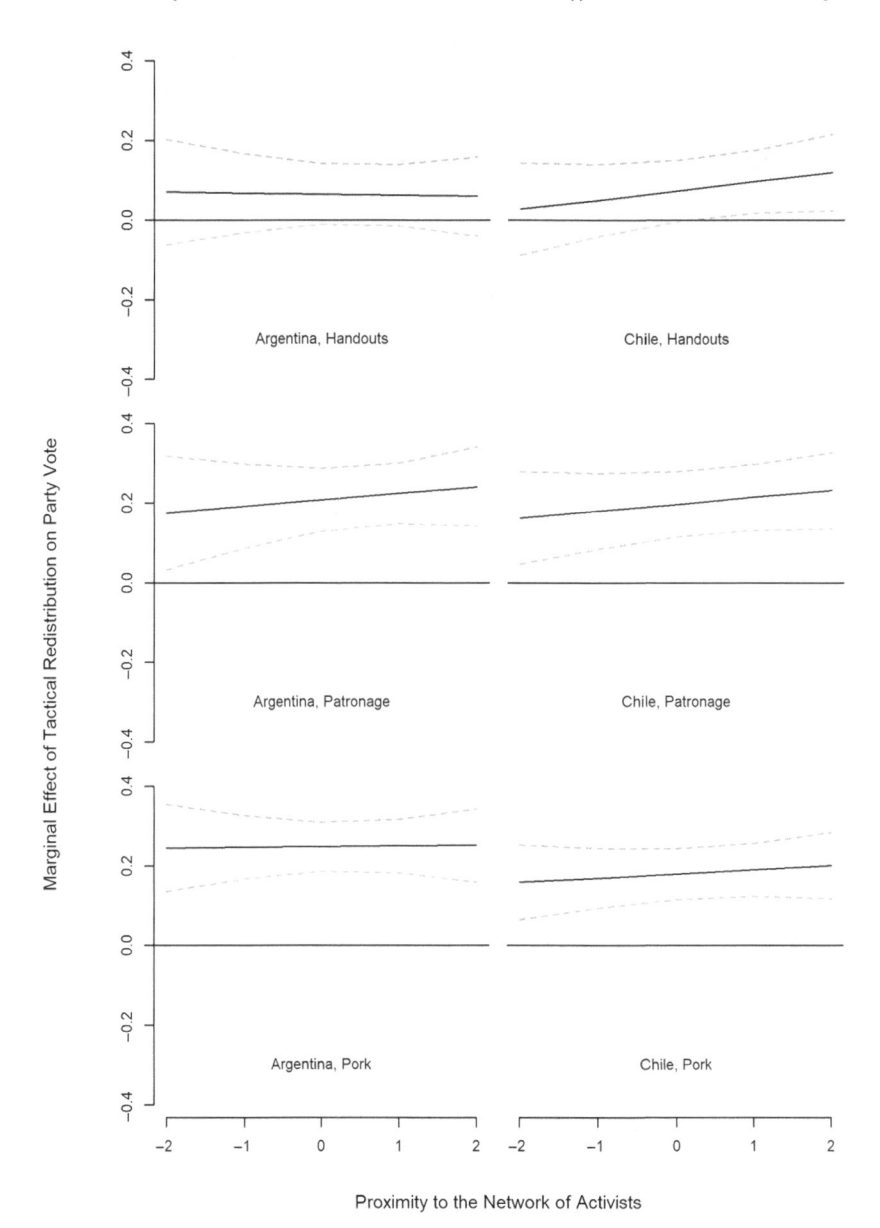

FIGURE 7.3. The effect of targeted distribution on vote choice conditional on network proximity for voters of higher socioeconomic status (C voters)

connected to partisan networks. These are the voters with incentives to exchange information with partisan activists and who, therefore, increase redistributive efficiency of targeted delivery. Argentine partisan networks provide information to distinguish, among voters of the same income, who are more sensitive to distributive expectations. Even though activists in Chile also target handouts to poorer voters, as described by Luna (2014), the informative effect of ideological networks among them is weaker and, thereby, fails to significantly increase electoral returns from handout distribution, in line with expectations laid in hypothesis 1.

Finally, the effect of patronage and pork on poorer voters, conditional on political networks, is large, positive, and significant for Argentina only; a finding we discuss at length in Chapter 8. In particular, returns from patronage require a selection of clients through partisan networks, which allow parties to efficiently distinguish those voters that provide the largest return to spending. As before, the effect is weaker for public works that cannot be discriminated across voters than for the two more excludable goods, in line with hypothesis 2 (attenuation effect). We expect this attenuation effect to be weaker among richer voters, who value the benefit less than poorer voters, and thereby have weaker incentives to sustain strong information flows regarding their wants and needs with party activists.

Figure 7.3 shows the results for voters of higher socioeconomic status in both countries. For richer voters in Argentina (column 1), we find that the effect of proximity to the network on the expectations of receiving handouts, gifts, and favors (clientelism) is not significant, as expected given the lower marginal value of these goods for middle-income voters. In Chile, this effect is significant, albeit small, for proximate voters, but the curve is almost flat. The effect of political connection remains significant for the expectations of receiving a public-sector job (and larger than handouts) in both countries. Yet the curve is flatter for voters of higher socioeconomic status in Argentina and it is now significant for voters of higher socioeconomic status in Chile. Patronage results reflect the higher sensitivity of Chilean middle-class voters to public-sector job expectations (as shown in Chapter 6), a subject to which we return in Chapter 8 when we analyze the targeting of public-sector wage premiums. In both countries, the curve turns flat for distributive expectations for public works, although the electoral impact is higher in Argentina than in Chile, even if not as pronounced as for poorer voters. The attenuation effect, moreover, is very small, given the lower information value of political network among richer voters in Argentina, suggesting that those voters' expectations of public work are not as affected by connections to activists' networks as those of poorer voters.

In short, our findings provide evidence of the selective effect of informative networks for shaping the electoral impact of targeted distribution. The informational aspects of activists' networks are particularly relevant to connecting poorer voters who lack alternative sources of access to scarce resources in Argentina. As a result, we observe the strongest attenuation effects as we increase the excludability of private goods (and the ability of activists to discriminate) among those voters. Hence, the strategic decision of investing in political networks – which in Argentina involves the recruitment of community and social activists into political parties' ranks – seems to provide the highest electoral gain for targeted distribution among poorer voters. Voters who are more dependent on those networks for accessing scarce resources have incentives to seek and provide information to political activists in their communities, who in turn can use this information to reduce the deadweight losses of distribution and therefore produce stronger information effects. Finally, these effects multiply the impact of territorial activists on the vote in Argentina. Not only are connected voters more likely to vote for the party due to mobilization, persuasion, and other tasks pursued by activists, but also partisan networks' efficiency in distribution increases the impact of targeted distribution on the vote. A defection of party activists may also endanger the effect of targeted distribution on electoral behavior, thereby reducing the agency of politicians to define how to allocate these private goods.

## 7.4 PARTISAN NETWORKS AS PERSUASION DEVICES

Following our discussion of the diverse functions and characteristics of partisan networks and after investigating their conditional effect on targeted distribution, we now test their capacity to transmit information about the parties' policy offers. We analyze the importance of networks as persuasion devices. Partisan networks allow parties to not only deliver targeted benefits, but also disseminate policy messages to voters. In particular, we expect ideological activists to excel at this task, given their expertise on the parties' policy offers, as illustrated by our interviews in Chapter 5.

Activists serve a crucial role in interpreting and rendering complex policies accessible to voters. As important, knowledge of voters is critical to knowing which messages should be communicated and to what goal so that parties may transform policy offers into votes through ideological persuasion. The literature suggests that voters with weaker priors – often the less educated – and voters paying attention should be most sensitive to information effects (Zaller, 1992). Education is a major component of our index of socioeconomic status – the correlation between both variables is 0.81 in Argentina and 0.63 in Chile – and therefore we should expect poorer voters to be more affected by the information provided by political activists. Among those poorer voters, those who do not meet activists randomly in a square or street corner but are instead better connected to activists' networks should be more politically attuned and pay more attention to the party message. Remember that our measure of connection requires voters and activists to know each other and to have the ability to contact each other if needed. Hence, we expect stronger effects of ideological distance conditional on connections to activists' networks among poorer voters (hypothesis 3).

Using the vote models presented in Table 7.A.1 in the appendix, we estimate the conditional impact of partisan networks on voters' ideological distance from the party – controlling for all determinants of the vote including the interactions of partisan networks with distributive expectations and competence. Here, we test the joint effect of being more connected to partisan networks and being ideologically proximate to a party on electoral behavior by interacting partisan networks and ideological distance. The analysis was also replicated among poorer voters – those in the D categories – and richer voters – those in the C categories (Tables 7.A.2 and 7.A.3 in the appendix.)

We present the results of the three analyses in Figure 7.4, where the two top plots correspond to the aggregate analysis, the two middle plots correspond to middle-class voters, and the bottom two plots correspond to poorer voters. All the plots on the left correspond to Argentina and those on the right to Chile. The horizontal axis describes the proximity to partisan networks, with a range of [−2, 2], where −2 describes a respondent that knows two standard deviations fewer activists than the prevalence rate for that party, a value of zero describes a respondent that knows the prevalence rate of activists of that party, and a value of 2 denotes a respondent that knows 2 standard deviations more activists than the prevalence rate. The vertical axis describes the marginal effect of ideological distance on party vote, conditional on the number of activists known by the respondent.

The general results from the top two plots show that the effect of ideological distance on vote choice is larger for Chilean than Argentine

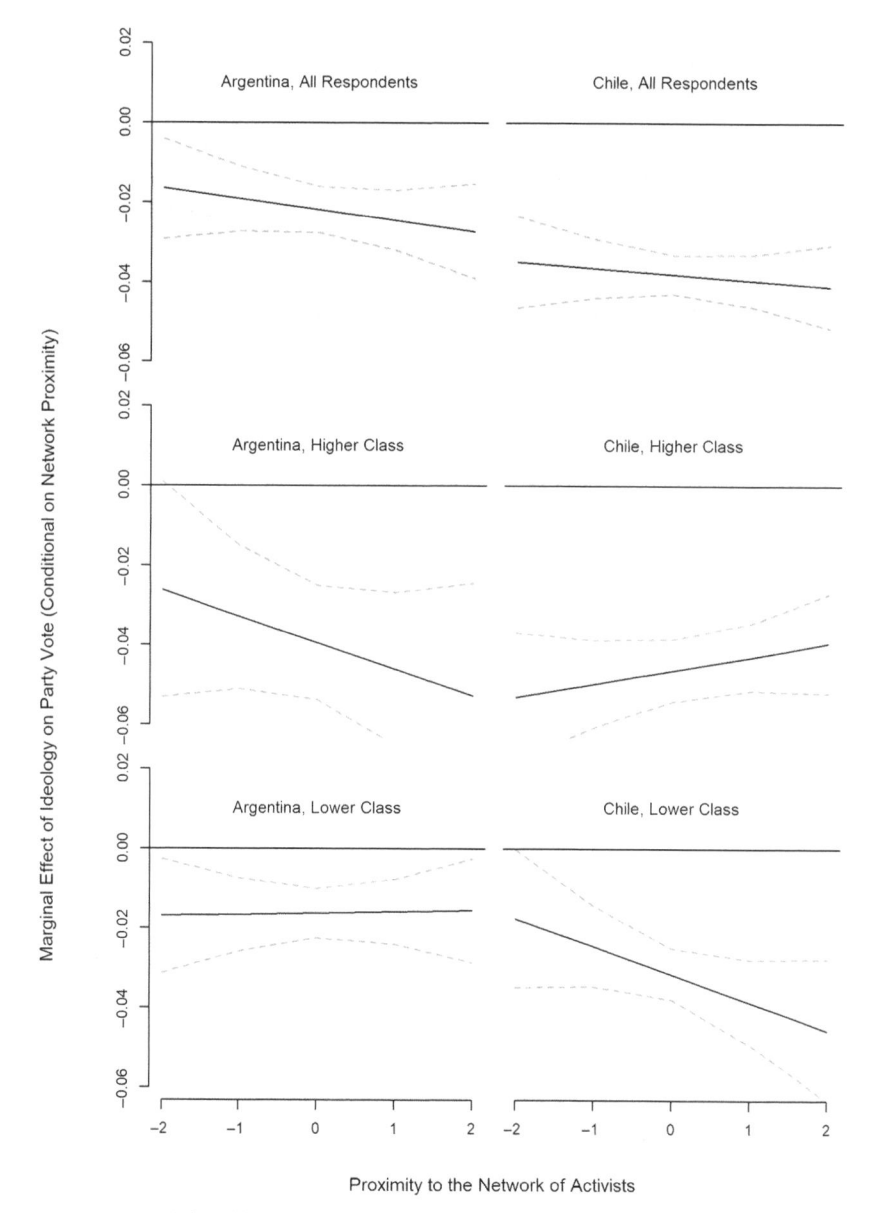

FIGURE 7.4. The effect of ideological distance on vote choice conditional on network proximity in Argentina and Chile

voters and the effect only grows slightly for voters who are more connected to party networks in either country. More interesting is the comparison between poorer and richer voters in either country.

The left plots correspond to Argentina. In this country, the impact of ideological distance for middle-class voters increases, as they know more activists, but the confidence intervals are very wide, suggesting that the relationship may in fact be flat. For the poorer half of the voters, ideological distances result in a decline in party vote that is roughly similar, irrespective of their proximity to partisan networks. The effect, in general, is weaker than for richer voters. Remember that poorer Argentine voters had more difficulties using ideology as an informational shortcut and cared more about distributive expectations, competence, and network connections. Indeed, these were the most sensitive voters to the conditional impact of networks on distributive expectations. Hence, territorial activists have an important role regarding targeted distribution, but it is not clear that they have a similar role in terms of ideological persuasion among the poorer Argentine voters. In sum, we do not have strong support for any electoral effect of ideological distance conditional on partisan networks among Argentine voters.

Figure 7.4 allows a comparison between Chilean richer and poorer voters in the right-side plots. Chilean voters of upper-socioeconomic status (middle plot) care about their ideological distance from a party irrespective of their connectivity to party networks, perhaps because, as our interviews suggest, they form their opinions mainly through the media. Hence, although richer Chilean voters are more connected to party networks – who involved activists of higher socioeconomic status – and although richer Chilean voters care more about policy offers, partisan networks seem not to shape the impact of ideological distance on their vote. The contrast with poorer voters is remarkable. Among them, higher proximity to party activists increases the importance of ideological distance on their electoral behavior. That is to say that the impact of ideological distance for poorer Chilean voters heightens significantly as they become more connected to party networks, in line with our expectations (hypothesis 3). As a result, the impact of ideological distance on the vote for connected poorer voters is similar to the average effect of middle-class voters, whereas that of unconnected voters is half the size. As these voters were less educated than richer voters, but more politically attuned to activists given their connections, they should be more sensitive to their policy persuasion. These results are also in line with ideological patterns of activist recruitment and the connections between activists and ideologically akin voters described in Chapter 5. Therefore, Chilean partisan networks, which were not informative in terms of targeted distribution to poorer voters, seem to be more effective for ideological persuasion among this subset of voters.

In short, the extensive political networks in Argentina and Chile allowed political parties to target poorer voters in an effective way, as voters who were more connected to partisan networks were more sensitive to either distributive expectations or ideological distance, respectively. This divergence is produced by the types of information channels through these networks and the prior recruitment patterns. In Argentina, territorial networks provide information useful for targeting selective incentives to high-yield voters. In Chile, ideological networks communicate ideological content to more connected voters. The indirect effect of activists on two crucial dimensions of electoral choice in either country shapes the opportunities and constraints faced by politicians. Argentine activists limit the agency of politicians to shift patterns of targeted distribution, whereas Chilean activists restrain politicians' opportunities to modify policy offers.

## 7.5 SUMMARY AND CONCLUDING REMARKS

Building on results from previous chapters, we have shown here that partisan networks play important, albeit different, roles in Argentina and Chile. Results show that parties not only benefit from targeting voters with selective incentives but, more importantly, that party networks play a crucial role in gathering information and delivering the goods. Selecting clients and persuading voters are important activities of parties in Argentina and Chile, which are carried out through the deployment of vast networks of political activists. Interacting with political activists, this chapter shows, has a significant effect on how voters access benefits, how they perceive policy messages, and ultimately how they chose for which candidates to vote.

As non-policy resources, political networks are crucial mechanisms that connect voters to party members, allowing candidates to service voters both through the delivery of goods as well as policy. From the point of view of voters, it is not the abstract promise of a party with little credibility, but the daily interaction with activists that matters in defining distributive expectations (Calvo and Murillo, 2013). Our results confirm the electoral benefits of party networks, both when identifying high-yield voters, when communicating policy content, and – as shown in this chapter – in shaping the importance that voters attach to delivery and persuasion in making vote decisions.

Our results show that party networks matter both in Chile and in Argentina. They increase the party's vote directly through mobilization efforts, as well as indirectly by delivering benefits and communicating policy content. The electoral benefits of party networks are larger in Argentina, as they yield broader electoral gains both directly and indirectly. In Chile, by contrast, party networks provide fewer votes through mobilization and yield smaller gains through persuasion. In both cases, however, party activists and face-to-face interaction have broader impacts among poorer voters.

Results in this chapter show that activists' networks have stronger effects in shaping the preferences of poorer voters in both countries. The conditional effect of targeted benefits on the vote is enhanced by party networks in Argentina, while the conditional effect of ideological distance is increased among poor voters in Chile. In line with our description in Chapter 5 and the interviews with politicians, our quantitative evidence shows that not all political networks specialize in the same tasks. Argentine networks are more efficient in reducing deadweight costs in the delivery of targeted benefits. Argentine networks efficiently communicate information that increases the electoral gains of targeting connected voters. In Chile, where networks have less informative value for targeted benefits, parties are better off communicating policy content and delivering handouts with the aim of reaching swing voters.

The implications of these findings for our framework help us understand politicians' opportunities in either country. Politicians' decisions discouraging the participation of activists would have an electoral cost that includes not just the direct effect of the partisan networks we measure in Chapter 6, but also the indirect effects generated by partisan activists on poorer voters in both countries, as shown in this chapter. Hence, our results have implications for short-term strategic decisions by politicians. Politicians can rely on partisan networks to reach voters. Because partisan networks have both direct and indirect (or conditional) effects on the vote, they reinforce patterns of recruitment and operation, generating path dependency on future party strategies, as politicians are aware of the cost of losing activist support. Chile, activists reinforce the limits of party to shift their policy offers, given not just their direct, but also their indirect effect on the vote through the conditional effects generated by partisan activists, who are themselves more connected to ideologically akin voters. By contrast, shifting distribution may be a more efficient way of trying to reach undecided voters for Chilean politicians, as already identified by the recent literature (Barozet, 2004; Luna, 2014). In the case of Argentina, activists do not anchor the parties' policy offers as they are not connected with more ideologically akin voters and they do not have strong conditional effects on ideological distance. Argentine activists, however, do shape the vote – both directly and indirectly – through their role in shaping distributive expectations, itself a crucial variable to explain the vote, especially among poorer voters. Argentine parties, thus, have more agency to shift their policy offers, but are heavily dependent on activists to efficiently target distribution to the most sensitive voters.[11] Thus, they limit politicians' agency for redefining criteria of targeted distribution.

Finally, this chapter provides an empirical answer to the core-swing debate that has been featured prominently in the discipline. Our results conform to the model proposed by Dixit and Londregan (1996), showing that targeting core or swing voters requires parties to measure the sensitivity of voters to particular types of policy and non-policy benefits. Where deadweight losses are important and voter information valuable, as in Argentina, the allocation of targeted benefits has been consistently directed to core voters – those connected to party activists – in line with findings by Stokes et al. (2013). Where deadweight losses are small and party networks inefficient, as in Chile, targeted benefits have been directed to swing voters and networks used to communicate policy content. Results show that strategies for targeted distribution are therefore conditional on the existence of information mechanism to reduce "leakage" in the distribution and increase the electoral returns derived from this non-policy resource. Hence, the answer to the core-swing debate should be conditional on informational mechanisms and will vary according to the context.

---

[11] As noticed by Stokes et al. (2013), the power of Argentine activists vis-à-vis politicians is sustained on information asymmetries, which as we show provide a valuable resource for politicians and constrain their ability to replace well-informed activists.

# 8

# Targeting Patronage in Argentina and Chile

In this chapter, we focus on public-sector wages to measure whether wage premiums conform to the varied sensitivities of voters of different socioeconomic groups in each country, as identified in Chapter 6. This chapter shows that distributive expectations about patronage have larger electoral effects in Argentina than in Chile and that electoral sensitivity toward public jobs is higher among poorer voters in Argentina and among middle-class voters in Chile. Therefore, we expect policymakers to use public-sector employment to reward the most sensitive voters in each country. In this chapter, we test these expectations using household income data. Public-sector wages provide a critical test of our argument, given that patronage expectations have been shown to have larger effects on the vote than handouts and to be uncorrelated with the voters' ideological preferences in either country. Wages, moreover, are more sensitive to political decisions than sheer employment, given limits on firing civil servants in both countries. Consequently, public-sector wages provide a crucial test for electorally minded decisions by politicians that hope to win elections.

In Chapter 6, we showed that Argentine and Chilean voters care for their ideological proximity to parties, as well as for the provision of non-policy benefits such as competence to manage the economy, their proximity to activists' networks, and the delivery of targeted goods. We also showed significant heterogeneity among respondents, with voters from different socioeconomic groups displaying distinctive sensitivities for the policy and non-policy benefits offered by parties. Low-income Argentine voters, for example, are more likely to change their vote in response to public-sector job offers than richer Argentine voters. Similarly, upper-income Chilean voters are more readily swayed by higher managerial competence than low-income voters. However, politicians' agency to tailor electoral offers varies. The conditions shaping competence evaluations are often hard to change in a short period, whereas decisions as to who should receive handouts, or what policy should be changed in a party's platform, can be done within a single electoral cycle. Some benefits, moreover, are associated with others. In Chile, shifting policy offers may also affect the incentives of activists to work for the party, thus limiting the agency of politicians to shift benefits that may impinge indirectly on other electoral resources. Public-sector job expectations have strong electoral effects in both countries – albeit larger in Argentina than in Chile – and do not correlate with voters' ideological preferences in either country. Because politicians have agency over public-sector employment and because the electoral effect of public-sector job expectations varies across socioeconomic status in different ways in Chile and Argentina, we can test whether or not fiscal revenue is used to target the voters that our measures in Chapter 6 identify as most electorally sensitive to patronage.

To provide an independent test of the model implications – i.e. parties allocate non-policy benefits disproportionally to respondents that our survey identified as highly sensitive voters – we use household income data collected by the statistical bureaus of each country. The data provides an independent measure of wage allocation among Argentine and Chilean voters, allowing us to test whether politicians allocate patronage resources in ways that are consistent with our model expectations.

In understanding the targeting of public spending on public employment, we consider that in both countries public officers are prevented from hiring to cover vacancies unless new agencies are created due to the existence of civil service provisions that preclude firing (Grindle, 2012). As a result, political elites have more agency over wages than job positions, even if the change in wage targeting is not immediate, as we show below. To assess the distributive implications of public-sector wages, we therefore analyze wage differentials between public- and private-sector jobs; that is, whether the same job, controlling for skill levels, pays more in the public or the private sector. If the public sector pays higher, we code this difference as a wage premium paid by public revenue. Our analysis centers on the targeting of wage premiums to socioeconomic groups of voters, given their electoral sensitivity to public-sector distributive expectations as described in Chapter 6 and summarized below.

Our expectations are as follows. First, we expect higher wage premiums among public-sector employees in Argentina than in Chile. This expectation is rooted in the higher value that Argentine respondents attached to patronage jobs when making vote decisions. We define a wage premium as a salary that is greater than the compensation expected by similar workers in comparable private-sector jobs controlling for education, tenure, and other personal characteristics.

Second, we expect patronage wages and employment to benefit voters that provide the highest marginal electoral return to targeted distribution. In the case of Argentina, our results in Chapter 6 identified lower-income workers (D1, D2, E) as being the most sensitive to expectations about public-sector job distribution in deciding their vote. In the case of Chile, we identified middle- and lower-middle-income (C2 and C3) voters as having a higher propensity to switch their electoral loyalty based on expectations of receiving patronage benefits.

We test these predictions on individual-level wages and employment data collected among private- and public-sector employees in Chile and Argentina. Our analyses take advantage of myriad individual-level data on private- and public-sector wages, educational achievement, type of recruitment, and tenure collected by various bureaus of statistics. We show that, in Argentina, lower-income and lower-skilled public-sector employees receive wage premiums that are significantly larger than those received by moderate-to-high-skilled/income workers. By contrast, in Chile, medium- and high-skilled public-sector employees receive larger premium wages than those of lower-skilled workers. Moreover, when we run our analysis separating by income (and controlling for education), we also find that wage premiums are targeted to lower-income workers in Argentina but not in Chile. In all, we show that Argentine public employees who are poorer are granted considerable premium wages, whereas in Chile wage premiums are distributed to public employees with higher skills and socioeconomic status.

## 8.1 PUBLIC EMPLOYMENT AND TARGETED DISTRIBUTION

Public-sector employees are primarily recruited and compensated to provide services to citizens. However, public-sector employment can also serve a variety of economic and political functions. Public employees, by sheer numbers and organization, have a dramatic influence on the world's labor markets, rising minimum wages, guidelines that regulate labor market standards, and – in some cases – the course of elections (Hammouya, 1999). Public-sector employment can boost overall employment in hard times and lower wage pressure in good times (Wallerstein and

Austen-Smith, 2008). Employment rules in the public sector may also set standards that alter the behavior of private employers. An expansion of public-sector employment can be used to sustain aggregate consumption during economic downturns and to reduce social conflict in distressed localities (Rodrik, 1997). Larger numbers of provincial public employees may pressure central governments to increase transfers to local governments (Treisman, 1999) and they are also crucial in allowing incumbents to sustain activists' networks (Grindle, 2012; Oliveros 2013, 2016).

The nature of bureaucratic recruitment makes spending in public-sector employment the largest targeted distribution program in many democracies. However, such targeted distribution often goes unnoticed so long as employees fulfill their contractual obligations (Alesina, Baqir, and Easterly, 1997). In Chile, public employees represent one-and-a-half times the number of retirees, while in Argentina the number of public employees is twice that of individuals receiving a pension or retirement benefits and almost three times the number of recipients enrolled in Argentina's broadest social program: the Universal Child Benefit (*Asignación Universal por Hijo*). The share of public employees in Argentine localities is even larger than in Chile and a significant share of Argentine families owe their monthly subsistence to public-sector employment. Hence, in both countries, the number of voters affected by public wage decisions is quite significant.

The sheer size of the public-sector labor force around 2009 explains its effect on the private-sector labor markets, as well as the potential electoral gains for self-interested politicians. In Argentina and Chile, public-sector employees represent approximately 16 percent and 12 percent of total employment, respectively.[1] In both countries there is significant territorial variation, ranging from a minimum of 12 percent in the city of Buenos Aires to over 40 percent in a few provinces in the Northwest of Argentina (EPH, 2009), and from 10 percent to 21 percent across Chile's regions (CASEN, 2009).[2] In Chile, the share of all salaried workers that are public-sector employees by *Comuna* ranges from a minimum of about 2 percent to a maximum of approximately 69 percent, with a median of 9 percent at the municipality level.

---

[1] Weighted estimates from the National Household Surveys by INDEC (Argentina) and CASEN (Chile). Un-weighted estimates are 19 percent and 13 percent for Argentina and Chile, respectively.

[2] In both countries, the smallest public sectors are in the densely populated urban areas of Buenos Aires and Santiago, while the largest public sectors are in smaller districts in the south and north.

In both countries, public-sector employees perform administrative, technical, and professional duties that are necessary for the proper functioning of the public administration. Here, we analyze the compensation they are assigned by focusing on the targeting of wage premiums among different groups of voters. In particular, we expect wage premiums to be targeted to the socioeconomic categories of voters that are most sensitive to patronage in defining their vote as described in Chapter 6: middle-class voters in Chile and poorer voters in Argentina.

## 8.2 TARGETING PUBLIC-SECTOR WAGE PREMIUM IN ARGENTINA AND CHILE

Politicians can expect two distinct types of political benefits from patronage spending. First, politicians can use public-sector employment to finance their political machines. Parties may subsidize their activities and increase network capacity by adding activists to the public-sector rolls. Although public-sector jobs are crucial to sustain partisan networks, activists represent a small fraction of public-sector employees.[3] A larger fraction provide jobs and salaries to significant shares of the electorate, broadening dependence on those transfers and generating incentives for politicians to target public employment expenditures with the goal of shaping electoral behavior to maximize the vote.

Analyses in this chapter take advantage of individual income data collected by the national statistical agencies of Argentina and the Ministry of Planning in Chile. In Argentina, we pooled together thirty-three large individual income surveys (*Serie Continua, Encuesta Permanente de Hogares* or *EPH*) collected by the Argentine Bureau of Statistics (INDEC) between 2003 and 2011. Each survey includes approximately 50,000 respondents, for a total of 1.8 million respondents. Among all respondents, 540,235 were private-sector employees while 158,754 where public-sector employees. In Chile, we use four very large income surveys conducted in 1996, 2003, 2006, and 2009, by the National Institute of Statistics (Chile). These National Surveys of Socio-Economic Characteristics (or CASEN) include 220,338 respondents, of which

---

[3] In a 1997 Siempro survey in Argentina, activists were 4.2 percent of public-sector employees and 1.36 percent of the total population, which represents a ratio of 4.16, although their percentage was not very high among public-sector workers. In Chile, 1.17 percent of public employees reported participation in political parties in contrast to 0.19 percent in the population according to CASEN (2003), which represents a ratio of 7.3.

189,883 were private-sector employees and 30,455 were public-sector employees.

The dependent variable of our analysis is the wage (ln) of the main occupation for all salaried employees in Argentina and Chile. This is measured in Argentine and Chilean pesos without adjusting for price changes across surveys in each country. Because we include fixed effects by survey, inflation is not a concern, with all estimates describing within-country and survey differences between the public- and private-sector wages. To ensure comparability in the analyses, samples in both countries do not include self-employed workers, small business owner, retirees, and any respondent that is not defined contractually as an employee. We do not consider other sources of income such as rents, debts, alimony, and secondary jobs held by the respondents. Therefore, all analyses compare primary wages of salaried employees of each country by survey.

### a) Public-Sector Wage Premiums and Educational Achievement

We start by presenting bivariate analyses of public- and private-sector wages conditional on educational achievement before exploring the distribution of public-wage premiums, while controlling for other covariates.[4] First, we plot the evolution of public-sector wages before and after 2007 in both Argentina and Chile, the time at which we conducted the surveys reported in previous chapters. Figures 8.1 and 8.2 describe the non-linear relationship between education and wages in Argentina and Chile. The vertical axis describes the natural log of wages, while the horizontal axis describes the level of educational attainment. In all figures, the straight solid and dotted lines describe the median public and private wages at the time of the survey. The gap between the two lines describes the wage premium for the whole sample. The curved solid and dotted lines describe the median public and private wage conditional on educational achievement. Again, the gap between the two curved lines describes the wage gap between the public and private sector for any given level of education, which we use as a measure of wage premium.

---

[4] The educational achievement variable in Argentina ranges from zero (No education) to seven (Completed college education). In Chile, the variable describes the number of years of education, from zero through twenty. Similar graphs that consider the number of years of education are also available from the authors. We use educational attainment for consistency with the quantile regression analyses reported later in this chapter.

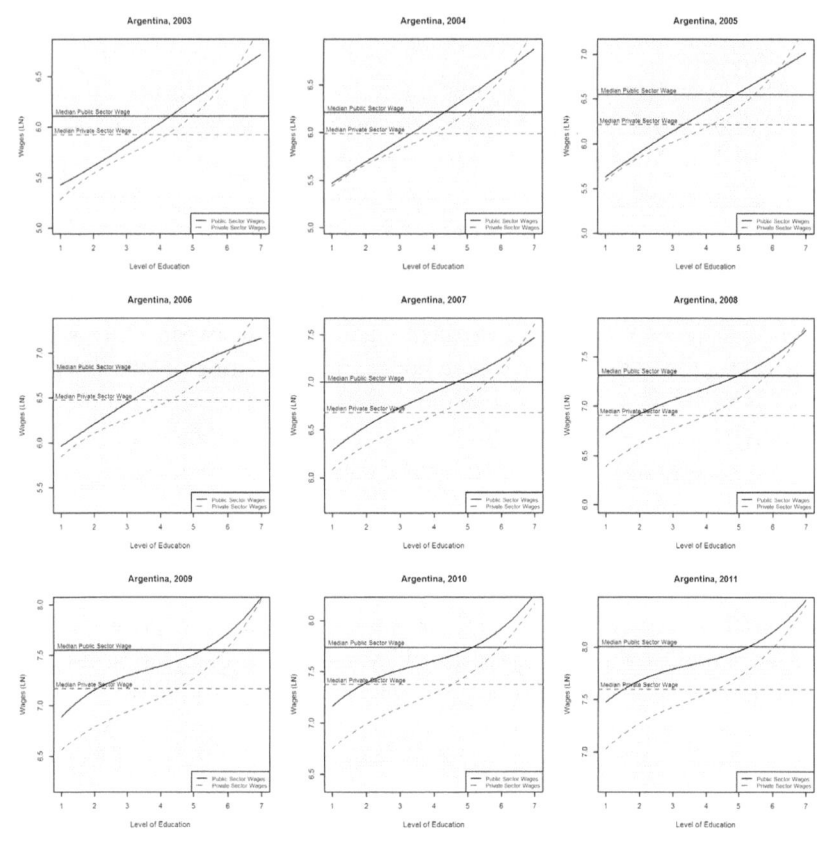

FIGURE 8.1. Private- and public-sector wages in Argentina, 2003–2011
*Note*: Estimated from the National Household Income Survey (EPH-Indec).
Education: 1–No schooling, 2–Incomplete elementary, 3–Elementary, 4–
Incomplete high school, 5–Complete high school, 6–Incomplete college, 7–College
or higher. Lines computed using B-splines with four degrees of freedom for the
private- and public-sector wages.

Given the broader electoral gains from patronage spending among
Argentine voters, we expected public-sector wage premiums to be larger
there than in Chile. This expectation is confirmed by the data. Although
we find that fiscal revenue is used to redistribute via public-sector compensation in both countries, an uncontrolled estimation of the median
public-sector wage premium establishes levels of around 22 percent in
Argentina (in 2007) and 15 percent in Chile (in 2006) – even when the
public-sector wage premium was slightly larger in Chile than Argentina in
1996. More importantly, Figure 8.1 shows that public-sector salaries in

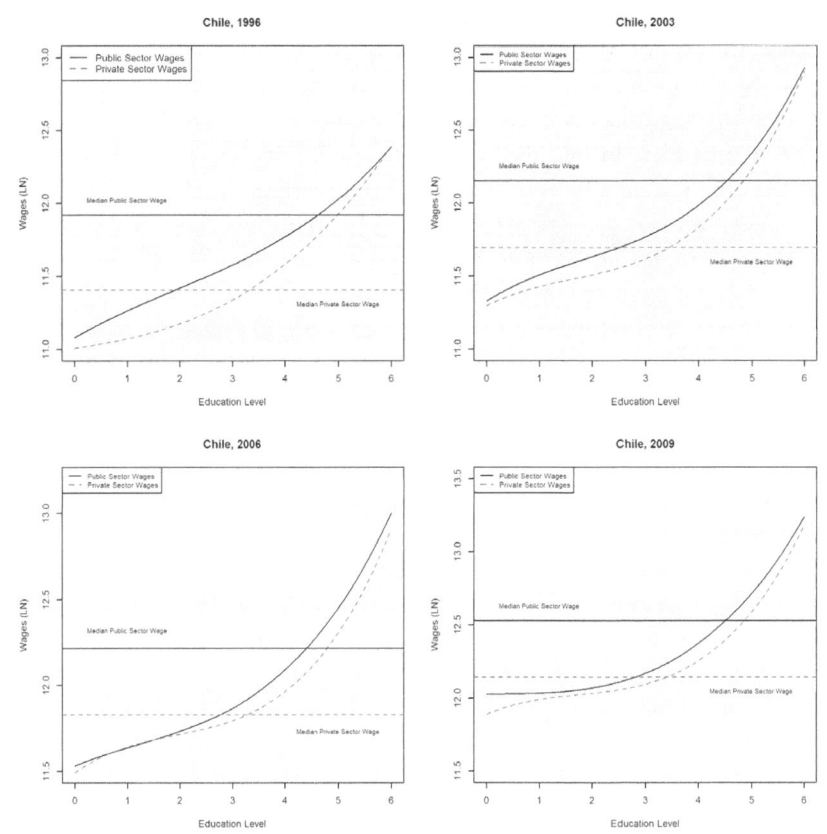

FIGURE 8.2. Private- and public-sector wages in Chile, 1996 through 2009
*Note*: Estimated from the National Income Survey, CASEN. Education: 0–No schooling, 1–Incomplete elementary, 2–Elementary, 3–Incomplete high school, 4–Complete high school, 5–Incomplete college, 6–College or higher. Lines computed using B-splines with four degrees of freedom for the private- and public-sector wages.

Argentina consistently benefited comparatively less-educated public employees, who perceived significantly larger premium wages than similarly educated private sector workers. Meanwhile, workers with the highest levels of education received wages that were on par or below those of the private sector.

Figure 8.1 shows the change over time between 2003 and 2011, which corresponds to the Peronist administrations of Nestor Kircher (2003–2007) and his wife Cristina Fernandez de Kirchner (2007–2011) described in Chapter 4. Given the higher propensity of poorer voters to vote Peronist and the higher sensitivity of poorer voters to patronage expectations, politicians seem to be responding to voters' preferences in this regard. Public-sector wage premiums increased between 2003 and 2007, although increases disproportionally favored employees in the lowest quantiles. In fact, from 2003 through 2004, workers with completed high school education received the largest wage premiums.

Then, after 2005, relative salaries of public sector workers in the bottom quantiles begin to grow at a rapid pace, significantly outpacing gains among educated workers. As education is a large portion of our index of socioeconomic status, these findings are in line with our expectations of public wage dispersion, favoring poorer voters who were more electorally sensitive to patronage expectations. The temporal change between 2003 and 2011 – the year when Cristina Kirchner was re-elected with a majority of the popular vote – shows considerable agency in politicians' targeting of public employment spending, even when change was incremental.

The evolution in public-sector wage premiums in Chile (Figure 8.2) contrasts with that of Argentina. The public-sector wage premium in Chile in the mid-1990s, just a few years after democratization, was larger and disproportionally favored wage earners with low-to-middle levels of education, while wage premiums were negative for workers with the highest education levels. Over the next ten years, wage premiums in the Chilean public sector declined and its distribution changed to favor those workers with the most education. Hence, by 2009, wage premiums were smaller and disproportionally benefited educated workers. Given the weight of education on the index of socioeconomic status, the results in this section are in line with those in Chapter 6, with middle-class voters better attuned to patronage spending in Chile. During this period, the *Concertación* was in power in Chile, but we do not observe clear patterns of socioeconomic voting in Chile, leading us to expect politicians of all parties targeted groups of voters who were more electorally sensitive to patronage expectations.

Hence, our bivariate analyses for both countries show patters that are in line with our expectations, where politicians target sensitive voters with wage premiums. Returns from skills in the public sectors of both countries, as well as the evolution of wage premiums, are consistent with our expectations, to the benefit of middle-class voters in Chile and poorer voters in Argentina. We now model wage premiums as a function of the socioeconomic status of survey respondents to maximize comparability with the estimates of Chapter 6, before including covariates for control.

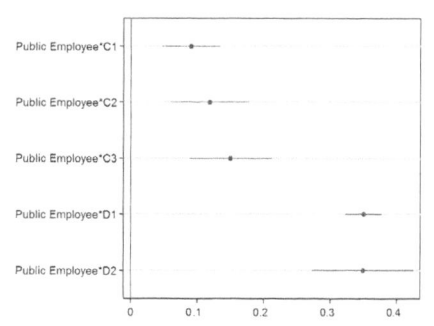

FIGURE 8.3. Public-sector wage premium by socioeconomic level, Argentina, 2009
*Note*: Estimates from Table 8.A.3 in the appendix to this chapter.

### b) Public-Sector Wage Premiums and Socioeconomic Status

In line with our expectations, we have shown that public-sector wage premiums are larger and benefit less-educated workers in Argentina more than in Chile. To make our findings more comparable with the socioeconomic categories employed in Chapter 6, we estimate public-sector wage premiums based on the same classification system. Using the EPH and the CASEN, as described by the INDEC in Argentina and by the AIM in Chile, we recreate those socioeconomic variables, once again making the educational attainment of respondents the main component.[5] Consequently, it is not surprising that results using socioeconomic variables closely approximate the results in Figures 8.1 and 8.2 and that Figures 8.3 (Argentina) and 8.4 (Chile), which present our estimates by socioeconomic level, mostly conform to our expectations.

In the case of Argentina, wage premiums are considerably larger for the employees in the lower socioeconomic categories (D1 and D2).[6] In 2009, the public employees in the lowest socioeconomic category (D2)

---

[5] To compute the NSE (Nivel Socio-Economico) in Argentina and the GSE (Grupo Socio-Economico) in Chile, we follow the guidelines of Sacco (2011), the accepted standard for estimating the respondents' NSE using the national household income survey. We use the same design for Chile, although we have only six of the eight required indicators. The estimates of GSE in Chile, consequently, are less precise than that of Argentina.

[6] The sample of respondents in the lowest socioeconomic income category, E, is not represented in the data. This is because the INDEC does not include any full-time employees in the lowest category. Consequently, the lowest socioeconomic category for full-time employees in Argentina is D2.

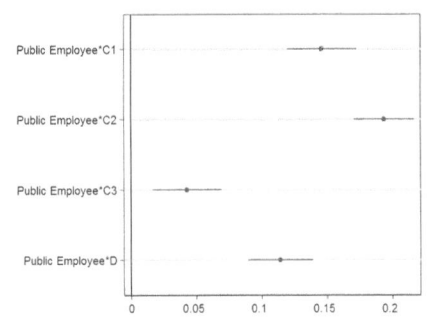

FIGURE 8.4. Public-sector wage premium by socioeconomic level, Chile, 2009
*Note*: Estimates from Table 8.A.3 in the appendix to this chapter.

received a 37-percent wage premium vis-à-vis their private counterparts: i.e. $\exp(0.32) = 1.37 = 37$ percent. Not far behind, upper-lower-income employees (D1) received a 33.6 percent wage premium: i.e. $\exp(0.29) = 1.336 = 33.6$ percent. By contrast, public-sector employees from the upper socioeconomic groups (C2–C3) received wages comparable to those of the private sector, while the upper-middle-income (C1) respondents received a very small premium.

Figure 8.4 shows different results for public-sector employees in Chile, who received smaller wage premiums – as shown by the different scale used in the x-axis – and whose wage premiums were consistently higher for the upper-socioeconomic groups. The socioeconomic group that received the largest wage premium as the middle-income (C2) voters were the group identified by our survey as the one providing the biggest returns from patronage spending. While wage premiums were smaller than in Argentina, workers in this middle-income category still received a 22 percent premium above the expected salary of private-sector employees in the same socioeconomic category. Not far behind, workers in the upper-middle-income (C1) category received a 16 percent premium over their private-sector counterparts. Meanwhile, premiums were small, although statistically significant, for individuals in the D category. To our surprise, respondents in the lower-middle-income (C3) category received the lowest wage premium, barely above 5 percent, a group that provided considerably higher returns than those of upper-middle (C1) income or lower-income (D) voters in our survey.

In all, results show that rewards went disproportionally to the most sensitive lower-income (D) voters with higher premium wages in Argentina. Further, these rewards comfortably exceeded premiums in the

Chilean public sector, as expected, given the stronger impact of public-job distributive expectations on the vote in Argentina. As expected, wage premiums for Chilean employees were concentrated in the higher-income categories. However, unlike results in Chapter 6, public-sector workers from the top socioeconomic category (C1) received premiums that exceeded those anticipated in Chapter 6, whereas lower-middle-income (C3) workers were not rewarded to the extent anticipated by our model. Consequently, while estimates strongly support the use of public-sector wages for targeting highly sensitive voters in Argentina, results are less conclusive in the case of Chile. This analysis, however, does not consider other variables affecting wage premiums, so in the next section we move to a different strategy that allows us to control for a set of covariates shaping compensation in the public sector.

## 8.3 TARGETING OF PUBLIC-SECTOR WAGE PREMIUMS: A QUANTILE REGRESSION ANALYSIS

We now include controls not only for education and socioeconomic status, but also for a number of other important confounding factors, such as the gender composition of the private and public sectors, the longevity (tenure) of the appointments, and the age of employees in our analysis of wage premiums. Below we estimate quantile regression models that control for a larger number of covariates for individuals at different levels of the income scale to assess the patterns associated with public-wage spending.

To test for public-sector wage premiums across income groups, we take advantage of recent research that analyzes inter-group wage inequality through quantile regression techniques (Koenker, 2005).[7] Unlike OLS, which minimizes the sum of square distances to the mean of the wage distribution, quantile regression extends previous research on absolute regression – which fits a line through the median of the sample distribution – and places different lines through each quantile of the dependent variable. For example, the median quantile fits a line that separates observations above and below the median income earner. Similarly, we can estimate the effect of covariates on the top 80th quantile, with a line that separates observations that are above and below a 0.8

---

[7] Quantile regression is a statistical strategy to estimate the conditional quantile distribution of a continuous dependent variable as a linear function of covariates (Koenker, 2005; Koenker and Bassett, 1978).

share of wage earners. Quantile regression techniques allow us to use covariates to model how variables such as education, tenure, or gender shape the expected income of employees in the top, median, or bottom quantiles.

The implications of our voting model in terms of voters' sensitivity to targeted distribution suggest that public-sector wage premiums should differ by income quantile in both Argentina and Chile. In Argentina, we expect voters at the lowest quantiles of income category to receive the largest wage premiums. This is consistent with results that showed poorer voters to be the ones with the highest sensitivity to patronage spending in terms of electoral behavior. By contrast, in Chile, we expect that better-off voters in the higher income categories should be given larger wage premiums, in order to maximize the electoral returns of patronage spending. In our model, the most sensitive Chilean voters in this category were those in the middle- (C2) and lower-middle- (C3) income categories. Therefore, we expect that the wage premium favoring public-sector employees will be larger among workers with relatively lower incomes in Argentina (low-quantile workers) than in Chile, where we expect wage premiums to benefit middle-class voters (middle-to-upper quantile). We also expect the size of the public-sector wage premiums to be larger in Argentina than in Chile, once we control for other covariates in the analysis.

As in the previous section, the dependent variable in our analysis is the wage (ln) of the primary job of employees in both Argentina and Chile. Wages are measured in Argentine and Chilean pesos without adjusting for price changes across surveys in each country, but with fixed effects by country/survey. As covariates we include: (i) a *public employee* variable that takes the value of one if the respondent receives a salary from a public agency, or a public company, and zero otherwise. Parameter estimates of this variable capture wage premiums in public-sector wages vis-à-vis the private sector. Our models include (ii) a variable describing the *level of education* of employees, which controls for the effect of skill differences among employees recruited into the public and private sector. They also include interactions between the number of years of schooling and the variable public sector, to distinguish the effect of education on wages within and across public- and private-sector employees. Using these covariates, we run restricted quantile models that include our key independent variables. After describing the effect of public employment and education on wages, we estimate full models with a number of other controls which we know affect wages, including (iii) gender and (iv) age. In Tables 8.A.1 and 8.A.2 in the appendix to this chapter we also present results including controls for working hours and tenure (only for Argentina as the data is not available for Chile).

### a) Restricted Quantile Regression Models

We begin by running a restricted model with the natural log of employee wages as the dependent variable and using the public-sector employment variable and education as covariates. This provides a baseline description of the difference between public and private wages at each of the different quantiles. Results are shown in Figure 8.5 with the left plots describing

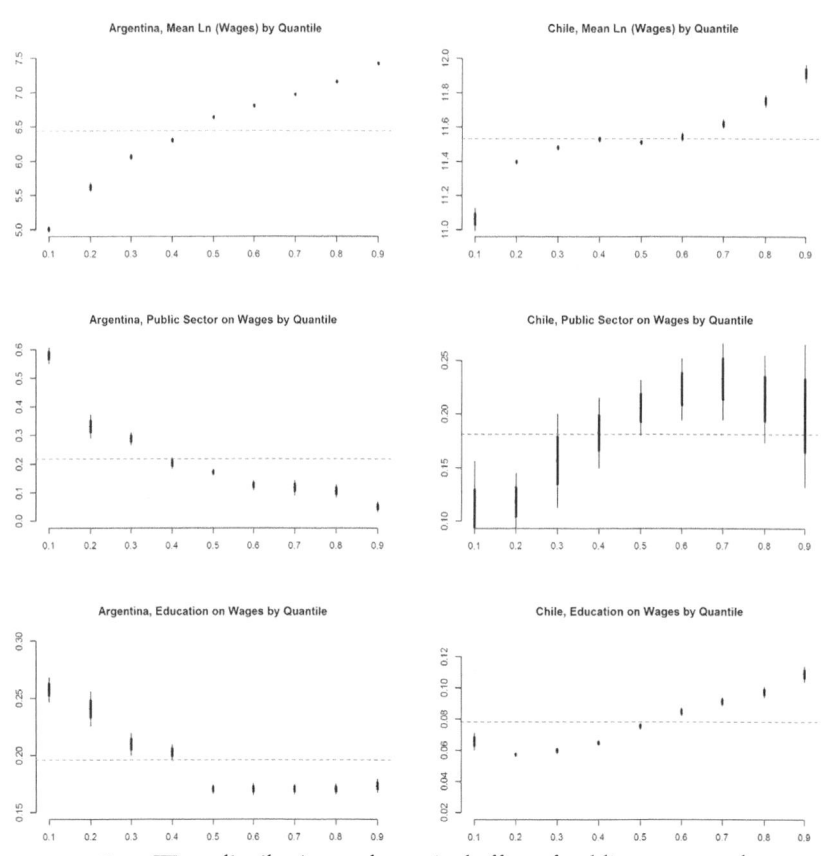

FIGURE 8.5. Wage distribution and marginal effect of public-sector employment and education on wages in Argentina, quantile regression estimates for Argentina (EPH, 2009) and Chile (CASEN, 2009)
*Note*: Estimates describe the marginal change in employee wages (ln) by quantile. Full estimate results are given in Table 8.A.1 (in the appendix to this chapter).

quantile estimates for Argentina, while the right plot describes model estimates for Chile. Each model has three parameters with estimates by quantile. First, a constant describing the mean private-sector wage (the dotted line in the graph); second, estimates of public-sector wage premium by quantile; and third, estimates of the returns by education by quantile. The horizontal axes describe the marginal effect of each covariate on the dependent variable wages (ln), with coefficient estimates measured at each of ten different quantiles, from the lowest 10 percent of income (0.1) to the top 90 percent of income (0.9).

Figure 8.5 presents the results of our analysis for both countries using the 2009 survey data, collected two years after our own surveys. These show the effect of public-sector wage premium in the middle plots, where the effect of being a public-sector employee controlling for education and income is shown. Consider, for example, the middle plot on the left side of Figure 8.5, which describes the difference in the wage of a public-sector employee and a private sector-employee in Argentina. We can see that a one-unit increase in private-sector wages leads to an increase larger than 0.25 among low-wage earners and a decline of −0.05 among the highest wage earners. Indeed, these results provide evidence of a positive premium directed at low-skilled/low-wage workers in the Argentine public sector, compared to the private sector, and a decline in wages among high-skilled/high-wage public-sector employees, even when controlling for education. These results thus provide stronger evidence to support our hypothesis about the targeting of public-sector wages to reward the most electorally sensitive groups of voters in Argentina.

By contrast, our results in the middle-right plot show that in Chile, once we control for education, the highest premium is allocated to those employees that are in the upper-middle quantiles. Whereas the first quantile has a very low premium, workers in the top three income quantiles (0.7) have the highest wage premiums. In all, models show that premium wages are disproportionally allocated to workers in the lower-income categories in Argentina, while they benefit middle-to-upper public-sector employees in Chile, as expected by the higher electoral sensitivity of voters in those socioeconomic categories.

### b) Unrestricted Quantile Models of Wage Premiums

Here we estimate models that include a broader set of employee variables to identify the origin of public-sector wage premiums in both countries. We consider a number of covariates, including the worker's age (ln), gender,

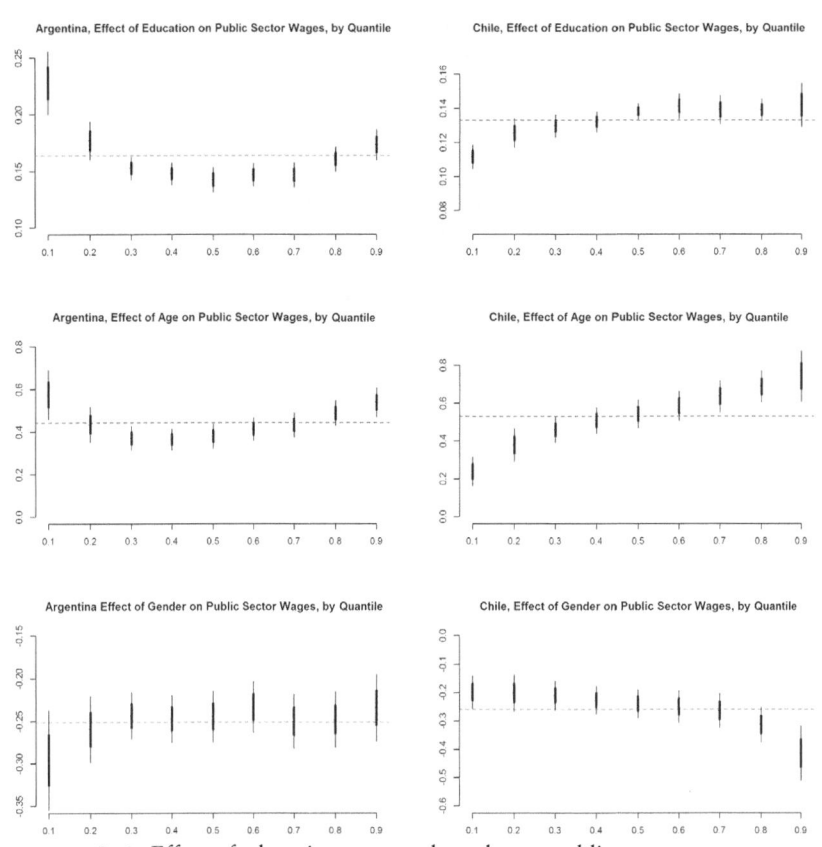

FIGURE 8.6. Effect of education, age, and gender on public-sector wages, Argentina (EPH, 2009) and Chile (Casen, 2009)
*Note*: Estimates describe the marginal change in employee wages (ln) by quantile. Full estimate results are given in Tables 8.A.2. and 8.A.3 in the appendix to this chapter.

and tenure on the job (only for Argentina). We also interact these variables with public employment. Figure 8.6 describes model results for the main covariates in Argentina and Chile, based on Tables 8.A.1 and 8.A.2 in the appendix. As in the estimates described in Figure 8.5, each plot in Figure 8.6 describes the marginal effect of each covariate on the wages (ln), for nine different wage quantiles. Thus, it allows us to establish the conditions that shape marginal increases in public-sector wages in either country.

In establishing the conditions behind the Argentine public-sector premium over private sector wages, both returns from skills (education) as well as other compositional characteristics matter, as shown by Figure 8.6. Figure 8.6 only analyzes public-sector employees in both countries, allowing for comparison within the public sector.[8] The first plot (upper-left) shows returns from education in the Argentine public sector for all income groups. Clearly, the most significant gains go to the lowest-income workers (quantile 0.1). By contrast, in Chile (upper-right plot), education generates positive returns, but the effect is considerably stronger for the higher quantiles.

The effect of older age (proxying for seniority) is very large and positive for Argentine public-sector employees at all income levels (middle-left plot). It benefits the lowest- and highest-income quantiles the most and the middle quantiles the least, although it is positive for all. In Chile, using age as a proxy for seniority – the middle-right plot – we observe a significant premium given to older employees at all income levels, although the effect diminishes for the lower quantiles and grows for higher quantiles, in contrast to the patterns we observe in Argentina.

The largest compositional effect on Argentine wages is associated with gender. The bottom plot shows the negative marginal effect of being a woman on public-sector wages. The effect is very large, showing a significant bias against women employees, which is more pronounced in the lower quantiles, even when it is not as large as in the private sector. In the private sector, women in the lowest quantile earn a remarkable 42-percent-lower wage vis-à-vis their male counterparts: e.g. $1 - \exp(-0.55) = 0.423$. The income difference for the largest quantile is a still-significant 26 percent: e.g. $1 - \exp(-0.3) = 0.74$. In the public sector, we see that women in the lowest quantiles are the most discriminated against, whereas the negative effect of gender bias declines in the upper quantiles. By contrast, female labor discrimination (in the bottom-right plot) in the Chilean public sector increases in the higher quantiles. As in Argentina, female public employees experienced a negative marginal effect on their wages compared to men, but the largest effect is at higher levels of income. More surprisingly, although not shown in this graph, gender discrimination is worse in the public than in the private sector. We find that unexpected gender effects are deserving of further attention, given that Chilean public-sector wage premiums are higher on those quantiles, despite gender discrimination.

---

[8] Results for tenure in Argentina and hours worked in both countries are in the appendix to this chapter.

In short, in line with our expectations, the results in this section show that public-sector wage premiums are targeted to poorer voters in Argentina and to middle-class voters in Chile. These results are robust to the inclusion of other covariates that also affect wage determination, which we have analyzed in this last section. Additionally, wage inequality has different determinants in each country. Returns from education in the Argentine public sector are greater than those in the private sector in the lowest quantiles and below the private sector for upper quantiles, whereas in the Chilean public sector they are always greater than the private sector and increase in the higher quantiles for all employees (public and private). Finally, we show that public-sector wage premiums are also shaped by compositional issues related to differences in the age and gender of public employees.

## 8.4 CONCLUDING REMARKS

In previous chapters, we show that not all voters value equally the non-policy benefits provided by parties. Further, we estimate voting models showing that voters from different socioeconomic strata have differing propensities to change their vote if expecting to receive patronage benefits. In this chapter, we test whether public-sector wages reward those groups of voters who display the most intense electoral sensitivity for patronage resources in Chapter 6.

To test the implications of our model, we take advantage of household income data collected by the statistical agencies of Argentina and Chile. We consider wage premiums as a good indicator of the investment of politicians in different socioeconomic groups and measure whether the most sensitive voters – e.g. voters who provide the highest electoral return to patronage spending – are also the ones receiving the highest wage premiums. We expected support for two distinct findings: first, larger public-sector wage premiums in Argentina than in Chile, given the larger effect of patronage expectations on the vote in the former country; second, wage premiums that benefit the most electorally sensitive voters in each country – low-income voters in Argentina and middle-to-upper income voters in Chile.

Our results confirm both expectations. First, public-sector wage premiums are considerably larger in Argentina than in Chile. These differences are particularly noteworthy at the lower-level quantiles, with wage premiums in Argentina being almost four times larger than those in Chile. Second, Argentina provides higher public-sector wage premiums to low-income voters, whereas the Chilean public sector provides higher premiums to voters in the middle-to-upper quantiles – both results are in line with the sensitivity of these groups of voters to patronage expectation presented in Chapter 6.

Our results are robust to the inclusion of a number of covariates which also affect wage determination. In analyzing those covariates, we show that returns to education are much larger at the upper quantiles in Chile than in Argentina. In the highest quantiles, returns per year of education in Chile almost doubled those observed in Argentina. Using a variety of quantile specifications, this chapter confirms that wage premiums disproportionally reward lower-income public-sector employees in Argentina. Results are also supportive of our argument in Chile, although estimates of premium wages for the upper-middle-income (C3) socioeconomic group were below expectations. Our findings also confirm perceptions of the Chilean public sector as being more meritocratic than its Argentine counterpart (Iacovella, 2006: 543; Longo 2006), with lower political gains also resulting in lower wage premiums. However, different from prior accounts, we find an electoral rational for rewarding sensitive voters in the upper quantiles of the wage distribution in Chile (but not in Argentina).

Our findings regarding public-sector wage premiums involve a period of high fiscal revenue as the commodities' boom fed the treasuries of both countries. Hence, these patterns were not the result of fiscal constraints but of agency in distributing the windfall produced by an exogenous shock, which fed into both economies. Moreover, we are confident that these correlations are not generated by reverse causation, with higher wage premiums generating larger expectations on the benefited groups of voters. Figures 8.A.1 and 8.A.2 in the appendix to this chapter provide information on the correlation between socioeconomic status and voters' distributive expectation in our survey. As in Chapter 4, these figures combine expectations by political party, but instead of organizing respondents on the ideological spectrum, they separate them by socioeconomic status. Figure 8.A.1 shows that there is no variation on distributive expectations regarding public-sector jobs from the main political parties across voters of different income levels in Chile. Therefore, the patterns of sensitivity we measured in Chapter 6 were not accompanied by changes in public-job expectations. Figure 8.A.2 shows the same correlation for Argentine voters across different socioeconomic categories for each of the main parties. We only found slightly higher expectations with respect to the PJ among the lower-income (D2), but not the upper-lower-income (D1), respondents, both of whom benefitted from wage premiums. In sum, we are confident that the results presented here are in line with the expectations of our theory and provide evidence that politicians respond to the incentives generated by voters' intense preferences.

# 9

## Back to Policy Offers

Since democratization, political parties in Argentina and Chile have pursued different policy strategies to win the support of voters. Our framework proposes that such policy differences are closely related to the constraints and opportunities that are provided by non-policy endowments. In Chapter 1 we noted that if two candidates offer the exact same policy but one of them has a non-policy advantage – e.g. higher perceived managerial competence – then voters should opt for the advantaged party on Election Day (Miller and Schofield, 2003; Schofield, 2003). We then asked if the losing candidate should still cater to the preferences of the median voter or, instead, cultivate a smaller subset of voters further to the left or right of the political spectrum. In previous chapters we focused on the advantages that non-policy politics provided to parties. We now turn our attention to how non-policy politics shapes the policy offers that parties make. In this chapter we describe how the availability of non-policy endowments shapes the parties' optimal policy responses.

In doing so, we relate our argument to the already described difference in patterns of electoral competition across both studied countries. On the one hand, as we noted, Peronists and Radicals switched policy positions in response to changes in the preferences of voters, forming coalitions with smaller parties on the left and right of the political spectrum. For example, President Carlos S. Menem forged close ties with the conservative Unión de Centro Democrático (Democratic Center Union) (U.Ce.De) to enact sweeping market reforms in the early 1990s (Gibson, 1996; Stokes, 1999).[1] It was

---

[1] At the time, the UCR was veering to the right as well, selecting Governor Eduardo Angeloz as its 1988 presidential candidate. Meanwhile, the influence of the more progressive

also the strategy of President Nestor Kirchner in 2003, when he steered Peronists back to the left and recruited activists from the Frente Grande, FREPASO, Socialists, as well as a large number of former-UCR majors and governors. The realignments of Peronists and Radicals followed voters' concerns with high inflation in early 1990 and with high unemployment in early 2000.[2]

On the other hand, Chilean parties advocated consistent policy positions and cultivated steady constituencies since democratization in 1989. They also coalesced into stable policy coalitions, oftentimes at arm's length of the preferences of the median Chilean voter (Luna, 2010; Navia et al., 2009). In spite of the moderate positions held by a majority of voters, Chileans have elected non-centrist presidential candidates since 1999. In all, while the largest parties in Argentina offered policies that closely aligned with the public's policy mood, Chilean parties have stayed the course by seemingly ignoring the electoral preferences of voters at large and focusing instead on the policy preferences of their core constituency.

In this chapter, we provide a rationale for such different types of multiparty competition. More specifically, we describe the effect of non-policy endowments on the parties' ability to switch their prior policy positions. We model the constraints and opportunities that result from differences in the availability of non-policy resources and, in doing so, provide new insights into the non-policy determinants of policy offers in Argentina and Chile.

The organization of this chapter is as follows: First, we describe the expectations from our theory, explaining how non-policy endowments constrain or facilitate policy switches in multiparty systems. Our model is concerned with the optimal policy offer that parties should make, given their non-policy advantages or disadvantages. Second, we describe the optimal strategies of parties when voters alter their non-policy preferences, or when in the presence of non-policy heterogeneity among voters. Finally, we discuss at greater length whether non-policy incentives shape the observable strategies of politicians in Argentina and Chile and how

---

"Renovacion y Cambio" faction led by former-President Raul R. Alfonsín faltered. The shift to the right by the Peronists and the Radicals in the early 1990s explains the emergence of the FREPASO in 1993, a center-left party originally founded by left-leaning dissidents from the Peronists.

[2] According to Schiumerini (2016: 21), Argentines grew supportive of state intervention due to disappointment with neoliberal reforms and "the policies of kirchnerismo tracked the preferences of the electorate, rather than the other way around."

they may differ from their optimal choices, as well as the implications of our analysis for the subsequent political evolution of parties in both countries.

### 9.1 NON-POLICY ADVANTAGES AND OPTIMAL POLICY OFFERS

In the last twenty years, significant advances in spatial models of voting have begun to close the gap between formal results and empirical observations of electoral competition. In an excellent review of the literature, Adams (2012) describes the extent to which models and empirical observations are beginning to converge as formal researchers incorporate more realistic utility functions to explain voters' preferences, whereas collective efforts to collect survey data allow scholars to empirically test their models. This process includes probabilistic voting models, more realistic assumptions about the relative costs of switching policies, a better understanding of valence determinants of vote choice, and distinct levels of voters' attention to policy changes.[3]

Just as scholarly attention shifts from positional issues to valence ones, comparative data now provides evidence of significant cross-country variation in non-policy assessments. Studies using the Comparative Study of Electoral Systems (CSES), for example, show significant variation in the importance that voters attach not only to ideology, but to valence considerations as well. As shown in this book, there are also significant differences in the extent to which ideology and non-policy assessments relate to each other. For example, while voters' ideological positions and economic competence assessments are uncorrelated in Argentina, they are closely connected in Chile. Such differences, we argue, constrain the policy offers that parties can make when seeking to maximize the vote.

#### a) Generalized Non-Policy Advantage

As noted by Adams (2012: 408), political parties or candidates who are viewed as more competent, trustworthy, and charismatic "may enjoy election advantages that are not tied directly to the current positions they stake out on positional dimensions." Parties with a critical advantage should do better electorally by taking on the positions of the median

---

[3] See Adams, Merrill, and Grofman (2005); Ansolabehere and Snyder (2000); Bruter et al. (2010); Clarke et al. (2011); Clark and Leiter (2014); Groseclose (2001); Laver and Sergenti (2012); Schofield and Sened (2006); Serra (2010, 2011).

voter, because other parties will not be able to match their policies and attract as many voters. Vote-seeking parties in that situation will have incentives to cash in on their stronger position by selecting centrist positions and crowding out disadvantaged parties.[4] Building on those insights, we combine our survey data with an algorithm developed by Adams, Merrill, and Grofman (2005) to estimate the optimal policy offer of parties in Argentina and Chile. We measure whether or not parties that enjoy a non-policy advantage move toward the policy preference of the median voter and whether disadvantaged parties move to more extreme policy locations. Our expectation is that, assuming a normal distribution of voters, parties that all voters perceive, on average, as having a non-policy advantage (e.g. better at managing the economy) should take on the policy preferences of the more central voters, whereas disadvantaged parties should move centrifugally toward more extreme policy positions.

### b) Non-Policy Advantage for a Subset of Ideologically Akin Voters

When parties' non-policy assessments are intertwined with policy preferences, changing policy stances may fail to deliver a larger number of votes. Parties benefiting from higher non-policy assessments among a subgroup of voters, who also share policy preferences, may derive uncertain benefits from shifting their policy offers. The association of policy preferences with perceptions about non-policy endowments makes it harder to assess the potential impact of modifying electoral offers on voters who may also update their non-policy assessments of the party in response to the policy shift. A detailed discussion of the mechanism behind this effect is presented by Schofield (2003) in his *Valence Competition in the Stochastic Spatial Model*, when focusing on party activists as a crucial non-policy resource:

> By contributing time and money to the candidate, activists allow the candidate to advertise his (or her) policies and persuade otherwise uncommitted voters that the candidate is a suitable choice. In this case, the activist-generated valence will be a function of the candidate position. It is natural to assume that the effect of contributions will be concave (displaying decreasing marginal returns). Consequently, the valence effect of activist contributions will be concave.
> (Schofield, 2003: 373)

---

[4] Citing the seminal work of Schofield (2003), Adams (2012: 407) states: "political parties with weak valence images will tend to shift their positions away from those of high-valence parties, because if low-valence parties match the policy offerings of high-valence parties, the low-valence parties will then suffer electoral catastrophe because voters will choose parties strictly on the basis of valence considerations."

In this case, as voters are less connected with party activists, the party faces decreasing campaign returns. Therefore, to maximize electoral returns, the party needs to weigh the policy preferences of the median voter and the declining marginal returns from demobilized activists who have intense and shared policy preferences. As we described in Chapter 7, in reference to the informational value of territorial activists in terms of returns for distribution – to avoid Dixit and Londregan's (1996) "leaky bucket" – seeking the policy preference of the median voter may generate efficiency losses by reducing ideological activists' campaign efforts and efficiency in persuading voters. Therefore, when non-policy assessments vary among groups of voters with distinct ideological preferences, political parties have fewer incentives to shift their policy offers and are more likely to move in the ideological direction preferred by voters with whom they enjoy a non-policy advantage. Hence, we expect political parties with a perceived non-policy advantage among a sub-group k of voters will move to a weighted location between the preference of the median voter, $\mu^m$ and the preference of median voter of the group k, $\mu_k^m$.

Two important preconditions for parties moving to policy locations other than the median voter are: (i) the ideological weight parameter has to be strictly smaller than zero, $\alpha < 0$ and (ii) the ideological distance and the non-policy assessment of parties cannot be strictly independent from each other. Conversely, as $\alpha \to 0$ and when the voters have policy and non-policy assessments of parties that are strictly orthogonal to each other, the party's equilibrium converges toward the overall median voter.[5]

### c) Voter Heterogeneity and Policy Offers

Voters are not only heterogeneous on policy and non-policy preferences, but also along demographic dimensions such as gender, social status, ethnicity, and religion. Different demographic groups can assign different weight to parties' policy offers in making their electoral choices, while also sharing distinctive policy preferences. For instance, we have shown that richer Chilean voters care more about ideological distance (higher $\alpha$) when casting their ballot and have more right-wing policy preferences than their poorer counterparts.

---

[5] For a formal proof see appendix 4.1 in Adams, Merrill, and Grofman (2005).

Following our general argument, we expect that differences in the salience that voters attach to policy and non-policy benefits will make some voters more influential than others when parties define their optimal ideological offers. Because parties should target the most sensitive voters with each type of benefit (*parameter effect*), voters with higher $\alpha$ should be more relevant to the definition of parties' equilibrium positions. In the case of policy offers, this effect should heighten the influence of preferences held by the most sensitive groups of voters (*compositional effect*). Because the most sensitive voters may have different preferences from the median voter, voter heterogeneity on demographic categories can influence the optimal policy positions of parties. The mechanism involved in this influence, thereby, includes both the salience that each group of voters assigns to policy offers (*parameter effect*) and their aggregated ideological preferences (*compositional effect*).

The rest of the chapter describes our statistical operationalization of these effects to assess the incentives they generate for vote-seeking parties. We estimate optimal policy offers using the algorithm of Adams, Merrill, and Grofman (2005) for multiparty settings. We use synthetic data to illustrate comparative statics of the model. Then, drawing on our own data in Argentina and Chile, we describe how differences in the weight that richer and poorer voters give to policy and non-policy benefits yield significant biases in responsiveness.

## 9.2 ESTIMATING THE OPTIMAL POLICY OFFERS OF PARTIES

We start with the utility function described in Chapter 2 (Eq. 2.1), where individuals weigh the policy and non-policy offers made by parties as well as their non-policy endowments:

$$U(V_{ik}) = -\alpha_i(x_i - L_k)^2 + \beta_i T_{ik} + \gamma_{ik} \qquad \text{(Eq. 2.1)}$$

Where $x_i$ describes the self-reported location of a voter in the left–right policy dimension, $L_k$ describes the reported policy proposal $L$ of party $k$, $(x_i - L_k)^2$ describes the distance between the voter and the location of the proposal of party $k$, the term $-\alpha$ describes the disutility for a policy that is further removed from the voter's preferred location, $\beta T_{ik}$ describes utility $\beta$ for the non-programmatic term $T_{ik}$, and $\delta_{ik}$ describes a voter-specific random utility term. We then assume that voters select the party or candidate that provides the highest utility from a multinomial logit distribution, with vote choice as the dependent variable:

$$\Pr(V_{ik}) = \frac{e^{U(V_{ik})}}{\sum_{k=1}^{K} e^{U(V_{ik})}} \forall i, k \qquad \text{(Eq. 9.1)}$$

In previous chapters, we provide estimates of the weight parameters $\alpha$ and $\beta$ from our survey data, considering a variety of non-policy benefits: competence, distributive expectations, and connections to party networks. Here, we estimate the multinomial logit model in Equation (9.2), with parameters by socioeconomic group and country.

Once we estimate the vote choice parameters, we then feed these values to the equilibrium algorithm. The equilibrium algorithm derives the optimal policy location taking the parameters estimated in Equations (9.1) and (9.2) as inputs then searching iteratively for optimal policy offer that maximizes its vote share $EV_k(\mathbb{L}, \alpha)$:

$$EV_k(\mathbb{L}, \alpha) = \sum_j P_{ik}(\mathbb{L}, \alpha) \qquad \text{(Eq. 9.2)}$$

In Equation (9.3), Adams, Merrill, and Grofman (2005) differentiate the optimal location of each party $L_k^o \in \mathbb{L}$ when $\alpha = 0$, solving for the last occurrence of $L_k^o$ to find the location at which party $k$ maximizes its vote share:

$$L_k^o = \frac{\sum_i P_{ik}(\mathbb{L}, 0)[1 - P_{ik}(\mathbb{L}, 0)]x_i}{\sum_j P_{jk}(\mathbb{L}, 0)[1 - P_{jk}(\mathbb{L}, 0)]} \qquad \text{(Eq. 9.3)}$$

By iteratively solving for each party preferred location, $max(L_k^o)$, the algorithm finds the set of party policy locations where no party can unilaterally select a new policy position without losing votes.[6] Notice that estimating the equilibrium strategy of party $k$ does not require information about the actual vote choice of the respondents as in Equations (9.1) and (9.2). The algorithm also has no stochastic component and mechanically updates the spatial location of each party in response to changes in the location of all other parties, with fixed proximity and non-proximity parameters.[7] Further, it is important to note that the observed position and the optimal position need not to be the same, $L_k \neq L_k^o$, given that the ideological position perceived by voters could differ from the optimal policy location. We coded this algorithm in WinBUGS 3.1.4 and in

---

[6] For proof of the conditions that guarantee the existence and uniqueness of Nash equilibria for each party see Adams, Merill, and Grofman (2005), appendix 4.1.
[7] We use WinBUGS 1.4.2 (Spiegelhalter et al., 2003) and R 2.15 to estimate the conditional choice models and to retrieve the equilibrium location of parties.

# Back to Policy Offers

TABLE 9.1. *Parameters and variables in the synthetic dataset*

| Term | Description |
| --- | --- |
| $x_i$ | Ideological location of voter $i$ on a left-right dimension: <br> Dataset 1: One hundred voters, $x_i \sim N(5,2)$ <br> Dataset 2: One hundred voters, $x_i \sim U[0,10]$ |
| $-\alpha_i$ | Weight that voters attach to policy proximity (disutility of ideological distance). <br> Datasets 1 and 2: $\alpha_i \equiv \{-0.02, -0.04, -0.06, -0.08, -0.1, -0.12, -0.14\}$ |
| $\beta_i$ | Weight that voters attach to the non-policy benefit $T$ provided by party $k$, $T_{ik}$. <br> Datasets 1 and 2: $\beta_i \equiv \{0.2, 0.4, 0.6, 0.8, 1, 1.2, 1.4\}$ |
| $T_{ik}$ | Non-policy endowment $T$ of party $k$ as assessed by voter $i$. <br> Datasets 1 and 2: $T_{ik} \equiv \{1:7 \text{ for each } k \in K\}$ |
| $f(T_{ik}, x_i \mid \rho)$ | Level of association of the policy and non-policy parameters:[8] <br> Datasets 1 and 2: $\rho \equiv \{0, 0.2, 0.4, 0.6\}$ <br> where rho = 0 indicates no functional relationship between $T_{ik}$ and $x_i$ |

R 3.1, generating similar results. Both the WinBUGS and R code are in Section 9.A in the appendix to this chapter, while replication materials are available to download on the authors' websites.

## a) Describing the Impact of Non-Policy Resources on Optimal Policy Offers

The algorithm Adams, Merrill, and Grofman (2005) propose allows us to operationalize the implications of our theoretical framework and to illustrate the effect of non-policy endowments on the optimal policy offers of parties using synthetic data. The synthetic dataset includes 3,294,172 draws of 100 voters with normally distributed ideological preferences and 3,294,172 draws of 100 voters with uniformly distributed ideological preferences. Consistent with our survey data, the ideological space ranges from a minimum of zero on the left of the political spectrum to a

---

[8] The level of association between the policy and non-policy parameters for each of the five parties was drawn from the following R function:

create.valence <- function(alpha,V, S){ val.temp<-abs(rnorm(voters,V*(1-rho*(abs(ideology-S))/10),.1))}

Where the parameter rho takes on values of zero (no association), 0.2, 0.4, 0.6 (high association).

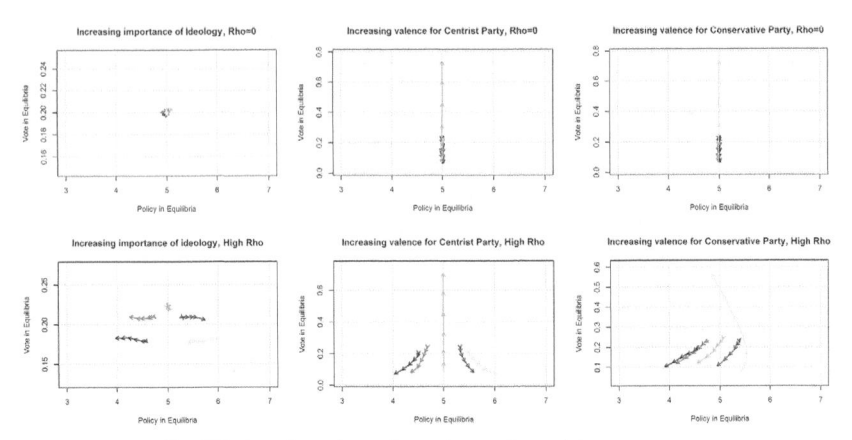

FIGURE 9.1. Equilibrium location of parties and model parameters
*Note*: All plots from the normally distributed synthetic data with five parties.

maximum of ten on the right, with other model parameters as described in Table 9.1.

The total number of elections used to evaluate the equilibrium location of parties combines seven different values of $-\alpha_i$, seven different values of $\beta_i$, four values describing the association between the policy and non-policy dimensions, and seven non-policy assessments scores for five different parties. This creates $7 \times 7 \times 4 \times 7 \times 7 \times 7 \times 7 \times 7 = 3,294,172$ electoral scenarios with normally distributed ideological preferences and 3,294,172 with uniformly distributed ideological preferences, for a total of 6,588,344 parameter configurations.

Figure 9.1 describes the effect of the parameters of interest on parties' equilibrium positions providing six different scenarios. In all six plots, the horizontal axis describes the left–right equilibrium position of parties while the vertical axis describes the expected vote share at their equilibrium location. The plots in Figure 9.1 describe systems with five competing parties and a normal distribution of ideological preferences among voters, while using arrows to describe changes in the equilibrium location and vote for parties as we increase or decrease model parameters.

### *Downsian Convergence*

The top three plots describe scenarios of Downsian convergence with changes in the salience of ideology and introducing asymmetries in non-policy resources, while keeping policy and non-policy offers by parties orthogonal in voters' perception. First, we start describing a Downsian convergence scenario in the top-left plot, where voters perceived parties as being equally endowed with the non-policy trait $T_{ik}$. These non-policy endowments are statistically independent from the policy preferences, $x_i$, so that $T_{i1} = T_{i2} = \ldots = T_{i5}$ and $\rho = 0$. As policy and non-policy assessments are strictly orthogonal ($\rho = 0$), parties will converge to the location of the median voter. This is true even when we decrease the value of $\alpha$ from zero to -0.14, thus making ideology more salient in electoral choices. Irrespective of how much weight voters attach to policy offers, the position of parties will only diverge from the median voter if non-policy assessments are not strictly independent from non-policy preferences.[9] This will be important in the Argentine case, where policy and non-policy endowments are perceived as orthogonal to each other for the two largest parties, whose equilibrium policy locations are shifted toward the center of the ideological space.

The upper-middle and upper-right plots also provide examples of Downsian convergence, where a party has a significant non-policy advantage but the policy and non-policy dimensions remain strictly orthogonal to each other ($\rho = 0$). In this case, all the parties remain at the center of the policy space, but the advantaged party benefits electorally by increasing its vote share at the expense of the disadvantaged parties. As the non-policy advantage of one party increases, its vote share goes up but its policy position remains unchanged. Assuming that all parties are vote maximizers, in the strictest sense, either moderate or conservative parties should be more than willing to move to their equilibrium location, where the preference of the median voter lays if they enjoy a non-policy advantage, as shown in the center or right plot, respectively.

### Non-Downsian Equilibria

The bottom three plots focus on scenarios where not all parties have incentives to converge, highlighting how asymmetries on non-policy endowments correlated with voters' policy preferences generate distinct incentives regarding optimal policy offers. This was done by setting $\rho = 0.6$. Like Adams, Merrill, and Grofman (2005), we expect that

---

[9] Schofield (2003) provides a formal description of this problem: "The consequence of the variation of [valence] across the candidates is that, when all candidates choose positions at the origin of the electoral distribution, they are not all viewed as identical by the electorate. Indeed, the highest valence candidate will gain a plurality for certain." (Schofield, 2003: 372) A pure-strategy Nash equilibrium at the bliss point, therefore, could only be assured when non-policy endowments are identical across candidates or when non-policy endowments are perceived as strictly independent.

increasing the voters' perceived salience for ideological considerations will drive parties to more extreme policy locations. When the mean non-policy endowments are relatively similar across parties, but different voters perceive different parties as offering better non-policy benefits, larger values of $\alpha$ will push parties further in the direction of the median preference of the mass of voters, for whom the party enjoys a larger non-policy advantage, thereby generating a centrifugal effect.

First, in the lower-left plot, we increase the disutility of ideological distance, $-\alpha$, for all voters, from zero to $-0.14$, which drives parties on the left of the political spectrum toward four, while parties on the right of the political spectrum move toward six.[10] Given that parties are equally endowed with similar non-policy resources, the vote shares of these parties remain almost unchanged.

Second, the lower-middle and lower-right plot of Figure 9.1 describe cases where one party is perceived by voters as having a non-policy advantage while, at the same time, the policy and non-policy dimensions correlate to each other ($\rho = 0.6$). In this case, the party that has an advantage moves to take on the policy preferences of the median voter, while other parties are pushed toward onto less central policy offers. This scenario reflects Schofield's (2003) model, where an advantaged party occupies the center of the policy space, while other parties move in the direction of the mass of voters where their policy disadvantage is less severe. Because we are assuming vote-seeking parties, both the centrist and the conservative parties move to the location of the median voter, as their non-policy advantages becomes sufficiently large to gain more voters than defections among their core supporters in the center and right plots, respectively.

Our synthetic examples illustrate how asymmetries in non-policy endowments provide opportunities for policy responsiveness, conditional on voters having a disutility for policy distance (high $\alpha$) and on the association between policy and non-policy benefits (high $\rho$). Given that in most political systems there are asymmetries in non-policy endowments and policy and non-policy dimensions are not strictly uncorrelated (at least for some of the parties), we can estimate optimal policy offers and analyze under what conditions parties are responsive to the preferences of

---

[10] Estimates of Equations (9.1) and (9.2) in a dozen countries of Europe and Latin America returned values for the non-policy weight $\beta$ in the range of 0.6 and 1.2 and between $-0.03$ and $-0.16$ for $\alpha$. Values of $\beta = 0.6$ and $\alpha = -0.14$ are within the samples retrieved from actual data.

Back to Policy Offers

the median voter or to the preferences of their own ideological core constituency.

We have illustrated the way in which our theoretical framework works to define optimal policy offers by parties relying on synthetic data. Using the descriptive evidence from earlier chapters, this framework allows us to explain the less central and more consistent policy offers observed among Chilean parties. Chilean voters attach more weight to ideological considerations, $\alpha$, and perceive parties' policy and non-policy offers as closely connected, so that distinct groups of voters see different parties as having a non-policy advantage. Moreover, none of the parties have an asymmetric non-policy advantage, allowing them to capture the center of the policy space where the median voter is located. As a result, as in the lower-left plot of Figure 9.1, the optimal policy offers of Chilean parties are further to the left and right of the political spectrum.

Argentine voters attach less weight to ideological considerations and perceive the Peronist party as enjoying significant non-policy advantages – on partisan networks, distributive expectations, and macroeconomic competence – with voters on the left and right of the political spectrum having roughly similar perceptions of parties' non-policy endowments. This non-policy advantage, therefore, should generate centripetal incentives similar to the ones described in the upper-center and right plots of Figure 9.1. Consequently, we expect the Peronists to be responsive to changes in the policy preferences of the median voter. Indeed, as non-policy resources are uncorrelated with voters' ideological views for the two main political parties in Argentina, both should concentrate on the center of the ideological space, and the PJ should receive more votes, given its various non-policy advantages.

## 9.3 THE EQUILIBRIUM LOCATION OF PARTIES IN ARGENTINA AND CHILE

What policy offers should political parties in Argentina and Chile make? Using all the information from prior chapters, we analyze the expected distribution of policy offers in both countries as well as the impact that distinct groups of voters have on those positions. We start by describing the effect of non-policy politics on the policy offers of Argentine and Chilean parties and then describe how varying levels of policy attention and preferences by distinct groups of voters yield different incentives for optimal policy offers on Election Day.

## a) Estimating Equilibrium Policies in Argentina and Chile

We begin by establishing an equilibrium baseline for each political party in Argentina and Chile. Subsequently, we compare the effect of different parameters and explore how changes in the sample of voters yield different policy offers. In this way, we not only describe the effect of the model parameters on the policy offers of Argentine and Chilean parties but, as important, the compositional effect that results from giving more attention to different groups of voters.

To analyze the optimal policy offers in Argentina and Chile, we draw from Tables 6.A.1 and 6.A.2 in the appendix to Chapter 6, which describe the weight that voters attach to ideological considerations, $-\alpha$, to economic competence, $\beta_1$, to their proximity to partisan networks, $\beta_2$, and to expectations of receiving handouts, patronage, and pork: $\beta_{3,1}, \beta_{3,2}, \beta_{3,3}$. The values of these parameters are reported in Table 9.2. Policy estimates combine the survey data with the parameter estimates reported in Table 9.2. For example, the equilibrium location of Chilean parties conditional on patronage spending solves for $L_k^*$ in Equation (9.5), using model 2 of Chile in Table 9.2:

$$U(V_{ik}) = -0.0373 \left(Ideology_i - L_k^*\right)^2 + 1.0368\ Competence_{ik}$$
$$+ \ldots + 0.1757\ Patronage_{ik} \qquad \text{(Eq. 9.5)}$$

Notice that all variables and parameters are already available, except the equilibrium locations and vote share, which are solved for by the algorithm. The variables for ideology, competence, and patronage were reported by respondents in the survey, while the parameters of the model were estimated from the vote choice multinomial model in Chapter 6. For our baseline equilibrium position, we iteratively solve for each party's location. Equilibrium locations for the Argentine and Chilean parties are depicted in Figure 9.2, which uses the parameters from model 2 in Table 9.2, combined with all observations in our survey. As in Figure 9.1, the equilibrium locations are reported in the horizontal axis and the expected vote share on the vertical axis.

The optimal ideological locations for each party in Argentina and Chile are presented in Figure 9.2. The algorithm provides reasonable estimates of the location of parties, although it neither uses the location of parties reported by respondents, nor does it consider information about their actual vote choice. In all, parties move in the expected

TABLE 9.A.2. *Multinomial estimates of key model parameters,* $-\alpha, \beta_1, \beta_2, \beta_{3,1}, \beta_{3,2}, \beta_{3,3}$, *from Tables 6.A.1 and 6.A.2 in Appendix 6*

| | Argentina | | | | | Chile | | | |
|---|---|---|---|---|---|---|---|---|---|
| | Model1 | Model2 | Model3 | Model4 | | Model1 | Model2 | Model 3 | Model4 |
| Ideological distance $(-\alpha)$ | -0.0205*** (0.003) | -0.0205*** (0.003) | -0.0184*** (0.003) | -0.0194*** (0.003) | Ideological distance $(-\alpha)$ | -0.0381*** (0.003) | -0.0373*** (0.003) | -0.0364*** (0.003) | -0.0359*** (0.003) |
| Competence to manage the economy ($\beta_1$) | 1.1262*** (0.066) | 1.0926*** (0.066) | 1.021*** (0.067) | 0.9889*** (0.068) | Competence to manage the economy ($\beta_1$) | 1.0474*** (0.056) | 1.0368*** (0.056) | 1.0273*** (0.056) | 1.0142*** (0.056) |
| Proximity to network of activists ($\beta_2$) | 0.4917*** (0.054) | 0.4661*** (0.054) | 0.4362*** (0.055) | 0.4186*** (0.056) | Proximity to network of activists ($\beta_2$) | 0.3321*** (0.041) | 0.3279*** (0.041) | 0.3267*** (0.041) | 0.3219*** (0.041) |
| Handouts ($\beta_{3,1}$) | 0.0923*** (0.032) | | | -0.0347 (0.036) | Handouts ($\beta_{3,1}$) | 0.0679** (0.032) | | | 0.0014 (0.036) |
| Patronage ($\beta_{3,2}$) | | 0.2433*** (0.038) | | 0.1707*** (0.042) | Patronage ($\beta_{3,2}$) | | 0.1757*** (0.035) | | 0.134*** (0.039) |
| Pork ($\beta_{3,3}$) | | | 0.2439*** (0.028) | 0.1975*** (0.030) | Pork ($\beta_{3,3}$) | | | 0.1552*** (0.026) | 0.1314*** (0.027) |

*Note:* Estimation details in Chapter 6. Parameters relevant for the equilibrium exercise are reported in this table.

194                           *Non-Policy Politics*

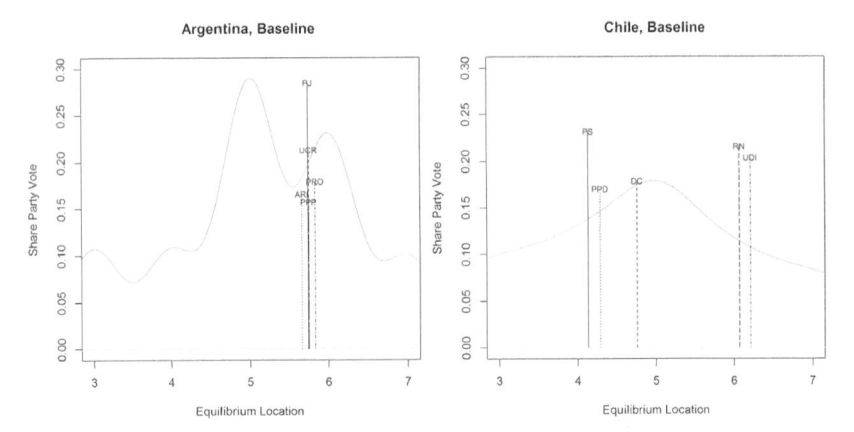

FIGURE 9.2. Equilibrium location of parties in Argentina and Chile, 2007
*Note*: Equilibrium location of parties in Argentina and Chile with parameter estimates from Table 9.2. Background line describes the density of the self-reported ideological location of voters in the survey (sample means of $\alpha = -0.027$ for Argentina and $\alpha = -0.043$). The ideological scale has been reduced to 3–7 for visualization purposes.

direction using how much voters weigh the policy and non-policy benefits in the portfolio of parties as inputs.

The left plot in Figure 9.2 shows equilibrium locations and expected vote shares in Argentina, where the PJ enjoys larger endowments of non-policy resources. Results display strong centripetal effects, with parties gravitating toward the center of the ideological scale. This is due to the lack of correlation between the voters' policy preferences and non-policy endowments described in Chapters 4 and 5. While the Peronists enjoy a sizable advantage and occupy the exact location of the median voter, crowding out is limited by the fact that there are very small penalties (and advantages) from moving to the left or right of the ideological space. This is similar to the scenario depicted in the bottom-center plot of Figure 9.1. The most important effect of an asymmetry in non-policy endowments is observed in the expected vote shares, which are much larger for the Peronists, although the differences in the optimal ideological location is extremely small. Indeed, all Argentine parties are concentrated between 5.5 and 6. Both the PJ and the UCR are in the middle of the distribution, while the ARI is to its left and the PRO to its right, but with a very small distance between all of them.

In Chile, where policy preferences and non-policy endowments correlate with each other, we see larger dispersion in the optimal policy location of parties. We find the optimal policy offer of Socialists to be on the left, winning a larger share of votes than the other parties. The optimal position of the Christian Democrats is at the center, while the UDI and the RN are located on the right. As it is possible to observe, the equilibrium location of parties is attenuated toward the center when compared to the ideological placement by voters in the survey described in Chapter 4.[11] Figure 9.2 is similar to the bottom-left plot in Figure 9.1, where there is little asymmetry in non-policy endowments and voters' perceptions of non-policy resources are correlated with their ideological location. In this case, the Socialists have a small non-policy advantage, resulting in a larger expected vote share (on the vertical axis) and a slightly more moderate position than would be expected otherwise. Results from the equilibrium model describe the mechanism that limits policy responsiveness in Chile, with a slight centripetal effect for the Socialists and the two right-wing parties, but no significant changes in the rank-ordering from left to right.

The optimal party locations in both countries are different from where voters perceived the parties to be (see Chapter 4) because they are more concentrated toward the center. Thus, the optimal policy positions suggest incentives for convergence toward the median voter in both countries. Yet, these incentives are much stronger in Argentina than in Chile. In both cases, moreover, all parties keep their relative position in the policy space. These equilibrium positions provide the baseline for our next analysis, where we assess the impact of parametric and compositional effects on parties' policy attention.

## b) Voter Heterogeneity, Parametric Effects, and Compositional Effects on Policy Responsiveness

Our analysis of voter heterogeneity has emphasized the distinct attention that richer and poorer voters pay to policy in making their electoral choices, as well as their diverse policy preferences. Therefore, understanding the implications of our model for analyses of policy responsiveness to different groups of voters requires identifying the opportunities generated by both the parametric and the compositional effects on political parties'

---

[11] To "push" parties in a centrifugal direction, Adams, Merrill, and Grofman (2005) propose a "discount model," which allow voters to vote strategically and force parties closer to their positions. Alternative specifications with "discount" as well as models that adjust for assimilation and contrast can be requested from the authors.

equilibrium policy positions. In this section, we show those effects using our own Chilean data because only in Chile did we find statistically significant differences in the level of attention to policy paid by the upper-middle-income (C1) voters and lower-income (D) voters in their electoral calculus.

Our theory indicates that parties should pay more attention to the voters with more intense policy preferences (those with larger negative $-\alpha$ values). However, such attention should also induce distinct party offers because the median voter among richer Chilean voters is located in a different place than the median voter among the subset of poor voters. The median richer voter in Chile is considerably to the right of the median poorer voter (Chapter 4). Second, the more ideologically intense voters will also induce centrifugal incentives on the parties, pulling them away from median voters, as shown in the bottom-left plot of Figure 9.1. Their higher sensitivity increases the utility loss among voters for parties that move further away from them, thereby keeping parties rooted to more extreme policy locations than the median voter.

Remember that our model results show two different effects that shape parties' opportunities for choosing their optimal policy position: parameter effects (different importance that groups of voters attach to the policy and non-policy benefits delivered by parties) and a compositional effect (different median voter by groups of voters that have different distributions of policy preferences). Both effects shape the incentives of parties to move in the policy space. The higher salience of ideology increases centrifugal incentives of all parties, whereas different median voters shift the incentives of all parties to pay attention to voters in a particular location of the policy space.

A cautionary note about the impact of shifting the salience of ideological distance, $\alpha$, in those two countries needs to be offered; although levels are higher in Chile than in Argentina, the range of variation is quite limited in both countries. In Argentina, the minimum $\alpha = -0.02$ and the maximum $\alpha = -0.03$, whereas in Chile the minimum $\alpha = -0.03$ and the maximum $\alpha = -0.06$. That is, even the maximum level of $\alpha$ for Chile is about the same as the average one for Finland in 2011, Germany in 2009, Iceland in 2009, or Israel in 2006 and lower than the average one for the Netherlands in 2010 and Spain in 2008 (Calvo, Chang, and Hellwig, 2014). However, even when the differences across both countries are not as marked as the literature suggests with regards to the impact of policy preferences on voting behavior, the range of values is higher in Chile than in Argentina.

Back to Policy Offers 197

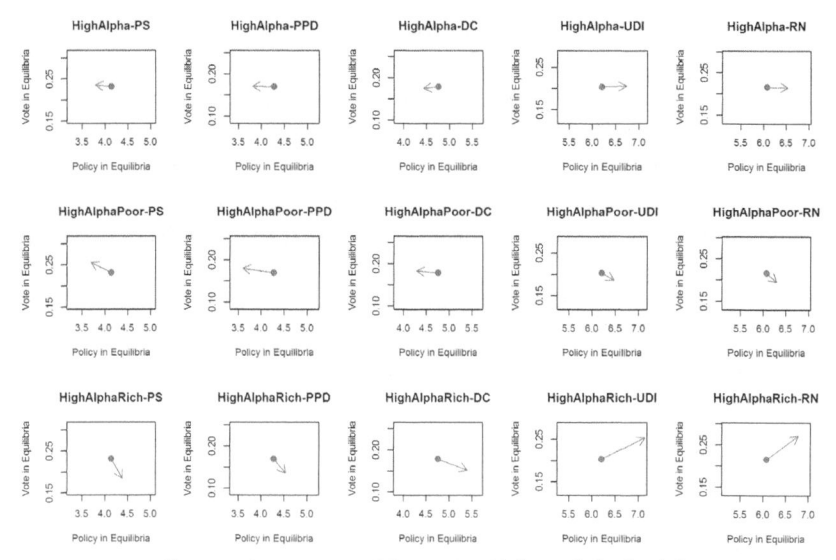

FIGURE 9.3. Changes in party equilibrium in Chile with high alpha
*Note*: Each figure describes the change from the baseline equilibrium (dot of the arrow) to the new location (head of the arrow) when model parameters are changed. The first row displays changes in equilibrium for all parties when the weight of ideology ($\alpha$) increases. The second row displays changes in equilibrium when the weight of ideology ($\alpha$) increases only among poor voters. The third row displays changes in equilibrium when the weight of ideology ($\alpha$) increases only among richer voters.

To better understand these effects (group preference composition and intensity of policy preferences), we present below a variety of models that map changes in party equilibrium for different parameter values and voter samples based on our Chilean data. Figure 9.3 departs from the baseline equilibrium positions defined for all five Chilean parties (setting $\alpha = -0.043$) in Figure 9.2. These equilibrium positions are marked by the dot at the center of each square, which corresponds to each of the five main political parties – with ideology in the horizontal axis and their vote share in the vertical axis.

The top plots in Figure 9.3 use the same data as before, but increase the average $\alpha$ of Chilean voters, thus setting $\alpha = -0.12$, while keeping all other variables at their means to calculate the new equilibrium positions, which are marked by the end of the arrows in each of the squares. These top five plots show that higher (more negative) values of $-\alpha$ generate centrifugal incentives for all five political parties. The PS and PPD are pushed to the left, as is the DC to a lesser extent, whereas the UDI and RN are pushed to the right. The centrifugal effect moves the PS from 4.14 to 3.78, the DC from 4.76 to 4.42, and the PPD from 4.28 to 3.8, showing the pull of the three *Concertación* parties to the left. By contrast, the two right-wing parties are pulled to the right, with RN moving from 6.21 to 6.73 and UDI from 6.07 to 6.54 (Table 9.A.1 in the appendix to this chapter). These results show the impact of shifting the parameter, $\alpha$, on the equilibrium positions of Chilean parties (parameter effect) and their centrifugal force.

The next two rows (middle and bottom) illustrate compositional effects. The middle row repeats the same exercise as the top row (keeps $\alpha = -0.12$ ), but restricts the sample to only the lower-income (D) respondents in our survey, which constitutes half of the sample. The bottom row, by contrast, also sets $\alpha = -0.12$ but considers the preferences of only the upper-middle-income (C1) voters, who are about 9 percent of our sample. We choose these two groups for our exercise because, in Chapter 6, we found significant differences on policy sensitivity between them. What kind of incentives does the different composition of poorer and richer voter preferences have on parties' optimal policy locations? Remember that poorer Chilean voters have more left-wing preferences than the average median voter, whereas the opposite is true for the richest Chilean voters (Chapter 4). Moreover, we are keeping constant a higher value of $\alpha$ to assess the incentives generated by this combination on political parties, but in reality the $\alpha$ for upper-middle-income (C1) voters is -0.055 and -0.03 for lower-income (D) voters, thereby generating diverse patterns of influence on parties' optimal policy positions. Hence, although the proportion of upper-middle-income (C1) voters in the electorate is only 9 percent, each of those richer voters is more influential on the general equilibrium policy positions of parties than each single lower-income (D) voter, thereby generating incentives to bias parties' ideological responsiveness.

The medium row shows that the more left-wing preferences of poorer voters push the equilibrium position of the PS, DC and PPD even more to the left than in the top plot. The PS moves from 4.14 to 3.69, the DC from 4.76 to 4.28, and the PPD from 4.28 to 3.6 (Table A.9.1 in the appendix to this chapter). Meanwhile, the share of PS vote increases by 2 percentage points and that of each of the other two *Concertación* parties grows by 1 point. By contrast the movement to the right by RN and UDI is attenuated in comparison with the top plot – that is, RN moves to 6.73 and UDI to 6.54 – and their share of votes fall by 2 percentage points each, as poorer voters are less likely to vote for the right-wing parties (Table A.9.1 in the

# Back to Policy Offers

appendix to this chapter). Thus, these results are strongly shaped by the more left-wing preferences of poorer Chilean voters, combined with an increase in the intensity of the effect of their ideological preferences on the vote, thereby highlighting the impact of compositional differences among voters' preferences on parties' incentives to choose a policy position.

The strongest impact generated by restricting the sample to the richest (C1) voters is on the total share of votes (bottom row of Figure 9.3). Votes fall substantially for the three parties in the *Concertación* and increase for the two right-wing parties. The PS declines from 23 percent to 18 percent, the DC from 18 percent to 15 percent, and the PPD from 17 percent to 14 percent; whereas RN grows from 20 percent to 25 percent and UDI from 22 percent to 27 percent (Table A.9.1 in the appendix to this chapter). Additionally, given the higher $\alpha$, these voters generate incentives for RN and the UDI to move substantially to the right, from 6.21 to 7.14 and from 6.07 to 6.79, respectively. Moreover, the more right-wing preferences of these voters (compositional effect) leads to even the *Concertación* parties shifting to a new equilibrium slightly to the right of their baseline position, with the PS moving from 4.14 to 4.38, the DC from 4.76 to 5.40, and the PPD from 4.28 to 4.54 (Table A.9.1 in the appendix to this chapter).

These last two rows, therefore, include the compositional effects of the more left-wing preferences of poorer Chilean voters and the more right-wing preferences of the richest ones, which heightened the incentives for changing party equilibria already produced by shifting the ideological salience parameter, $\alpha$. What is more remarkable is how the compositional preferences of the richest voters tamed the centrifugal effect produced by a higher $\alpha$ only for the *Concertación* parties, which are pushed toward the center. The importance of this effect is remarkable because the richest (C1) voters are effectively the most sensitive to parties' policy position (highest $\alpha$), although their $\alpha = -0.055$ is lower than the one used in this exercise.

What does this example tell us about voter heterogeneity and its potential to bias the attention of political parties? If Chilean political parties were to focus their attention only on poorer voters because they were to increase their ideological sensitivity, the incumbent parties in the *Concertación* should offer more left-wing policies. The effect on the right-wing parties would move them in a centrifugal direction in a milder way, driven by the smaller number of poorer voters on the right. By contrast, if politicians were only paying attention to the top 9 percent of voters (who in our real data are the most sensitive to parties' ideological offers), the effect on *all* parties would be a pull to the right. Even the two left-wing parties would have to move to the right in response to the incentives created by higher ideological salience of this group of voters, given their set of policy preference and their association with non-policy preferences, as described below. This effect should moderate the *Concertación* beyond the impact of institutional veto points derived from Pinochet's constitution and their own process of ideological revisionism in exile.

In sum, the incentives generated by changes in the sensitivity of voters along with the diverse composition of their preferences can lead parties to adopt distinct, electorally optimal positions. Given the higher $\alpha$ of richer voters, the original equilibrium positions of Chilean parties are already giving them a louder voice than their poorer counterparts and pulling left-wing parties toward more centrist positions, although not as much as in this exercise.

### c) The Effect of Non-Policy Resources on Policy Offers

Here, we add to the parametric and compositional effects produced by voters' policy preferences, by including the impact of the distribution of non-policy resources discussed in the prior sections. Remember that whether parties' non-policy resources are associated with the policy preferences of groups of voters, or orthogonal to their ideological views, generates different incentives on parties' search for equilibrium policy positions. Hence, our goal here is to illustrate the effect of the functional relationship between policy and non-policy benefits, in terms of the opportunities generated for parties' seeking to reach optimal policy positions to maximize their vote. We therefore compare the impact of increasing the $\alpha$ with that of increasing the $\beta$ for non-policy benefits that are either correlated with voters' ideological location – in this case competence evaluations – or are not associated with voters' policy preferences: distributive expectations. We choose these non-policy resources because our Chilean data shows a correlation, $\rho$, among non-policy resources – such as competence evaluations – and voters' ideological position, but none with distributive expectations, which were orthogonal to voters' policy preferences (Chapter 4).

Figure 9.4 departs from the Chilean baseline equilibria from the top plot in Figure 9.2 to define the dots in the center of each of the party squares, with all parameters set at their means except those in the analysis. The horizontal axis indicates ideological position and the vertical axis

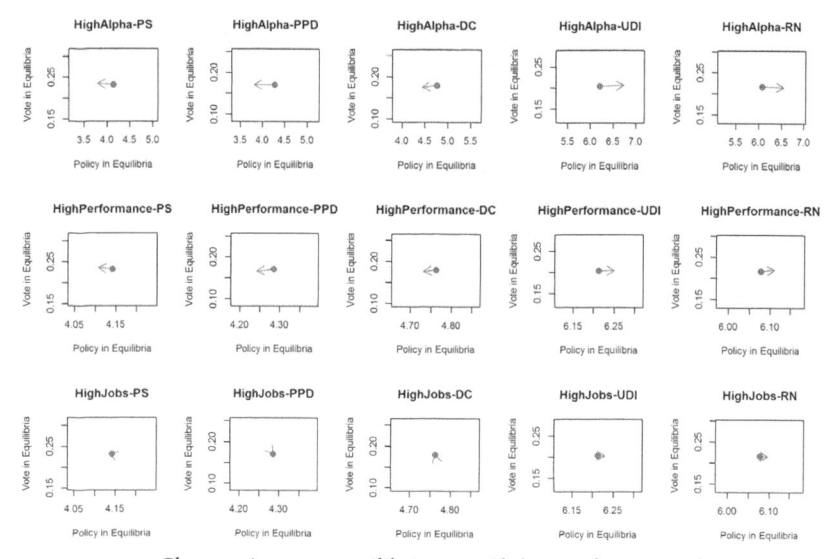

FIGURE 9.4. Changes in party equilibrium in Chile as a function of model parameters (all voters)
*Note*: Each figure describes the change from the baseline equilibrium (beginning of the arrow) to the new location (head of the arrow) when model parameters are changed. The first row displays changes in equilibrium for all parties when the importance of ideology (α) increases. The second row displays changes in equilibrium when increasing the importance that voters attach to economic competence. The third row displays changes in equilibrium when increasing the importance that voters attach to patronage spending.

represents the share of the vote. It presents three rows of squares. The first row keeps all parameters at their means but increases $\alpha$ using the maximum values of sensitivity we found in Chapter 6, rather than $\alpha = 0.12$ as in the prior exercise. That is, in the first row we set $\alpha = -0.055$ – the value for upper-middle-income (C1) voters. The resulting centrifugal effects are similar to the top row in the prior figure, but more moderate and represent the effect of these upper-middle-income (C1) voters on Chilean politicians (attenuated by their number within the electorate).

The second row sets the competence parameter to $\beta_1 = 1.5$, the value of upper-middle-income (C1) voters – the most sensitive to performance – and the bottom row sets $\beta_2 = 0.5$ as reported for middle-income (C2) voters – the most sensitive to patronage distributive expectations. Given the argument we present in the first section of this chapter, we expect that increasing the $\beta$ of economic competence should have a similar centrifugal effect as increasing the $\alpha$ on parties' incentives to seek the optimal policy position. That is, we expect the correlation between ideological views and perceptions of economic competence to increase the cost of seeking the median voter for Chilean parties. By contrast, the bottom row increases the $\beta$ of distributive expectations regarding patronage, which are orthogonal to the ideological preferences of Chilean voters. Hence, we do not expect this last exercise to generate the same magnitude of centrifugal incentives that we expect from the top two ones.

The top row shows smaller centrifugal incentives for all five parties than when we set $\alpha = 0.12$, but the direction remains the same. The movement is in the expected direction, with the PS shifting to the left from 4.24 to 4.16, the DC moving in the same direction from 4.82 to 4.78, and the PPD from 4.35 to 4.31. RN moves to the right from 6.09 to 6.18, as does the UDI from 5.97 to 6.05 (Table A.9.1 in the appendix to this chapter). As expected, the second row – where the $\beta$ of economic competence is higher – generates similar incentives on parties, with consistent direction of change, albeit in a less pronounced way. The PS moves from 4.24 to 4.19, the DC from 4.82 to 4.78, and the PPD from 4.39 to 4.34; all three *Concertación* parties move very little to the left. By contrast, RN moves slightly to the right from 6.09 to 6.13 and the UDI from 5.98 to 6.02 (Table A.9.3 in the appendix to this chapter). The correlation between voters' ideological preferences and economic performance evaluations in Chile explains this (albeit smaller) centrifugal effect, which follows the effect of higher salience ($\alpha$) for ideology.

Finally, the bottom row shows that increasing the salience of public-job expectations produces no effect on either the ideological position of parties, or their vote share. Given the lack of correlation between Chilean voters' distributive expectations and ideological positions, parties are not subject to centrifugal incentives. Hence, when non-policy benefits are not associated with the ideological locations of distinct groups of voters, they do not impose costs on parties that want to converge toward the median voter. However, in the case of Chile, this effect is attenuated by the stronger salience ($\beta$) of those non-policy resources associated with policy preferences, such as macroeconomic competence or partisan networks.

In short, our results show that shifting the values of parameters corresponding to the salience of ideology or economic performance – which is correlated to the ideological preferences of Chilean voters – from their mean to their maximum levels generates centrifugal incentives on parties, moving them away from more centrist equilibrium positions. These centrifugal incentives generated by restricting the analysis to shifting the parameters of intensity ($\alpha$ and $\beta$) is different from the effects produced by changing the composition of voters when we restricted the sample to either the upper-middle-income (C1) voters or the lower-income (D) voters, which are all pulling in different directions. Both effects, however, operate in the general equilibrium position of political parties depicted by Figure 9.2.

## 9.4 OPTIMAL POLICY POSITION AND POLITICIANS' STRATEGIES

In this section, we assess whether or not the equilibrium locations of the parties described in Figures 9.3 and 9.4 correspond to the policy offers that parties hope to communicate to voters, by assessing the views of legislators in both countries and comparing them with the views of voters in our survey. That is, we compare the parties' equilibria with the locations reported in surveys by elites and voters of Argentina and Chile, expecting elites to seek positions that are more in line with the ideal policy offers we calculate for their parties than where voters perceive their parties to be located in our survey.

To recover the position of party elites, we rely on the *Political Elites of Latin America* (PELA) Dataset of the Universidad of Salamanca, which carries out systematic interviews with Latin American legislators. We use the 2007–2010 wave for Argentina and the 2006–2010 wave for Chile, comparing the reported ideological location of each party by members and non-members. That is, we compare the party positions reported by legislators of each party as well as the party positions reported by legislators of other parties. We consider the difference in party location between party members and non-members as an aspirational location by the legislators for their party, to be compared with the equilibrium positions discovered in the previous section. We then repeat the exercise by comparing the location of parties that is given by survey respondents that vote for each party and the location by respondents that will not vote for the party in a hypothetical election. Again, we consider the location reported by voters of the party as a sincere aspirational measure. Figure 9.5 and 9.6 present the result of both exercises.

Figure 9.5 summarizes the different locations of political parties in Chile. The upper section of Figure 9.5 uses arrows, with the starting location describing the position where the party is seen by legislators of other parties and the arrow head describing the aspirational position reported by party legislators. In all cases, the arrow shows a centripetal effect, with party members reporting a more centrist position than that

204                    Non-Policy Politics

**Chile**

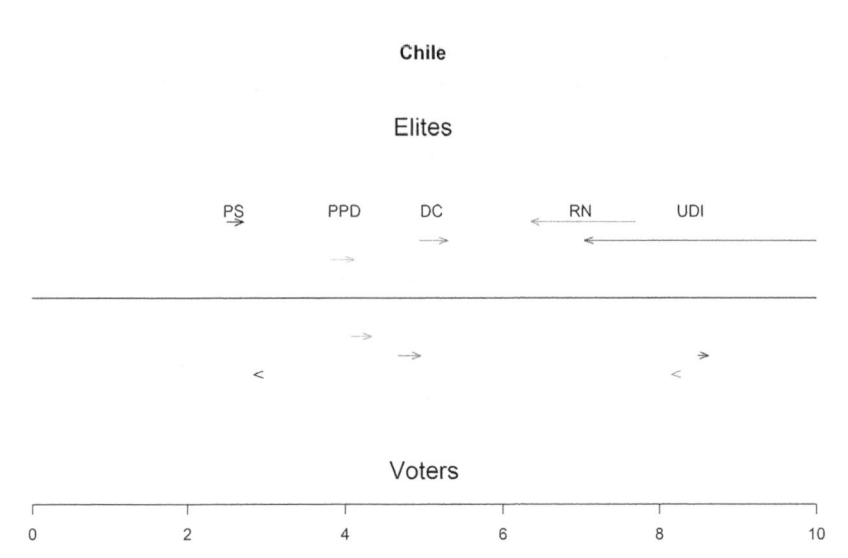

Elites

PS  PPD  DC           RN        UDI

Voters

|0    2    4    6    8    10|

Reported Ideology

FIGURE 9.5. Elite and voter locations of political parties in Chile

**Argentina**

Elites

PJ-K
UCR   PRO
ARI

PJ-K    PRO
ARI   PJ-NoK
UCR

Voters

|0    2    4    6    8    10|

Reported Ideology

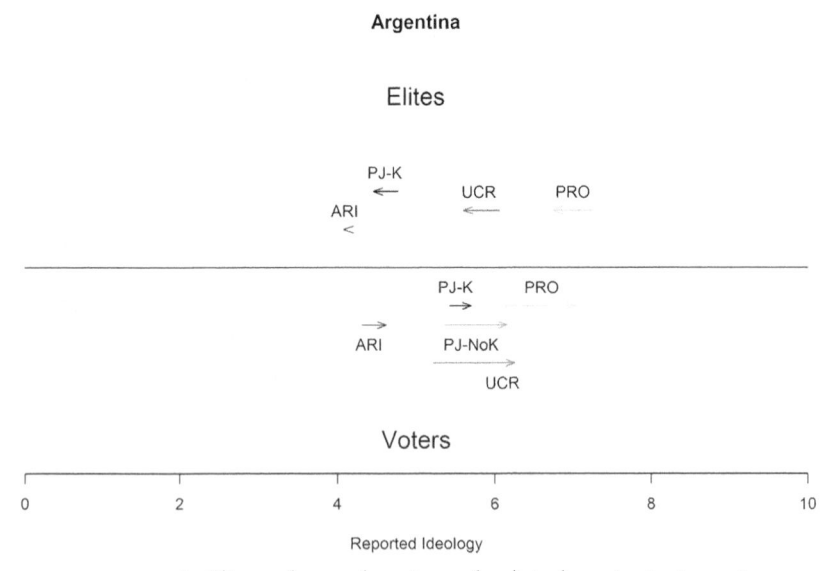

FIGURE 9.6. Elite and voter locations of political parties in Argentina

reported by legislators from other parties. This centripetal assessment of party locations by legislators does not perfectly match the optimal policy positions in Figure 9.2, which are more concentrated at the center, but respects both the rank ordering and, more importantly, the direction of the policy change that conforms to model predictions. The effect is stronger for the right-wing parties, and especially for the UDI.

The centripetal perception by politicians contrasts with the views of voters in the bottom half of Figure 9.5. Although respondents to our survey maintain the relative rank ordering of parties from left to right, there is very little difference in the placement of parties by their own voters and by voters of other parties. Additionally, the direction of the difference between both sets of respondents is not centripetal for the PS or the UDI. This difference suggests that Chilean politicians seek to occupy more centrist positions that those espoused by their supporters and closer to the optimal policy positions predicted by the model, even if this information is not always internalized by voters.

Figure 9.6 repeats the same exercise as Figure 9.5 but for the main political parties in Argentina.[12] Remember that in Figure 9.2, all Argentine parties experienced a strong centripetal effect when they reached their optimal policy position: the result of weak correlations between policy and non-policy preferences among groups of voters (Chapters 4 and 5) along with weaker salience for ideological proximity in the electoral calculus of voters (Chapter 6). The reported location of the parties by both elites and voters corresponds to this centripetal pull. While the range of ideological locations reported by party members in Chile went from a minimum of three to a maximum of seven, the range in Argentina was considerably smaller, from four for the ARI to 6.7 for the PRO.

Interestingly, while the location of the parties reported by voters closely matches the equilibria in Figure 9.2, legislators for both the FPV and the ARI report aspirational positions that are further to the left.[13] Indeed, voters of the FPV placed their party closer to the optimal location predicted by the model than the parties' legislators, which would lead to lower vote returns in all of our model specifications. While we cannot account for this effect, it may be related to the relatively weak salience of

---

[12] PELA values used in Figures 9.5 and 9.6 are in Table A.9.3 in the appendix to this chapter.
[13] Whereas we are able to distinguish Peronist voters from among those who are Kirchnerista and non-Kirchnerista, the PELA sample only has Kircherist legislators, given their overwhelming majority in Congress during this period.

ideology among the majority of Argentine voters, which reduces the electoral risks, along with the more left-wing preferences of richer voters, who give more weight to ideological considerations. In any case, differences in policy positions are minimal and both the UCR and PJ concentrated on the center.

## 9.5 POLICY AND NON-POLICY OFFERS IN ELECTORAL COMPETITION IN CHILE AND ARGENTINA

Our survey provides a snapshot of party politics in Argentina and Chile in the first decade of the twenty-first century. Our analysis of the incentives generated by non-policy politics in these countries, we argue, informs our understanding of electoral dynamics, policy positioning, and subsequent political developments in both countries. Hence, in this section, we complement the analysis of ideal policy positions by parties with a discussion of how these could reflect the evolution of electoral dynamics in Argentina and Chile.

### a) Policy Anchoring, Voter Disaffection and Party Fragmentation in Chile

Our survey was fielded in 2007, two years into the first administration of Socialist president Michelle Bachelet. This was a period of heightened economic redistribution, preceded by the implementation of major health reforms that increased the number of insured voters (*AUGE*) and the implementation of a limited cash transfer program that repackaged different social programs for the poor (*Chile Solidario*).[14] The first administration of Bachelet, however, would also signal the end of the coalitional arrangement that dominated Chilean politics after democratization in 1989. In 2008, the model of coalitional competition that emerged from the transition would start to unravel as public protests against social inequality – started by students protesting for the high cost of education – re-entered the previously demobilized political scene (Huneeus, 2016; Luna, 2014, 2016). Do our findings help us understand changes in Chilean party systems and its increasing fragmentation in the second decade of the millennium?

---

[14] These reforms were implemented partly under the presidency of Socialist Ricardo Lagos (2000–2006) and immediately before the 2008 expansion of non-contributory pensions (Garay, 2016; Pribble, 2015).

We have documented the incentives generated by Chilean voters' preferences that politicians faced by 2007. Voting patterns had been very stable and parties of the right and the left had been electorally successful. Between 1989 and 2005, the legislative representation of the PS and the PPD, and especially that of the UDI, grew at the expense of the DC and RN. Electoral volatility was low and even when around a third of voters changed their preferences between elections, the percentage jumping across ideological coalitions was limited to between 5 percent and 10 percent of voters in the 1993–2009 period (Avendaño and Sandoval, 2016: 186, 192). The incentives generated by voter preferences along with the binominal electoral system favored parties in both ideological coalitions – with a slightly larger seat premium for the *Concertación* (Siavelis and Morgenstern, 2008: 185; Zucco, 2007) – although the median Chilean voter was centrist.

This apparent divorce between voters and politicians was accompanied by a pro-rich policy bias resulting from the distribution of voters' preferences, along with the influence of business sectors in policymaking (Murillo, 2009; Pribble, Huber, and Stephens, 2009). Meanwhile, divisions within the *Concertación* and the legislative representation of the right-wing parties further restricted the scope of redistributive outcomes (Garay, 2016; Pribble, 2015). In the 2009 presidential election, these internal tensions produced a rupture and the candidacy of former-Socialist Marco Henriquez Ominami, who refused to support the Christian Democratic candidate, former-President Eduardo Frei, and divided the *Concertación* vote. The right-wing candidate, RN Sebastian Piñeira benefited from this division. He ran a moderate campaign based on his management skills as a successful businessman – he was the richest person in the country – to increase the salience of competence and reach beyond those right-wing voters who gave better marks to RN on this non-policy dimension. Although the vote was divided on ideological preferences, centrist voters defined the election as he won in a run-off (Morales and Sanchez, 2010; Navia and Godoy, 2014: 58, 66). Hence, the aspirational moderation of right-wing parties that we showed in Figure 9.5 seems reflected in the 2009 electoral campaign and allowed the election of the first right-wing president since the transition to democracy.

Perception of voter discontent with parties brought the elites toward personalist campaign strategies (Luna, 2014), as well as institutional fixes such as establishing voluntary voting without mandatory prior registration in 2013 and the establishment of larger districts with proportional representation in 2015. However, protests expanded under Piñeira from students, indigenous peoples and environmental groups to labor unions (Delamaza, Maillet, and Martinez, 2016). Protests did not stop even when Bachellet returned to the presidency in 2014 leading a broader coalition on the left, which expanded the *Concertación* to include the Communist Party as well as new left-wing Socialist splinters. Hence, policy anchoring kept the party coalitions on both sides of the policy spectrum, whereas social mobilization probably increased the intensity of ideological sensitivity among left-wing voters, pushing the Socialists in that direction – a feature that could be observed in the aspiration of Socialists voters in Figure 9.5.

In line with our expectations, the vacuum of the policy center hastened party system fragmentation in this context. As parties remained anchored to their ideological position, they experienced fractures, which mostly led to splinters from the main parties becoming new parties, seeking to occupy the political center. The correlation of Chilean voters' policy and non-policy benefits, which anchored traditional parties, led to the emergence of centrist alternatives in response to voters' dissatisfaction. Those new parties included: the *Partido Progresista* (Progressive Party), founded by Marco Henriquez Ominami in 2010 on the center-left; a more centrist party called *Ciudadanos* (Citizens), founded in 2013 as a splinter of the *Concertación*, led by former-Finance Minister Andres Velasco; the PRI (Independent Regionalist Party), founded in 2014 by former-DC legislators; and two center-right parties emerging from RN in 2014 – Evopoli (Political Evolution) and Amplitud (Amplitude). Hence, the incentives we identified for legislators seeking the median voter resulted in the emergence of new political parties, attempting to attract the median centrist vote and reshaping the options that voters have for consideration.

Our framework focuses on politicians' short-term incentives, given their non-policy endowments to face the challenge of the next election. Over time, voters' reactions may generate incentives for the entry of new parties, which are not tied to the same legacies of voter evaluations as their predecessors. We saw, for instance, how the ARI and the PRO, although indirectly linked to old Radical politicians, did not inherit the deleterious competence evaluations of this party in our survey. Party fragmentation in Chile was heightened by an electoral reform that established automatic registration, made the vote voluntary, and introduced proportional representation in legislative elections, as well as a scandal on electoral financing. In fact, in the first round of the 2017 presidential elections, the vote was divided among many candidates to the point that the two most voted for combined did not get two-thirds of the vote. These were Nueva Mayoria, represented by Alejandro Guillier, and the right-wing coalition consisting of UDI, RN, and two new center-right parties, led by Sebastian Piñeira. The latter won the run-off election by benefiting from better competence evaluations than his contenders.[15] In particular, the contrast between the Chilean economic performance during his prior administration, which coincided with the commodities' boom, and that of outgoing President Bachellet, which coincided with declining prices of Chilean export products that negatively affected her popularity, was crucial.[16]

### b) Argentina: From Hegemony to Competition?

Our picture of Argentina in 2007, at the end of Nestor Kirchner's administration, suggested the appearance of a new predominant party system replacing the more competitive one that had emerged, for the first time, in the aftermath of democratic transition. The asymmetry between Peronism and its contenders was associated with non-policy resources, in particular voters' assessments of its macroeconomic competence and the dramatic drop in their views of Radicals skills in that regard. The lack of association between these non-policy endowments and voters' ideological preferences facilitated policy switching. Indeed, the Peronist party left its prior neoliberal policies and reconverted into an expression of the left-wing wave covering Latin America during the onset of the millennium (Levitsky and Roberts, 2013). Whereas that policy shift followed prior changes in public opinion (Schiumerini, 2016), we show that the crucial determinant of the vote in the aftermath of a deep recession was the evaluation of economic competence. The weight of those assessments on the vote, moreover, was more salient for poorer voters, who had been more exposed to the dire consequences of economic volatility.

The incumbent Peronist party won the 2007 presidential election by a wide margin and delivered not only economic growth – thanks to the commodity boom – but also redistribution to those poorer voters judging economic performance by their wellbeing. Major social policies were adopted in the aftermath of the 2008 economic crisis, a year when

---

[15] See www.elmostrador.cl/noticias/pais/2017/10/25/encuesta-cep-no-hay-por-donde-ganarle-a-pinera/
[16] See www.americasquarterly.org/content/why-pinera-frontrunner-return-chiles-president

President Cristina Kirchner's popularity was deeply hurt by her fight against rural producers in an unsuccessful attempt to increase export taxes. In 2009, the AUH (universal allowance for children) universalized a right of parents in the formal sector by unifying existing programs (Jefes y Jefas, Familias, PEC) with a significantly higher allowance and limited discretion in distribution. It accompanied a national workfare program decentralized to majors in its implementation (Argentina Trabaja), who retained political discretion over delivery (Garay, 2016: 287–292).[17] A 2008 pension reform policy ended the private system and granted non-contributory pensions, which allowed access to retirement to 97 percent of outsiders who were 65 years or older by 2010 (Garay, 2016: 277).[18] By 2011, incumbent President Cristina Kirchner easily won re-election by an even larger margin than in 2007 – and with overwhelming support of lower-income voters (Calvo and Murillo, 2012).

Her re-election suggested the re-establishment of Peronist predominance. Yet, there were tensions between center-left and center-right factions, leading to an erosion in competence evaluations as a consequence of declining commodities' prices and a weakening economy, especially among the most sensitive poorer voters hurt by growing inflation. These tensions produced a Peronist division, which weakened incumbent support in the 2013 midterm elections and brought two serious Peronist contenders to the 2015 presidential elections. Taking advantage of the declining popularity of the incumbent PRO candidate, Mauricio Macri, shifted to the center by making an alliance with the UCR and the Civic Coalition (heir to the ARI). Although he only received a third of the vote, the division of the Peronist vote allowed him to narrowly win the run-off election. The promise of economic improvement by a candidate who did not carry the heavy weight of the deleterious Radical economic competence assessments facilitated his victory (Murillo and Levitsky, forthcoming). As the young PRO is a center-right party, we expect that its performance would favor voters' reliance on ideology in judging its performance, and in 2017 there is

---

[17] For a general discussion on the politics of decentralization in Latin America see Falleti (2005, 2010).
[18] According to Nora Lustig, in Argentina, "the main redistributive intervention has been the pension moratorium – in essence a large-scale noncontributory pension program. [It] is largely responsible for the increase in the number of old-age pensioners from 3.6 to 6.3 million between 2003 and 2009, with the largest increase taking place among women" (www.commitmentoequity.org/publications_files/Argentina/ArgentinaSummaryAugust2013_revisedJan2014.pdf) accessed on July 1, 2016.

evidence that voters' ideological self-placement increasingly predicts assessments of presidential performance.[19]

In sum, our framework showed how the PJ advantage on non-policy resources – sustained by good economic performance during the commodities' boom – was crucial to explaining its electoral strength. Indeed, the decline in economic performance since 2013, with the decline in the price of agricultural commodities, is crucial to explain its electoral decline. Additionally, the weight of incumbency experience on these evaluations can be seen in the better marks received by the PRO than the UCR at the time of the 2015 election. If the PRO develops a stronger assessment among more like-minded voters, its capacity to occupy the political center could diminish, moving in the direction of the constraints faced by Chilean parties.

## 9.6 SUMMARY AND CONCLUDING REMARKS

What are the implications of our framework for explaining policy offers and policy switches in Argentina and Chile? In this chapter, we have shown that non-policy politics provides crucial constraints and opportunities for parties in defining their expected policy offers. Three findings are of the utmost importance for explaining the updating of parties' policy offers. First, when non-policy endowments are orthogonal to and independent from the voters' policy preferences, parties converge toward more centripetal positions. In those cases, parties with a non-policy advantage see their vote share increase above and beyond the vote of disadvantaged parties. However, most parties still take on more centripetal positions and adjust their policy offers in response to changes in the median voter preferences. That is, when the policy preferences of the median voter change, as happened in Argentina in the early 1990s and in the early 2000, parties adjust their policy offers to match the preferences of voters.

Second, our model shows that when perceptions about non-policy *endowments* correlate with policy preferences, so that voters on the left or right of the political spectrum see different parties as being advantaged, parties move to non-centrist positions. That is, when views of non-policy endowments correlate with voters' policy preferences, parties are less able to freely switch policy positions and maintain consistent offers over time.

---

[19] See "La derecha y la izquierda en tiempos de Cambiemos," El Estadista, December 27, 2017. (http://elestadista.com.ar/?p=13727)

As a result, shocks to the median voter preferences are not met by rapid policy switches as in Argentina.

Third, when parties have a non-policy advantage among all voters, but such an advantage is larger among a subset of them, the parties' policy offers is a weighted combination of the preferences of the median voter and the mass of voters that display the largest non-policy advantage. The PS in Chile, we have shown, is perceived as more capable by voters on the left of the political spectrum but also had an overall advantage in the electorate at large. As a result, its optimal policy offer is shifted centripetally, closer to the median Chilean voter than the position espoused by its own activists. In all, our model explains the mechanisms that make non-policy politics a critical determinant of the policy offers made by parties.

To explain the effect of non-policy politics on the policy offers of parties, we use synthetic data and survey data from Argentina and Chile. We gain leverage to see the effect of policy shocks by comparing the optimal response to preferences of subgroups of voters. For the case of Chile, we show that heterogeneity among voters drives non-policy politics to bias the policy offers that parties make.

Results given in this chapter also drive attention to non-policy differences between richer and poorer voters. These differences are more significant in Chile where our model predicts larger-than-expected moderation by both the *Concertación* and the right-wing parties. This was the result of richer voters giving a larger weight to ideological considerations than their poorer, but more progressive, voters. By contrast, in Argentina, the larger weight of richer voters' was expected to drive the Peronists into a more leftist position.

In explaining the effect of non-policy politics on the policy offers of parties, this chapter provides a theoretical account of policy stability in Chile and of policy switches in Argentina. In Chile, we argued, intertwined non-policy assessments and policy preferences inhibit parties from moving too close to the median voters. For example, if the PS moved to the position of the median voter, non-policy losses in perceived competence would outweigh any positional gains in the ideological space. As a result, Chilean parties were unable to freely adjust to changes in the preferences of the median voter.

By contrast, in Argentina, independence between non-policy assessments and voters' policy preferences drove parties toward the median voter. The effect was more pronounced for the non-policy advantaged Peronists, which could take on the preferences of the median voter every time that there is a change in her preferences. Smaller parties, on the other hand, gravitate close to the center but have non-policy deficits that crowd them out from the position of the median voter. In all, Peronist politicians constantly shifted their policy offers in response to changes in the median voter preferences, while sustaining their electoral support. Peronist presidents had been particularly successful, exercising unprecedented freedom to change policy offers, switching to market reform and back to statism without making significant sacrifices to their vote shares.

In short, our theory provides a vote-seeking rational for policy stability in Chile and for policy switches in Argentina. It explains these different outcomes as the result of vote maximizing strategies by parties that are bound by non-policy assessments, which are sticky and difficult to modify in the short-term. Our theory shows that even though parties may struggle to change their reputations for managerial competence among voters, Chilean parties are unable to profit from policy switches, while Argentine parties are unable to profit from policy stability. Switches impose costs in Chile and benefits in Argentina, and political entrepreneurs are ready to abide by the strategies that are more conducive to winning office.

# 10

# Non-Policy Politics and Electoral Responsiveness

How does non-policy politics shape vote choices in modern democracies? How does it change the policy calculus of parties and the policy offers made by candidates? How does it shape democratic patterns of multi-party competition? Our theory provides a response to these important questions. Whereas the political science literature long considered policy responsiveness as critical for democratic representation, a dominant Downsian consensus relegated non-policy politics to supporting roles or questioned its existence as a pathology soon to be extinguished. Donald Stokes (1963) forcefully rejected such Downsian *reductionism*, arguing in favor of a valence-driven model of politics. In the last twenty years, scholars have recognized the theoretical importance of such non-policy dimensions, bringing back not just Stokes' valence issues but other non-policy dimensions such as religion, ethnicity, affective politics, identity politics, partisan activism, and clientelism. These dimensions are fundamental to democratic responsiveness.

Our theory owes much to this emerging scholarship. We also characterize democratic responsiveness through a broader portfolio of policy offers and non-policy endowments. We consider these broader portfolios critical for explaining the electoral choices of voters and the strategic behavior of parties. We then take a further step and describe biases in the delivery of non-policy endowments and strategic incentives to deliver policy offers.

Out of all possible non-policy resources, our research focuses on the effect of managerial competence, the delivery of selective incentives, and the exchange of information and goods through partisan networks. These three different non-policy endowments feature prominently in recent research. More important, these non-policy endowments provide examples of three families of non-policy endowments that are based on reputation (valence), institutional resources (targeted distribution), and party organization (networks). We show that these non-policy endowments are relatively fixed in the short-term, are difficult to acquire, and play a crucial role in delivering elections to parties and candidates. Political parties have different endowments, which allow them to promise diverse non-policy benefits. These endowments, therefore, enhance the electoral prospects of parties with many resources, while damaging the opportunities of those who have few. Finally, our research provides evidence that non-policy politics alters the strategic calculus of parties, as well as the policy offers that they make.

Non-policy politics has always been critical for electoral success. Parties routinely signal managerial competence, mobilize their members, and deliver selective incentives to win elections. They invest significant resources in maintaining and expanding party networks and rely heavily on activists to spread their policy messages, as well as their non-policy products. Parties cultivate brand names to deliver policies but also cultivate reputations that signal competence, confidence, and trustworthiness. Non-policy politics, servicing citizens around the world, figures prominently in the life of democratic parties and voters' expectations when deciding on Election Day.

In this book, we illuminate our conceptualization of electoral responsiveness with empirical information about voter preferences and politicians' strategies in Argentina and Chile. In doing so, we have shown that voters' demand constrained politicians in the short-term but that supply politics matters as well in the long-term. Conflicts within the *Concertación* and the Peronists in presidential elections created opportunities for their rivals, while exogenous shocks – such as changes in commodity prices – influenced voters' perceptions of economic competence. Investment by interest groups and the mobilization of social movements with intense preferences may also shape policy outcomes and alter the voters' perceptions of politicians' capacity.[1] In the long-term, therefore, our research acknowledges that the supply-side incentives will alter non-policy endowments as well as the voters' expectations. In the short-term,

---

[1] Kitschelt et al. (2010) argue that the types of linkages between voters and parties in Latin America are subjected to changes in political and economic conditions, rather than being stable and resulting from the institutional freezing of long-term social cleavages as originally suggested by Lipset and Rokkan (1967).

however, we show how vote-seeking politicians are constrained by voters' preferences, thereby highlighting the importance of the demand side on parties' electoral strategies.

Our argument assumes that democracies with working political parties, which allow free flows of information, generate the incentives that make vote-seeking politicians operate as our framework suggests: combining distinct strategies to attract diverse groups of voters.[2] In doing so, we seek to bridge the divide between the literature on advanced democracies, more focused on policy and competence, and the scholarship on new democracies, more centered on targeted distribution. Indeed, the combination of policy and non-policy resources in the electoral portfolio of politicians may be most apparent in Latin America, because it is a region with a relatively long electoral experience due to early decolonization, whereas the Third Wave of democracy spread more widely despite very high levels of economic inequality. Our broader conceptualization of electoral responsiveness is not specific to Latin America, however. It can be extended to widely different democracies, adapting the dimensions of non-policy politics used to explain the incentives generated by electoral competition on politicians, as well as the categories of voters they identify for targeting their offers.

## 10.1 VOTER HETEROGENEITY AND NON-POLICY POLITICS

In this book, we provide evidence that voters care about the policy offers and the non-policy benefits delivered by parties. We show significant variation in voters' preferences and sensitivity for policy and non-policy offers, which in turn inform party behavior. Voters, we argue, attach different weights to the policy and non-policy benefits provided by parties. Such heterogeneity does not simply describe differences in policy preferences across groups of voters but, more importantly, describes differences in the weight that voters assign to their expectations of access to the different benefits provided by parties. In doing so, our theory provides a crucial mechanism to explain why parties deliver different combinations of benefits to distinct groups of voters.

Unveiling differences in the weight that voters attach to policy offers and non-policy resources also allows us to explain significant biases in the delivery of benefits. Voters who care more intensely about particular

---

[2] We always assume niche political parties trying to shape specific policy agendas rather than to win elections operate under a different logic.

types of policy and non-policy benefits, we argue, should be given priority if parties hope to win elections. Heterogeneity among voters could result in patterns of segmented representation – when different groups of voters specialize in distinct types of benefits – or they could benefit a particular constituency – when some voters demand "more of everything" at higher rates than their peers do. For instance, in Chapter 8, our research shows that differences in the weight that voters attach to the delivery of public-sector jobs inform the behavior of politicians in Argentina and Chile.

In describing how voter heterogeneity is met with the delivery of policy and non-policy benefits, our research shows that electoral responsiveness can bias public resources to the benefit of more intense voters. The opportunities and constraints that non-policy politics provides to parties are a powerful force for a biased allocation of benefits. Whether those alleviate or exacerbate existing inequities is by no means a trivial discussion and requires further research.

Our conceptualization of political parties as organizations that deliver policy and non-policy benefits to heterogeneous groups of voters provides both a theoretical framework and general predictions for polities regardless of their national wealth, number of parties, or consolidation status. Our framework does not assume distinct types of political parties, either programmatic or non-programmatic, but organizations endowed with a diverse array of electoral resources and the flexibility to use all of them to win the support of voters. In the short-term, the policy and non-policy preferences of voters provide predictable opportunities and constraints for vote-maximizing politicians. Preferences, however, change over time in response to exogenous shocks and endogenous learning. By conceptualizing parties as organizations that invest a portfolio of resources, rather than specializing in a particular type of voter, we are able to see preferences as fixed in the short-term and evolving over time, with parties adjusting to changes in the political environment and investing in non-policy resources to produce party brands with greater electoral strength.

In this research, however, we are agnostic and provide no theory on how voters' preferences evolve or on the origin of their distribution across distinct groups of voters. Instead, we take preferences as given and provide a theory that explores how parties deliver policy and non-policy benefits to voters given their preferences. However, the influence of competence assessments, we find, suggests that if voters cannot distinguish the origin of positive performance, politicians have incentives toward short-term fixes to the economy aligned with the preferences of voters – in line with the literature on political business cycles.

Finally, our theory also provides a rationale for party switches in democratic settings. As shown in Chapter 9, when voters perceive policy and non-policy benefits as closely related to each other, politicians pay a significant electoral price for abandoning their prior policy positions. By contrast, we argue, when the policy and non-policy preferences of voters are weakly correlated or orthogonal, advantaged parties may freely pursue the policy preferences of the median voter and constantly switch their policies in response to the evolving preferences of voters. Thus, different types of non-policy endowments have similar effects on the likelihood of policy switches, depending on their association with voters' policy preferences. If politicians require ideological activists who are more connected with similar voters for policy persuasion, they will face significant constraints in their ability to depart from the policies espoused by the members of those networks. By contrast, territorial activists who reach voters across the ideological spectrum do not generate similar constraints. Hence, in the short-term, voters' non-policy preferences shape the agency of vote-seeking politicians attempting to modify their prior policy offers. Non-policy politics, consequently, is a crucial explanatory variable for understanding policy switches in democratic politics. Whereas those policy switches may benefit the party electorally in the short-term (Stokes, 2001), over time they may corrode party differentiation and, if combined with deleterious performance, may affect party brands (Lupu, 2016).

In what follows, we discuss in greater detail how recent research has sought to bridge the gap between the distinct policy and non-policy traditions of party politics. Building on that work, we seek to provide a comprehensive framework for understanding electoral competition across different types of polities. We then describe how our research connects to the larger literature on electoral responsiveness and discuss the normative implications of our work.

## 10.2 THEORETICAL IMPLICATIONS: PARTY-VOTER LINKAGES AND ELECTORAL RESPONSIVENESS

In this section, we discuss the conventional wisdom on electoral competition in advanced and new democracies and how our theoretical framework contributes to an emerging literature that helps bridge the gap between these two traditions. We start by describing the distinction between programmatic and clientelistic parties and the way in which we expand the non-policy resources to include targeted distribution – widespread in the literature on new democracies – as well as competence evaluations and activists' networks – more prevalent in the analysis of advanced democracies. We also discuss how the emphasis on voter heterogeneity, emerging from the study of segmented strategies in unequal democracies, could be included as a case of our general framework, which has a broader application across democracies.

## a) The Two Worlds of Democracy

The literature on party-voter linkages was originally built on the experience of Western democracies and assumes party specialization. In the path-breaking work of Martin Shefter (1994), parties' historical access to state resources was crucial in defining either a programmatic or patronage specialization for mass mobilization.[3] Similarly, extending this analysis to Third Wave democracies, and summarizing the previous literature, Kitschelt (2000) argues that either clientelistic or programmatic linkages between parties and voters could be used to establish both responsiveness and accountability to voters, but that each was associated with different political, economic, and institutional conditions.[4] In Kitschelt's view, over-time specialization should make either type of linkage relatively stable within a single polity unless their political economies changed in a significant way.[5] This view has a profound impact in the literature, which often assumes a modernization trajectory where political parties in richer and older democracies would be less likely to subsist on patronage, given civil service laws and the excessive costs of private distribution to richer voters (Keefer, 2007; Kitschelt and Kselman,

---

[3] Shefter's (1994) supply-side argument suggests that the timing of democratization and civil service bureaucracies defines whether party leaders rely on patronage or programmatic appeals to mobilize activists and voters, explaining that Sweden and Germany skipped clientelistic parties, whereas Greece, Spain, and Italy succumbed to them.

[4] Whereas programmatic responsiveness is based on the idea that party labels could be associated to cognitive shortcuts publicizing policy (Aldrich, 1995; Hinich and Munger, 1994), it also assumes politicians' responsiveness to policy mandates (Manin, Przeworski, and Stokes, 1999). Kitchelt and Wilkinson (2007), by contrast, explore clientelistic linkages and the conditions that make those more likely, whereas our own work builds on this emphasis on the mechanism connecting voters and parties in defining clientelistic or programmatic expectations for the distribution of private and club goods in Argentina and Chile (Calvo and Murillo, 2013).

[5] "At low dosages, all linkage mechanisms may be compatible. As politicians intensify their cultivation of a particular type of linkage, however, they reach a production possibility frontier at which further intensifications of one linkage mechanism can occur only at the expense of toning down other linkage mechanism." (Kitschelt, 2000: 855).

2013).[6] Stokes et al. (2013) establish an explicit association between poverty and clientelism, suggesting that economic development reduces the returns and viability of this electoral strategy due to budget constraints, as shown by the experience of Britain and the US.

This prevailing view explains that the recent literature on electoral competition in advanced democracies is dominated by analyses of policy positions and valence issues to a much larger extent than targeted distribution, and it certainly ignores clientelistic strategies even when pork is recognized as a crucial component of politicians' electoral behavior.[7] Significantly, we build our theoretical framework on the insights emerging from this literature, which introduces the weight of non-policy valence issues such as competence evaluations and the role of partisan activists, most notably on the work of Adams, Merrill, and Grofman (2005); Shofield and Sened (2006); and Ansolabehere and Snyder (2000). However, we have also included targeted distribution as one of those non-policy dimensions.

Running parallel to these developments in the study of electoral competition in advanced democracies, the work on younger and poorer democracies – which boomed after the Third Wave Democratization – departed from the assumption of an idealized programmatic competition. Such programmatic competition in advanced democracies was contrasted with the increasing prevalence of clientelistic strategies among newcomers. This electoral strategy was associated with credibility problems experienced by political parties without an extended trajectory, in contexts where ethnic diversity and poverty affected voters' expectations and trust on politicians' promises. Keefer (2007) and Keefer and Vlaicu (2008) focus on democratic youth and poverty to explain the credibility problems of political parties and their need to rely on clientelism (immediate distribution) rather than programmatic promises (future policy) to build party brands. Credibility is also at the core of the emphasis on ethnicity as

---

[6] Kitschelt and Kselman (2013) argue the relationship is curvilinear but still with lower probability of clientelism at higher levels of economic development. This argument resonates with the traditional literature on parties, such as Huntington (1968) and Sartori (2005).

[7] An important exception to those views is Piattoni (2001), who shows that clientelism and patronage can survive in richer democracies. The discussion of targeted distribution and pork in the literature on advanced democracies is mostly detached from that of political parties' programmatic offers, although formal models, such as Dixit and Londregan (1996) and Lindbeck and Weibull (1987) include both policy preferences and targeted distribution. See, for instance, Ansolabehere and Snyder (2007), Snyder (1989), and Dahlberg and Johansson (2002).

a mechanism to inform voters' distributive expectations, in the pathbreaking studies of Chandra (2004) and Posner (2005) in India and Zambia, respectively. In both cases, political parties rely on ethnic identification to build credibility for their distributive promises during electoral campaigns. Therefore, demographic identities are used as a source of information, given the weakness of partisan networks.

Whereas these two literatures evolved on parallel tracks, detaching programmatic promises from clientelistic linkages, we bring them both together by considering targeted distribution among the non-policy dimensions in the voter utility function, while exploring their relationship with policy offers and the patterns of their allocation across categories of voters. Indeed, we show in Chapters 7 and 8 that targeted distribution is allocated in different ways and with diverse electoral efficiency in Argentina and Chile. In this way, we bring the study of targeted distribution together with those of other non-policy resources and account for the combination of diverse electoral strategies, even when controlling for economic and political development as well as party organization. More importantly, we provide a framework that includes different types of nonpolicy resources, which can be applied to political parties across older and younger democracies.

### b) Not All Voters Are Equal

Our work assumes that parties can combine policy and non-policy offers, and building on the recent literature on younger democracies, it shows how parties can take advantage of voter heterogeneity to tailor different offers to distinct groups of voters. These democracies enjoy, in many cases, higher discretion to spend public funds or high levels of economic inequality that facilitates fundraising among private donors to pay for targeted distribution, both of which ease the tailoring of electoral strategies to distinct groups of voters.

In building our argument, we took as a point of departure the concept of portfolio diversification coined by Magaloni et al. (2006) to depict how the Mexican PRI relied alternatively on policy or targeted distribution to seek the support of voters with diverse propensity to support it: either core or swing voters. In our earlier work, we have shown how electoral returns to core constituents may vary, depending on voters' socioeconomic status (Calvo and Murillo, 2004). Here, we extend the concept of portfolio diversification to the broader endowment of electoral resources that politicians can use in targeting sets of voters, based on distinct demographic features or individuals within these groups. In doing so, we build on prior scholarship on the importance of demographic categories for defining distinctive electoral strategies. Analyzing Argentine electoral politics, Weitz-Shapiro (2014) shows the impact of the different distributive preferences of poorer and middle-class voters on politicians' electoral strategies, whereas Luna (2014) illustrates how the latter segment their electoral offers by combining policy benefits for richer core voters and targeted distribution for poorer swing voters in Latin America. Indeed, Thachil (2014) shows a similar strategy in India, where the BJP (Indian's People Party) promises policy to high-caste voters while distributing goods and services to lower-caste voters. Building on this literature on segmented electoral strategies, we propose here a general framework which explores the heterogeneity of voter preferences (in our cases by socioeconomic status) to show how these shape the opportunities for portfolio diversification for all political parties in both Argentina and Chile.

Our theoretical framework contributes to bridging the gap between the literatures on advanced and new democracies by emphasizing how diverse non-policy resources shape politicians' electoral strategies and by providing an empirical approach to test these effects. Its emphasis on voter heterogeneity is also relevant for our understanding of biases favoring distinct groups of voters. While the focus on voter heterogeneity has been included in analyses of new democracies, we believe that it can be extended to advanced democracies where inequality is not only increasing, but also becoming more politically salient. Whereas recent studies focused on its effects on shaping policy preferences (Bartels, 2008; Gilens, 2012), we call for further research applying it also to the non-policy preferences of the citizenry, especially perceptions about economic competence, given the extensive literature on economic voting. Such a line of research should be fruitful for advancing our understanding of the evolving patterns of electoral competition in advanced democracies experiencing increasing income inequality.

### c) Back to the Literature: Democracy and Distributive Politics

By building a theoretical framework that applies to both old and new democracies, we can contribute to closing the gap between the literatures of advanced and new democracies, while generating insights that can be applied to each of them. First, by exploring, rather than assuming, the association between non-policy and policy preferences of voters, we highlight the conditions shaping politicians' agency in both types of polities. Most of the literature on multiparty competition in advanced democracies assumes the association of both types of preferences, thus emphasizing the centrifugal impact of non-policy competence assessments and party activists (e.g. Adams, Merrill, and Grofman, 2005; Schofield and Sened, 2003). However, by taking an agnostic view on such associations and leaving it to empirical evaluation, we were able to bring the insight of two-party models into our multiparty framework by showing how higher valence allows political parties to move in the policy space when it is not closely connected with voters' policy preferences (e.g. Ansolabehere and Snyder, 2000). The effects of non-policy resources on policy offers, therefore, rest on their association and should not be assumed but explored. Similarly, the effect of exogenous shocks or even endogenous mistakes that shape non-policy resources, such as voters' competence evaluations or activists' commitment to the party, over time should also constrain politicians' agency for modifying policy offers when seeking to maximize electoral support.

Second, building on Dixit and Londregan's (1993) model, we point to the informative role of partisan networks in reducing the waste in targeted distribution by appealing to the metaphor of a "leaky bucket." This information is crucial to solving for the optimal allocation of targeted distribution for maximizing electoral returns. The answer to the core-swing debate in the distributive politics literature, therefore, depends on how informative these partisan networks are (and whether they can be replaced by alternative sources of information that allow for individualizing voters' needs and wants).[8] We found core effects in Argentina but not in Chile, given the different way in which partisan networks operate in each country. Therefore, Argentine politicians' dependence on activists to avoid a "leaky bucket" in targeted distribution reduces their ability to adapt their distributive strategies in the short-term, because they risk reducing the electoral returns derived from the same level of spending. By contrast, Chilean politicians have more freedom to change patterns of distribution, since they lack informative partisan networks modulating the efficiency of distribution. Conversely, Chilean politicians are more

---

[8] In line with our empirical analysis in Chapter 6, Zarazaga (2016) provides a formal model for the impact of information on the efficiency of targeted distribution by partisan networks, illustrated with qualitative evidence from Argentina. He also assumes that voters have diverse policy and non-policy preferences, with targeted distribution being granted to those voters where efficiency is the largest given their other preferences.

constrained in their capacity to modify policy offers, given the connection between voters and ideologically akin activists.

In short, we propose a theoretical framework that brings together the literatures on electoral competition in established and newer democracies. Its flexibility is based on its own agnosticism, in terms of the association between voters' policy and non-policy preferences across and within polities. This framework also allowed us to investigate the interactions between partisan networks and distributive expectations, providing crucial insights for an empirical solution to the core-swing debate in the literature on clientelism. The flexibility of this demand-driven theory of politicians' electoral strategies is that it can include different types of non-policy resources and distinct categories of voters, thereby facilitating the dialogue between the two traditions on the study of democracy and our understanding of electoral competition in democratic regimes more generally.

## 10.3 BROADENING ELECTORAL RESPONSIVENESS AND ITS NORMATIVE IMPLICATIONS

Democratic representation involves responsiveness to citizens. Representatives are expected to pay attention to voters' preferences to get elected and to pay a price if they ignore their views by losing re-election, thus providing the citizenry with a crucial mechanism for keeping politicians' accountable.[9] Although policy responsiveness is at the heart of this process, the lack of explicit policy mandates in representative democracies suggest that voters may be, in fact, selecting representatives whom they trust to make good decisions for them. The central criticism of electoral responsiveness as a mechanism of sanction for breaking mandates comes from Manin's (1997) argument that governments, which are responsive to public opinion, may be unrepresentative because mandates are not instructions but only signals of voters' preferences because voters do not give explicit instructions to their government.[10] Even though the literature

---

[9] For a discussion of the different models of representation, see Pitkin (1967). Manin, Przeworski, and Stokes (1999) summarize the literature on democratic representation and its connection with the concept of policy responsiveness.

[10] See Schumpeter (1942) and Fearon (1999) for arguments about citizens selecting representatives rather than policy mandates. Indeed, Mansbridge's (2003) concept of gyroscopic representation involves representatives who do not necessarily follow mandates because they should look for the better interest of voters, which includes bargaining that cannot be observed by voters.

on democratic representation has not solved the debate between the sanction and selection models of representation, empirically elections remain the main mechanism for accountability to voters. Voter preferences are the center of this mechanism, which assumes no clear alternative to voters' own assessment to adjudicate what is better for them. Politicians, in turn, are responsive to voters' policy and non-policy preferences because they want to be elected.

Political responsiveness to voters' preferences requires alternative electoral options and capacity to monitor politicians. Indeed, the literature on policy responsiveness emphasizes the attention requirements necessary to evaluate politicians, or at least the possibility to rely on like-minded elites, advocates, or interest groups to provide the voters – who lack the necessary expertise – with cogent collective assessments to follow the political process (Gilens, 2012; Page and Shapiro, 1992). Politicians take advantage of voters' lack of attention or expertise, as shown by the American political behavior literature, which has documented the incentives of politicians to disregard the policy preferences of the median voter. This literature provides examples of higher policy responsiveness to richer (Bartels, 2008; Gilens, 2012) or core voters (Lax and Phillips, 2009) than to the median voter. It also points to politicians' efforts at hiding their lack of responsiveness with obfuscation techniques, such as providing biased information (Jacobs and Shapiro, 2000), relying on ambiguity when presenting their policy offers (Tomz and Van Houweling, 2009, 2010), and taking advantage of the lack of public attention (Jones and Baumgartner, 2005). Indeed, Achen and Bartels (2016) even associate politicians' lack of responsiveness with voters' inability to connect policies to outcomes, which leads politicians to continue investing in partisanship as a non-policy resource.

Our broader conceptualization of responsiveness, which includes not only policy preferences, but also non-policy assessments, such as competence evaluations and distributive expectations, has lower attention requirements for monitoring politicians. At least partially, prior experience can contribute more to voters' non-policy assessments than to discerning the connection between policy promises and outcomes. Indeed, Stokes (1963) suggests that valence issues are easier to gauge than policies for the citizenry, whereas Kitschelt (2000) and Keefer (2007) point to the facility with which voters can figure out whether politicians fulfill their distributive promises of delivering private or club goods, such as a public-sector job or pavement on their street. The lower informational requirement of these non-policy dimensions should make it easier for voters to make politicians accountable to their electoral promises, thereby increasing their responsiveness in a broader sense. However, it may also generate incentives for adopting short-term fixes in response to contemporary perceptions and expectations, which could have long-term deleterious consequences.

We therefore expect higher responsiveness to voters' non-policy preferences as these broaden the range of options of politicians and are easier for voters to monitor. However, increasing responsiveness to non-policy preferences may allow politicians to reduce their attention to citizens' policy preferences – especially for voters who are more sensitive to non-policy than policy offers ($\beta > \alpha$) – thus generating trade-offs in terms of policy responsiveness. As voters' electoral sensitivity change according to the type of offers, politicians can be responsive on one dimension at the expense of the others in the voter utility function. These biases in policy attention resulting from the diverse components of responsiveness in our conceptualization have been associated with negative trade-offs for voters in the literature. For instance, many scholars assume that politicians will cater to the policy preferences of richer voters and non-policy preferences of poorer voters, especially because the latter derive a higher marginal utility from targeted distribution, thus producing pro-rich policies.[11]

Our approach does not assume trade-offs, but investigates how non-policy preferences may generate biases in favor of richer or poorer voters. For instance, assessments of economic competence were associated with policy preferences in Chile but not in Argentina. Therefore, we expect these evaluations to accentuate the policy influence of Chilean richer voters, who are the most sensitive to both parties' ideological position and macroeconomic competence, in line with the fiscal conservatism that characterized this country during the period of study. Moreover, we have seen that patronage expectations, although not associated with policy preferences, are the highest not among poorer but middle-class voters in Chile, further weakening politicians' responsiveness to less well-off voters, as documented in Chapter 8.

By contrast, we do not expect assessment of economic competence to necessarily generate a pro-rich bias in Argentina because they are unconnected to voters' ideological preferences and have the strongest impact on poor voters' electoral choices, thus allowing the parties to move in the

---

[11] This is an assumption of Acemoglu and Robinson's (2005) argument about democracy and redistribution and is explicitly discussed as a possible consequence by many studies of clientelism, including Kitschelt (2000), Luna (2014), and Stokes et al. (2013).

policy space. Indeed, analysis of redistribution through taxes and social policy in Latin America circa 2010, finds that Argentina redistributes more than Chile, suggesting similar class biases to those we encountered (Lustig, Lopez-Calva, and Ortiz-Juarez, 2013). However, there is also evidence that many (but not all) social programs delivering private goods tend to be politicized in Argentina toward core voters, but not in Chile during the period we study (Garay, 2016; Luna and Mardones, 2017). Such patterns coincide with our expectations of how activist networks constrain politicians in both countries.[12]

In short, our broader conceptualization of responsiveness does not elude but shares the problems already identified for policy responsiveness in terms of how representation works, as pointed out at the onset of this section. However, by including non-policy dimensions, it increases the areas in which voters can make politicians' responsive while lowering informational demands they face. In our view, that expansion increases their capacity to make politicians' accountable, although it is important to empirically assess whether non-policy responsiveness generates trade-offs with policies affecting them in the longer run. Indeed, those trade-offs should be investigated rather than assumed to better understand the biases of each polity and the consequences of those biases for distinct sets of voters.

Finally, the operationalization of our framework provides an important tool for the exploration of policy and non-policy biases by facilitating the evaluation of how voter preferences can shape them. That is, beyond the effect of mechanisms for electoral financing or the actions of interest groups, we point here to another crucial element shaping the opportunities and constraints faced by politicians when defining the allocations of resources in their electoral portfolio and the policy and non-policy promises they make to the electorate. We expect others will follow us in extending its applicability to other polities.

---

[12] Our prior work, moreover, shows that the effect of activists' networks on distributive expectations for all three types of goods analyzed in Chapter 6 is only significant for the PJ and UCR in Argentina. By contrast, we do not find this effect for any of the parties in Chile (Calvo and Murillo, 2013: 868–869).

# APPENDICES

## Appendix to Chapter 2

### 2.A THE EFFECT OF NON-POLICY ENDOWMENTS ON POLICY OFFERS: A STACKELBERG LEADERSHIP MODEL

The second contribution of our research is that the optimal policy offer that a party should make to voters will change when there are asymmetries in non-policy endowments: when voters perceive one of the parties as less competent, as having a smaller party network, or as less capable of delivering patronage jobs. We introduce a *Stackelberg* model of party competition where non-policy endowments shape the optimal policy offers made by parties. The *Stackelberg* leadership model (Bernhardt and Ingerman, 1985; Von Stackelberg, 2010) is frequently used in economics to describe the strategic behavior of two oligopolistic firms, one of which has an endowment advantage/disadvantage and delivers benefits at a lower/higher cost.[1] In what follows, we introduce a two-party Stackelberg model where one party has a non-policy endowment disadvantage and, consequently, makes an optimal policy offers that is further removed from the median voter

Equilibrium in our version of the model is dependent on two important preference constraints that can be empirically verified. First, voters perceive parties as unequally equipped to provide non-policy benefits. Second, the policy preferences of voters correlate with perceptions of non-policy endowments. This could be the result of motivated reasoning,

---

[1] See Berhardt and Ingman (1985) for an example where the leader and follower have different reputations. Their Stackelberg game considers an incumbent that moves first and a follower that responds to the leader's policy offer.

as discussed earlier in Chapter 2, or the result of verifiable differences in social capital, organization, or access to public office. If either of these two constraints is not satisfied, then the model reverts to a policy only probabilistic model with Downsian convergence to the median voter.

An important constraint to this model is that once the leader finds its optimal Stackelberg solution, it cannot defect and pursue a non-Stackelberg strategy, which would mirror the optimal offer of the follower. This constraint also highlights another characteristic of the Stackelberg model, whereby an initial move by the follower would lead to a different optimal move by the leader.

The model assumes that we have two parties, the *Leader* (party 1) and the *Follower* (party 2). We consider the same equation earlier in Chapter 2, and consider that party 2 has a non-policy disadvantage, $\overline{T_1} > \overline{T_2}$:

$$U(V_{i1}) = -\alpha(x_i-L_1)^2 + \beta T_{1i} \qquad \text{(Eq. 2.A.1)}$$

$$U(V_{i2}) = -\alpha(x_i-L_2)^2 + \beta T_{2i} \qquad \text{(Eq. 2.A.2)}$$

$$0 < -\alpha(x_i-L_1)^2 - [\alpha(x_i-L_2)^2 + \beta T_i] \qquad \text{(Eq. 2.A.3)}$$

For simplicity, we assume that $T_i \equiv T_{2i}-T_{1i}$, with $T_i$ representing the disadvantage of party 2 with respect to 1. Voter $i$ selects party 1 when it provides a larger utility than party 2, so that the condition $0 < -\alpha(x_i-L_1)^2-[\alpha(x_i-L_2)^2 + \beta T_i]$, where $T_i < 0$ is satisfied. Assuming that preferences are normally distributed, there is a cutpoint $x_i = \Phi[U(V_{i1})-U(V_{i2})]$ that distinguishes voters that prefer the *leader*, party 1, over the *follower*, party 2.

As in the rest of the book, we assume that the voters' policy preference $x_i$ and perception of party's non-policy endowment $T_i$ correlate with each other. That is, $x_i$ and $T_i$ are drawn from a bivariate normal distribution with correlation $\rho x T$:

$$f := (x, T, \rho) \to \frac{1}{2} \frac{e^{-\frac{x^2 + T^2 - 2\rho x T}{2 - 2\rho^2}}}{\pi\sqrt{1-\rho^2}} \qquad \text{(Eq. 2.A.4)}$$

Figure 2.A.1 provides two different examples of the bivariate normal distribution, the first one describing a non-policy disadvantage that is considerably larger among conservative voters, while the second describes a party with a small non-policy disadvantage that is more significant among leftist voters. The horizontal axis describes the policy dimension, while the vertical one describes the non-policy endowment.

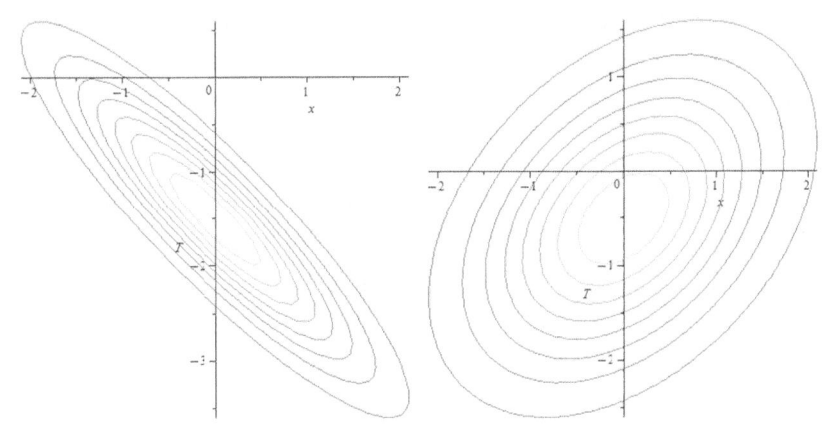

FIGURE 2.A.1. Bivariate normal distributions of policy preference $x_i$ and non-policy endowment $T_i$ in the vertical axis, two examples.
*Note*: Left plot party 1 advantage on the left, $x_i = 0, T_i = -1.5, \rho = -0.9$. Right plot party 2 disadvantage more pronounced on the left, $x_i = 0, T_i = -0.5, \rho = 0.3$.

On the left graph, we see an example where most voters are below the horizontal line. Consequently, all but a small group of very leftist voters perceive the disadvantaged party as having less of the non-policy endowment, $T$. On the second graph, the correlation between policy preferences and non-policy endowments is small, thereby a majority of voters perceive the disadvantaged party as having less of the non-policy endowment $T$, although the non-policy disadvantage is rather small.

A correlation parameter that is different from zero respects the basic constraint in Adams, Merrill, and Grofman's (2005, appendix to chapter 4) as well as in Schofield and Sened (2006) models, which produce out-of-center optimal policy offers only if the policy and non-policy terms – valence and activists respectively – correlate with each other. For any $\rho \neq 0$, therefore, we may rewrite the vote equation as:

$$X = -\alpha(x_i - L_1)^2 + [-\alpha((x_i + \rho T_i) - L_2)^2 + \beta(T_i + \rho x_i)] \quad \text{(Eq. 2.A.5)}$$

In the Stackelberg leadership model, the advantaged firm – the *leader* – moves first. In making the first move, however, it knows that the follower anticipates the leader's best move and that the follower knows that the leader knows this. There are many reasons that justify the *leader* moving first. Although there are only two parties competing in this game, the leader may anticipate threats from new entrants. In the multiparty setting, however, we allow all parties to have different non-policy endowments and to iterate over the policy space until all of them reach equilibria (if one exists).

232                     *Non-Policy Politics*

The Stackelberg game is solved by finding the game's sub-game perfect equilibrium through backward induction, with the *leader* evaluating the optimal offer anticipated by the *follower*, optimizing its own response, and then committing to this best policy offer. In our case, we consider two parties with different quantities of the fix endowment $T$ that compete on policy $L$.

We begin with the leader, which expects the follower to differentiate the leaders' optimal response and solve the equation 2.A.6 so that $\frac{d}{dx}f(L_1) = \bar{x}_i$. That is, the leader's optimal offer takes on the position of the median voter. The follower then substitutes the leader's best policy offer into equation 2.A.6 and solves for her optimal policy response:

$$-(\bar{x}_i + \rho T_i - L_2)^2 + T_i + \rho \bar{x}_i \qquad \text{(Eq. 2.A.6)}$$

$$\frac{d}{dx}f(L_2) = \bar{x}_i + \rho T_i \qquad \text{(Eq. 2.A.7)}$$

Given that $T_i < 0$, the followers' endowment disadvantage, we know that the policy offer of party 2 – *the follower* – moves opposite to the region where voters perceive the leader, party 1, as *better*. Considering the same values entered in Figure 2.A.1, plots in Figure 2.A.2 show the displacement of the disadvantaged party away from optimal offer made by the advantaged party and in the direction of the voters that give the lowest $T_i$ scores to the leader. In the left plot of Figure 2.A.2, the displacement is

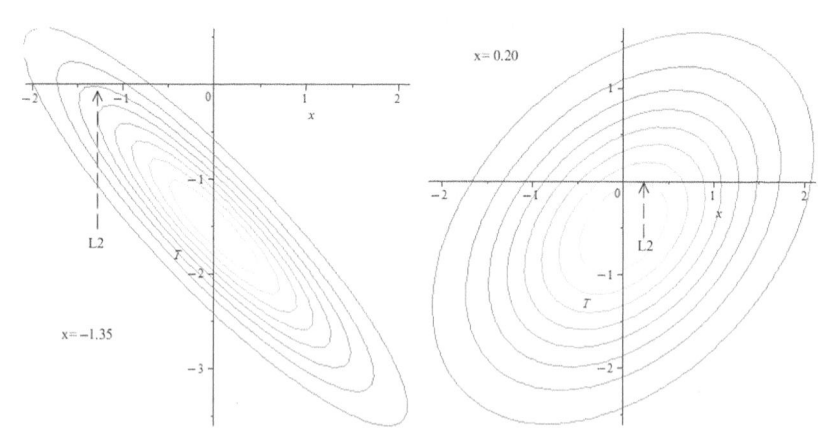

FIGURE 2.A.2. Bivariate normal distributions of policy preference $x_i$ and non-policy endowment $T_i$ in the vertical axis, two examples.
*Note*: Left plot party 2 disadvantage less pronounced among leftist voters, $x_i = 0, T_i = 1.5, \rho = -0.9$. Right plot party 2 disadvantage more pronounced among conservative voters, $x_i = 0, T_i = -0.5, \rho = -0.9$.

larger, to $L_2 = 0 + (-0.9)^*1.5 = -1.35$. Notice that while the optimal location for both parties changes, the expected vote shares of each party are strictly a function of the valence gap $T$.

Assuming that the vote is drawn from a Bernoulli distribution with normally distributed errors and $\bar{x}_i = 0$, we can then estimate the expected vote as $P_1 = \Phi(-t + \rho x)^{-1} = 0.817$; $P_2 = 0.183$. Meanwhile, on the right plot the optimal policy offer for the follower is a rather small change, $L_2 = 0.20$, with a vote for party 1 of 0.622 and a vote for party 2 of 0.378.

# Appendix to Chapter 4

Table 4.A.1. *Ideological self-placement and non-responses in Argentina and Chile*

|  | Argentina |  |  |  |  |  |  |
|---|---|---|---|---|---|---|---|
|  | C1 | C2 | C3 | D1 | D2 | E | Total |
| Self-reported ideological location | 134 | 261 | 480 | 391 | 482 | 67 | 1,815 |
|  | 88.16 | 77.22 | 70.59 | 63.37 | 60.17 | 53.17 | 66.88 |
| Non-response | 18 | 77 | 200 | 226 | 319 | 59 | 899 |
|  | 11.84 | 22.78 | 29.41 | 36.63 | 39.83 | 46.83 | 33.12 |
| Total | 152 | 338 | 680 | 617 | 801 | 126 | 2,714 |
|  | 100 | 100 | 100 | 100 | 100 | 100 | 100 |

|  | Chile |  |  |  |  |
|---|---|---|---|---|---|
|  | C1 | C2 | C3 | D | Total |
| Self-reported ideological location | 202 | 410 | 601 | 962 | 2,175 |
|  | 77.1 | 79.15 | 78.46 | 76.71 | 77.68 |
| Non-response | 60 | 108 | 165 | 292 | 625 |
|  | 22.9 | 20.85 | 21.54 | 23.29 | 22.32 |
| Total | 262 | 518 | 766 | 1,254 | 2,800 |
|  | 100 | 100 | 100 | 100 | 100 |

236                                  *Non-Policy Politics*

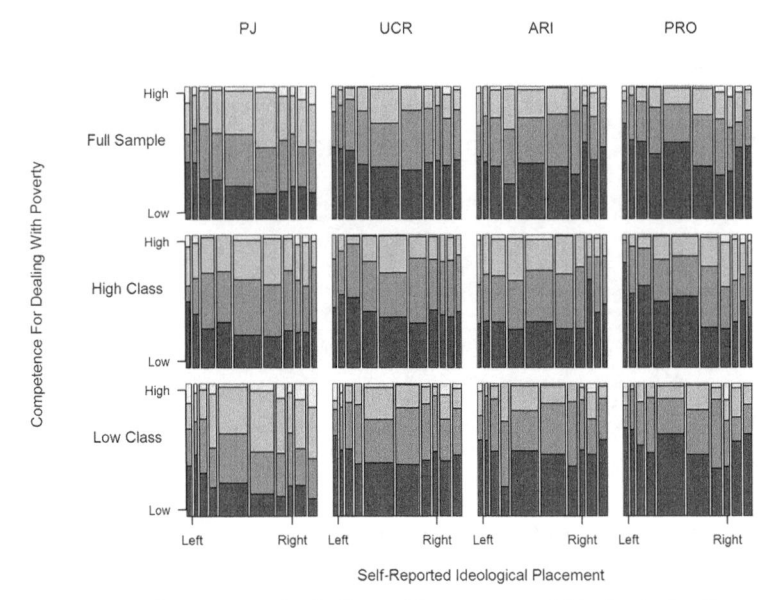

FIGURE 4.A.1. Competence in dealing with poverty and ideological self-placement in Argentina
*Note*: Mosaic plot with self-reported ideological location in the horizontal axis and perceptions of capacity to deal with poverty in the vertical axis, by class.

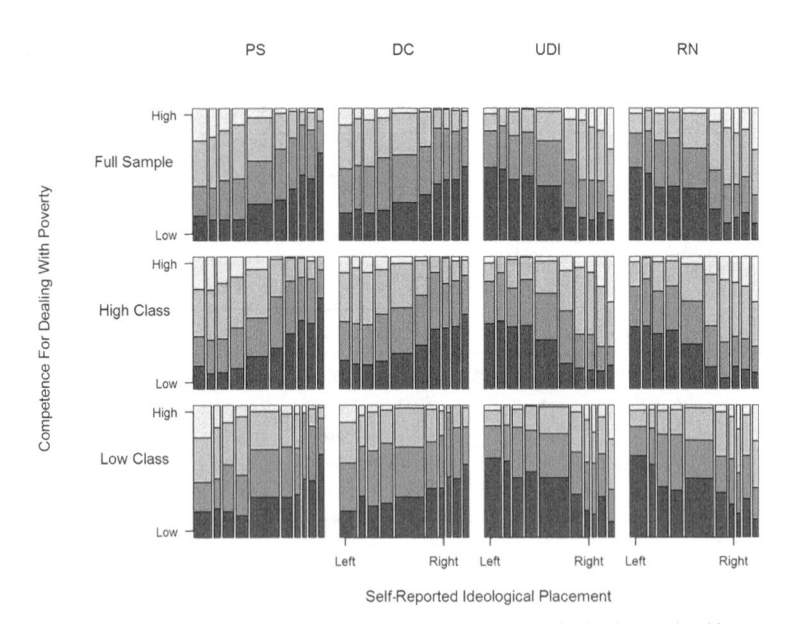

FIGURE 4.A.2. Competence in dealing with poverty and ideological self-placement in Chile
*Note*: Mosaic plot with self-reported ideological location in the horizontal axis and perceptions of capacity to deal with poverty in the vertical axis, by class.

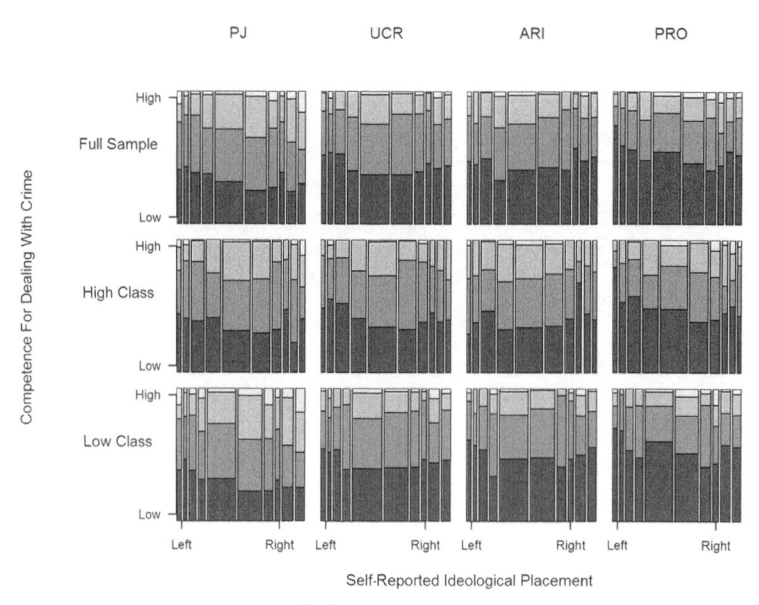

FIGURE 4.A.3. Competence in dealing with crime and ideological self-placement in Argentina
*Note*: Mosaic plot with self-reported ideological location in the horizontal axis and perceptions of capacity to deal with crime in the vertical axis, by class.

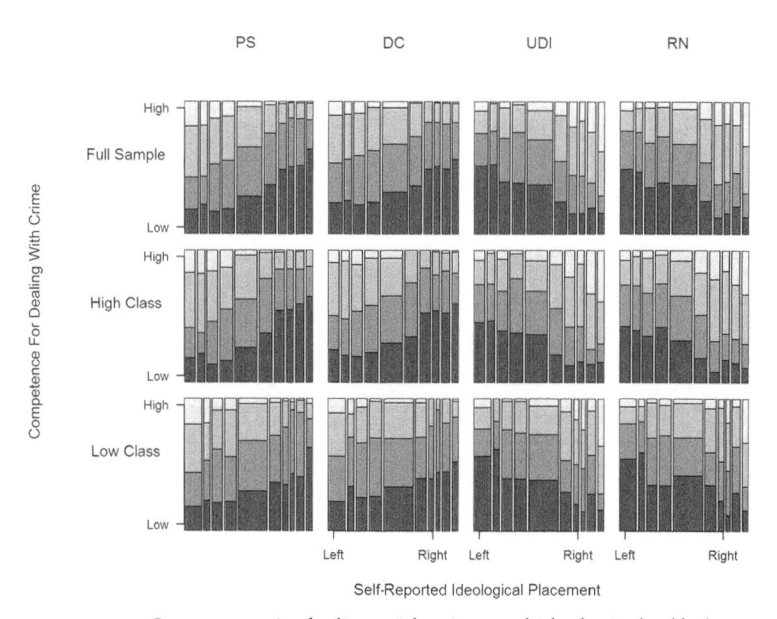

FIGURE 4.A.4. Competence in dealing with crime and ideological self-placement in Chile
*Note*: Mosaic plot with self-reported ideological location in the horizontal axis and perceptions of capacity to deal with crime in the vertical axis, by class.

# Appendix to Chapter 5

TABLE 5.A.1. *Networks of activists compared with volunteers*

| Networks of volunteers, Chile and Argentina (Percent of population) ||||
|---|---|---|---|
| **CHILE** | | **ARGENTINA** | |
| Volunteer PS | 0.195 | Volunteer PJ | 0.640 |
| Activist PS | 0.356 | Activist PJ | 0.766 |
| Volunteer DC | 0.167 | Volunteer UCR | 0.311 |
| Activist DC | 0.299 | Activist UCR | 0.420 |
| Volunteer PPD | 0.126 | Volunteer ARI | 0.037 |
| Activist PPD | 0.200 | Activist ARI | 0.056 |
| Volunteer UDI | 0.117 | Volunteer PRO | 0.019 |
| Activist UDI | 0.199 | Activist PRO | 0.029 |
| Volunteer RN | 0.124 | Volunteer PPP | 0.098 |
| Activist RN | 0.147 | Activist PPP | 0.108 |

## 5.A A STATISTICAL MODEL TO MEASURE POLITICAL NETWORKS

The model estimates the three sets of parameters that are key to the utility function described in Chapter 5: the relative size of each respondent's personal network $\alpha_i$, the relative prevalence of each group $k$ in the population $\beta_k$, and a parameter that explores individual-level deviations from the personal network and group prevalence. The overdispersed Poisson model uses the count of individuals known to each respondent as the dependent variable and estimates three sets of latent parameters:

$$y_{ik} \sim Poisson\left(e^{\alpha_i + \beta_k + \delta_{ik}}\right) \quad \text{(Eq. 5.A.1)}$$

where $\alpha_i$ describes the size of the personal network of respondent $i$, $\beta_k$ describes the expected prevalence of group $k$ in the population, and the overdispersion parameter $\delta_{ik}$ estimates a multiplicative factor with individual and group-level deviations from the personal network $\alpha_i$ and group prevalence $\beta_k$ (Gelman and Hill, 2007). We use a vector of known group offsets to rescale the parameters of interest to theoretically meaningful sets of values. In the first model, we estimate the size of personal networks using as offset the log of the frequencies of the known populations, $O_k \equiv \{o_1, \ldots, o_k\}$. Each of the different elements of $O_k$ describes group frequencies that we know e.g. $o_1$ = number of Silvias in the population.

$$y_{ik} \sim Poisson(O_k\, e^{\alpha_i + \beta_k + \delta_{ik}}), \text{where } O_k \equiv \{o_1, \ldots, o_k\} \quad \text{(Eq. 5.A.2)}$$

The posterior median of each individual respondent's parameter provides a vector, $A_i \equiv \{\hat{\alpha}_1, \ldots, \hat{\alpha}_i\}$, describing the log of the total number of people in each respondent's personal network: e.g. if $\hat{\alpha}_1 = 4.97$, the number of individuals in the personal network of respondent 1 is $N_p = \exp(4.97) = 145$. The vector of personal network parameters $\hat{\alpha}_1$ is then used as offset for the second model estimated using Equation (5.A.3):

$$y_{ik} \sim Poisson(A_i\, e^{\alpha_i + \beta_k + \delta_{ik}}), \text{where } A_i \equiv \{\hat{\alpha}_i, \ldots, \hat{\alpha}_i\} \quad \text{(Eq. 5.A.3)}$$

Hence, to estimate the prevalence of different political groups in the population, we first estimate a model that measures the size of the respondents' personal networks, $A_i \equiv \{\hat{\alpha}_1, \ldots, \hat{\alpha}_i\}$. Then, in a second stage, we use these first estimates to rescale the group parameters to meaningful quantities.

We estimate this model in WinBUGS 3.1.4 in R 3.1 as described in the code below. Alternative specifications using LMER, as described in Zheng et al. (2006) are available upon request:

```
####################################################
##
## WinBUGS over-dispersed poisson model.
##
####################################################
model {
  for (i in 1:N) {
    howmany[i] ~ dpois(lambda[i])
       log(lambda[i]) <- offset[i] + mu + b.greg[id[i]] +
       b.cat[category[i]] + epsilon[i]

       epsilon[i] ~ dnorm(0, tau.epsilon)
   }
```

```
mu ~ dnorm(0,.01)
mu.adj <- mu + mean(b.greg[])+ mean(b.cat[])
tau.epsilon <- pow(sigma.epsilon, -2)
sigma.epsilon ~ dunif(0,10)

for (i in 1: G) {
 b.greg[i] ~ dnorm(0, tau.greg)
 b.greg.adj[i] <- b.greg[i] - mean(b.greg[])
 }

tau.greg <- pow(sigma.greg, -2)
sigma.greg ~ dunif(0, 10)

for (t in 1:C) {
 b.cat[t] ~ dnorm(0, tau.cat)
 b.cat.adj[t] <- b.cat[t] - mean(b.cat[])
}

tau.cat <- pow(sigma.cat, -2)
sigma.cat ~ dunif(0, 10)
}
```

# Appendix to Chapter 6

## 6.A CODE FOR MULTINOMIAL CHOICE MODEL IN WINBUGS

Parameters by socioeconomic status were estimated using WinBUGS 3.1.4. The model below is a multinomial choice specification with random slopes indexed by the variable SES in the Argentine and Chilean surveys. Full replication materials may be downloaded from the authors' websites.

```
model
    {
      for (t in 1:J) {
                #Priors
        A[t] ~dnorm(0,.01)
             B[t] ~ dnorm(0,.01)
             C[t] ~ dnorm(0,.01)
             D[t] ~ dnorm(0,.01)
             #prob[t]<- mean(z[,t])
        }
for (i in 1 : I) { # Loop around groups
        Y[i,1:K] ~ dmulti(z[i,1:K] , 1)

for (k in 1 : K) { # Multinomial Choice Model

z[i,k]  <- phi[i,k] / sum(phi [i,])
log(phi[i,k])<- D[nse[i]]*capaz[i,k] +C[nse[i]]* bienes[i,k] +
        B[nse[i]]*network[i,k] +A[nse[i]]* (x[i,k])
            }}}
}
```

TABLE 6.A.1. *Determinants of the vote in Argentina, conditional (multinomial) choice model*

| | Model1 | Model2 | Model3 | Model4 | | Model1 | Model2 | Model3 | Model4 |
|---|---|---|---|---|---|---|---|---|---|
| Ideological distance | -0.0205*** (0.003) | -0.0205*** (0.003) | -0.0184*** (0.003) | -0.0194*** (0.003) | Large district (UCR) | | | | -0.4885** (0.200) |
| Competence to manage the economy | 1.1262*** (0.066) | 1.0926*** (0.066) | 1.021*** (0.067) | 0.9889*** (0.068) | Large district (ARI) | | | | 0.8071*** (0.272) |
| Proximity to network of activists | 0.4917*** (0.054) | 0.4661*** (0.054) | 0.4362*** (0.055) | 0.4186*** (0.056) | Large district (PRO) | | | | 0.7352** (0.301) |
| Handouts | 0.0923*** (0.032) | | | -0.0347 (0.036) | Large district (PPP) | | | | 0.5386* (0.298) |
| Patronage | | 0.2433*** (0.038) | | 0.1707*** (0.042) | Proper to distribute Handouts (UCR) | -0.0355 (0.033) | | | -0.0452 (0.037) |
| Pork | | | 0.2439*** (0.028) | 0.1975*** (0.030) | Proper to distribute Jobs (UCR) | | -0.0113 (0.029) | | -0.017 (0.046) |
| NSE C2(UCR) | 0.1393 (0.467) | -0.0226 (0.470) | 0.0699 (0.478) | -0.0405 (0.493) | Proper to distribute Pork (UCR) | | | 0.0143 (0.032) | 0.0378 (0.049) |
| NSE C3(UCR) | -0.1519 (0.437) | -0.2696 (0.439) | -0.1683 (0.447) | -0.3072 (0.463) | Proper to distribute Handouts (ARI) | -0.0963** (0.038) | | | -0.0488 (0.044) |

| | | | | | | | |
|---|---|---|---|---|---|---|---|
| NSE D1(UCR) | -0.5392 (0.451) | -0.6306 (0.452) | -0.5318 (0.459) | -0.5712 (0.472) | | -0.0994*** (0.032) | 0.002 (0.051) |
| NSE D2(UCR) | -0.3212 (0.436) | -0.4295 (0.436) | -0.387 (0.445) | -0.5258 (0.463) | Proper to distribute Jobs (ARI) Proper to allocate Public Works (ARI) | | -0.1243*** (0.034) -0.1118** (0.051) |
| NSE D3(UCR) | -0.4986 (0.614) | -0.512 (0.608) | -0.5257 (0.618) | -0.6735 (0.634) | Proper to distribute Handouts (PRO) | -0.0575 (0.042) | -0.035 (0.048) |
| NSE C2(ARI) | -0.419 (0.401) | -0.4432 (0.404) | -0.4411 (0.406) | -0.42 (0.408) | Proper to distribute Jobs (PRO) | -0.0527 (0.036) | -0.0533 (0.052) |
| NSE C3(ARI) | -0.9822** (0.378) | -0.9689** (0.381) | -0.9** (0.379) | -0.7786** (0.384) | Proper to allocate Public Works (PRO) | | -0.0034 (0.042) 0.0406 (0.056) |
| NSE D1(ARI) | -1.3298*** (0.401) | -1.3022*** (0.403) | -1.2295*** (0.402) | -1.1901*** (0.405) | Proper to allocate Public handouts (PPP) | -0.0158 (0.045) | -0.044 (0.050) |
| NSE D2(ARI) | -2.0045*** (0.443) | -2.076*** (0.447) | -1.9841*** (0.444) | -1.84*** (0.451) | Proper to allocate jobs (PPP) | 0.0175 (0.043) | 0.039 (0.072) |

(continued)

TABLE 6.A.1. (continued)

|  | Model1 | Model2 | Model3 | Model4 |  | Model1 | Model2 | Model3 | Model4 |
|---|---|---|---|---|---|---|---|---|---|
| NSE D3(ARI) | -1.7546** | -1.7883** | -1.8003** | -1.5629* | Proper to allocate Public Works (PPP) |  |  | 0.0165 | -0.0089 |
|  | (0.815) | (0.818) | (0.816) | (0.833) |  |  |  | (0.047) | (0.074) |
| NSE C2(PRO) | -0.1927 | -0.1914 | -0.2546 | -0.1832 | Women (UCR) | -0.0187 | 0.0121 | -0.0252 | -0.0058 |
|  | (0.410) | (0.417) | (0.426) | (0.430) |  | (0.192) | (0.195) | (0.195) | (0.201) |
| NSE C3(PRO) | -1.4424*** | -1.393*** | -1.3135*** | -1.1626*** | Women (ARI) | -0.3809* | -0.3593* | -0.4152* | -0.377* |
|  | (0.416) | (0.423) | (0.426) | (0.433) |  | (0.216) | (0.218) | (0.220) | (0.223) |
| NSE D1(PRO) | -1.829*** | -1.8016*** | -1.701*** | -1.6093*** | Women (PRO) | -0.4554* | -0.4366* | -0.4503* | -0.3754 |
|  | (0.442) | (0.447) | (0.451) | (0.456) |  | (0.238) | (0.240) | (0.244) | (0.249) |
| NSE D2(PRO) | -1.8974*** | -1.8431*** | -1.8254*** | -1.5976*** | Women (PPP) | -0.1449 | -0.1644 | -0.1746 | -0.1544 |
|  | (0.456) | (0.459) | (0.465) | (0.474) |  | (0.281) | (0.285) | (0.285) | (0.288) |
| NSE D3(PRO) | -2.4698** | -2.3959** | -2.3475** | -2.0372* | Constant (UCR) | -2.9239*** | -2.7986*** | -3.1396*** | -2.3391*** |
|  | (1.087) | (1.088) | (1.081) | (1.089) |  | (0.783) | (0.797) | (0.817) | (0.884) |
| NSE C2(PPP) | -1.1242** | -1.3301** | -1.2012** | -1.2276** | Constant (ARI) | -0.9713 | -0.7006 | -0.5099 | -1.6676* |
|  | (0.540) | (0.547) | (0.554) | (0.554) |  | (0.856) | (0.877) | (0.883) | (0.978) |
| NSE C3(PPP) | -1.3452*** | -1.5029*** | -1.2766*** | -1.2377*** | Constant (PRO) | -0.2713 | -0.3302 | -0.8922 | -1.8597* |
|  | (0.462) | (0.461) | (0.466) | (0.467) |  | (0.932) | (0.943) | (0.977) | (1.060) |
| NSE D1(PPP) | -2.0826*** | -2.2603*** | -2.0679*** | -2.0976*** | Constant (PPP) | -1.8732* | -1.8701* | -2.3599** | -2.9394** |
|  | (0.524) | (0.522) | (0.527) | (0.524) |  | (1.106) | (1.126) | (1.137) | (1.199) |
| NSE D2(PPP) | -2.172*** | -2.3478*** | -2.1246*** | -2.0283*** |  |  |  |  |  |
|  | (0.502) | (0.499) | (0.505) | (0.507) |  |  |  |  |  |
| NSE D3(PPP) | -1.5015** | -1.6991** | -1.5436** | -1.3136* |  |  |  |  |  |
|  | (0.694) | (0.697) | (0.702) | (0.715) |  |  |  |  |  |

|  |  |  |  |  |
|---|---|---|---|---|
| Personal network (UCR) | 0.3515*** (0.121) | 0.3319*** (0.123) | 0.3581*** (0.123) | 0.2762** (0.127) |
| Personal network (ARI) | 0.1534 (0.147) | 0.1669 (0.148) | 0.192 (0.148) | 0.2998* (0.153) |
| Personal network (PRO) | −0.0244 (0.164) | 0.0171 (0.164) | 0.072 (0.167) | 0.1534 (0.170) |
| Personal network (PPP) | 0.2385 (0.188) | 0.2427 (0.189) | 0.3241* (0.189) | 0.3646* (0.192) |
| LogLik | −1203.54 | −1183.1 | −1162.38 | −1138.9 |
| N | 1696 | 1696 | 1696 | 1696 |

*Note:* Conditions (multinomial) logit model with alternative-specific and individual-specific parameter estimates. Estimated in R 3.2 using the package *mlogit* (Croissant, 2012).

TABLE 6.A.2. *Determinants of the vote in Chile, conditional (multinomial) choice model*

|  | Model1 | Model2 | Model3 | Model4 |  | Model1 | Model2 | Model3 | Model4 |
|---|---|---|---|---|---|---|---|---|---|
| Ideological distance | -0.0381*** | -0.0373*** | -0.0364*** | -0.0359*** | Proper to Distribute Handouts (DC) | 0.0107 |  |  | -0.0186 |
|  | (0.003) | (0.003) | (0.003) | (0.003) |  | (0.029) |  |  | (0.039) |
| Competence to manage the economy | 1.0474*** | 1.0368*** | 1.0273*** | 1.0142*** | Proper to distribute Handouts (PPD) |  | 0.0297 |  | 0.0283 |
|  | (0.056) | (0.056) | (0.056) | (0.056) |  |  | (0.026) |  | (0.048) |
| Proximity to network of activists | 0.3321*** | 0.3279*** | 0.3267*** | 0.3219*** | Proper to distribute Handouts (UDI) |  |  | 0.0337 | 0.0204 |
|  | (0.041) | (0.041) | (0.041) | (0.041) |  |  |  | (0.025) | (0.042) |
| Handouts | 0.0679** |  |  | 0.0014 | Proper to distribute Handouts (RN) | -0.0514 |  |  | -0.1067** |
|  | (0.032) |  |  | (0.036) |  | (0.032) |  |  | (0.042) |
| Patronage |  | 0.1757*** |  | 0.134*** | Proper to distribute Jobs (DC) |  | 0.0218 |  | 0.0375 |
|  |  | (0.035) |  | (0.039) |  |  | (0.027) |  | (0.048) |
| Pork |  |  | 0.1552*** | 0.1314*** | Proper to distribute Jobs (PPD) |  |  | 0.0339 | 0.0508 |
|  |  |  | (0.026) | (0.027) |  |  |  | (0.027) | (0.042) |
| NSE C2(DC) | -0.2001 | -0.2056 | -0.1449 | -0.1669 | Proper to distribute Jobs (UDI) | -0.0398 |  |  | -0.0541 |
|  | (0.426) | (0.426) | (0.427) | (0.427) |  | (0.034) |  |  | (0.045) |

| | | | | | | | |
|---|---|---|---|---|---|---|---|
| NSE C3(DC) | 0.3639 | 0.3846 | 0.4417 | 0.4227 | Proper to distribute Jobs (RN) | | | -0.0089 |
| | (0.396) | (0.396) | (0.397) | (0.398) | | | | (0.052) |
| NSE D(DC) | 0.3618 | 0.3543 | 0.3903 | 0.3726 | Proper to allocate Public Works (DC) | | 0.012 | 0.0447 |
| | (0.388) | (0.386) | (0.387) | (0.389) | | | (0.028) | (0.045) |
| NSE C2(PPD) | −0.7427* | −0.781** | −0.6937* | −0.682* | Proper to allocate Public Works (PPD) | −0.0668** | | −0.0796* |
| | (0.396) | (0.397) | (0.398) | (0.400) | | (0.034) | | (0.044) |
| NSE C3(PPD) | −0.4908 | −0.5 | −0.4179 | −0.4236 | Proper to allocate Public Works (UDI) | | −0.0164 | 0.0257 |
| | (0.370) | (0.371) | (0.371) | (0.374) | | | (0.028) | (0.049) |
| NSE D(PPD) | −0.2061 | −0.2653 | −0.1991 | −0.1353 | Proper to allocate Public Works (RN) | | | −0.0139 | 0.0022 |
| | (0.353) | (0.353) | (0.353) | (0.357) | | | (0.026) | (0.043) |
| NSE C2 (UDI) | −0.3951 | −0.4359 | −0.3873 | −0.3911 | Women (DC) | 0.0782 | 0.0733 | 0.0811 | 0.067 |
| | (0.397) | (0.399) | (0.398) | (0.400) | | (0.172) | (0.173) | (0.173) | (0.174) |
| NSE C3(UDI) | −0.1769 | −0.1854 | −0.1064 | −0.1136 | Women (PPD) | −0.0511 | −0.076 | −0.0647 | −0.0566 |
| | (0.379) | (0.381) | (0.380) | (0.382) | | (0.180) | (0.180) | (0.181) | (0.182) |

(*continued*)

249

TABLE 6.A.2. (continued)

|  | Model1 | Model2 | Model3 | Model4 |  | Model1 | Model2 | Model3 | Model4 |
|---|---|---|---|---|---|---|---|---|---|
| NSE D (UDI) | -0.0196 (0.365) | -0.082 (0.365) | -0.0133 (0.363) | 0.0211 (0.367) | Women (UDI) | 0.4725** (0.190) | 0.4946*** (0.191) | 0.446** (0.191) | 0.4665** (0.193) |
| NSE C2 (RN) | -0.3836 (0.366) | -0.4409 (0.367) | -0.3683 (0.367) | -0.3922 (0.368) | Women (RN) | 0.1477 (0.181) | 0.1408 (0.181) | 0.1037 (0.181) | 0.113 (0.183) |
| NSE C3(RN) | -0.2475 (0.351) | -0.2771 (0.352) | -0.1658 (0.352) | -0.1997 (0.354) | Constant (DC) | -0.816 (0.681) | -0.88 (0.686) | -0.9348 (0.691) | -0.9094 (0.692) |
| NSE D(RN) | -0.259 (0.337) | -0.3555 (0.337) | -0.2678 (0.337) | -0.2529 (0.339) | Constant (PPD) | -0.167 (0.695) | -0.427 (0.699) | -0.4639 (0.701) | -0.4428 (0.707) |
| Personal network (DC) | 0.0143 (0.107) | 0.0068 (0.108) | 0.0038 (0.108) | 0.0033 (0.109) | Constant (UDI) | -1.0835 (0.730) | -1.1347 (0.733)* | -1.1799 (0.736) | -1.1965 (0.738) |
| Personal network (PPD) | 0.0225 (0.113) | 0.0358 (0.113) | 0.0141 (0.113) | 0.0165 (0.114) | Constant (RN) | -1.2367* (0.695) | -1.255* (0.698) | -1.3016* (0.701) | -1.2699* (0.704) |
| Personal network (UDI) | 0.1733 (0.118) | 0.1767 (0.119) | 0.1623 (0.119) | 0.171 (0.120) | | | | | |
| Personal network (RN) | 0.2993*** (0.113) | 0.2985*** (0.114) | 0.2991*** (0.114) | 0.3039*** (0.115) | LogLik N | -1824.28 1584 | -1815.83 1584 | -1809.91 1584 | -1802.01 1584 |

*Note*: Conditions (multinomial) logit model with alternative-specific and individual-specific parameter estimates. Estimated in R 3.2 using the package *mlogit* (Croissant, 2012).

TABLE 6.A.3. *Argentina vote choice model by socioeconomic class, multinomial model (WinBUGS), handouts*

| | | Mean | sd | 2.50% | 50% | 97.50% | Rhat |
|---|---|---|---|---|---|---|---|
| Ideological distance | C1 | -0.0366 | 0.0145 | -0.0698 | -0.0354 | -0.0099 | 1.0108 |
| | C2 | -0.0285 | 0.0078 | -0.0434 | -0.0288 | -0.0144 | 1.0085 |
| | C3 | -0.0257 | 0.0057 | -0.0389 | -0.0254 | -0.0152 | 1.0009 |
| | D1 | -0.0259 | 0.0065 | -0.0402 | -0.0255 | -0.0138 | 1.0044 |
| | D2 | -0.0298 | 0.0058 | -0.0420 | -0.0297 | -0.0185 | 1.0033 |
| | E | -0.0245 | 0.0123 | -0.0494 | -0.0240 | -0.0007 | 1.0084 |
| Network of activists | C1 | 0.4233 | 0.3938 | -0.3102 | 0.4053 | 1.1480 | 1.0019 |
| | C2 | 0.6482 | 0.3679 | -0.1053 | 0.6319 | 1.3432 | 1.0009 |
| | C3 | 0.6663 | 0.3474 | -0.0076 | 0.6768 | 1.3220 | 1.0066 |
| | D1 | 0.5211 | 0.3703 | -0.1850 | 0.5020 | 1.2340 | 1.0057 |
| | D2 | 0.5221 | 0.3839 | -0.2339 | 0.5204 | 1.2570 | 1.0046 |
| | E | 0.1933 | 0.4736 | -0.8278 | 0.2073 | 1.0680 | 1.0308 |
| Distributive expectations, handouts | C1 | 0.1405 | 0.1201 | -0.0930 | 0.1426 | 0.3643 | 1.0020 |
| | C2 | 0.1871 | 0.0802 | 0.0401 | 0.1816 | 0.3613 | 1.0014 |
| | C3 | 0.2433 | 0.0543 | 0.1469 | 0.2423 | 0.3527 | 1.0038 |
| | D1 | 0.3026 | 0.0663 | 0.1710 | 0.3026 | 0.4294 | 1.0108 |
| | D2 | 0.3898 | 0.0549 | 0.2914 | 0.3858 | 0.5002 | 1.0017 |
| | E | 0.7963 | 0.2108 | 0.4367 | 0.7760 | 1.2320 | 1.0012 |
| Competence to manage the economy | C1 | 0.9702 | 0.1849 | 0.6058 | 0.9711 | 1.3520 | 1.0010 |
| | C2 | 1.2615 | 0.1309 | 1.0170 | 1.2610 | 1.5170 | 1.0006 |
| | C3 | 1.4884 | 0.1184 | 1.2660 | 1.4840 | 1.7260 | 1.0019 |
| | D1 | 1.5719 | 0.1132 | 1.3530 | 1.5780 | 1.7860 | 1.0019 |
| | D2 | 1.6041 | 0.1016 | 1.4120 | 1.6025 | 1.8090 | 1.0029 |
| | E | 1.3623 | 0.2449 | 0.8984 | 1.3660 | 1.8820 | 1.0017 |
| Deviance | | 3441.1 | 7.8 | 3428.0 | 3440.0 | 3458.0 | 1.0035 |

TABLE 6.A.4. *Argentina vote choice model by socioeconomic class, multinomial model (WinBUGS), patronage*

|  |  | Mean | sd | 2.50% | 50% | 97.50% | Rhat |
|---|---|---|---|---|---|---|---|
| Ideological distance | C1 | -0.0337 | 0.0137 | -0.0615 | -0.0335 | -0.0093 | 1.0077 |
|  | C2 | -0.0284 | 0.0081 | -0.0443 | -0.0287 | -0.0134 | 1.0049 |
|  | C3 | -0.0232 | 0.0057 | -0.0354 | -0.0233 | -0.0125 | 1.0033 |
|  | D1 | -0.0271 | 0.0066 | -0.0400 | -0.0269 | -0.0146 | 1.0046 |
|  | D2 | -0.0311 | 0.0059 | -0.0434 | -0.0310 | -0.0201 | 1.0052 |
|  | E | -0.0214 | 0.0112 | -0.0441 | -0.0205 | -0.0008 | 1.0034 |
| Network of activists | C1 | 0.4380 | 0.4115 | -0.3385 | 0.4224 | 1.2312 | 1.0081 |
|  | C2 | 0.4645 | 0.3787 | -0.2716 | 0.4479 | 1.1700 | 1.0011 |
|  | C3 | 0.5301 | 0.3759 | -0.1873 | 0.5496 | 1.2301 | 1.0191 |
|  | D1 | 0.3988 | 0.3708 | -0.3113 | 0.3806 | 1.1250 | 1.0027 |
|  | D2 | 0.5999 | 0.3770 | -0.1313 | 0.6005 | 1.3150 | 1.0077 |
|  | E | 0.1802 | 0.4561 | -0.7111 | 0.1866 | 0.9996 | 1.0138 |
| Distributive expectations, patronage | C1 | 0.2286 | 0.0963 | 0.0647 | 0.2219 | 0.4243 | 1.0026 |
|  | C2 | 0.3233 | 0.0809 | 0.1734 | 0.3218 | 0.4948 | 1.0023 |
|  | C3 | 0.3523 | 0.0613 | 0.2419 | 0.3520 | 0.4777 | 1.0110 |
|  | D1 | 0.4033 | 0.0865 | 0.2347 | 0.4018 | 0.5823 | 1.0034 |
|  | D2 | 0.5392 | 0.0861 | 0.3909 | 0.5331 | 0.7215 | 1.0068 |
|  | E | 0.8091 | 0.2784 | 0.3306 | 0.7729 | 1.4400 | 1.0013 |
| Competence to manage the economy | C1 | 0.9362 | 0.1811 | 0.5718 | 0.9343 | 1.3170 | 1.0029 |
|  | C2 | 1.2400 | 0.1388 | 0.9905 | 1.2350 | 1.5220 | 1.0023 |
|  | C3 | 1.4563 | 0.1160 | 1.2479 | 1.4510 | 1.6980 | 1.0047 |
|  | D1 | 1.5482 | 0.1174 | 1.3330 | 1.5480 | 1.7831 | 1.0006 |
|  | D2 | 1.5559 | 0.1037 | 1.3590 | 1.5455 | 1.7700 | 1.0007 |
|  | E | 1.4024 | 0.2465 | 0.9646 | 1.4060 | 1.9212 | 1.0010 |
| Deviance |  | 3417.9 | 7.4 | 3404.0 | 3417.0 | 3434.0 | 1.0040 |

TABLE 6.A.5. *Argentina vote choice model by socioeconomic class, multinomial model (WinBUGS), pork*

| | | mean | sd | 2.50% | 50% | 97.50% | Rhat |
|---|---|---|---|---|---|---|---|
| Ideological distance | C1 | −0.0356 | 0.0140 | −0.0646 | −0.0360 | −0.0078 | 1.0166 |
| | C2 | −0.0250 | 0.0081 | −0.0413 | −0.0250 | −0.0100 | 1.0049 |
| | C3 | −0.0188 | 0.0057 | −0.0310 | −0.0186 | −0.0082 | 1.0011 |
| | D1 | −0.0244 | 0.0065 | −0.0380 | −0.0238 | −0.0125 | 1.0026 |
| | D2 | −0.0259 | 0.0058 | −0.0381 | −0.0256 | −0.0143 | 1.0029 |
| | E | −0.0209 | 0.0127 | −0.0478 | −0.0206 | 0.0026 | 1.0091 |
| Network of activists | C1 | 0.3144 | 0.4085 | −0.4925 | 0.3195 | 1.1270 | 1.0014 |
| | C2 | 0.3484 | 0.3754 | −0.4083 | 0.3367 | 1.0450 | 1.0052 |
| | C3 | 0.4209 | 0.3596 | −0.2820 | 0.4180 | 1.1260 | 1.0060 |
| | D1 | 0.2645 | 0.3806 | −0.4331 | 0.2445 | 1.0160 | 1.0021 |
| | D2 | 0.5202 | 0.3824 | −0.2299 | 0.5353 | 1.2490 | 1.0027 |
| | E | 0.1988 | 0.4586 | −0.7031 | 0.2116 | 1.0101 | 1.0111 |
| Distributive expectations, pork | C1 | 0.3791 | 0.0921 | 0.1974 | 0.3731 | 0.5564 | 1.0021 |
| | C2 | 0.3850 | 0.0619 | 0.2751 | 0.3811 | 0.5082 | 1.0008 |
| | C3 | 0.3722 | 0.0449 | 0.2903 | 0.3723 | 0.4576 | 1.0099 |
| | D1 | 0.4304 | 0.0563 | 0.3280 | 0.4304 | 0.5485 | 1.0061 |
| | D2 | 0.5013 | 0.0536 | 0.4049 | 0.4970 | 0.6130 | 1.0112 |
| | E | 0.6331 | 0.1545 | 0.3471 | 0.6198 | 0.9398 | 1.0016 |
| Competence to manage the economy | C1 | 0.8146 | 0.2004 | 0.4342 | 0.8117 | 1.2242 | 1.0017 |
| | C2 | 1.0237 | 0.1403 | 0.7597 | 1.0180 | 1.3120 | 1.0051 |
| | C3 | 1.3622 | 0.1165 | 1.1389 | 1.3580 | 1.5880 | 1.0015 |
| | D1 | 1.3772 | 0.1172 | 1.1689 | 1.3800 | 1.5970 | 1.0040 |
| | D2 | 1.4393 | 0.1088 | 1.2440 | 1.4330 | 1.6600 | 1.0007 |
| | E | 1.3292 | 0.2624 | 0.8363 | 1.3290 | 1.8600 | 1.0008 |
| Deviance | | 3207.4 | 7.6 | 3195.0 | 3207.0 | 3223.0 | 1.0007 |

TABLE 6.A.6. *Chile vote choice model by socioeconomic class, multinomial model (WinBUGS), handouts*

| | | Mean | sd | 2.50% | 50% | 97.50% | Rhat |
|---|---|---|---|---|---|---|---|
| Ideological distance | C1 | -0.0565 | 0.0144 | -0.0884 | -0.0555 | -0.0286 | 1.0072 |
| | C2 | -0.0415 | 0.0069 | -0.0551 | -0.0413 | -0.0297 | 1.0020 |
| | C3 | -0.0459 | 0.0056 | -0.0578 | -0.0457 | -0.0354 | 1.0030 |
| | D | -0.0335 | 0.0040 | -0.0418 | -0.0333 | -0.0264 | 1.0061 |
| Network of activists | C1 | 0.3557 | 0.4116 | -0.4402 | 0.3697 | 1.1590 | 1.0070 |
| | C2 | 0.8661 | 0.3517 | 0.1766 | 0.8741 | 1.5560 | 1.0036 |
| | C3 | 0.8328 | 0.3354 | 0.1581 | 0.8200 | 1.4552 | 1.0062 |
| | D | 1.3353 | 0.3346 | 0.6851 | 1.3385 | 2.0490 | 1.0049 |
| Distributive expectations, handouts | C1 | -0.1163 | 0.1096 | -0.3198 | -0.1133 | 0.0899 | 1.0006 |
| | C2 | 0.0541 | 0.0729 | -0.0865 | 0.0531 | 0.2084 | 1.0083 |
| | C3 | 0.2026 | 0.0686 | 0.0801 | 0.1941 | 0.3457 | 1.0009 |
| | D | 0.0542 | 0.0449 | -0.0336 | 0.0576 | 0.1431 | 1.0046 |
| Competence to manage the economy | C1 | 1.4518 | 0.1793 | 1.1420 | 1.4430 | 1.8240 | 1.0117 |
| | C2 | 1.0490 | 0.1197 | 0.8171 | 1.0430 | 1.2940 | 1.0205 |
| | C3 | 1.2049 | 0.1222 | 0.9844 | 1.2010 | 1.4510 | 1.0013 |
| | D | 0.9624 | 0.0702 | 0.8350 | 0.9577 | 1.1020 | 1.0019 |
| Deviance | | 3769.8 | 8.0 | 3756.0 | 3769.0 | 3787.0 | 1.0115 |

TABLE 6.A.7. *Chile vote choice model by socioeconomic class, multinomial model (WinBUGS), patronage*

|  |  | Mean | SD | 2.50% | 50% | 97.50% | R-hat |
|---|---|---|---|---|---|---|---|
| Ideological distance | C1 | −0.05546 | 0.01398 | −0.08585 | −0.05482 | −0.03008 | 1.005858 |
|  | C2 | −0.03975 | 0.00715 | −0.05375 | −0.03939 | −0.02681 | 1.003396 |
|  | C3 | −0.04377 | 0.00561 | −0.05584 | −0.04384 | −0.0331 | 1.003233 |
|  | D | −0.03325 | 0.00388 | −0.04125 | −0.03295 | −0.0267 | 1.001558 |
| Network of activists | C1 | 0.329524 | 0.40874 | −0.42096 | 0.3467 | 1.133 | 1.006004 |
|  | C2 | 0.834773 | 0.3576 | 0.11182 | 0.8133 | 1.526 | 1.002112 |
|  | C3 | 0.836756 | 0.33497 | 0.17308 | 0.8179 | 1.471275 | 1.007706 |
|  | D | 1.291809 | 0.31836 | 0.6874 | 1.283 | 1.93905 | 1.00153 |
| Distributive expectations, patronage | C1 | −0.04968 | 0.10787 | −0.2644 | −0.04297 | 0.1677 | 1.009611 |
|  | C2 | 0.298906 | 0.09499 | 0.1221 | 0.2961 | 0.4841 | 1.01461 |
|  | C3 | 0.255969 | 0.06850 | 0.132775 | 0.2498 | 0.405 | 1.003456 |
|  | D | 0.16343 | 0.04882 | 0.059299 | 0.1673 | 0.2575 | 1.007873 |
| Competence to manage the economy | C1 | 1.45923 | 0.19096 | 1.124 | 1.454 | 1.85605 | 1.015836 |
|  | C2 | 1.016215 | 0.11703 | 0.78757 | 1.014 | 1.249 | 1.012984 |
|  | C3 | 1.201626 | 0.11219 | 0.9862 | 1.199 | 1.432 | 1.007617 |
|  | D | 0.951106 | 0.07449 | 0.8181 | 0.9489 | 1.097 | 1.00084 |
| Deviance |  | 3745.893 | 7.74252 | 3732 | 3745 | 3751 | 1.009667 |

TABLE 6.A.8. *Chile vote choice model by socioeconomic class, multinomial model (WinBUGS), pork*

|  |  | Mean | sd | 2.50% | 50% | 97.50% | Rhat |
|---|---|---|---|---|---|---|---|
| Ideological distance | C1 | -0.0533 | 0.01437 | -0.08541 | -0.05264 | -0.02746 | 1.002458 |
|  | C2 | -0.03929 | 0.007053 | -0.0528 | -0.03903 | -0.02709 | 1.002487 |
|  | C3 | -0.04157 | 0.00584 | -0.05395 | -0.04134 | -0.03059 | 1.004051 |
|  | D | -0.03222 | 0.003951 | -0.04064 | -0.03222 | -0.02489 | 1.006474 |
| Network of activists | C1 | 0.316317 | 0.396951 | -0.39042 | 0.3132 | 1.162 | 1.002885 |
|  | C2 | 0.853829 | 0.341141 | 0.17736 | 0.86195 | 1.524 | 1.005544 |
|  | C3 | 0.873842 | 0.343063 | 0.1975 | 0.8449 | 1.543 | 1.007798 |
|  | D | 1.257598 | 0.331652 | 0.633455 | 1.2565 | 1.944 | 1.001044 |
| Distributive expectations, pork | C1 | 0.077603 | 0.098 | -0.1089 | 0.07894 | 0.2632 | 1.006348 |
|  | C2 | 0.227513 | 0.062911 | 0.101487 | 0.2267 | 0.3535 | 1.018673 |
|  | C3 | 0.186294 | 0.054789 | 0.087167 | 0.1885 | 0.2907 | 1.009069 |
|  | D | 0.158334 | 0.03522 | 0.089719 | 0.1598 | 0.2259 | 1.005033 |
| Competence to manage the economy | C1 | 1.460185 | 0.189736 | 1.132975 | 1.4435 | 1.861 | 1.011589 |
|  | C2 | 1.017607 | 0.128322 | 0.775147 | 1.008 | 1.279025 | 1.02181 |
|  | C3 | 1.185795 | 0.116314 | 0.9771 | 1.188 | 1.434075 | 1.00902 |
|  | D | 0.941918 | 0.073702 | 0.806172 | 0.9403 | 1.086 | 1.004181 |
| Deviance |  | 3735.347 | 7.765037 | 3721 | 3735 | 3752 | 1.013371 |

256

# Appendix to Chapter 7

TABLE 7.A.1. *The conditional effect of partisan networks on targeted distribution, ideological distance, and competence*

| | ARGENTINA | | | | CHILE | | |
|---|---|---|---|---|---|---|---|
| | Model1 Handouts | Model2 Patronage | Model3 Pork | | Model1 Handouts | Model2 Patronage | Model3 Pork |
| Ideological distance | −0.0191*** (0.003) | −0.0187*** (0.003) | −0.0177*** (0.003) | Ideological distance | −0.0372*** (0.004) | −0.037*** (0.004) | −0.0359*** (0.004) |
| Proximity to network of activists | 0.3511** (0.160) | 0.4187*** (0.160) | 0.2597 (0.168) | Proximity to network of activists | 0.3717* (0.205) | 0.3691* (0.207) | 0.4425** (0.214) |
| Distribution of goods | 0.0749** (0.032) | 0.1953*** (0.037) | 0.2655*** (0.028) | Distribution of goods | 0.0359 (0.045) | 0.1233** (0.052) | 0.1637*** (0.036) |
| Managerial competence (Economy) | 1.1513*** (0.064) | 1.1258*** (0.065) | 1.0195*** (0.066) | Managerial competence (Economy) | 0.9096*** (0.077) | 0.8984*** (0.078) | 0.8918*** (0.078) |
| Ideological Distance* Network of activists | 0.0002 (0.003) | 0.0004 (0.003) | 0.0017 (0.003) | Ideological distance* Network of activists | −0.0138** (0.006) | −0.0134** (0.006) | −0.0139** (0.006) |
| Distribution of Goods* Network of activists | 0.0505** (0.021) | 0.033 (0.022) | 0.0194 (0.019) | Distribution of goods* Network of activists | 0.0105 (0.028) | 0.0066 (0.030) | −0.0165 (0.022) |
| Managerial competence* Network of activists | 0.0127 (0.056) | −0.0026 (0.057) | 0.0332 (0.058) | Managerial competence* Network of activists | 0.0186 (0.067) | 0.02 (0.067) | 0.0207 (0.069) |

| | | | | | |
|---|---|---|---|---|---|
| UCR | −1.5529*** (0.092) | −1.5636*** (0.093) | −1.5482*** (0.094) | DC | −0.3305*** (0.122) | −0.3267*** (0.122) | −0.3228*** (0.123) |
| PRO | −1.9074*** (0.106) | −1.8655*** (0.105) | −1.7275*** (0.107) | PPD | −0.5041*** (0.128) | −0.4862*** (0.128) | −0.477*** (0.129) |
| ARI | −2.1778*** (0.117) | −2.142*** (0.117) | −2.0429*** (0.119) | RN | −0.1805 (0.140) | −0.1616 (0.140) | −0.121 (0.141) |
| PPP | −2.4623*** (0.138) | −2.4289*** (0.138) | −2.2869*** (0.138) | UDI | −0.2001 (0.135) | −0.175 (0.136) | −0.1325 (0.137) |
| LogLik | −1256.4 | −1241.4 | −1217.7 | LogLik | −1833.2 | −1823.3 | −1816 |
| N | 1696 | 1696 | 1696 | N | 1584 | 1584 | 1584 |

*Note*: Conditional Logit Model with alternative specific variables. Standard errors in parentheses with confidence levels reported as follows: * $p < 0.1$, ** $p < 0.05$, *** $p < 0.01$. The base party category is the Peronist (Justicialista) in Argentina and the Socialists (PS) in Chile. Estimated in R 3.2 using the package *mlogit* (Croissant, 2012).

TABLE 7.A.2. *Effect of networks on distribution and ideological distance by SES in Chile*

|  | Chile higher-status voters ||| | Chile lower-status voters |||
| --- | --- | --- | --- | --- | --- | --- | --- |
|  | Model1 Handouts | Model2 Patronage | Model3 Pork |  | Model1 Handouts | Model2 Patronage | Model3 Pork |
| Ideological distance | -0.0488*** (0.005) | -0.0478*** (0.005) | -0.0471*** (0.005) | Ideological distance | -0.0331*** (0.004) | -0.0327*** (0.004) | -0.0317*** (0.004) |
| Proximity to network of activists | 0.3087* (0.173) | 0.3072* (0.175) | 0.3428** (0.174) | Proximity to network of activists | 0.4112** (0.201) | 0.3845* (0.202) | 0.4422** (0.208) |
| Distribution of goods | 0.08* (0.048) | 0.1948*** (0.050) | 0.172*** (0.039) | Distribution of goods | 0.0226 (0.046) | 0.1145** (0.052) | 0.1414*** (0.036) |
| Managerial competence (Economy) | 1.1907*** (0.083) | 1.1716*** (0.083) | 1.1552*** (0.083) | Managerial competence (Economy) | 0.9094*** (0.076) | 0.8982*** (0.076) | 0.8888*** (0.076) |
| Ideological distance* Network of activists | 0.0034 (0.004) | 0.0033 (0.004) | 0.0037 (0.004) | Ideological distance* Network of activists | -0.0076 (0.005) | -0.0072 (0.005) | -0.0075 (0.005) |
| Distribution of goods* Network of activists | 0.0276 (0.023) | 0.015 (0.021) | 0.0139 (0.020) | Distribution of goods* Network of activists | 0.0033 (0.027) | 0.012 (0.029) | -0.011 (0.022) |
| Managerial competence* Network of activists | -0.0312 (0.056) | -0.0211 (0.055) | -0.0394 (0.058) | Managerial competence* Network of activists | 0.0018 (0.065) | 0.0013 (0.065) | 0.0046 (0.066) |
| DC | -0.4997*** (0.121) | -0.4817*** (0.121) | -0.4553*** (0.121) | DC | -0.3474*** (0.122) | -0.3468*** (0.122) | -0.3409*** (0.123) |

|        |              |              |              |        |              |              |              |
|--------|--------------|--------------|--------------|--------|--------------|--------------|--------------|
| PPD    | −0.684***    | −0.6615***   | −0.6507***   | PPD    | −0.5227***   | −0.5066***   | −0.4951***   |
|        | (0.126)      | (0.127)      | (0.127)      |        | (0.127)      | (0.127)      | (0.128)      |
| RN     | −0.2821**    | −0.2261*     | −0.2271*     | RN     | −0.1931      | −0.1753      | −0.1416      |
|        | (0.136)      | (0.137)      | (0.137)      |        | (0.139)      | (0.139)      | (0.140)      |
| UDI    | −0.0369      | 0.0235       | 0.0335       | UDI    | −0.2178      | −0.1939      | −0.162       |
|        | (0.128)      | (0.129)      | (0.129)      |        | (0.134)      | (0.134)      | (0.135)      |
| LogLik | −954.1535    | −947.2747    | −945.8512    | LogLik | −867.005     | −864.468     | −859.0094    |
| N      | 879          | 879          | 879          | N      | 705          | 705          | 705          |

*Note:* Conditional Logit Model with alternative specific variables. Standard errors in parentheses with confidence levels reported as follows: * $p < 0.1$, ** $p < 0.05$, *** $p < 0.01$. The base party category is the Socialists (PS) in Chile. Estimated in R 3.2 using the package *mlogit* (Croissant, 2012).

TABLE 7.A.3. *Effect of networks on distribution and ideological distance by SES in Argentina*

|  | Argentina higher-status voters ||| | Argentina lower-status voters |||
| --- | --- | --- | --- | --- | --- | --- | --- |
|  | Model1 Handouts | Model2 Patronage | Model3 Pork |  | Model1 Handouts | Model2 Patronage | Model3 Pork |
| Ideological distance | -0.0206*** (0.005) | -0.021*** (0.005) | -0.0187*** (0.005) | Ideological distance | -0.0204*** (0.005) | -0.0193*** (0.005) | -0.017*** (0.005) |
| Proximity to network of activists | 0.6709*** (0.211) | 0.7312*** (0.216) | 0.6003*** (0.220) | Proximity to network of activists | 0.006 (0.284) | 0.2937 (0.264) | 0.0805 (0.276) |
| Distribution of goods | 0.0486 (0.045) | 0.2335*** (0.048) | 0.2552*** (0.037) | Distribution of goods | 0.1069** (0.047) | 0.2311*** (0.065) | 0.2409*** (0.043) |
| Managerial competence (Economy) | 1.1581*** (0.091) | 1.134*** (0.092) | 1.0246*** (0.092) | Managerial competence (Economy) | 1.1345*** (0.097) | 1.0961*** (0.096) | 1.0158*** (0.098) |
| Ideological distance* Network of activists | -0.0103** (0.005) | -0.0118** (0.005) | -0.0111** (0.005) | Ideological distance* Network of activists | 0.0033 (0.004) | 0.0036 (0.004) | 0.0049 (0.004) |
| Distribution of goods* Network of activists | 0.017 (0.027) | 0.0114 (0.028) | 0.0085 (0.024) | Distribution of goods* Network of activists | 0.1364*** (0.037) | 0.0653* (0.038) | 0.0442 (0.029) |
| Managerial competence* Network of Activists | -0.0675 (0.072) | -0.0972 (0.073) | -0.0671 (0.074) | Managerial competence* Network of activists | 0.0803 (0.097) | 0.0398 (0.097) | 0.0889 (0.099) |
| UCR | -1.2666*** (0.136) | -1.2882*** (0.139) | -1.2582*** (0.139) | UCR | -1.7715*** (0.130) | -1.7453*** (0.128) | -1.75*** (0.129) |

|  |  |  |  |  |  |  |
|---|---|---|---|---|---|---|
| PRO | −1.3904*** | −1.3051*** | −1.2353*** | PRO | −2.4047*** | −2.4155*** | −2.3018*** |
|  | (0.137) | (0.136) | (0.137) |  | (0.179) | (0.179) | (0.181) |
| ARI | −1.5854*** | −1.5086*** | −1.4866*** | ARI | −2.7956*** | −2.7851*** | −2.6981*** |
|  | (0.146) | (0.146) | (0.148) |  | (0.206) | (0.208) | (0.207) |
| PPP | −1.8203*** | −1.7459*** | −1.6414*** | PPP | −2.9823*** | −2.9523*** | −2.8335*** |
|  | (0.181) | (0.182) | (0.183) |  | (0.218) | (0.214) | (0.214) |
| LogLik | −677.1998 | −662.3427 | −650.4798 | LogLik | −543.162 | −545.2609 | −535.7337 |
| N | 714 | 714 | 714 | N | 982 | 982 | 982 |

*Note:* Conditional Logit Model with alternative specific variables. Standard errors in parentheses with confidence levels reported as follows: * $p < 0.1$, ** $p < 0.05$, *** $p < 0.01$. The base party category is the Peronist (Justicialista) in Argentina. Estimated in R 3.2 using the package *mlogit* (Croissant, 2012).

# Appendix to Chapter 8

TABLE 8.A.1. *Quantile regression of public employment and education on employee wages (LN) in Argentina, INDEC (2009)*

| | Quantile 0.1 | Quantile 0.2 | Quantile 0.3 | Quantile 0.4 | m 0.5 | Quantile 0.6 | Quantile 0.7 | Quantile 0.8 | Quantile 0.9 |
|---|---|---|---|---|---|---|---|---|---|
| Education | 0.228*** (0.001) | 0.177*** (0.001) | 0.153*** (0.001) | 0.148*** (0.001) | 0.142*** (0.001) | 0.147*** (0.001) | 0.147*** (0.001) | 0.160*** (0.001) | 0.173*** (0.001) |
| Age (LN) | 0.574*** (0.007) | 0.434*** (0.005) | 0.370*** (0.005) | 0.365*** (0.005) | 0.379*** (0.005) | 0.413*** (0.006) | 0.431*** (0.005) | 0.487*** (0.005) | 0.537*** (0.005) |
| Woman | −0.296*** (0.004) | −0.260*** (0.003) | −0.244*** (0.003) | −0.247*** (0.003) | −0.245*** (0.003) | −0.234*** (0.003) | −0.250*** (0.003) | −0.248*** (0.003) | −0.235*** (0.003) |
| Tenure (LN) | 1.058*** (0.009) | 0.853*** (0.006) | 0.658*** (0.006) | 0.529*** (0.006) | 0.457*** (0.006) | 0.374*** (0.007) | 0.319*** (0.006) | 0.256*** (0.007) | 0.291*** (0.007) |
| Constant | 2.309*** (0.026) | 3.679*** (0.018) | 4.513*** (0.018) | 4.908*** (0.017) | 5.118*** (0.018) | 5.222*** (0.021) | 5.401*** (0.018) | 5.404*** (0.019) | 5.307*** (0.020) |
| Observations | 21,207 | 21,207 | 21,207 | 21,207 | 21,207 | 21,207 | 21,207 | 21,207 | 21,207 |

*Note*: Quantile regression models (Koenker, 2005) was estimated in R 3.2 using quantreg (Koenker, 2013). Standard errors in parenthesis. *$p < 0.1$; **$p < 0.05$; ***$p < 0.01$.

TABLE 8.A.2. *Quantile regression of public employment and education on employee wages (LN) in Chile, CASEN (2009)*

### Quantile regression models, Chile

| | Quantile 0.1 | Quantile 0.2 | Quantile 0.3 | Quantile 0.4 | Quantile 0.5 | Quantile 0.6 | Quantile 0.7 | Quantile 0.8 | Quantile 0.9 |
|---|---|---|---|---|---|---|---|---|---|
| Education | 0.112*** (0.0002) | 0.126*** (0.0002) | 0.130*** (0.0002) | 0.132*** (0.0002) | 0.138*** (0.0002) | 0.141*** (0.0002) | 0.139*** (0.0002) | 0.139*** (0.0002) | 0.142*** (0.0003) |
| Age (LN) | 0.239*** (0.002) | 0.380*** (0.002) | 0.459*** (0.002) | 0.509*** (0.002) | 0.542*** (0.002) | 0.585*** (0.002) | 0.635*** (0.002) | 0.686*** (0.002) | 0.742*** (0.003) |
| Woman | −0.199*** (0.001) | −0.202*** (0.001) | −0.211*** (0.001) | −0.228*** (0.001) | −0.240*** (0.001) | −0.250*** (0.001) | −0.264*** (0.001) | −0.314*** (0.001) | −0.415*** (0.002) |
| Hours (LN) | 0.574*** (0.002) | 0.468*** (0.002) | 0.408*** (0.001) | 0.306*** (0.001) | 0.263*** (0.001) | 0.237*** (0.001) | 0.248*** (0.002) | 0.196*** (0.002) | 0.221*** (0.002) |
| Constant | 7.710*** (0.011) | 7.627*** (0.010) | 7.671*** (0.009) | 7.966*** (0.009) | 8.063*** (0.008) | 8.096*** (0.009) | 8.065*** (0.010) | 8.272*** (0.010) | 8.234*** (0.014) |
| Observations | 8,850 | 8,850 | 8,850 | 8,850 | 8,850 | 8,850 | 8,850 | 8,850 | 8,850 |

*Note:* Quantile regression models (Koenker, 2005) was estimated in R 3.2 using quantreg. Standard errors in parenthesis. *$p < 0.1$; **$p < 0.05$; ***$p < 0.01$.

TABLE 8.A.3. *Mean wages by socioeconomic class in the private and public sector*

| Variables | (1) Argentina wages (LN) 2009 | (2) Chile wages (LN) 2009 |
|---|---|---|
| C1 | 7.926*** | 13.04*** |
|  | (0.0145) | (0.00810) |
| C2 | 7.359*** | 12.36*** |
|  | (0.0166) | (0.00500) |
| C3 | 7.433*** | 12.18*** |
|  | (0.0169) | (0.00426) |
| D |  | 12.04*** |
|  |  | (0.00384) |
| D1 | 6.832*** |  |
|  | (0.00501) |  |
| D2 | 6.521*** |  |
|  | (0.0122) |  |
| C1*Public employees | 0.0902*** | 0.146*** |
|  | (0.0224) | (0.0134) |
| C2*Public employees | 0.118*** | 0.194*** |
|  | (0.0300) | (0.0117) |
| C3*Public employees | 0.150*** | 0.0429*** |
|  | (0.0316) | (0.0134) |
| D*Public employees |  | 0.114*** |
|  |  | (0.0125) |
| D1*Public employees | 0.350*** |  |
|  | (0.0138) |  |
| D2*Public employees | 0.349*** |  |
|  | (0.0389) |  |
| Observations | 52,584 | 60,819 |
| R-squared | 0.985 | 0.998 |

*Note*: OLS estimates with all categories and no constant to facilitate comparison.

Appendix to Chapter 8

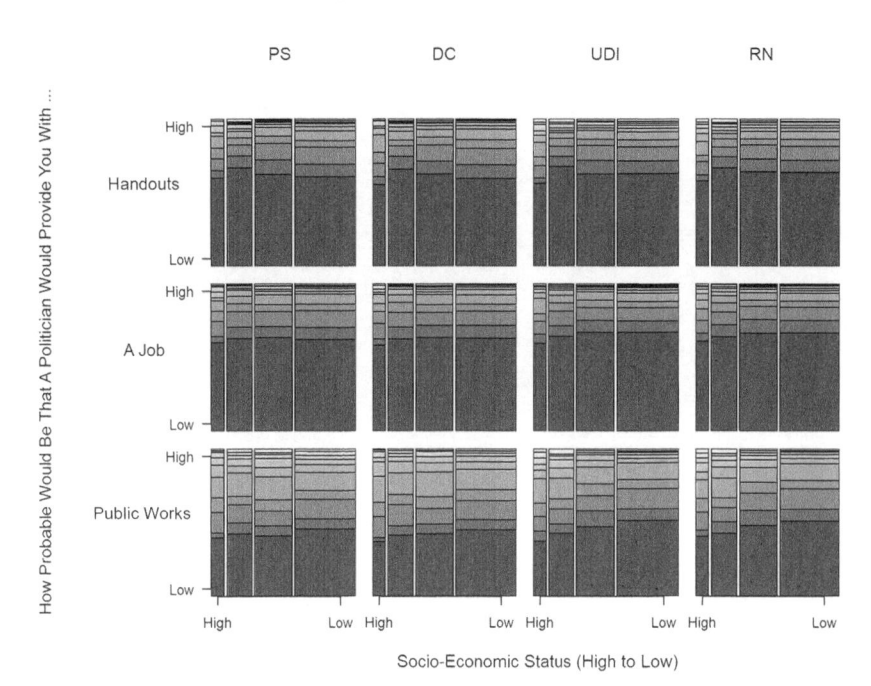

FIGURE 8.A.1. Association between distributive expectations and SES, Chile

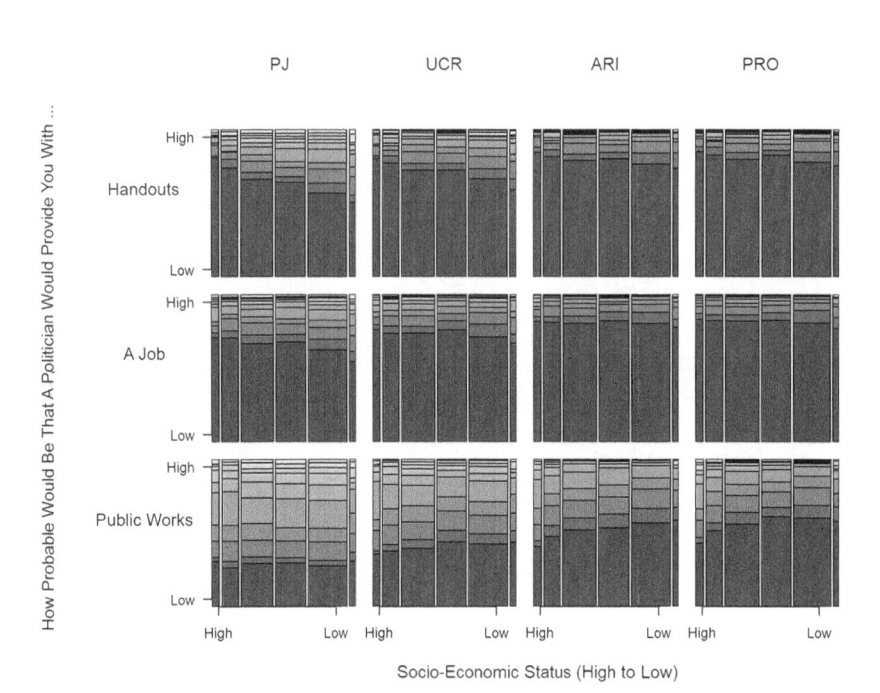

FIGURE 8.A.2. Association between distributive expectations and SES, Argentina

# Appendix to Chapter 9

## 9.A EQUILIBRIUM MODEL IN WINBUGS

Code below implements Adams, Merrill, and Grofman (2005) equilibrium algorithm in WinBUGS 3.1.4. It takes as input the survey data from Chile and Argentina and the model parameters estimated in Section 5.A in the appendix to Chapter 5 (Parameters A, B, C, and D). It returns the parameter $nash[t]$ with equilibrium locations for each party $t$ and expected vote share $p[,]$. Full replication materials may be downloaded from the authors' websites.

```
model
    {
    for (t in 1:K) {
    #Nash Equilibrium Algorithm 1
    nash[t] ~ dnorm(nash.mu[t],100) #Small Random Noise for Updating.
nash.mu[t] <- mean(w1[,t])/mean(w2[,t])+xbar
                }

        for (i in 1 : I) { # Loop around groups
    for (k in 1 : K) {# Updating Multinomial Model with given values for A,B,C,D.
p[i,k]    <- phi[i,k] / sum(phi[i,])
log(phi[i,k]) <- D*performance[i,k]+ B*network[i,k]+ C*goods[i,k] +
        A*pow(M*(x[i] -nash[k]),2)
        w1[i,k] <- p[i,k] * (1-p[i,k])* (x[i] -xbar)
        w2[i,k] <- p[i,k] * (1-p[i,k])
    }
  }
}
```

TABLE 9.A.1. *Optimal ideological location of parties and expected vote in Chile, 2007*

| | Nash Chile | | | | | | Vote Chile | | | | |
|---|---|---|---|---|---|---|---|---|---|---|---|
| | PS | DC | PPD | UDI | RN | | PS | DC | PPD | UDI | RN |
| Baseline | 4.268 | 4.811 | 4.431 | 6.051 | 5.952 | Baseline | 22.44% | 18.27% | 17.23% | 20.37% | 21.70% |
| Poor | 4.210 | 4.665 | 4.339 | 5.614 | 5.539 | Poor | 23.99 | 19.10 | 18.30 | 18.82 | 19.80 |
| Rich | 4.875 | 5.488 | 5.072 | 6.730 | 6.602 | Rich | 18.56 | 16.05 | 14.32 | 24.21 | 26.87 |
| High alpha | 3.981 | 4.607 | 4.093 | 6.430 | 6.276 | High alpha | 22.74 | 17.94 | 17.19 | 20.52 | 21.61 |
| High performance | 4.186 | 4.702 | 4.288 | 6.187 | 6.074 | High performance | 23.58 | 17.23 | 15.82 | 20.57 | 22.80 |
| High jobs | 4.265 | 4.813 | 4.430 | 6.073 | 5.974 | High jobs | 22.80 | 18.43 | 17.13 | 20.20 | 21.44 |
| High alpha poor | 3.895 | 4.450 | 3.939 | 6.076 | 5.921 | High alpha poor | 24.26 | 18.72 | 18.26 | 19.02 | 19.74 |
| High alpha rich | 4.649 | 5.432 | 4.849 | 6.928 | 6.754 | High alpha rich | 18.80 | 15.72 | 14.14 | 24.39 | 26.95 |
| High performance poor | 4.115 | 4.583 | 4.157 | 5.823 | 5.731 | High performance poor | 26.42 | 17.99 | 16.64 | 18.68 | 20.26 |
| High performance rich | 4.704 | 5.288 | 4.869 | 6.792 | 6.729 | High performance rich | 18.76 | 14.32 | 12.69 | 24.50 | 29.73 |
| High jobs poor | 4.198 | 4.676 | 4.336 | 5.634 | 5.550 | High jobs poor | 24.57 | 19.32 | 18.10 | 18.56 | 19.45 |
| High jobs rich | 4.898 | 5.501 | 5.094 | 6.728 | 6.623 | High jobs rich | 18.84 | 16.46 | 14.35 | 24.02 | 26.33 |

*Note*: Estimated using Adams, Merrill, and Grofman (2005) equilibrium algorithm on the survey data from Argentina, varying model parameters described in Table 9.1.

TABLE 9.A.2. *Optimal ideological location of parties and expected vote in Argentina, 2007*

| | Nash Argentina | | | | | | Vote Argentina | | | | |
|---|---|---|---|---|---|---|---|---|---|---|---|
| | PJ | UCR | ARI | PRO | PPP | | PJ 26.28% | UCR 21.12% | ARI 17.41% | PRO 18.52% | PPP 16.67% |
| Baseline | 5.780 | 5.765 | 5.680 | 5.838 | 5.772 | Baseline | | | | | |
| Poor | 5.890 | 5.837 | 5.819 | 5.872 | 5.817 | Poor | 31.20 | 22.21 | 14.88 | 14.55 | 17.15 |
| Rich | 4.905 | 5.351 | 5.250 | 5.368 | 5.208 | Rich | 18.41 | 19.47 | 20.82 | 26.81 | 14.48 |
| High alpha | 5.793 | 5.761 | 5.395 | 6.039 | 5.803 | High alpha | 26.22 | 21.09 | 17.50 | 18.57 | 16.62 |
| High performance | 5.796 | 5.802 | 5.661 | 5.832 | 5.770 | High performance | 27.24 | 21.41 | 16.92 | 19.06 | 15.37 |
| High jobs | 5.750 | 5.750 | 5.679 | 5.839 | 5.762 | High jobs | 28.62 | 21.23 | 16.51 | 17.64 | 16.00 |
| High alpha poor | 5.895 | 5.836 | 5.812 | 5.877 | 5.811 | High alpha poor | 31.20 | 22.21 | 14.88 | 14.55 | 17.15 |
| High alpha rich | 4.913 | 5.347 | 5.249 | 5.366 | 5.209 | High alpha rich | 18.40 | 19.48 | 20.83 | 26.81 | 14.48 |
| High performance poor | 5.827 | 5.822 | 5.768 | 5.888 | 5.808 | High performance poor | 34.05 | 23.14 | 13.37 | 13.15 | 16.29 |
| High performance rich | 4.854 | 5.415 | 5.342 | 5.360 | 5.339 | High performance rich | 16.40 | 17.69 | 20.88 | 31.97 | 13.07 |
| High jobs poor | 5.880 | 5.830 | 5.808 | 5.864 | 5.809 | High jobs poor | 32.06 | 22.21 | 14.59 | 14.21 | 16.92 |
| High jobs rich | 4.910 | 5.353 | 5.252 | 5.363 | 5.165 | High jobs rich | 21.88 | 19.47 | 19.43 | 26.05 | 13.18 |

*Note:* Estimated using Adams, Merrill, and Grofman (2005) equilibrium algorithm on the survey data from Argentina, varying model parameters described in Table 9.1.

TABLE 9.A.3. *Ideological location of parties in Argentina and Chile as reported by legislators, 2006–2010*

| colspan="5" | Ideological position as reported by the party's own legislators | colspan="5" | Ideological position as reported by legislators of the other parties |
| --- | --- | --- | --- | --- | --- | --- | --- | --- | --- |
| PS | PPD | DC | RN | UDI | PS | PPD | DC | RN | UDI |
| 2.72 | 4.125 | 5.31 | 6.36 | 7.04 | 2.54 | 3.88 | 5.01 | 7.48 | 8.91 |
| PJ | UCR | ARI | PRO | | PJ | UCR | ARI | PRO | |
| 4.77 | 6.06 | 4.11 | 7.23 | | 4.45 | 5.6 | 4.08 | 6.75 | |

*Note*: Data from the Legislative Elite Observatory of Latin America, University of Salamanca.

# Appendix with List of Cited Politicians

### ARGENTINA

01. UCR candidate to provincial legislator, August 5, 2009, Cordoba.
02. UCR National Representative and former Senator, July 20, 2009, Ciudad de Buenos Aires.
03. PJ National Representative, July 14, 2009, Ciudad de Buenos Aires.
04. Former PJ National Representative and campaign manager of PJ vice-presidential candidate, July 15, 2009, Ciudad de Buenos Aires.
05. City Councilor and President of City Council of San Isidro, from Acción Vecinal, August 12, 2009, San Isidro.
06. Campaign manager of PRO for the election of Mayor in the City of Buenos Aires in 2007, July 15, 2009, Ciudad de Buenos Aires.
07. National Representative Coalicion Civica, July 26, 2009, National Congress, Ciudad de Buenos Aires.
08. UCR National Representative elected in coalition with Coalicion Civica/ARI, July 29, 2009, Ciudad de Buenos Aires.
09. Former PJ Mayor in the Great Buenos Aires, July 27, 2009, Ciudad de Buenos Aires.
10. PJ broker of Great Buenos Aires, August 27, 2009, Carrefour of Vicente Lopez.
11. UCR broker in Great Buenos Aires, August 5, 2009, San Martin.
12. Coalicion Civica/GEN National Representative, August 11, 2009, National Congress, Ciudad de Buenos Aires.

### CHILE

01. National Representative PPD, April 14, 2009, Valparaiso.
02. UDI Representative, April 13, 2009, Santiago.
03. DC National Representative, April 13, 2009, Santiago.
04. PPD activist, July 17, 2009, Santiago.
05. UDI City Councilor, July 7, 2009, Pudahuel.
06. RN Mayor, July 7, 2009, Puente Alto.
07. Former PS city Councilor, April 13, 2009, Santiago.
08. RN National Representative, April 13, 2009, Santiago.
09. PS activist and campaign chief for candidate to mayor, July 16, 2009, Santiago.
10. Chief of Staff of PS National Representative, July 7, 2009, Santiago.
11. Former DC City Council and ex-chief party official, April 15, 2009.
12. UDI National Representative, April 14, 2009, Valparaiso.
13. PS National Representative, April 14, 2009, Valparaiso.
14. UDI activist and campaign manager for UDI National Representative, July 9, 2009, Santiago.
15. Assistant to UDI Representative, July 6, 2009.
16. DC Mayor, April 15, 2009, Santiago.

# References

Abal Medina, J., and Suárez Cao, J. (ND). Analisis critico del sistema electoral argentino. Evolucion histórica y desempeño efectivo. (Unpublished manuscript).

Abal Medina, J., Suárez Cao, J., and Cavarozzi, M. (2002). La competencia partidaria en la Argentina: sus implicancias sobre el régimen democrático. In *El asedio a la política: Los partidos latinoamericanos en la era neoliberal* (163-185). Beunos Aires: Homo Sapiens.

Acemoglu, D., and Robinson, J. A. (2005). *Economic Origins of Dictatorship and Democracy*. Cambridge: Cambridge University Press.

Achen, C. H. (1992). Social psychology, demographic variables, and linear regression: Breaking the iron triangle in voting research. *Political Behavior, 14*(3), 195-211.

Achen, C. H., and Bartels, L. M. (2004). Musical chairs: Pocketbook voting and the limits of democratic accountability. Paper presented at the Annual Meeting of the American Political Science Association, Chicago, IL.

(2016). *Democracy for Realists: Why Elections Do Not Produce Responsive Government*. Princeton, NJ: Princeton University Press.

Acuña, C. (1995). Algunas notas sobre los juegos, las gallinas, y la política de los pactos constitucionales, In C. Acuña (Ed.) *La nueva Matriz Política Argentina*. Buenos Aires: EUDEBA.

Adams, J. (2012). Causes and electoral consequences of party policy shifts in multiparty elections: Theoretical results and empirical evidence. *Annual Review of Political Science. 15*(1), 401-419. doi:10.1146/annurev-polisci-031710-101450

Adams, J., Merrill, S., and Grofman, B. (2005). *A Unified Theory of Party Competition : A Cross-National Analysis Integrating Spatial and Behavioral Factors*. Cambridge: Cambridge University Press.

Agüero, F., Tironi, E., Valenzuela, E., and Sunkel, G. (1998). Votantes, partidos e información política: la frágil intermediación política en el Chile post-autoritario. *Revista de ciencia política, 19*(2), 159-193.

Alcañiz, I. (2016). *Environmental and Nuclear Networks in the Global South: How Skills Shape International Cooperation.* New York: Cambridge University Press.

Alcañiz, I., and Hellwig, T. (2011). Who's to blame? The distribution of responsibility in developing democracies. *British Journal of Political Science, 41*(02), 389–411. doi:10.1017/S0007123409990317

Alcañiz, I., Calvo, E., and Rubio, J. M. (2016). Educadamente desiguales: Género y salario en el Sector Público argentino (2003–2010). *Desarrollo Economico, 55*(217), 343–357.

Alcantara, M., and Freidenberg, F. (2001). Los partidos poclitios en America Latina. *Ediciones Universidad de Salamanca. América Latina Hoy, 27,* 17–35

Alcántara, M., and Tagina, M. L. (2013). *Elecciones y política en América Latina 2009–2011.* México: Instituto Federal Electoral.

Aldrich, J. H. (1995). *Why Parties?: The Origin and Transformation of Political Parties in America.* Chicago, MA: The University of Chicago Press.

Alesina, A., and Rosenthal, H. (1995). *Partisan Politics, Divided Government, and the Economy.* Cambridge: Cambridge University Press.

Alesina, A., Baqir, R., and Easterly, W. (1997). *Public Goods and Ethnic Divisions.* Cambridge, MA: National Bureau of Economic Research.

Alonso, P. (2000). *Entre la revolución y las urnas. Los orígenes de la Unión. Cívica Radical y la política argentina en los años '90.* Buenos Aires: Editorial Sudamericana.

(2010). *Jardines secretos, legitimaciones públicas: El Partido Autonomista Nacional y la política argentina de fines del siglo XIX.* Buenos Aires: Edhasa.

Ames, B. (1987). *Political Survival: Politicians and Public Policy in Latin America.* Berkeley, CA: University of California Press.

Ansolabehere, S., and Snyder Jr, J. M. (2000). Valence politics and equilibrium in spatial election models. *Public Choice, 103*(3), 327–336.

(2007). Party control of state government and distribution of public expenditures. *Scandinavian Journal of Economics, 108* (4), 547–569.

Auyero, J. (2001). *Poor People's Politics: Peronist Survival Networks and the Legacy of Evita.* Durham, NC: Duke University Press.

Auyero, J., and Swistun, D. A. (2009). *Flammable: Environmental Suffering in an Argentine Shantytown.* New York: Oxford University Press.

Avendaño, O., and Sandoval, P. (2016). Desafección política y estabilidad de los resultados electorales en Chile, 1993–2009. *Perfiles latinoamericanos, 24* (47), 175–198.

Baker, A., Ames, B., and Renno, L. R. (2006). Social context and campaign volatility in new democracies: Networks and neighborhoods in Brazil's 2002 elections. *American Journal of Political Science, 50*(2), 382–399.

Baldwin, K. (2016). *The Paradox of Traditional Leaders in Democratic Africa.* New York: Cambridge University Press.

Bambaci, J., Spiller, P., and Tommasi, M. (2007). The bureaucracy. In P. Spiller and M. Tommasi (Eds.) *The Institutional Foundations of Public Policy in Argentina.* Cambridge: Cambridge University Press.

Barozet, E. (2004). Elementos Explicativos de la Votación de los Sectores Populares en Iquique: Lógica y Eficiencia de las Redes Clientelares. *Politica*, 43, 205–251.

(2006). Relecturas de la noción de clientelismo: una forma diversificada de intermediación política y social. *Debate (Ecuador)*, 69, 77–101.

Barozet, E., and Aubry, M. (2005). De las reformas internas a la candidatura presidencial autónoma: Los nuevos caminos institucionales de Renovación Nacional. *Politica*, 45, 165–196.

Barrueto, F., and Navia, P. (2015). Evolución de las preferencias políticas y de políticas públicas entre el sector popular y el resto de la sociedad chilena entre 1990 y 2010. *Perfiles Latinoamericanos*, 23(46) México jul./dic., 61–89.

Bartels, L. M. (2002). Beyond the running tally: Partisan bias in political perceptions. *Political Behavior*, 24(2), 117–150.

(2008). *Unequal Democracy : The Political Economy of the New Gilded Age*. New York, Princeton, NJ: Russell Sage Foundation, Princeton University Press.

Bartle, J., and Bellucci, P. (2009). *Political Parties and Partisanship: Social Identity and Individual Attitudes*. London and New York: Routledge.

Bascuñán, C. (1990). *La izquierda sin Allende*. Santiego, Chile: Editorial Planeta.

Bateson, R. (2012). Crime victimization and political participation. *American Political Science Review*, 106(03), 570–587.

Baumgartner, F. R., and Jones, B. D. (1993). *Agendas and Instability in American Politics*. Chicago, IL: University of Chicago Press.

Bawn, K., Cohen, M., Karol, D., Masket, S., Noel, H., and Zaller, J. (2012). A theory of political parties: Groups, policy demands and nominations in American politics. *Perspectives on Politics*, 10(03), 571–597.

Bélanger, É., and Meguid, B. M. (2008). Issue salience, issue ownership, and issue-based vote choice. *Electoral Studies*, 27(3), 477–491.

Beramendi, P., and Rueda, D. (2014). Inequality and institutions: the case of economic coordination. *Annual Review of Political Science*, 17, 251–271.

Bernhardt, M. D., and Ingerman, D. E. (1985). Candidate reputations and the 'incumbency effect'. *Journal of Public Economics*, 27(1), 47–67.

Bértola, L., and Ocampo, J. A. (2012). *The Economic Development of Latin America Since Independence*. Oxford: Oxford University Press.

Bianchi, S., and Sanchís, N. (1988). *El Partido Peronista Femenino* (Vol. 208). Buenos Aires: Centro editor de América latina.

Bishop, G. F. (1976). The effect of education on ideological consistency. *Public Opinion Quarterly*, 40(3), 337–348.

Blais, A., Martin, P., and Nadeau, R. (1998). Can people explain their own vote? Introspective questions as indicators of salience in the 1995 Quebec referendum on sovereignty. *Quality & Quantity*, 32(4), 355.

Bleck, J., van de Walle, N. (2013). Valence issues in African elections navigating uncertainty and the weight of the past. *Comparative Political Studies*, 46(11), 1394–1421.

Boix, C. (2003). *Democracy and Redistribution*. Cambridge: Cambridge University Press.

Borzutzky, S. (2002). *Vital Connections: Politics, Social Security, and Inequality in Chile.* Notre Dame, IN: University of Notre Dame Press.

Botana, N. R. (1984). *El Orden Conservador.* Buenos Aires: Editorial Sudamericana.

Brader, T., Tucker, J. A., and Duell, D. (2013). Which parties can lead opinion? Experimental evidence on partisan cue taking in multiparty democracies. *Comparative Political Studies,* 46(11), 1485–1517.-

Brambor, T., Clark, W. R., and Golder, M. (2006). Understanding interaction models: Improving empirical analyses. *Political Analysis,* 14(1), 63–82. doi: 10.1093/pan/mpi014

Brooks, C., and Manza, J. (2006). Why do Welfare States Persist? *Journal of Politics,* 68 (4), 816–827.

Brusco, V., Nazareno, M., and Stokes, S. C. (2004). Vote buying in Argentina. *Latin American Research Review,* 39(2), 66–88.

Bruter, M., Erikson, R., and Strauss, A. (2010). Uncertain candidates, valence, and the dynamics of candidate position taking. *Public Choice,* 144, 153–168.

Carnes, N., and Lupu, N. (2015). Rethinking the comparative perspective on class and representation: evidence from Latin America. *American Journal of Political Science,* 59(1), 1–18.

Calvo, E., and Escolar, M. (2005). *La nueva politica de partidos en la Argentina : crisis politica, realineamientos partidarios y reforma electoral.* Buenos Aires: Prometeo-Pent.

Calvo, E., and Hellwig, T. (2011). Centripetal and centrifugal incentives under different electoral systems. *American Journal of Political Science,* 55(1), 27–41. doi: 10.1111/j.1540-5907.2010.00482.x

Calvo, E., and Moscovich, L. (2017). Inequality, protests, and the progressive allocation of cash transfers in the Argentine provinces. *Latin American Politics and Society,* 59(2), 3–26.

Calvo, E., and Murillo, M. V. (2004). Who delivers? Partisan clients in the Argentine electoral market. *American Journal of Political Science,* 48(4), 742–757.

  (2005). A new law of Argentine politics. In M. V. Murillo and S. Levitsky (Eds.) *Argentine Democracy : The Politics of Institutional Weakness.* University Park, PA: Pennsylvania State University.

  (2012). The persistence of Peronism. *Journal of Democracy,* 23(2), 148–161.

  (2013). When parties meet voters assessing political linkages through partisan networks and distributive expectations in Argentina and Chile. *Comparative Political Studies,* 46(7), 851–882.

Campbell, A., Converse, P. E., Miller, W. E., and Stokes, D. E. (1964). *The American Voter: An Abridgment.* New York: Wiley.

Campello, D. (2013). What is left of the Brazilian Left? *Available at SSRN 2243118.*

Campello, D., and Zucco Jr., C. (2015). Presidential success and the world economy. *The Journal of Politics,* 78 (2).

Cantú, F., and Saiegh, S. M. (2011). Fraudulent democracy? An analysis of Argentina's "Infamous Decade" using supervised machine learning. *Political Analysis,* 409–433.

Carey, J. M., and Siavelis, P. (2006). Election insurance and coalition survival. Informal institutions and democracy: Lessons from Latin America. In Gretchen Helmke and Steven Levitsky (Eds.) *Informal Institutions and Democracy: Lessons from Latin America* (160). Baltimore, MD: John Hopkins University Press.

Castro, M. O. (2008). *El ocaso de la república oligárquica: poder, política y reforma electoral, 1898–1912*. Buenos Aires: Edhasa.

Cavarozzi, M. (1984). *Sindicatos y política en Argentina*: Buenos Aires: Centro de Estudios de Estado y Sociedad.

Chandra, K. (2004). *Why Ethnic Parties Succeed : Patronage and Ethnic Head Counts in India*. Cambridge, UK; New York: Cambridge University Press.

Chen, J., and Rodden, J. (2013). Unintentional gerrymandering: Political geography and electoral bias in legislatures. *Quarterly Journal of Political Science*, 8(3), 239–269.

Ciria, A. (1983). *Política y cultura popular: la Argentina peronista, 1946–1955*. Beunos Aires: De la Flor.

Clark, M. (2009). Valence and electoral outcomes in Western Europe, 1976–1998. *Electoral Studies*, 28(1), 111–122.

Clark, M., and Leiter, D. (2014). Does the ideological dispersion of parties mediate the electoral impact of valence? A cross-national study of party support in nine Western European democracies. *Comparative Political Studies*, 47(2), 171 – 202.

Clarke, H. D., Sanders, D., Stewart, M. C., and Whiteley, P. F. (1992). *Performance Politics and the British Voter*. New York: Cambridge University Press.

(2011). Valence politics and electoral choice in Britain, 2010. *Journal of Elections, Public Opinion and Parties*, 21(2), 237–253.

Converse, P. E. (1962a). Information flow and the stability of partisan attitudes. *Public Opinion Quarterly*, 26(4), 578–599.

(1962b). *The Nature of Belief Systems in Mass Publics: Survey Research Center*. Ann Arbor, MI: University of Michigan.

Corstange, D. (2009). Sensitive questions, truthful answers? Modeling the list experiment with LISTIT. *Political Analysis*, 17(1), 45–63.

(2016). *The Price of a Vote in the Middle East: Clientelism and Communal Politics in Lebanon and Yemen*. New York: Cambridge University Press.

Cox, G. (1999). Electoral rules and electoral coordination. *Annual Review of Political Science*, 2, 145–161.

Cox, G. W. (2007). Swing voters, core voters and distributive politics. Paper presented at the Elections and Redistribution, Yale University.

Cox, G. W., and McCubbins, M. D. (1986). Electoral politics as a redistributive game. *The Journal of Politics*, 48(2), 370–389.

Crisp, B. F., and Simoneau, W. M. (2018). Electoral systems and constituency service. In Herron, E. S., Pekkanen, R. J., and Shugart, M. S. (Eds.) *The Oxford Handbook of Electoral Systems*, 345–361. New York: Oxford University Press.

Croissant, Y. (2012). Estimation of multinomial logit models in R: The mlogit Packages. *R package version 0.2-2*. http://cran. r-project. org/web/packages/ mlogit/vignettes/mlogit. pdf

Dahlberg, M., and Johansson, E. (2002). On the vote-purchasing behavior of incumbent governments. *American Political Science Review*, 96(01), 27–40. doi:10.1017/S0003055402004215

Dávila, M. (2010). Tecnocracia y democracia en el Chile contemporáneo: el caso de los gobiernos de la Concertación (1990–2010). *Revista de sociología*, 24, 199–217.

De la Maza, G. (2010). Construcción democrática, participación ciudadana y políticas públicas en Chile. PhD Dissertation, Department of Languages and Cultures of Latin America, Faculty of Humanities, Leiden University.

De la Maza, G., Maillet, A., and Martinez, C. (2016). ¿El despertar de la fuerza? Análisis exploratorio de la politización de los conflictos socioterritoriales y sus consecuencias en Chile (2005–2014). Paper presented at the Annual Repal Conference, MIT, Cambridge.

De La O, A. L. (2013). Do conditional cash transfers affect electoral behavior? Evidence from a randomized experiment in Mexico. *American Journal of Political Science*, 57(1), 1–14.

De Privitellio, L. (2011). Las elecciones entre dos reformas: 1900–1955. In H. Sabato, M. Ternavasio, L. de Privitellio, and A. Persello (Eds.) *Historia de las elecciones en la Argentina*. Buenos Aires: El Ateneo.

Diaz-Cayeros, A., Estevez, F., and Magaloni, B. (2016). *The Political Logic of Poverty Relief: Electoral Strategies and Social Policy in Mexico*. New York: Cambridge University Press.

Díaz, J. B., Rolf Lüders, S., and Gert Wagner, H. (2005). *Chile, 1810–2000, La República en Cifras*: Mimeograph, Instituto de Economía, Pontificia Universidad Católica de Chile.

Dixit, A., and Londregan, J. (1996). The determinants of success of special interests in redistributive politics. *The Journal of Politics*, 58(4), 1132–1155.

(1998). Ideology, Tactics, and Efficiency in Redistributive Politics. *The Quarterly Journal of Economics*, 113(2), 497–529.

Downs, A. (1957). *An Economic Theory of Democracy*. New York: Harper Collins.

Drake, P. W. (1978). *Socialism and Populism in Chile, 1932–52*. Champaign, IL: University of Illinois Press.

Duch, R. M., and Stevenson, R. T. (2008). *The Economic Vote : How Political and Economic Institutions Condition Election Results*. New York: Cambridge University Press.

Eifert, B., Miguel, E., and Posner, D. N. (2010). Political competition and ethnic identification in Africa. *American Journal of Political Science*, 54(2), 494–510.

Escolar, M. (2013). La ilusión unitaria: Política territorial y nacionalización política en Argentina. *Revista SAAP*, 7(2), 441–451.

Escudero, L. (2001). Argentina. In M. Alcántara Sáez and F. Freidenberg (Eds.) *Partidos Políticos de América Latina: Cono Sur*. Salamanca: Universidad de Salamanca.

Espinoza, E. (2008). Mapa de las redes de poder en el seno de la élite política chilena desde el retorno de la democracia. El caso de los diputados (1990–2005). Paper presented in the Congress on Technology and Cultures.

# References 283

A Cros-Disciplinary Dialogue. Looking to the Future in Latin America and the Caribbean. October 20–November 2, 2008, Universidad de Santiago de Chile, Chile.

Espinoza, V., and Madrid, S. (2010). *Trayectoria y Eficacia Política de los Militantes en Juventudes Políticas. Estudio de la elite política emergente.* Santiago de Chile: Instituto de Estudios Avanzados.

Etchemendy, S., and Garay, C. (2010). Between moderation and defiance: Argentina's left populism in comparative perspective (2003–2009). In S. Levitsky and K. Roberts (Eds.) *Latin America's Left Turn: Causes and Implications.* Baltimore, MD: Johns Hopkins University Press.

Falleti, T. G. (2005). A sequential theory of decentralization: Latin American cases in comparative perspective. *American Political Science Review*, 99(3), 327–346.

(2010). *Decentralization and Subnational Politics in Latin America.* Cambridge: Cambridge University Press.

Fearon, J. D. (1999). Electoral accountability and the control of politicians: Selecting good types versus sanctioning poor performance. In A. Przeworski, S. Stokes, and B. Manin (Eds.) *Democracy, Accountability, and Representation* (55–97). Cambridge: Cambridge University Press.

Ferreres, O. (2005). *Dos siglos de economía argentina.* Fundación Norte y Sur.

Finan, F., and Schechter, L. (2012). Vote-buying and reciprocity. *Econometrica*, 80(2), 863–881.

Fiorina, M. P. (1981). *Retrospective Voting in American National Elections.* New Haven, CT: Yale University Press.

Flores-Macias, G. (2012). *After Neoliberalism? The Left and Economic Reforms in Latin America.* Oxford: Oxford University Press.

Folke, O., Hirano, S., and Snyder, J. M. (2011). Patronage and elections in US states. *American Political Science Review*, 105(03), 567–585.

Fuentes, C. (1999). *Partidos y coaliciones en el Chile de los 90. Entre pactos y proyectos.* Santiago de Chile: Lom Editores.

Galway, T. (2014). *Machine Made: Tammany Hall and the Creation of Modern American Politics.* New York: WW Norton & Company.

Gamboa, R., and Morales, M. (2015). Deciding on the electoral system: Chile's adoption of proportional representation in 1925. *Latin American Politics and Society*, 57(2), 41–66.

Gamboa, R., and Salcedo, R. (2009). El Faccionalismo en el Partido Socialista de Chile (1990–2006): características y efectos políticos en sus procesos de toma de decisión. *Revista de ciencia política (Santiago)*, 29(3), 667–692.

Gamboa, R., Lopez, M. A., and Baeza, J. (2013). La evolución programática de los partidos chilenos 1970–2009: De la polarización al consenso, Revista de ciencia política, 33(2), 443–467.

Gamboa Valenzuela, R. (2011). Reformando reglas electorales: La cédula única y los pactos electorales en Chile (1958–1962). *Revista de ciencia política (Santiago)*, 31(2), 159–186.

Gans-Morse, J., Mazzuca, S., and Nichter, S. (2014). Varieties of clientelism: machine politics during elections. *American Journal of Political Science*, 58(2), 415–432.

Garay, C. (2007). Social policy and collective action: Unemployed workers, community associations, and protest in Argentina. *Politics & Society*, 35 (2), 301–328.
    (2016). *Social Policy Expansion in Latin America*. New York: Cambridge University Press.
Garreton, M. A. (2012). *Neoliberalismo corregido y progresismo limitado. Los gobiernos de la Concertación en Chile, 1990–2010*. Santiago de Chile: Santiago Editorial Arcis-CLACSO.
Gelman, A., and Hill, J. (2007). *Data Analysis Using Regression and Multilevel/Hierarchical Models*. Cambridge; New York: Cambridge University Press.
Gerber, A., and Green, D. (1999). Misperceptions about perceptual bias. *Annual Review of Political Science*, 2(1), 189–210.
Gerchunoff, P., and Torre, J. C. (1992). What role for the state in Latin America. In S. Teitel (Ed.) *Towards a New Development Strategy for Latin America: Pathways from Hirschman's Thought* (259–280). Washington, DC: Inter-American Development Bank.
Gibson, E. L. (1996). *Class & Conservative Parties: Argentina in Comparative Perspective*. Baltimore, MD: Johns Hopkins University Press.
Gibson, E. L., and Calvo, E. (2000). Federalism and low-maintenance constituencies: Territorial dimensions of economic reform in Argentina. *Studies in Comparative International Development*, 35(3), pg: 32.
    (2001). Federalismo y Sobrerrepresentación: La Dimensión Territorial de la Reforma Económica en la Argentina. In E. F. Calvo and J. M. H. Abal Medina (Eds.) *El Federalismo Electoral Argentino* (179–204). Buenos Aires: EUDEBA.
Gilens, M. (2012). *Affluence and Influence: Economic Inequality and Political Power in America*. Princeton, NJ: Princeton University Press.
Gingerich, D. W. (2010). Understanding off-the-books politics: Conducting inference on the determinants of sensitive behavior with randomized response surveys. *Political Analysis*, 18(3), 349–380. doi: 10.1093/pan/mpq010
Giraudy, A. (2007). The distributive politics of emergency employment programs in Argentina (1993–2002). *Latin American Research Review*, 42(2), 33–55.
Gonzalez-Ocantos, E., Kiewiet de Jonge, C., Meléndez, C., Osorio, J., and Nickerson, D. (2010). Vote Buying and Social Desirability Bias: Experimental Evidence from Nicaragua. Paper presented at the Yale Conference on Redistribution, Public Goods and Political Market Failures, New Haven.
Granberg, D., and Brent, E. (1980). Perceptions of issue positions of presidential candidates: Candidates are often perceived by their supporters as holding positions on the issues that are closer to the supporters' views than they really are. *American Scientist*, 68(6), 617–625.
Greene, S. (2004). Social identity theory and partisan identification. *Social Science Quarterly*, 85(1), 136–153.
Green, D. P., Palmquist, B., and Schickler, E. (2004). *Partisan Hearts and Minds: Political Parties and the Social Identities of Voters*. New Haven, CT: Yale University Press.
Grindle, M. S. (2012). *Jobs for the Boys*. Cambridge, MA: Harvard University Press.

Groseclose, T. (2001). A model of candidate location when one candidate has a valence advantage. *American Journal of Political Science*, 45(4), 862–886.

Grossman, G. M., and Helpman, E. (2002). *Interest Groups and Trade Policy*. Princeton, NJ: Princeton University Press.

Grzymała-Busse, A. (2007). *Rebuilding Leviathan: Party Competition and State Exploitation in Post-Communist Democracies*. Cambridge, UK: Cambridge University Press.

 (2015). *Nations under God: How Churches Use Moral Authority to Influence Policy*. Princeton, NJ: Princeton University Press.

Gutiérrez, R. A., and Isuani, F. (2013). Luces y sombras de la política ambiental argentina entre 1983 y 2013. *Revista SAAP*, 7(2), 317–328.

Habyarimana, J., Macartan, H., Posner, D. N., and Weinstein, J. M. (2009). *Coethnicity: Diversity and the Dilemmas of Collective Action*. New York: Russell Sage Foundation, Princeton University Press.

Hammouya, M. (1999). *Statistics on Public Sector Employment: Methodology, Structures and Trends* (Vol. W.P.144). Geneva: International Labour Organization.

Hellwig, T., and Samuels, D. (2008). Electoral accountability and the variety of democratic regimes. *British Journal of Political Science*, 38(01), 65–90. doi:10.1017/S0007123408000045

Hinich, M. J., and Munger, M. C. (1994). *Ideology and the Theory of Political Choice*. Ann Arbor, MI: University of Michigan Press.

Hite, K. (2000). *When the Romance Ended: Leaders of the Chilean Left, 1968–1998*. New York: Columbia University Press.

Holland, A. C. (2013). Right on crime?: Conservative party politics and Mano Dura policies in El Salvador. *Latin American Research Review*, 48(1), 44–67.

Hora, R. (2001). *The Landowners of the Argentine Pampas: A Social and Political History 1860–1945*. Oxford: Clarendon Press.

Horowitz, J. (2010). *Argentina's Radical Party and Popular Mobilization, 1916–1930*. University Park, PA: Penn State University Press.

Huneeus, C. (2000). *El Regimen de Pinochet*. Santiago: Editorial Sudamericana.

 (2016). La oposición en el autoritarismo El caso del Partido Demócrata Cristiano durante el régimen del general Pinochet en Chile. *Revista Mexicana de Ciencias Políticas y Sociales*, 61(227), 247–271.

Huntington, S. P. (1968). *Political Order in Changing Socities*. New Haven, CT: Yale University Press.

Iacovella, M. (2006) Análisis comparativo por subsistemas. In Koldo Echevarria (Ed.) *Informe sobre la situación del servicio civil en América Latina*. Washington, DC: Inter-American Development Bank.

Iyengar, S. (1994). *Is Anyone Responsible?: How Television Frames Political Issues*. Chicago, IL: University of Chicago Press.

Iyengar, S., and Kinder, D. R. (2010). *News That Matters: Television and American Opinion*. Chicago, IL: University of Chicago Press.

Jacobs, L. R., and Shapiro, R. Y. (2000). *Politicians Don't Pander: Political Manipulation and the Loss of Democratic Responsiveness*. Chicago, IL: University of Chicago Press.

Jacoby, W. G. (1991). Ideological identification and issue attitudes. *American Journal of Political Science*, 178–205.

Jones, B. D., and Baumgartner, F. R. (2005). *The Politics of Attention: How Government Prioritizes Problems*. Chicago, IL: University of Chicago Press.

Jones, M. P., Lauga, M., and León-Roesch, M. (2005). Argentina. In D. Nohlen (Ed.) *Elections in the Americas: A Data Handbook* (Vol. 2, South America, 59–122). New York, NY: Oxford University Press.

Kaplan, N., Park, D. K., and Ridout, T. N. (2006). Dialogue in American political campaigns? An examination of issue convergence in candidate television advertising. *American Journal of Political Science*, 50(3), 724–736.

Kaplan, S. B. (2016). Partisan technocratic cycles in Latin America, *Electoral Studies*.

Karol, D. (2009). *Party Position Change in American Politics: Coalition Management*. Cambridge; New York: Cambridge University Press.

Kasara, Kimuli. (2017). Tax me if you can: Ethnic geography, democracy, and the taxation of agriculture in Africa. *American Political Science Review* 101(1), 159–172.

Kaufman, R. (2011). The political left, the export boom, and the populist temptation. In S. Levitsky and K. Roberts (Eds.) *The Resurgence of the Latin American Left* (93–116). Baltimore, MD: John Hopkins University Press,

Kedar, O. (2005). When moderate voters prefer extreme parties: policy balancing in parliamentary elections. *American Political Science Review*, 99(2), 185–199.

Keefer, P. (2007). Clientelism, credibility, and the policy choices of young democracies. *American Journal of Political Science*, 51(4), 804–821.

Keefer, P., and Vlaicu, R. (2008). Democracy, credibility, and clientelism. *Journal of Law Economics & Organization*, 24(2), 371–406. doi: 10.1093/jleo/ewm054

Kitschelt, H. (1994). *The Transformation of European Social Democracy*. Cambridge; New York: Cambridge University Press.

  (2000). Linkages between citizens and politicians in democratic polities. [Review]. *Comparative Political Studies*, 33(6–7), 845–879.

Kitschelt, H., and Kselman, D. M. (2013). Economic development, democratic experience, and political parties' linkage strategies. *Comparative Political Studies*, 46(11), 1453–1484.

Kitschelt, H., and Wilkinson, S. (2007). *Patrons, Clients, and Policies : Patterns of Democratic Accountability and Political Competition*. Cambridge; New York: Cambridge University Press.

Kitschelt, H., Hawkins, K. A., Luna, J. P., Rosas, G., and Zechmeister, E. J. (2010). *Latin American Party Systems*. Cambridge; New York: Cambridge University Press.

Koenker, R. (2005). *Quantile Regression*. New York: Cambridge University Press.

  (2013). quantreg: Quantile Regression. R package version 5.05. *R Foundation for Statistical Computing: Vienna) Available at:* http://CRAN. R-project. org/package= quantreg.

Koenker, R., and Bassett Jr, G. (1978). Regression quantiles. *Econometrica: Journal of the Econometric Society*, 33–50.
Laver, M., and Sergenti, E. (2012) *Party Competition: An Agent-Based Model*. Princeton, NJ: Princeton University Press.
Lax, J. R., and Phillips, J. H. (2009). How should we estimate public opinion in the states? *American Journal of Political Science*, 53(1), 107–121.
Leiras, M. (2007). *Todos los caballos del rey: la integración de los partidos políticos y el gobierno democrático de la Argentina*. Buenos Aires: Prometeo.
Levitsky, S. (2003). *Transforming Labor-Based Parties in Latin America: Argentine Peronism in Comparative Perspective*. Cambridge, UK; New York: Cambridge University Press.
Murillo, M. V., and Levitsky, S. (2019) Crisis, boom, and the restructuring of the Argentine party system (1999–2015). In N. Lupu, V. Oliveros, and L. Schiumerini (Eds.) *Campaigns and Voters in Developing Democracies: Argentina in Comparative Perspective*. Ann Arbor, MI: Michigan University Press.
Levitsky, S., and Roberts, K. M. (2013). *The Resurgence of the Latin American Left*: Baltimore, MD: John Hopkins University Press.
Lewis-Beck, M. S., and Ratto, M. C. (2013). Economic voting in Latin America: A general model. *Electoral Studies*, 32(3), 489–493.
Lindbeck, A., and Weibull, J. W. (1987). Balanced-budget redistribution and the outcome of political competition. *Public Choice*, 52(3), 273–297.
Lipset, S. M., and Rokkan, S. (1967). *Party Systems and Voter Alignments: Cross-National Perspectives (Contributors: Robert R. Alford and others)*. New York: Free Press.
Llach, L. (2007). *The Wealth of the Provinces: The Rise and Fall of the Interior in the Political Economy of Argentina, 1880–1910*: Doctorial Dissertation, Harvard University.
Lodola, G. (2005). Protesta popular y redes clientelares en la Argentina: el reparto federal del Plan Trabajar (1996–2001). *Desarrollo Economico*, 515–536.
Londregan, J., and Romer, T. (1993). Polarization, incumbency, and the personal vote. *Political Economy: Institutions, Competition, and Representation*, 355–377.
Longo, F. (2006). Análisis comparativo por índices. In K. Echevarria (Ed.) *Informe sobre la situación del servicio civil en América Latina*. Washington, DC: Inter-American Development Bank.
Loxton, J. (2016). Authoritarian successor parties and the new right in Latin America. In S. Levitsky, J. Loxton, B. Van Dyck, and J. I. Domínguez (Eds.) *Challenges of Party-Building in Latin America* (245–272). New York: Cambridge University Press.
Luna, F. (1972). *Argentina de Péron a Lanusse, 1943–1973*. Barcelona: Planeta.
Luna, J. P. (2008). Partidos Políticos y Sociedad en Chile: Trayectoria Histórica y Mutaciones Recientes. In A. Fontaine, I. Walter, J. Navarrete, and C. Larroulet (Eds.) *Reforma de los Partidos Políticos en Chile*. Santiago: PNUD.
  (2010). Segmented party voter linkages in Latin America: The case of the UDI. *Journal of Latin American Studies*, 42(2), 325–356.

(2014). *Segmented Representation: Political Party Strategies in Unequal Democracies*. Oxford: Oxford University Press.

(2016). Chile's crisis of representation. *Journal of Democracy*, 27(3), 129–138.

(2017). Sistema de partidos y campaña electorales a nivel local. Quienes logran ser electos y re-electos. In J. P. Luna and R. Mardones (Eds). *La columna vertebral fracturada: revisitando intermediarios políticos en Chile*. Santiago de Chile: Ril Editores.

Luna, J. P., and Altman, D. (2011). Uprooted but stable: Chilean parties and the concept of party system institutionalization. *Latin American Politics and Society*, 53(2), 1–28.

Luna, J. P., and Mardones, R. (2017). Politicas de Distribucion Selectivas: Uso Politico de Fondos Sociales Focalizados en Chile. In J. P. Luna and R. Mardones (Eds.) *La Columna Vertebral Fracturada: Revisitando Intermediarios Politicos en Chile*. Santiago de Chile: RIL Editores.

Luna, J. P., and Rosenblatt, F. (2012). ¿Notas para una autopsia? Los partidos políticos en el Chile actual. In F. J. Diaz and L. Sierra (Eds.) *Democracia con partidos*. CEP-CIEPLAN.

(2017). La Columna Vertebral ¿Fracturada? In J. P. Luna and R. Mardones (Eds). *La columna vertebral fracturada: revisitando intermediarios políticos en Chile*. Santiago de Chile: Ril Editores.

Luna, J. P., Rosenblatt, F., and Toro, S. (2011). *Desk Review on Programmatic Parties*. Estocolmo: IDEA-International, no publicado.

Lupu, N. (2011). *Party Brands in Crisis: Partisanship, Brand Dilution and the Breakdown of Political Parties in Latin America*. Princeton, NJ: Princeton University Press.

(2013). Party brands and partisanship: Theory with evidence from a survey experiment in Argentina. *American Journal of Political Science*, 57(1), 49–64.

(2016). *Party Brands, Partisan Erosion, and Party Breakdown Latin American Party Systems: Institutionalization, Decay, and Collapse*. New York: Cambridge University Press.

Lupu, N., and Stokes, S. (2009). The social bases of political parties in Argentina, 1912–2003. *Latin American Research Review*, 44(1), 58–87.

Lustig, N., Lopez-Calva, L. F., and Ortiz-Juarez, E. (2013). Declining inequality in Latin America in the 2000s: the cases of Argentina, Brazil, and Mexico. *World Development*, 44, 129–141.

MacKinnon, M. M. (2002). Los años formativos del Partido Peronista: resultados de una investigacion, *Desarrollo Economico*, 117–127.

Machado, F., Scartascini, C., and Tommasi, M. (2011). Political institutions and street protests in Latin America. *Journal of Conflict Resolution*, 55(3), 340–365.

Madrid, R. L. (2012). *The Rise of Ethnic Politics in Latin America*. Cambridge: Cambridge University Press.

Magaloni, B. M., Diaz-Cayeros, A., and Estevez, F. (2006). Clientelism and portfolio diversification: A model of electoral investment with applications to Mexico. In H. Kitschelt and S. Wilkinson (Eds.) *Patrons, Clients, and*

Policies : *Patterns of Democratic Accountability and Political Competition*. Cambridge, UK ; New York: Cambridge University Press.

Magar, E., Rosemblum, M. R., and Samuels, D. (1998). The absence of centripetal incentives in double-member districts: The case of Chile. *Comparative Political Studies*, 31(6), 714–739.

Mainwaring, S., and Scully, T. (1995). *Building Democratic Institutions: Party Systems in Latin America*. Stanford, CA: Stanford University Press.

Malamud, A., and De Luca, M. (2015). *La Politica en Tiempos de Los Kirchner*. Beunos Aires: Eudeba.

Manin, B. (1997). *The Principles of Representative Government*. Cambridge: Cambridge University Press.

Manin, B., Przeworski, A., and Stokes, S. (1999). Elections and representation. In A. Przeworski, S. Stokes, and B. Manin (Eds.) *Democracy, Accountability, and Representation* (29–54). Cambridge: Cambridge University Press.

Mansbridge, J. (2003). Rethinking representation. *American Political Science Review*, 97(04), 515–528.

Mares, I., and Young, L. (2016). Buying, expropriating, and stealing votes. *Annual Review of Political Science*, 19, 267–288.

McCarty, C., Killworth, P. D., and Rennell, J. (2007). Impact of methods for reducing respondent burden on personal network structural measures. *Social Networks*, 29(2), 300–315. doi: 10.1016/j.socnet.2006.12.005

McCarty, C., Killworth, P. D., Bernard, H. R., Johnsen, E., and Shelley, G. A. (2000). Comparing two methods for estimating network size. *Human Organization*, 60, 28–39.

McGuire, J. W. (1997). *Peronism without Perón: Unions, Parties, and Democracy in Argentina*. Stanford, CA: Stanford University Press.

Meltzer, A. H., and Richard, S. F. (1981). A rational theory of the size of government. *The Journal of Political Economy*, 914–927.

Miller, G., and Schofield, N. (2003). Activists and partisan realignment in the United States. *American Political Science Review*, 97(02), 245–260.

Miller, W. E., and Shanks, J. M. (1996). *The New American Voter*. Cambridge, MA: Harvard University Press.

Ministerio del Interior. (2008). *Historia Electoral Argentina (1912–2007)*. Buenos Aires: Ministerio de Interior.

Mora y Araujo, M., and Llorente, I. (Eds.) (1980). *El Voto Peronista: Ensayos sobre la Sociología Electoral Argentina*. Buenos Aires: Editorial Sudamericana.

Morales, M. Q., and Bugueño, R. (2001). La UDI, como expresión de la nueva derecha en Chile. *Estudios Sociales (Chile)*, 215–248.

Morales, M., and Navia, P. (2010). El sismo electoral de 2009. In M. Morales and P. Navia (Eds.) *El sismo electoral de 2009*. (9–56). Santiago de Chile: Ediciones Universidad Diego Portales.

Morales, M., and Sanchez, M. J. (2010). La segunda es la vencida: Piñeira y sus bases de apoyo. In M. Morales y P. Navia (Eds.) *El sismo electoral de 2009*. Santiago de Chile: Ediciones Universidad Diego Portales.

Morris, E. (2010). *The Rise of Theodore Roosevelt*. New York: The Modern Library.

Moseley, M. W. (2018). *Protest State: The Rise of Everyday Contention in Latin America*. Oxford: Oxford University Press.

Munoz, P. (2018). *Buying Audiences: An Informational Theory of Campaign Clientelism in Weak Party Systems*. New York: Cambridge University Press.

Murillo, M. V. (2001). *Labor Unions, Partisan Coalitions and Market Reforms in Latin America*. Cambridge, UK; New York, NY: Cambridge University Press.

(2009). *Political Competition, Partisanship, and Policymaking in Latin American Public Utilities*. New York: Cambridge University Press.

Murillo, M. V., and Visconti, G. (2017). Economic performance and incumbents' support in Latin America. *Electoral Studies*, 45, 180–190.

Murillo, M. V., Oliveros, V., and Vaishnav, M. (2010). Electoral revolution or democratic alternation? *Latin American Research Review*, 45(3), 87–114.

(2011). Economic constraints and presidential agency. In S. Levitsky and K. Roberts (Eds.) *The Resurgence of the Latin American Left* (52–70). Baltimore, MD: John Hopkins University Press.

Murmis, M., and Portantiero, J. C. (1974). *Estudios sobre los orígenes del peronismo*. Buenos Aires: Siglo Veintiuno Editores.

Navia, P. (2004). *Las grandes alamedas: el Chile post Pinochet* (1st edn.). Santiago de Chile: Tercera-Mondadori.

Navia,. P., and Godoy, R. (2014). The Alianza quest to win power democratically. In K. Sehnbruch and P. Siavelis (Eds.) *Democratic Chile: The Politics and Policies of a Historic Coalition, 1990–2010*. Boulder, CO: Lynne Rienner Publishers.

Navia, P., Morales Quiroga, M., and Briceño Espinoza, R. (2009). *El genoma electoral chileno : dibujando el mapa genético de las preferencias políticas en Chile* (1st edn.). Santiago, Chile: Ediciones Universidad Diego Portales.

Navia, P., and Osorio, R. (2015). It's the Christian Democrats' fault: Declining political identification in Chile, 1957–2012. *Canadian Journal of Political Science*, 48(4), 815–838.

Navia, P., Osorio, R., and Valenzuela, F. (2013). Sesgo político en las lunas de miel presidenciales: El Mercurio y La Tercera, 1994–2010. *Intermedios. Medios de comunicación y democracia en Chile* (35–57). Santiago, Chile: Ediciones Universidad Diego Portales.

Navia, P., and Rojas, P. (2005). Representación y tamaño de los distritos electorales en Chile, 1988–2002. *Revista de ciencia política (Santiago)*, 25(2), 91–116.

Negretto, G. L. (2013). El papel de la Constitución en la nueva democracia argentina. *Revista SAAP*, 7(2), 297–305.

(2013). *Making Constitutions: Presidents, Parties, and Institutional Choice in Latin America*. New York: Cambridge University Press.

Nichter, S. (2008). Vote buying or turnout buying? Machine politics and the secret ballot. *American Political Science Review*, 102(01), 19–31. doi:10.1017/S0003055408080106

Nohlen, D. (2005). *Elections in the Americas: A Data Handbook: Volume 2 South America* (Vol. 2): Oxford University Press on Demand.

O'Donnell, M. (2005). *El aparato : los intendentes del Conurbano y las cajas negras de la política* (1st edn.). Buenos Aires: Aguilar.

Olivella, S., and Tavits, M. (2014). Legislative effects of electoral mandates. *British Journal of Political Science*, 44(2), 301–321.

Oliveros, V. (2013). *A Working Machine: Patronage Jobs and Political Services in Argentina*. PhD Dissertation, Columbia University.
  (2016). Making it personal: Clientelism, favors, and the personalization of public administration in Argentina. *Comparative Politics*, 48(3), 373–391.
Page, B. I., and Shapiro, R. Y. (1992). *The Rational Public : Fifty Years of Trends in Americans' Policy Preferences*. Chicago, IL: University of Chicago Press.
Pedrosa, F. (2005). *Las relaciones personales también importan. Instituciones informales, redes y partidos políticos*. Paper presented at the Actas Primer Congreso Latinoamericano de Antropología Simposio Análisis de redes sociales: aplicaciones en antropología.
Perez, O. (2015). The impact of crime on voter choice in Latin America. In R. E. Carlin, M. M. Singer, and E. J. Zechmeister (Eds.) *The Latin American Voter: Pursuing Representation and Accountability in Challenging Contexts*. Ann Arbour, MI: University of Michigan Press.
Pérez, G. J., and Pereyra, S. (2013). *La protesta social entre las crisis de la democracia argentina, Revista SAAP*, 7(2), 463–471.
Persello, A. V. (2005). El Partido Radical, oposición y gobierno. *Estudios Sociales*, 11(1), 67–84.
Petrocik, J. R. (1996). Issue ownership in presidential elections, with a 1980 case study. *American Journal of Political Science*, 40(3), 825–850.
Piattoni, S. (2001). *Clientelism, Interests, and Democratic Representation: The European Experience in Historical and Comparative Perspective*. Cambridge: Cambridge University Press.
Pinto, C. (2006). *UDI: la conquista de corazones populares (1983–1987)*. Santiago de Chile: A & V.
Pirro, J. C. M. (2009). *El peronismo después del peronismo: resistencia, sindicalismo y política luego del 55*. Beunos Aires: Siglo Veintiuno Editores.
Pitkin, H. F. (1967). *The Concept of Representation*. Berkeley, CA: University of California Press.
Plumb, D. (1998). El Partido por la democracia: The Birth of Chile's Postmaterialist Catch-All Left. *Party Politics*, 4(1), 93–106.
Pollack, M. (1999). *New Right in Chile*. USA: Springer.
Posner, D. N. (2005). *Institutions and Ethnic Politics in Africa*. Cambridge; New York: Cambridge University Press.
Pribble, J. (2015). *Welfare and Party Politics in Latin America*. New York: Cambridge University Press.
Pribble, J., and Huber, E. (2011). Social policy and redistribution: Chile and Uruguay. In S. Levitsky and K. Roberts (Eds.) *The Resurgence of the Latin American Left* (117–138). Baltimore, MD: John Hopkins University Press.
Pribble, J., Huber, E., and Stephens, J. D. (2009). Politics, policies, and poverty in Latin America, *Comparative Politics*, 41(4), 387–407.
Rahn, W. M. (1993). The role of partisan stereotypes in information processing about political candidates. *American Journal of Political Science*, 472–496.

Ratto, M. C. (2011). El proceso de atribución de responsabilidades en América Latina: un estudio sobre el voto económico entre 1996 y 2004. *Revista SAAP*, 5(1), 59–92.
  (2013). Rechazo a la democracia o al partido de gobierno? Despejando el camino para el estudio de la accountability electoral o algunas reflexiones sobre la relación entre crisis económica y voto en los últimos 30 años. *Revista SAAP*, 7(2).
Remmer, K. L. (2012). The rise of leftist–populist governance in Latin America The roots of electoral change. *Comparative Political Studies*, 45(8), 947–972.
Rhodes, S. (2005). *Social Movements and Free Market Capitalism in Latin America*. Albany, NY: SUNY Press.
Roberts, K. M. (1998). *Deepening Democracy?: The Modern Left and Social Movements in Chile and Peru*. Stanford, CA: Stanford University Press.
  (2013). Market reform, programmatic (de) alignment, and party system stability in Latin America. *Comparative Political Studies*, 46(11), 1422–1452.
Roberts, K. M., and Wibbels, E. (1999). Party systems and electoral volatility in Latin America: a test of economic, institutional, and structural explanations. *American Political Science Review*, 93(3), 575–590.
Robinson, J., and Verdier, T. (2002). *The Political Economy of Clientelism*(3205). London: Centre for Economic Policy Research.
Rock, D. (1972). Machine politics in Buenos Aires and the Argentine Radical Party, 1912–1930. *Journal of Latin American Studies*, 4(02), 233–256.
  (1975). *Politics in Argentina, 1890–1930 : The Rise and Fall of Radicalism*. Cambridge, UK.: Cambridge University Press.
Rodden, J. (2002). The dilemma of fiscal federalism: Grants and fiscal performance around the world, *American Journal of Political Science*, 670–687.
  (2006). *Hamilton's Paradox: The Promise and Peril of Fiscal Federalism*. New York: Cambridge University Press.
Rodrik, D. (1997). *What Drives Public Employment?*. Cambridge, MA: National Bureau of Economic Research.
Rouquié, A., and Zadunaisky, D. (1984). *El estado militar en América Latina*: Buenos Aires: Emecé.
Sabato, H. (2001). *The Many and the Few: Political Participation in Republican*. Buenos Aires, Redwood City, CA: Stanford University Press.
Sabato, H., and Ternavasio, M. (2015). El voto en la república. Historia del sufragio en el siglo XIX. In H. Sabato, M. Ternavasio. L. Di Privitello, and A. V. Persello (Eds.) *Historia de las elecciones en la, Argentina* (17–134). Beunos Aires: Editorial El Ateneo.
Sanders, D., Clarke, H. D., Stewart, M. C., and Whiteley, P. (2011). Downs, stokes and the dynamics of electoral choice. *British Journal of Political Science*, 41(02), 287–314.
Sartori, G. (2005). *Parties and Party Systems: A Framework for Analysis*. Colchester, UK: ECPR Press.
Scartascini, C., Stein, E. H., Tommasi, M., Jones, M. P., Saiegh, S., Magaldi de Sousa, M., Martínez-Gallardo, C., et al. (2010). *How Democracy Works: Political Institutions, Actors and Arenas in Latin American Policymaking*. Washington, DC: Inter-American Development Bank.

Schaffer, F. C. (2007). *Elections for Sale: The Causes and Consequences of Vote Buying*. Boulder, CO: Lynne Rienner Publishers.

Schaffer, J., and Baker, A. (2015). Clientelism as persuasion-buying: Evidence from Latin America. *Comparative Political Studies*, 48(9), 1093–1126.

Schefter, M. (1994). *Political Parties and the State: The American Historical Experience*. New York: Cambridge University Press.

Schiumerini, L. (2016). Macri's victory: A right-wing mandate? Paper presented at the Conference on Campaigns and Voters in a Developing Democracy: Argentina's 2015 Election in Comparative Perspective, Tulane University, New Orleans, LA, May 19–20, 2016.

Schlozman, K. L., Verba, S., and Brady, H. E. (2012). *The Unheavenly Chorus Unequal Political Voice and the Broken Promise of American Democracy*. Princeton, NJ: Princeton University Press.

Schofield, N. (2003). Valence competition in the spatial stochastic model. *Journal of Theoretical Politics*, 15(4), 371–383.

Schofield, N., and Sened, I. (2006). *Multiparty Democracy: Elections and Legislative Politics*. Cambridge; New York: Cambridge University Press.

Schumpeter, J. A. (1942). *Capitalism, Socialism and Democracy*. New York: Harper Torchbooks.

Scully, T. R. (1992). *Rethinking the Center: Party Politics in Nineteenth-and Twentieth-Century Chile*. Stanford, CA: Stanford University Press.

Scully, T., and Valenzuela, J. S. (1993). *From Democracy to Democracy: Continuities and Changes of Electoral Choices and the Party System in Chile*. Notre Dame, IN.: Helen Kellogg Institute for International Studies, University of Notre Dame.

Serra, G. (2010) Why primaries? The party's tradeoff between policy and valence. *Journal of Theoretical Politics*, 23(1), 21–51.

(2011). Polarization of what? A model of elections with endogenous valence. *Journal of Politics*, 72(2), 426–437.

Siavelis,. P. M. (2000). *The President and Congress in Postauthoritarian Chile : Institutional Constraints to Democratic Consolidation*. University Park, PA: Pennsylvania State University Press.

Siavelis, P., and Morgenstern, S. (2008). *Pathways to Power: Political Recruitment and Candidate Selection in Latin America*. University Park, PA.: Pennsylvania State University Press.

Smith, W., Acuña, C., and Gamarra, A. (Eds.) (1994). *Democracy, Markets, and Structural Reform in Latin America*. New Brunswick, NJ: Transaction.

Snyder, J. M. (1989). Election Goals and the Allocation of Campaign Resources, *Econometrica*, 57(3), 637–660.

Soto, Á. (2001). *La irrupción de la UDI en las poblaciones 1983–1987*. Paper presented at the Annual Meeting of the Latin American Studies Association.

Spiegelhalter, D., Thomas, A., Best, N., and Lunn, D. (2003). WinBUGS user Manual 1.4. Retrieved from www.mrc-bsu.cam.ac.uk/bugs

Steinmo, S. (1993). *Taxation and Democracy: Swedish, British, & American Approaches to Financing the Modern State*. New Haven, CT: Yale University Press.

Stokes, D. (1963). Spatial models of party competition. *The American Political Science Review*, 57(2), 368–377.

(1992). Valence politics. *Electoral Politics*, 141–164.
Stokes, S. C. (1999). What do policy switches tell us about democracy? In A. Przeworski, S. Stokes, and B. Manin (Eds.) *Democracy, Accountability, and Representation* (98–130). Cambridge: Cambridge University Press.
  (2001). *Mandates and Democracy: Neoliberalism by Surprise in Latin America.* Cambridge ; New York: Cambridge University Press.
  (2005). Perverse accountability: A formal model of machine politics with evidence from Argentina. *American Political Science Review*, 99(3), 315–325.
  (2007). *Political Clientelism* Oxford handbooks of political science. (xi, 1021). Oxford; New York: Oxford University Press
Stokes, S. C., Dunning, T., Nazareno, M., and Brusco, V. (2013). *Brokers, Voters, and Clientelism: The Puzzle of Distributive Politics*. New York: Cambridge University Press.
Suárez Cao, J., Cavarozzi, M., and Abal Medina, J. M. (2002). La competencia partidaria en la Argentina: sus implicancias sobre el régimen democrático. In *El asedio a la política: Los partidos latinoamericanos en la era neoliberal* (163–185). Buenos Aires: Homo Sapiens.
Szwarcberg, M. (2012). Uncertainty, political clientelism, and voter turnout in Latin America: Why parties conduct rallies in Argentina. *Comparative Politics*, 45(1), 88–106.
  (2015). *Mobilizing Poor Voters: Machine Politics, Clientelism, and Social Networks in Argentina*. Cambridge University Press. https://doi.org/10.1017/CBO9781316286913
Tagina, M. L. (2012). Factores contextuales, predisposiciones de largo plazo y accountabilty electoral en Argentina en tiempos del kirchnerismo. In *Política y Gobierno, XIX*(2).
Tcach, C. (1991). *Sabatinismo y peronismo*. Buenos Aires: Sudamericana.
Thachil, T. (2014). Elite parties and poor voters: Theory and evidence from India. *American Political Science Review*, 108(02), 454–477.
Tomz, M., and Van Houweling, R. P. (2009). The electoral implications of candidate ambiguity. *American Political Science Review*, 103(01), 83–98.
  (2010). Candidate Repositioning. *Unpublished manuscript*.
Torcal, M., and Mainwaring, S. (2003). The political recrafting of social bases of party competition: Chile, 1973–95. *British Journal of Political Science*, 33(1), 55–84: Cambridge Journals Online. doi:10.1017/S0007123403000036
Torre, J. C. (1974). *El proceso político interno de los sindicatos en Argentina*. Buenos Aires: Instituto Torcuato Di Tella, Centro de Investigaciones Sociales.
  (2003). Los huérfanos de la política de partidos Sobre los alcances y la naturaleza de la crisis de representación partidaria. *Desarrollo Economico*, 42 (168), 647–665.
  (2006). *La vieja guardia sindical y Perón: sobre los orígenes del peronismo* (2nd edn.). Argentina: Editorial de la Universidad Nacional de Tres de Febrero.
Tow, A. (2016). www.andytow.com/atlas/totalpais/. Retrieved from www.andytow.com/blog/
Treisman, D. (1999). Political decentralization and economic reform: A game-theoretic analysis. *American Journal of Political Science*, 43(2), 488–517.

Tsebelis, G. (1990). *Nested Games: Rational Choice in Comparative Politics*. Berkeley, CA: University of California Press.
Valenzuela, A. (1977). *Political Brokers in Chile*. Durham, NC: Duke University Press.
  (1978). *The Breakdown of Democratic Regimes: Chile* (Vol. 4). Baltimore, MD: Johns Hopkins University Press.
  (1998). *La política de partidos y la crisis del presidencialismo en Chile: una propuesta para una forma parlamentaria de gobierno*. Paper presented at the Las crisis del presidencialismo.
Valenzuela, G. U. (1992). *Historia política de Chile y su evolución electoral: desde 1810 a 1992*. Santiago, de Chile: Editorial Jurídica de Chile.
Valenzuela, J. P. (1997). *Descentralización fiscal: Los ingresos municipales y regionales en Chile*. Santiago de Chile: ECLAC.
Valenzuela, J. S. (1985). *Democratización vía reforma: la expansión del sufragio en Chile* (Vol. 6) Buenos Aires: Instituto de Desarrollo Económico y Social.
  (1999). Reflexiones sobre el presente y futuro del paisaje político chileno a la luz de su pasado. *Estudios Públicos*, 75, 273–290.
Valobra, A. M. (2008). La ciudadanía política de las mujeres y las elecciones de 1951. *Anuario del Instituto de Historia Argentina 8*, 53–89.
Vavreck, L. (2009). *The Message Matters: The Economy and Presidential Campaigns*. Princeton, NJ: Princeton University Press.
Visconti, G. (2017). *Crime Victimization and Policy Preferences*. Columbia University. New York. (unpublished manuscript)
Vommaro, G., Morresi, S., and Bellotti, A. (2015). *Mundo Pro: anatomía de un partido fabricado para ganar*. Beunos Aires: Planeta.
Von Stackelberg, H. (2010). *Market Structure and Equilibrium*: Heidelberg: Springer Science & Business Media.
Wallerstein, M., and Austen-Smith, D. (2008). *Selected Works of Michael Wallerstein : The Political Economy of Inequality, Unions, and Social Democracy*. Cambridge; New York: Cambridge University Press.
Wattenberg, M. P. (2009). *The Decline of American Political Parties, 1952–1996*: Cambridge, MA: Harvard University Press.
Weitz-Shapiro, R. (2012). What wins votes: Why some politicians opt out of clientelism. *American Journal of Political Science*.
  (2014). *Curbing Clientelism in Argentina: Politics, Poverty, and Social Policy*. New York: Cambridge University Press.
Weyland, K. (1977). Growth with equity in Chile's new democracy? *Latin American Research Review*, 32(1), 37–67.
Wibbels, E. (2000). Federalism and the politics of macroeconomic policy and performance. *American Journal of Political Science*, 44(4), 687–702. doi:10.2307/2669275
Wilkinson, S. I. (2006). *Votes and Violence: Electoral Competition and Ethnic Riots in India*. New York: Cambridge University Press.
World Bank (2015). http://databank.worldbank.org/data/home.aspx
Zaller, J. (1992). *The Nature and Origins of Mass Opinion*. New York: Cambridge University Press.

Zaller, J., and Feldman, S. (1992). A simple theory of the survey response: Answering questions versus revealing preferences. *American Journal of Political Science*, 36(3), 579.

Zarazaga, R. (2015). Plugged in brokers: A model of vote-buying and access to resources. *Journal of Applied Economics*, 18(2), 369–390.

  (2016). Party machines and voter-customized rewards strategies. *Journal of Theoretical Politics*, 28(4), 678–701.

Zechmeister, E. J., and Corral, M. (2013). Individual and contextual constraints on ideological labels in Latin America. *Comparative Political Studies*, 46( 6), 675–701.

Zheng, T., Salganik, M., and Gelman, A. (2006). How many people do you know in prison?: Using overdispersion in count data to estimate social structure in networks. *Journal of the American Statistical Association*, 101, 474.

Zucco, C. (2007). Where's the bias? A reassessment of the Chilean electoral system. *Electoral Studies*, 26(2), 303–314.

  (2013). When payouts pay-off: Conditional cash transfers and voting behavior in Brazil 2002–10. *American Journal of Political Science*, 57(4), 810–822.

# Index

Allende, 52
ARI, 61, 67, 74, 78, 89, 91, 100, 105, 109, 114–115, 119, 141, 194, 205, 208, 210, 239, 259, 263, 273–275
*attenuation effect*, 139–140, 143, 146, 152
AUH, 210

Bachelet, 58, 206

CASEN, 163–164, 167, 169, 267
*Chile Solidario*, 87, 206
Civic Coalition, 61, 91, 210
clientelism, 31, 51–52, 77, 83, 98, 100, 114, 133, 146, 149, 152, 214, 220, 224, 226, 286, 295
clientelistic
 goods, 101
 linkages, 219, 221
 parties, 23, 218–219
 strategies, 220
competence, 23
 economic, 21, 31, 45, 57, 60, 62, 64, 71, 74–75, 81, 105, 108, 113, 116, 118, 123, 127, 133, 145, 182, 192, 202, 215, 222
 managerial, 7–8, 11, 14, 19, 38, 64, 121, 129, 161, 180, 213–214
 policy, 22, 223
 signals, 21
compositional effect, 176, 185, 192, 196, 199
Concertacion, 53

core voters, 23, 29, 33, 101, 133–135, 138–139, 148, 159, 222, 225, 227
Cristina Fernandez de Kirchner, 61, 167, 210
crowding out, 183, 194

DC, 52, 58, 67, 75, 88, 96, 98, 101, 104, 109, 112, 115–116, 118, 142, 197–198, 202, 207–208, 239, 259–260, 272, 274, 276
distributive expectations, 23, 31, 42, 46, 57, 59, 62–63, 71, 76–77, 79–80, 83, 87, 100, 107–109, 111, 114, 119, 121–123, 127, 129, 131–132, 136, 140, 142–143, 145, 152, 154, 156–157, 159–161, 171, 178, 186, 191, 200, 202, 221, 224–225, 227
*Downsian Convergence*, 188

economic voting, 11, 18, 21, 105, 168, 222
electoral
 benefits, 14, 16, 29, 132, 148, 157
 campaign, 15, 24, 59, 89–91, 95, 97, 105, 114–115, 136, 207, 221
 portfolio, 19, 23, 44–45, 67, 120, 126, 216, 227
 system, 49–50, 62, 95, 182, 207
 volatility, 51, 207

gender, 77, 111–112, 143–144, 171–172, 174, 176–177, 184

handouts, 11, 14–16, 19, 23, 31, 42, 47, 65, 76–78, 80–82, 87, 100–101, 107,

109–110, 114, 120, 139–140,
142–143, 145–146, 149, 152, 158,
160–161, 192
heterogeneity
socio-economic, 94
voter, 10, 12, 17, 23, 26, 28, 31, 35,
37–38, 64, 81, 107–108, 134, 138,
148, 160, 181, 184, 195, 199, 212,
216–217, 221

Identification
partisan, 12, 17, 96, 103
ideological
distance, 37, 46, 68, 86, 105, 108, 110,
112, 117, 121, 123–124, 127, 129,
132, 136, 141–143, 149, 154, 156,
158, 184, 190
position, 8, 28, 44, 58, 62, 64, 68, 72, 81,
83, 116, 119, 149, 182, 186, 200, 202,
208, 226
proximity, 20, 27, 36–37, 58, 107, 109,
113, 119–121, 123, 129, 135, 141,
144, 160, 205
self-placement, 25, 29, 69, 71, 75–77, 79,
87, 94–95, 100, 211
INDEC, 89, 163–164, 169, 266
inequality, 30, 171, 177, 206, 216, 221–222
information effect, 132, 138–139, 143, 146,
149, 153
issue
ownership, 20
Issue
valence, 10, 20, 71, 214, 220, 225

Justicialista, 54, 67, 259, 263

Latin America, 11–12, 19, 21–22, 30, 47,
71, 128, 190, 203, 209, 215–216, 222,
227, 274, 278–279, 281, 283–284,
286–288, 290–291, 293
leaky bucket, 135, 141, 184, 223
linkages
network, 13, 19
party, 19, 25, 28, 48, 110, 215, 218, 221
policy, 77

Nestor Kircher, 167, 181, 209
Networks
activists, 8, 14, 25, 44, 57, 60, 82–84, 89,
91, 93, 131, 138, 142, 145, 154,
156–157, 160, 219

personal, 84–86, 111, 143, 239
size, 25, 47, 65, 83, 85, 89, 92, 121
Party
clientelistic, 218
programmatic, 23, 217–218, 220
patronage
jobs, 8, 10, 14, 24, 38, 162, 229
spending, 130, 164, 166, 168, 170, 172,
177, 192
Piñeira, Sebastian, 59, 207–209
Pinochet, Augusto, 52–53, 56, 59, 200
PJ, 54, 56–57, 59–62, 67, 75, 78, 81, 87–88,
90–92, 95, 98, 100–101, 109,
113–114, 119, 132, 141, 144, 178,
191, 194, 206, 211, 227, 239,
273–275
Political Elites of Latina America-PELA,
203, 205
portfolio, 43, 194
diversification, 26, 221–222
PRO, 29, 61–62, 67, 74, 78, 88–89, 91, 94,
100, 102, 105, 109, 112, 114–115,
119, 142, 194, 205, 208, 210–211,
239, 259, 263, 273–275
programmatic
linkages, 219
PS, 52–53, 58, 67, 75, 79–80, 88, 92, 97,
101, 109, 112–116, 118, 125, 142,
145, 197–198, 202, 205, 207, 212,
239, 259, 261, 272, 274, 276
public goods, 132–133
club, 139
local, 138–139, 146, 148
public works, 11, 14–16, 24, 31, 65, 76–78,
80, 108–111, 142–143, 145–146,
152
public-sector employees, 161, 163–164,
170, 172, 174, 176, 178
public-sector wages, 123–124, 160–162,
165–167, 171–172, 174–177

RN, 53, 58–59, 67, 75–76, 88–89, 92–94,
97, 102–104, 109, 112, 115–116, 118,
142, 195, 197–198, 202, 207–208,
239, 259, 261, 272, 274, 276

segmented representation, 10, 217
selective incentives, 14, 17, 38, 43, 64,
77–79, 108–109, 114, 120, 122,
132–133, 135, 157, 214–215

*Stackelberg*, 35, 41, 229–230, 232, 295
swing voters, 23, 26, 103, 135, 138, 158–159, 221

targeted distribution, 10, 12–13, 15–16, 19, 22–23, 25, 30–31, 37–38, 45, 47, 51, 60–62, 64–65, 71, 76–78, 80, 87, 96, 100–101, 104–105, 111, 115, 123, 127, 130–133, 135, 137–140, 144–146, 148–149, 153, 156–157, 159, 162–163, 172, 215–216, 218, 220–221, 223, 226

UCR, 49, 51, 54–57, 59–62, 67, 74–75, 78, 80–81, 85, 88, 90–91, 95, 98–99, 101, 109, 114–115, 119, 132, 141, 180, 194, 206, 210–211, 227, 239, 259, 262, 273–275
UDI, 53, 58–59, 67, 75, 88–89, 93–95, 97, 101, 103, 109, 112, 115–116, 118, 142, 195, 197–198, 202, 205, 207, 209, 239, 259, 261, 272, 274, 276, 287, 289, 291, 293

valence, 6, 10, 13–14, 19, 36, 71, 109, 143, 182–183, 187, 189, 214, 220, 223, 225, 231, 233, 285
Voter
    median, 6–7, 18, 27–28, 33, 35, 40, 44, 118, 127–128, 180
    poorer, 31, 37, 39, 45, 53, 59–60, 69–70, 73–75, 81, 100, 124, 127–128, 130, 133, 140, 148–149, 152, 154, 157–159, 164, 168, 172, 177, 185, 198, 209–210, 226
    richer, 31–32, 38, 45, 66–67, 80, 94, 108, 120, 132, 146, 148, 152, 154, 156, 196, 198, 200, 206, 212, 219, 226
voter utility function, 46, 68–69, 221, 226

wage premium, 161–162, 165–166, 168, 170, 172, 174